Attachment and Loss

VOL. III: LOSS

Attachment and Loss

VOLUME III

LOSS

SADNESS AND DEPRESSION

■■

John Bowlby

BASIC BOOKS, INC., PUBLISHERS • NEW YORK

To

MY PATIENTS

who have worked hard to educate me

Contents

Part II: The Mourning of Adults

Acknowledgements

Once again in preparing this volume I have been helped and encouraged by many friends and colleagues who have given most generously of their time and thought. To all of them I am deeply grateful.

One to whom I am especially indebted is Colin Murray Parkes. At a time in the early nineteen-sixties when I was struggling to clarify the nature of mourning he drew my attention to Darwin's ideas and to the part played by the mourner's urge to recover the lost person. Subsequently we joined forces and he began his studies of widows, first in London and later in Boston, which have made such a big contribution to our understanding. He has read through the chapters in Part II of this volume, on the mourning of adults, and has made a large number of valuable criticisms and suggestions. Others to have read through these chapters and to have made valuable suggestions are Robert S. Weiss and Emmy Gut. Whilst I believe that, as a result, the chapters have been much improved, I alone am responsible for the deficiencies that remain.

Beverley Raphael kindly checked the accuracy of my exposition of her work in Chapter 10, and George Brown did the same for my exposition of his in Chapters 14 and 17. The final section of Chapter 4 owes much to a discussion with Mary Main. Among those who have contributed in other ways are Mary Salter Ainsworth and Dorothy Heard, both of whom read through drafts of almost every chapter and made many valuable suggestions.

Once again the script has been prepared by my secretary, Dorothy Southern, who from start to finish has typed every word of these volumes, often many times over, with unflagging zeal and devotion. Library services have been provided with traditional efficiency by Margaret Walker and the staff of the Tavistock Library. For preparation of the list of references and other editorial help I am indebted to Molly Townsend, who has also prepared the index. To each of them my warmest thanks are due.

The many bodies that from 1948 onwards supported the research on which the work is based are listed in the first volume. To all of them I remain deeply indebted. During the time that this volume has been in preparation I have received hospitality from the Tavistock Clinic and the Tavistock Institute of Human Relations which, since my retirement, have generously made available office space and other facilities.

For permission to quote from published works, thanks are due to the publishers, authors and others listed below. Bibliographical details of all the works cited are given in the list of references at the end of the volume.

Tavistock Publications, London, and International Universities Press Inc., New York, in respect of *Bereavement: Studies of Grief in Adult Life* by C. M. Parkes; International Universities Press Inc., New York, in respect of 'Aggression: its role in the establishment of object relations' by R. A. Spitz, in *Drives, Affects and Behavior* edited by R. M. Loewenstein; of 'Notes on the development of basic moods: the depressive affect' by M. S. Mahler, in *Psychoanalysis: A General Psychology* edited by R. M. Loewenstein, L. M. Newman, M. Schur & A. J. Solnit; and of 'Contribution to the metapsychology of schizophrenia' in *Essays on Ego Psychology* by H. Hartmann; Academic Press Inc., New York, in respect of 'Episodic and semantic memory' by E. Tulving, in *Organization of Memory* edited by E. Tulving and W. Donaldson; McGraw Hill Book Co., New York, in respect of 'Social use of funeral rites' by D. Mandelbaum, in *The Meaning of Death* edited by H. Feifel; Prentice-Hall International, Hemel Hempstead, Herts., in respect of 'The provisions of social relationships' by R. S. Weiss, in *Doing Unto Others* edited by Z. Rubin; John Wiley, New York, in respect of 'Death, grief and mourning in Britain' by G. Gorer, in *The Child and his Family* edited by C. J. Anthony and C. Koupernik and of *The First Year of Bereavement* by I. O. Glick, R. S. Weiss and C. M. Parkes; Basic Books, New York, in respect of *Marital Separation* by R. S. Weiss; the Editor, *Psychological Review* in respect of 'A new look at the new look' by M. H. Erdelyi; the Editor, *Psychosomatic Medicine*, in respect of 'Is Grief a Disease?' by G. Engel; the University of Chicago and the Editor, *Perspectives in Biology and Medicine*, in respect of 'Toward a neo-dissociation theory' by E. Hilgard; International Universities Press Inc., New York and the Editor, *Psychoanalytic Study of the Child*, in respect of 'Children's reactions to the death of important objects' by H. Nagera and of 'Anaclitic Depression' by R. A. Spitz; the Editor, *American Journal of Psychiatry*, in respect of 'Symptomatology and management of acute grief' by E. Lindemann; the Editor, *Journal of the American Psychoanalytic Association*, in respect of 'Separation-individuation and object constancy' by J. B. McDevitt; the Editor, *Archives of General Psychiatry*, in respect of 'Children's reactions to bereavement' by S. I. Harrison, C. W. Davenport and J. F. McDermott Jnr.

Preface

This is the third and final volume of a work that explores the implications for the psychology and psychopathology of personality of the ways in which young children respond to a temporary or permanent loss of mother-figure. The circumstances in which the enquiry was launched are described in the prefaces to the earlier volumes. The overall strategy, which entails approaching the classic problems of psychoanalysis prospectively, is presented in the first chapter of the first volume. It can be summarized as follows—the primary data are observations of how young children behave in defined situations; in the light of these data an attempt is made to describe certain early phases of personality functioning and, from them, to extrapolate forwards. In particular the aim is to describe certain patterns of response that occur regularly in early childhood and, thence, to trace out how similar patterns of response are to be discerned in the later functioning of the personality.

There are many reasons why my initial frame of reference was, and has in many respects remained, that of psychoanalysis. Not the least is that, when the enquiry began, psychoanalysis was the only behavioural science that was giving systematic attention to the phenomena and concepts that seemed central to my task—affectional bonds, separation anxiety, grief and mourning, unconscious mental processes, defence, trauma, sensitive periods in early life. Yet there are many ways in which the theory advanced here has come to differ from the classical theories advanced by Freud and elaborated by his followers. In particular I have drawn heavily on the findings and ideas of two disciplines, ethology and control theory, that existed only in germinal form at the end of Freud's life. In this volume, moreover, I draw on recent work in cognitive psychology and human information processing in an attempt to clarify problems of defence. As a result the frame of reference now offered for understanding personality development and psychopathology amounts to a new paradigm and is thus alien to clinicians long used to thinking in other ways. The consequent difficulties of communication are as unfortunate as they are inevitable.

Nevertheless, I am much heartened by finding another psychoanalyst who has, independently, adopted a theoretical position almost identical to my own. This is Emanuel Peterfreund whose monograph *Information, Systems and Psychoanalysis* was published in 1971. Interestingly enough, although influenced by the same scientific considerations as myself, the problems that Dr Peterfreund was initially concerned to solve, problems of 'the clinical analytic process and the phenomena of insight', were entirely different from mine. Despite that, however, the theoretical frames of reference elaborated by each of us have proven 'strikingly consistent', to borrow the words he uses in a brief footnote added to his work (p. 149) just before it went to press.

Our two works are in many respects complementary. Special features of Dr Peterfreund's work are, first, his trenchant critique of current psychoanalytic theory; secondly, his brilliant exposition of the basic concepts of information, information processing and control theory; and thirdly, his systematic application of these concepts to the clinical problems with which every analyst treating patients is daily confronted. In particular, he demonstrates how the phenomena subsumed under the terms transference, defence, resistance, interpretation and therapeutic change are explicable by reference to the paradigm we both advocate. Analysts who find my work puzzling, not only because of the unfamiliar paradigm but because my prospective approach is also strange, are therefore encouraged to read Dr Peterfreund's work. Where my work differs from his lies in the central place I give to the concept of attachment behaviour as constituting a class of behaviour having its own dynamic, distinct from feeding behaviour and sexual behaviour, and of at least an equal importance.

There are a number of other psychoanalysts now who are also drawing attention to the merits of a paradigm based on current concepts in biology, control theory and information processing. An example is the work of Rosenblatt and Thickstun (1977).

The first steps I took towards formulating my own schema were in a series of papers published between 1958 and 1963. The present three-volume work is a further attempt. The first volume, *Attachment*, is devoted to problems originally tackled in the first paper of the series, 'The Nature of the Child's Tie to his Mother' (1958).

The second volume, *Separation: Anxiety and Anger*, covers ground originally tackled in two further papers, 'Separation Anxiety' (1960a) and 'Separation Anxiety: A Critical Review of the Literature' (1961a). This, the third volume, deals with problems of grief and mourning and with the defensive processes to which anxiety and loss can give rise. It comprises a revision and amplification of material first published in the subsequent papers of the earlier series— 'Grief and Mourning in Infancy and Early Childhood' (1960b), 'Processes of Mourning' (1961b) and 'Pathological Mourning and Childhood Mourning' (1963)—and draws also on drafts of two further papers concerned with loss and defence that were written during the early 1960s and received limited circulation, but remained unpublished.

Since then I have had the immense advantage of having my friend, Colin Murray Parkes, as a close colleague. This has meant that not only have I had privileged access to his valuable collection of data on adult bereavement but have also had constant opportunity to keep in close touch with his thinking.

Many of the basic data from which I start are set out in the opening chapters of the earlier volumes (see especially Volume I, Chapter 2, and Volume II, Chapters 1 and 3) and have become fairly well known. In the opening chapter of this one, therefore, only a brief summary is given. Yet, in order to remind the reader of the poignancy of the responses observed and to draw his attention to data that I believe to be of special import for understanding the genesis of psychopathological processes, some further illustrative material is given.

In the body of this volume a number of case reports culled from the publications of other clinicians are presented. Since most of them have been extensively rewritten an explanation is called for. Reasons for rewriting are of three kinds. In some cases the original record is too long and requires abbreviation. In many others it is permeated with technical terms that not only obscure the simple narrative of events and responses on which I am focusing but are incompatible with the paradigm I adopt. Finally, in several cases I have thought it useful to present the sequence of events and the patient's responses to them in a more consistently historical way than in the original; and I have made special note of the source from which each part of the record is, or appears to have been, derived. Naturally in this rewriting I have done my utmost to preserve the essence of the original. One difficulty, however, is un-avoidable. When a record is abbreviated some factual material is omitted and the criteria of selection that I have used may well be different from those that the original author would himself have adopted. To any who feel that in my account of their data distortions have crept in I offer my sincere apologies.

Part I: Observations, Concepts and Controversies

CHAPTER I

The Trauma of Loss

Definition of scientific phenomena should be based on the phenomena as we see them. We have no business to base our definition on ideas of what we think phenomena *ought* to be like. The quest for such touchstones seems to arise from a private conviction that simple laws and absolute distinctions necessarily underlie any connected set of phenomena.

C. F. A. PANTIN, *The Relation between the Sciences*

Prelude

During the present century a number of psychoanalysts and psychiatrists have sought causal links between psychiatric illness, loss of a loved person, pathological mourning and childhood experience.

For several decades the sole starting point for these studies was a sick patient. Then, during the nineteen-forties, clinicians began to pay attention to the intense distress and emotional disturbance that immediately follow the experience of loss. In some of these later studies the loss was that of a spouse; in others it was that of a mother by a young child. Although each of these three starting points yielded findings of great interest, it was some years before the way that each set of data could be related to the others began to be appreciated. A constant difficulty was that generalizations made in connection with the earlier, retrospective, set were often misleading, whilst the theoretical explanations offered for them were ill-suited to both of the later, prospective, sets.

In this volume I seek to bring these diverse sets of data into relation with each other and to outline a theory that is applicable to them all. As in the two previous volumes, precedence is given throughout to data that derive from prospective studies.

Since loss as a field for enquiry is a distressing one the student is faced with emotional problems as well as intellectual ones.

Loss of a loved person is one of the most intensely painful experiences any human being can suffer. And not only is it painful to experience but it is also painful to witness, if only because we are so impotent to help. To the bereaved nothing but the return of the lost person can bring true comfort; should what we provide fall short of that it is felt almost as an insult. That, perhaps, explains a bias that runs through so much of the older literature on how human beings respond to loss. Whether an author is discussing the effects of loss on an adult or a child, there is a tendency to underestimate how intensely distressing and disabling loss usually is and for how long the distress, and often the disablement, commonly lasts. Conversely, there is a tendency to suppose that a normal healthy person can and should get over a bereavement not only fairly rapidly but also completely.

Throughout this volume I shall be countering those biases. Again and again emphasis will be laid on the long duration of grief, on the difficulties of recovering from its effects, and on the adverse consequences for personality functioning that loss so often brings. Only by taking serious account of the facts as they seem actually to be is it likely that we shall be able to mitigate the pain and disability and to reduce the casualty rate.

Unfortunately, despite enormously increased attention to the subject during recent years, empirical data regarding how individuals of different ages respond to losses of different kinds and in differing circumstances are still scarce. The best we can do therefore is to draw on such systematic data as are available and to make prudent use of the far greater array of unsystematic accounts. Some of the latter are autobiographical but most derive from clinical observation of individuals who are in treatment. For that reason they are both a goldmine and a snare—a goldmine by providing valuable insight into the various unfavourable courses that responses to loss can take, and a snare because of the false generalizations to which they can lead. These have been of two kinds. On the one hand it has been assumed that certain features now known to be especially characteristic of unfavourable courses of response are ubiquitous features of general importance; and, on the other, that responses now known to be common to all forms of response are specific to pathology. An example of the first type of mistake is the supposition that guilt is intrinsic to mourning, and of the second the presumption that a person's disbelief that loss has really occurred (often termed 'denial') is indicative of pathology. Healthy grieving, it will frequently be emphasized, has a number of features that once were thought to be pathological and lacks others that once were thought to be typical.

Since the route by which I entered the field was that of studying the effects on young children of loss of mother, it is to those data, and to some of the controversies to which they have given rise, that the reader's attention is directed in this, the first, of five introductory chapters.

In the second I review ideas that have emerged during the treatment of patients whose emotional problems seem to be related to loss, and also outline the types of theory to which such studies have given rise. In the course of that chapter a number of key questions are identified around each of which controversy persists and for which answers are sought in the chapters that follow.

In the third and fourth of these introductory chapters I give an outline of the conceptual framework that, having first been developed in connection with this study, I now bring to the presentation and interpretation of data. The stage thus set, I embark on the body of the work.

Grief in infancy and early childhood

Let us turn first to the data that originally gave rise to this study, observations of how a young child between the ages of about twelve months and three years responds when removed from the mother-figure[1] to whom he is attached and is placed with strangers in a strange place. His initial response, readers of earlier volumes will recall,[2] is one of protest and of urgent effort to recover his lost mother. 'He will often cry loudly, shake his cot, throw himself about, and look eagerly towards any sight or sound which might prove to be his missing mother.' This may with ups and downs continue for as long as a week or more. Throughout it the child seems buoyed up in his efforts by the hope and expectation that his mother will return.

Sooner or later, however, despair sets in. The longing for mother's return does not diminish, but the hope of its being realized fades. Ultimately the restless noisy demands cease: he becomes apathetic and withdrawn, a despair broken only perhaps by an intermittent and monotonous wail. He is in a state of unutterable misery.

[1] Although throughout this work the text refers usually to 'mother' and not to 'mother-figure', it is to be understood that in every case reference is to the person who mothers a child and to whom he becomes attached. For most children, of course, that person is also his natural mother.

[2] See Volume II, Chapter 2.

9

Although this picture must have been known for centuries, it is only in the past decades that it has been described in the psychological literature and called by its right name—grief. This is the term used by Dorothy Burlingham and Anna Freud (1942), by Spitz (1946b) in titling his film *Grief: A Peril in Infancy*, and by Robertson (1953) who for twenty-five years has made a special study of its practical implications. Of the child aged from eighteen to twenty-four months Robertson writes:

> If a child is taken from his mother's care at this age, when he is so possessively and passionately attached to her, it is indeed as if his world had been shattered. His intense need of her is unsatisfied, and the frustration and longing may send him frantic with grief. It takes an exercise of imagination to sense the intensity of this distress. He is as overwhelmed as any adult who has lost a beloved person by death. To the child of two with his lack of understanding and complete inability to tolerate frustration it is really as if his mother had died. He does not know death, but only absence; and if the only person who can satisfy his imperative need is absent, she might as well be dead, so overwhelming is his sense of loss.

At one time it was confidently believed that a young child soon forgets his mother and so gets over his misery. Grief in childhood, it was thought, is short-lived. Now, however, more searching observation has shown that that is not so. Yearning for mother's return lingers on. This was made plain in many of Robertson's early studies of young children in residential nursery and hospital and was amply confirmed in the two systematic studies of children in residential nurseries conducted by Heinicke (Heinicke 1956; Heinicke and Westheimer 1966).[3] Crying for parents, mainly for mother, was a dominant response especially during the first three days away. Although it decreased thereafter, it was recorded sporadically for each of the children for at least the first nine days. It was particularly common at bedtime and during the night. Searching for mother also occurred.

Although wishful thinking has probably contributed to the idea that a young child's grief is short-lived, certain features of his behaviour have proved misleading. For example, after the critical phase of protest, a child becomes quieter and less explicit in his communications. So far from indicating that he has forgotten his mother, however, observation shows that he remains oriented

[3] Particulars of Heinicke's studies are given in the first chapter of the second volume of this work.

strongly towards her. Robertson has recorded many cases of young children whose longing for the absent mother was apparent, even though at times so muted or disguised that it tended to be over-looked. Of Laura, the subject of his film *A Two-year-old Goes to Hospital* (1952), he writes: 'She would interpolate without emotion and as if irrelevantly the words "I want my Mummy, where has my Mummy gone?" into remarks about something quite different; and when no one took up the intruded remark she would not repeat the "irrelevance".' The same child would sometimes let concealed feelings come through in songs and, apparently unknown to herself, substitute the name of 'Mummy' for that of a nursery-rhyme character. On one occasion she expressed an urgent wish to see the steam-roller which had just gone from the roadway below the ward in which she was confined. She cried, 'I want to see the steam-roller, I want to see the steam-roller, I want to see my *mummy*, I want to see the steam-roller.'[4]

Another child, aged three and a half, who had been in hospital for ten days, was observed playing a repetitive game by himself of a kind which appeared at first sight to be quite happy. He was bowing, turning his head to the left and lifting his arm. This seemed harm-less enough, and also meaningless. When approached, however, he was heard to be muttering to himself, 'My mummy's coming soon— my mummy's coming soon'; and he was evidently pointing to the door through which she would enter. This was at least three hours before she could be expected.[5]

To the perceptive observer, such persistent orientation to the lost mother is evident even in much younger children. Thus Robertson also records the case of Philip who was aged only thirteen months when placed in a residential nursery. Although he was too young to verbalize any wish for his mother, the staff reported that during the days of fretting and later, whenever frustrated or upset, he would make the motions associated with the rhyme 'round and round the garden' with which his mother used to humour him when he was out of temper at home.

In the Hampstead Nurseries Anna Freud and Dorothy Burling-ham recorded many cases of persistent but muted longing for an

[4] For further discussion of how Laura responded during and after her stay in hospital see Chapters 23 and 25.

[5] This observation, made by James Robertson, is reported in Bowlby, Robertson and Rosenbluth (1952).

absent mother (Freud and Burlingham 1974).[6] A striking example is that of a boy aged three years and two months who had already experienced two separations from his mother, the first when he was evacuated to a foster-home where he fretted and the second when he was in hospital with measles. On being left in the nursery he had been admonished to be a good boy and not to cry—otherwise his mother would not visit him.

Patrick tried to keep his promise and was not seen crying. Instead he would nod his head whenever anyone looked at him and assured himself and anybody who cared to listen . . . that his mother would come for him, she would put on his overcoat and would take him home with her again. Whenever a listener seemed to believe him he was satisfied; whenever anybody contradicted him, he would burst into violent tears.

This same state of affairs continued through the next two or three days with several additions. The nodding took on a more compulsive and automatic character: 'My mother will put on my overcoat and take me home again.'

Later an ever-growing list of clothes that his Mother was supposed to put on him was added: 'She will put on my overcoat and my leggings, she will zip up the zipper, she will put on my pixie hat.' When the repetitions of this formula became monotonous and endless, somebody asked him whether he could not stop saying it all over again. Again Patrick tried to be the good boy that his mother wanted him to be. He stopped repeating the formula aloud but his lips showed that he was saying it over and over to himself.

At the same time he substituted for the spoken words gestures that showed the position of his pixie hat, the putting on of an imaginary coat, the zipping of the zipper, etc. What showed as an expressive movement one day was reduced the next to a mere abortive flicker of his fingers. While the other children were mostly busy with their toys, playing games, making music, etc., Patrick, totally uninterested, would stand somewhere in a corner, moving his hands and lips with an absolutely tragic expression on his face.

Unfortunately, shortly after Patrick's admission to the nursery his

[6] Reports of observations made in the Hampstead Nurseries were first published during the war in the U.K. (Burlingham and Freud 1942, 1944) and in the U.S.A. (Freud and Burlingham 1943). They are now reprinted in a volume of Anna Freud's collected works (Freud and Burlingham 1974) and page references given in the text are to that publication. In the account that follows the pseudonym Patrick, used originally in the 1943 edition but changed to Billie in 1974, has been retained because in earlier publications of my own in which the case is referred to (e.g. Bowlby *et al.* 1952) Patrick is the pseudonym used.

mother contracted influenza and was confined to hospital for more than a week. Only after her discharge, therefore, was it possible to arrange for her to stay with Patrick in the nursery.

Patrick's state changed immediately. He dropped his symptom and instead clung to his mother with the utmost tenacity. For several days and nights he hardly left her side. Whenever she went upstairs or downstairs, Patrick was trailing after her. Whenever she disappeared for a minute, we could hear his anxious questioning through the house or see him open the door of every room and look searchingly into every corner. No one was allowed to touch him; his mother bathed him, put him to sleep, and had her bed next to his (Freud and Burlingham 1974, pp. 19–20).

This case is discussed further in Chapter 23 since it illustrates vividly one of the common courses that childhood grieving can take and illumines certain features that occur typically when an adult's responses to loss take a pathological course. Features to be noted are: first, Patrick's persistent yearning for reunion with his mother; secondly, the pressure exerted on him by well-meaning adults to persuade him to desist from grieving and think of something else; thirdly, the tendency for his yearning none the less to persist but thenceforward to be expressed in an increasingly obscure form and directed towards an increasingly obscure goal; and fourthly, the circumstances in which he comes to enact the role of his missing mother. The latter provides, I suggest, a valuable clue to understanding the process of identification with the lost figure which Freud made the keystone of his theory of mourning.

A child's persistent longing for his mother is often suffused with intense, generalized hostility. This has been reported by several workers, e.g. Robertson (1953) and Spitz (1953), and was one of the most striking findings in the first of Heinicke's systematic studies. Heinicke (1956) compared the behaviour of two groups of children, both aged between sixteen and twenty-six months; one group was in a residential nursery, the other in a day nursery. Not only did the children in the residential nursery cry for their mothers more than did the day-nursery children, but they exhibited much violent hostility of a kind hardly seen at all in those in the day nursery. The targets of this hostility were so varied that it was difficult to discern towards whom it was principally directed.

Nevertheless, there is good reason to believe that in its origin much of the anger of separated children is directed towards the missing mother-figure. This was clearly so in the case of Reggie, a

13

small boy of two years and eight months (described in the early pages of Volume II) who had become intensely attached to one of the nurses in the Hampstead Nurseries but who refused to have anything to do with her when she visited a fortnight after she had left to get married. After her visit he had stared at the closing door and in bed that evening had made plain his ambivalent feelings: 'My very own Mary-Ann!' he exclaimed. 'But I don't like her' (Freud and Burlingham 1974).

In later chapters there is much further reference to the anger that is so commonly elicited by the departure of a loved person, whatever the reason may be that he has gone.

As in the case of a bereaved adult who misses and longs for a particular person and so cannot find comfort in other companions, so does a child in a hospital or residential nursery at first reject the ministrations of those caring for him. Although his appeals for help are clamant, often his behaviour is as contradictory and frustrating to the would-be comforter as is that of a recently bereaved adult. Sometimes he rejects them. At others he combines clinging to a nurse with sobs for his lost mother. Anna Freud and Dorothy Burlingham have recorded the case of a little girl of seventeen months who said nothing but 'Mum, Mum, Mum' for three days and who, although liking to sit on the nurse's knee and to have the nurse put her arm around her, insisted throughout on having her back to the nurse so as not to see her.

Nevertheless, the complete or partial rejection of the strange adult does not continue for ever. After a phase of withdrawal and apathy, already described, a child begins to seek new relationships. How these develop turns on the situation in which he finds himself. Provided there is one particular mother-figure to whom he can relate and who mothers him lovingly he will in time take to her and treat her almost as though she were his mother. In those situations, by contrast, in which a child has no single person to whom he can relate or when there is a succession of persons to whom he makes brief attachments, the outcome is different. As a rule he becomes increasingly self-centred and prone to make transient and shallow relationships with all and sundry. This condition bodes ill for his development if it becomes an established pattern.

Do young children mourn? a controversy
In the paper 'Grief and Mourning in Infancy and Early Childhood',

published 1960, in which I first drew attention to these observations, I pointed to the striking similarities between the responses of young children following loss of mother and the responses of bereaved adults. The number and extent of these similarities had not been emphasized before. This was in part because the traditional pictures of how children and adults respectively are thought to respond to loss had greatly exaggerated such real differences as exist, and in part because there was little understanding of the nature of attachment behaviour and its role in human life. Since the similarities between childhood and adult responses to loss are central to my thesis they are examined fully in Part III. 'Meanwhile', I had concluded in 1960,

since the evidence makes it clear that at a descriptive level the responses are similar in the two age-groups, I believe it to be wiser methodologically to assume that the underlying processes are similar also, and to postulate differences only when there is clear evidence for them. That certain differences between age-groups exist I have little doubt, since in infants and small children the outcome of experiences of loss seem more frequently to take forms which lead to an adverse psychological outcome. In my judgment, however, these differences are best understood as being due to special variants of the mourning process itself, and not to processes of a qualitatively different kind. When so conceived, I believe, we are enabled both to see how data regarding the responses of young children to a separation experience relate to the general body of psychoanalytic theory and also to reformulate that theory in simpler terms.

This line of argument was pursued in the two subsequent papers[7] in which I emphasized especially that

The mourning responses that are commonly seen in infancy and early childhood bear many of the features which are the hallmark of pathological mourning in the adult (1963, p. 504).

In particular, I drew attention to four pathological variants of adult mourning already described in the clinical literature and to the tendency for individuals who show these responses to have experienced loss of a parent during childhood or adolescence. The four variants, described here in the terms now preferred, are as follows:

– unconscious yearning for the lost person
– unconscious reproach against the lost person combined with conscious and often unremitting self reproach

[7] 'Processes of Mourning' (1961b) and 'Pathological Mourning and Childhood Mourning' (1963).

– compulsive caring for other persons
– persistent disbelief that the loss is permanent (often referred to as denial).

A sharp controversy followed these early papers. Of the many issues debated one calls for immediate comment: namely, the use of the term 'mourning'.

As explained in the original series of papers, it seemed useful to employ the term 'mourning' in a broad sense to cover a variety of reactions to loss, including those that lead to a pathological outcome, because it then becomes possible to link together a number of processes and conditions that evidence shows are interrelated— much in the way that the term 'inflammation' is used in physiology and pathology to link together a number of processes, some of which lead to a healthy outcome and some of which miscarry and result in pathology. The term 'mourning' was selected because it had been introduced into psychoanalysis in the translation of Freud's seminal paper on 'Mourning and Melancholia' (1917) and had for many years been in wide use by clinicians.

My thesis met with strong opposition, however, especially from psychoanalysts who were close to Freud and those who follow in that tradition.[8] The difficulties they raise are in part matters of substance and in part terminological. To enable us to identify the points of substance let us deal immediately with the problem of terms.

The terminological difficulties stem from the restrictive sense in which some of my critics interpret Freud's statement that 'Mourning has a quite precise psychical task to perform: its function is to detach the survivor's memories and hopes from the dead' (*SE* 13, p. 65).[9] The term 'mourning', these critics insist, must be applied only to psychological processes that have that single outcome: no other usage is permissible.

[8] See the three critical articles, by Anna Freud, Max Schur and René Spitz, that are printed in Volume 15 of *The Psychoanalytic Study of the Child* (1960) following the first of my three papers: see also Wolfenstein (1966).

[9] The abbreviation *SE* denotes the Standard Edition of *The Complete Psychological Works of Sigmund Freud*, published in 24 volumes by Hogarth Press Ltd, London, and distributed in America by W. W. Norton, New York. All quotations from Freud in the present work are taken from this edition.

Such terminological rigidity is alien to the spirit of science. For, once a definition is laid down, it tends to straitjacket thought and to control what the worker permits himself to observe; so that, instead of the definition being allowed to evolve to take account of new facts, facts not covered by the original definition are neglected. Thus, were we to accept the injunction to restrict the term mourning in the way proposed, we should have to limit it to psychological processes with an outcome that is not only predetermined as an optimum but which we now have good reason to know, and as Freud himself rightly suspected, is never completely attained (see Chapters 6 and 16). Processes leading to any variation of outcome would by definition be excluded and would thereby have to be described in other terms.

A restricted usage of that kind is unacceptable. One of the major contributions of psychoanalysis has been to help integrate psychopathology with general personality theory. To use different terms for a process or processes according to whether outcome is favourable or unfavourable endangers that integration. In particular, intractable problems would arise were it thought necessary to define at an early stage where healthy processes end and pathological ones begin. Should such a definition prove later to be mistaken confusion would reign. That, in fact, is what has occurred in our field.

Since I judge these considerations to outweigh all others, the usage adopted in the earlier papers is retained. Thus, the term 'mourning', with suitable qualifying adjectives, is used to denote a fairly wide array of psychological processes set in train by the loss of a loved person irrespective of their outcome. Even so, an alternative term already in broad usage is 'grieving' and arguments can be advanced for employing it instead of 'mourning'. In addition to its avoiding controversy over the restricted usage of mourning discussed above, it would avoid also another and quite different tradition of specialized usage stemming from anthropology which restricts mourning to the public act of expressing grief. Because public mourning is always in some degree culturally determined, it is distinguishable, at least conceptually, from an individual's spontaneous responses. (That usage is encouraged in Webster's *Dictionary of the English Language* and is adopted in a review by Averill 1968.) Yet a further reason for employing grieving in a broad sense would be that, as we have seen, it has already been so used by prominent psychoanalysts and there is therefore no dispute that very young children grieve.

Nevertheless, there are good reasons for retaining the term mourning and using it to refer to all the psychological processes, conscious and unconscious, that are set in train by loss. First, it has for long been so used in psychopathology. Secondly, by employing it thus, the term grieving is freed to be applied to the condition of a person who is experiencing distress at loss and experiencing it in a more or less overt way. Not only is this common usage but it is especially convenient when we come to discuss the paradoxical condition known as absence of grief (Deutsch 1937). To denote the public expression of mourning we can use 'mourning customs'.

Once we recognize differences in the use of the term mourning much of the controversy melts away. For example, as Miller (1971) points out, there is now widespread agreement among clinicians that, when loss is sustained during childhood, responses to it frequently take a pathological course. Nevertheless, we are still left with substantial points of difference.

The most important is whether a pre-adolescent child is capable in any circumstances of responding to loss of parent with healthy mourning which we can define, adapting a definition given by Anna Freud,[10] as the successful effort of an individual to accept both that a change has occurred in his external world and that he is required to make corresponding changes in his internal, representational, world and to reorganize, and perhaps to reorient, his attachment behaviour accordingly. On the one side of the controversy are a number of influential analysts who, impressed by the many patients they have treated whose response to a childhood loss had taken a pathological course, have concluded that a pathological form of response is inevitable and have sought to explain the alleged inevitability by postulating that a child's ego is too weak and undeveloped 'to bear the strain of the work of mourning'. This view, first advanced by Deutsch (1937), has been followed with minor variations of emphasis by many others, including Mahler (1961),

[10] 'The process of mourning *(Trauerarbeit)* taken in its analytic sense means to us the individual's effort to accept a fact in the external world (the loss of the cathected object) and to effect corresponding changes in the inner world (withdrawal of libido from the lost object, identification with the lost object)' (A. Freud 1960, p. 58).

Fleming and Altschul (1963), Wolfenstein (1966) and Nagera (1970). On the other are psychoanalytically trained students of the problem who, as a result of their observations, insist that, given support and honest information, it is possible for even quite young children to mourn a lost parent in as healthy a way as can an adult. This view, advanced by Robert and Erna Furman (R. A. Furman 1964a; E. Furman 1974) and also by Gilbert and Ann Kliman (G. Kliman 1965), is supported by descriptions of a number of children, aged from two years upwards, whose mourning for a lost parent was observed and recorded.

The second point of controversy concerns the nature of the responses that occur after loss of a parent during the first year or two of a child's life. It turns, among other things, on the question of when during development a child becomes capable of maintaining an image of his absent mother. This raises issues both of cognitive development and also of socio-emotional development. They are discussed in Chapter 25, with reference to the concepts of person permanence and of libidinal object constancy.

In regard to these and other controversies the views expressed in this volume are not very different from those expressed in my earlier papers. Such differences as there are arise mainly from consideration of the evidence, published since those papers were written, concerning the influence on his responses of the experiences a child has with parents and parent-substitutes before, during, and after his loss. These and other matters are discussed in Chapters 15 onwards.

Meanwhile, it may help the reader if his attention is drawn to the two complementary themes that run through this volume. One is that, as emphasized in the earlier papers, the responses to loss seen in early life have a great deal in common with responses seen in later life, and that sharp distinctions are both unwarranted and misleading. The second is that, as widely agreed, certain differences exist which call for detailed examination. At different points in the exposition one or other of these themes is given prominence; but it is hoped the reader will never forget the importance of both.

Detachment

Before closing this introductory chapter I wish to return to the third of the three phases into which Robertson and I have divided a young child's response to the loss of his mother-figure, namely the phase we have termed 'detachment'. This phase, already described in the opening chapters of the earlier volumes (Chapter 2 of Volume I and Chapter 1 of Volume II) but so far not discussed, is regularly seen whenever a child between the ages of about six months and three years has spent a week or more out of his mother's care and without being cared for by a specially assigned substitute. It is characterized by an almost complete absence of attachment behaviour when he first meets his mother again.[11]

This puzzling phenomenon was observed with especial care by Heinicke and Westheimer (1966) in their study of ten young children, aged from thirteen to thirty-two months, who spent a minimum of twelve days in one of three residential nurseries.[12]

On meeting mother for the first time after the days or weeks away every one of the ten children showed some degree of detachment. Two seemed not to recognize mother. The other eight turned away or even walked away from her. Most of them either cried or came close to tears; a number alternated between a tearful and an expressionless face.

In contrast to these blank, tearful retreats from mother, all but one of the children responded affectionately when they first met father again. Furthermore, five were friendly to Ilse Westheimer as well.

As regards detachment, two findings of earlier studies were clearly confirmed in this one. The first is that detachment is especially characteristic of the way in which a separated child behaves when he meets his mother again, and is much less evident with father; the second is that the duration of a child's detachment from mother correlates highly and significantly with the length of his time away.

In nine cases detachment from mother persisted in some degree throughout almost the first three days of reunion. In five children it was so marked that each mother complained, characteristically, that her child treated her as though she were a stranger; none of these children showed any tendency to cling to her. In the other

[11] It should be noted that this use of the term 'detachment' differs radically from that of workers who use it to refer either to a child's tendency to explore away from his mother or to the increasing self-reliance he shows as he gets older (a theme discussed in Volume II, Chapter 21).

[12] The précis of their findings that follows is taken from the first chapter of *Separation: Anxiety and Anger.*

four, detachment was less pronounced; phases during which they turned away from mother alternated with phases during which they clung to her. Only one child, Elizabeth, who was the oldest and whose separation was among the shortest, was affectionate towards her mother by the end of the first day home.

When a mother does not receive the natural responses she expects from her child she finds it both puzzling and wounding. Even when he is hurt he is likely still to make no attempt to seek her comfort and will even spurn her attempts to provide it. To anyone familiar with young children this behaviour seems very extraordinary. Some years ago Robertson observed it in a small boy who had been admitted to hospital at the age of thirteen months and had remained there for three years. During the month following his return home, during which he remained wholly detached, he burned his hand in the fire. Instead of howling and seeking comfort like the ordinary toddler, he smiled and kept to himself. (Reported in Ainsworth and Boston, 1952.)

The same behaviour was noted in one child of the Heinicke and Westheimer series (pp. 112–58):

Owen was aged 2 years and 2 months at the start of what proved to be an eleven-week separation. Both during the journey home with his father and after he had entered the house and met mother he remained characteristically numb, silent and unresponsive; in fact it was fifty minutes before he showed the first flicker of animation. Then, and during the next couple of days, he began sometimes to turn to his father; but his mother he continued to ignore. During his second day home he bumped his knee and, when he seemed about to cry, mother at once offered comfort. Owen however passed her by and went to father instead. Not unnaturally mother felt this as a cruel rebuff.

Clearly many different views can be taken of the phenomenon of detachment and it has already been the subject of some debate (A. Freud 1960; Bowlby 1963). The view I took in my earlier papers is that detachment is an expression of what in the psychoanalytic tradition has always been referred to as a defence or, and better, as the result of a defensive process. The suggestion I made is that defensive processes are a regular constituent of mourning at every age and that what characterizes pathology is not their occurrence but the forms they take and especially the degree to which they are reversible. In infants and children, it appears, defensive processes once set in motion are apt to stabilize and persist.

The thesis I have advanced, therefore, is that in a young child an experience of separation from, or loss of, mother-figure is especially apt to evoke psychological processes of a kind that are as crucial for psychopathology as inflammation and the resulting scar tissue are for physiopathology. This does not mean that a crippling of personality is the inevitable result; but it does mean that, as in the case, say, of rheumatic fever, scar tissue is all too often formed that in later life leads to more or less severe dysfunction. The processes in question, I have suggested, are pathological variants of some of those that characterize healthy mourning.

Although this theoretical position is closely akin to positions taken by others, it appears none the less to be different from them. Its strength lies in relating the pathological responses met with in older patients to responses to loss and threats of loss that are to be observed in childhood, thereby providing a possible link between psychiatric conditions of later life and childhood experience. In the latter half of the following chapter and in more detail in Bowlby (1960b) this formulation is compared to some of its predecessors. Whether or not it proves a useful way of ordering and understanding the data and, if so, what modifications or elaborations may be called for are questions to which this volume addresses itself.

CHAPTER 2

The Place of Loss and Mourning
in Psychopathology

Although we know that after such a loss the acute state of mourning will
subside, we also know we shall remain inconsolable and will never find a
substitute. No matter what may fill the gap, even if it be filled completely,
it nevertheless remains something else. And actually this is how it should
be. It is the only way of perpetuating that love which we do not want to
relinquish.
SIGMUND FREUD[1]

A clinical tradition

It is eighty years since Freud first adumbrated the idea that both
hysteria and melancholia are manifestations of pathological mourning following more or less recent bereavement,[2] and sixty since in
'Mourning and Melancholia' he advanced the hypothesis more
explicitly (1917). Since then there have been a host of other studies
all of which in different ways support it. Clinical experience and a
reading of the evidence leaves little doubt of the truth of the main
proposition—that much psychiatric illness is an expression of
pathological mourning—or that such illness includes many cases of
anxiety state, depressive illness and hysteria, and also more than
one kind of character disorder. Plainly Freud had discovered a large
and promising field of enquiry. Yet it is one that only in recent
years has been receiving the attention it deserves.

   Controversy, never absent, still abounds. To understand it we
turn to history. In doing so it is necessary to trace how ideas have
developed in regard to two distinct types of problem:

– ideas regarding the nature of mourning processes themselves and
  in what ways healthy and pathological processes differ
– ideas regarding why some individuals and not others should
  respond to loss in a pathological way.

   In regard to the first set of problems the early literature is concerned almost exclusively with the mourning of adults. In regard to

[1] In a letter to Ludwig Binswanger who had lost a son.
[2] According to Strachey (1957), the first reference is in a manuscript
dated 31st May 1897, a copy of which Freud sent to Fliess (Freud 1954).

23

the second it is concerned very largely with events and responses of childhood. Nevertheless, in regard to the nature of the childhood events, the phases of development during which children may be especially sensitive, and the way both the events and the responses evoked are conceptualized there are deep divisions between different schools of psychoanalytic thought.

In tracing how ideas regarding these issues developed during the years up to about 1960 opportunity is taken to indicate the directions in which presently available evidence seems to point.

Ideas regarding the nature of mourning processes, healthy and pathological

In the history of psychoanalytic thought the study of grief and mourning has usually been approached by way of the study of depressive illness in adults. Because of this we find that few attempts have been made by psychoanalysts to conceptualize the processes of grief and mourning as such. Until about 1960 only Freud, Melanie Klein, Lindemann, and Edith Jacobson had tackled the problem; and Lindemann appears to have been alone in having made the first-hand study of acute grief his main concern. Much of the clinical literature, indeed, deals exclusively with depressive illness, and some of it makes little or no reference to bereavement or other actual loss. Even when the roles of bereavement and mourning are clearly recognized, moreover, the bulk of clinical literature is concerned more with pathological variants of mourning than with the normal process. An account of the development of psychoanalytic theories of mourning is given in Bowlby (1961b).

It is a misfortune that, for half a century or longer, the clinical tradition should have remained thus one-sided since the balance might well have been redressed by drawing on contributions stemming from other traditions of psychological thought. Two of the most notable are those of Darwin (1872) and Shand (1920). Because of his concern with comparative studies, Darwin's interest in the expression of the emotions lay in the functions served and the muscles used. In keeping with conclusions reached on other grounds, his analysis traces much of an adult's expression in times of grief to the crying of an infant.[3] Shand, drawing for his data on the works of English poets and French prose-writers, not only delineates most

[3] In Chapters 6 and 7 of *The Expression of the Emotions in Animals and Man* Darwin analyses the muscle movements engaged and the expressions

24

of the main features of grief as we now know them but discusses in a systematic way its relation to fear and anger. As a sensitive and perspicacious study his book ranks high and deserves to be better known. Among sociologists and social psychologists whose publications date from the nineteen-thirties and whose work merits the attention of clinicians are Eliot (1930, 1955), Waller (1951) and Marris (1958).

Because the psychological processes engaged in mourning, both healthy and pathological, are manifold and intricately related to each other, points of controversy have been, and still are, numerous. It is convenient to consider them under eight headings:

(i) what is the nature of the psychological processes engaged in healthy mourning?

(ii) how is the painfulness of mourning to be accounted for?

(iii) how is mourning related to anxiety?

(iv) what sorts of motivation are present in mourning?

(v) what is the role in mourning of anger and hatred?

(vi) what is the role in mourning of identification with the person lost?

(vii) in what ways does pathological mourning differ from healthy mourning?

(viii) at what stage of development and by means of what processes does an individual arrive at a state which enables him thereafter to respond to loss in a healthy manner?

(i) All who have discussed *the nature of the processes engaged in healthy mourning* are agreed that amongst other things they effect, in some degree at least, a withdrawal of emotional investment in the lost person and that they may prepare for making a relationship with a new one. How we conceive their achieving this change, however, depends on how we conceptualize affectional bonds. Because it is at this point that the concepts adopted in this work differ most from those of Freud and other analysts, it is in regard to those processes that it becomes most necessary to attempt new formulations.

exhibited in anxiety, grief and despair, and advances the view that they all derive from an infant's screaming. 'In all cases of distress, whether great or small, our brains tend through long habit to send an order to certain muscles to contract, as if we were still infants on the point of screaming out; but this order . . . we are able partially to counteract' by means which are unconscious to us.

Traditionally in psychoanalytic writings emphasis has been placed on identification with the lost object as the main process involved in mourning, such identification being regarded as compensatory for the loss sustained. Furthermore, following Freud, the dynamics of mourning are commonly cast within a form of theory that (a) sees the process of identification as almost exclusively oral in character, and (b) sees libido as a quantity of energy that undergoes transformation. There are reasons for discarding each of these formulations. First, evidence suggests that identification is neither the only, nor even the main, process involved in mourning. Secondly, identification is almost certainly independent of orality, though it may sometimes become related to it. Thirdly, as is made clear in an earlier volume (Bowlby 1969), the hydrodynamic model of instinct, which pictures instincts on the model of a liquid that varies in quantity and pressure, has serious limitations. A different account of the processes of healthy mourning, framed within the new paradigm, is therefore required.

(ii) In attempts to account for the *painfulness* of mourning two main hypotheses have been advanced:

– because of the persistent and insatiable nature of the yearning for the lost figure, pain is inevitable
– pain following loss is the result of a sense of guilt and a fear of retaliation.

It should be noted that these hypotheses are not mutually exclusive, and that there are therefore three possible schools of thought. In the event, however, there are only two. The first, to which Freud belongs, holds that the pain of yearning is of great importance in its own right; it may or may not be exacerbated and complicated by a sense of guilt or fear of retaliation. The second, represented especially by Melanie Klein, pays less attention to yearning as something painful *per se* and holds that, since guilt and paranoid fear are believed always to be present in bereavement and always to cause distress, taken by itself the painfulness of yearning is of little more than secondary importance. The first of these schools is the one evidence seems to favour.

(iii) Our third theme, *the relation of mourning to anxiety*, is one already discussed in the previous volume. There I have adopted and elaborated the view advanced by Freud in the final pages of *Inhibitions, Symptoms and Anxiety* that when the loved figure is believed to be temporarily absent the response is one of anxiety, when he or she appears to be permanently absent it is one of pain and mourning. I have shown also how different this view is from that of Klein, which regards fear of annihilation and persecutory anxiety as being primary. In the decade before Freud's formulation Shand had already advanced a view substantially similar to his. Fear, he suggests, presupposes hope. Only when we are striving and hoping for better things are we anxious lest we fail to obtain them. 'So farewell hope, and with hope farewell fear', wrote Milton.[4] Because, however, hope may be present in any degree, there is a continuum in feeling between anxiety and despair. During grief, feeling often travels back and forth, now nearer to anxiety, now to despair.

(iv) In exploring this line of thought Shand has also contributed to an understanding of our fourth theme, the complex *motivation present in situations evoking grief*, or, to use the word he favours, sorrow. The urge to regain the person lost, he points out, is powerful and often persists long after reason has deemed it useless. Expressions of this urge are weeping and the appeal to others for assistance, an appeal which inevitably carries with it an admission of weakness: 'Thus the expressions and gestures of sorrow—the glance of the eyes indicating the direction of expectation, its watchings and waitings, as well as its pathetic cries—all are evidence that the essential end of its system is to obtain the strength and help of others to remedy its own proved weakness' (p. 315). This appeal Shand regards, I believe rightly, as stemming from primitive roots and as having survival value: 'the cry of sorrow . . . tends to preserve the life of the young by bringing those who watch over them to their assistance'. It is a mode of conceptualizing the data that is strongly supported by the findings of Darwin (1872) on the expressive movements occurring when grief is experienced. In the chapters to follow, Shand's and Darwin's ideas are strongly endorsed and given a central position. Main themes are that a mourner is repeatedly seized, whether he knows it or not, by an urge to call for, to search

[4] Another famous Englishman to have expressed similar sentiments is Winston Churchill. In describing his feelings during escape from a prison camp he writes, 'when hope had departed, fear had gone as well'.

for and to recover the lost person and that not infrequently he acts in accordance with that urge. 'Bereave', we note, stems from the same root as 'rob'.

Nevertheless, when we study the various clinical traditions of theorizing about mourning, we find that recognition of the urge to recover the lost person and, especially, the actions to which it gives rise, is conspicuous by its absence. True, there is no lack of reference to the emotions that accompany the urge. For example, Freud refers repeatedly to yearning for the lost object, a theme later taken up and elaborated by Jacobson (1957); Klein (1948) discusses defence as directed against pining; whilst Bibring (1953) draws attention to the mourner's wish to regain the lost object and the resulting helplessness and hopelessness that he experiences. What we miss is clear recognition that these emotions and wishes are but the subjective counterparts of a mourner's urge to act—to call for and to search for the lost person—and that not infrequently he engages in those very acts, fragmented and incomplete though they be.

(v) The fifth theme, and one of the most controversial, concerns the roles of *anger and hatred in mourning*. Although all are agreed that anger with the lost figure (often unconscious and directed elsewhere) plays a major role in pathological mourning, there has been much doubt whether its presence is compatible with healthy mourning. Freud's position is not altogether consistent. On the one hand are many passages in which he makes it clear that in his view all relationships are characterized by ambivalence,[5] and a corollary of this would seem to be that ambivalence must enter into all forms of mourning also. On the other hand is the view he expressed in 'Mourning and Melancholia', and it would appear never revised, that ambivalence is absent in normal mourning and, when present, transforms what would otherwise have been normal into pathological mourning: 'Melancholia . . . is marked by a determinant which is absent in normal mourning or which, if it is present, transforms the latter into pathological mourning. The loss of a

---

[5] E.g. 'Up to a point ambivalence of feeling of this sort, appears to be normal' ('The Dynamics of the Transference', *SE* 12, p. 106). 'This ambivalence is present to a greater or less amount in the innate disposition of everyone' (*Totem and Taboo*, *SE* 13, p. 60). 'The unconscious of all human beings is full enough of such death wishes, even against those they love' ('A case of Homosexuality in a Woman', *SE* 18, pp. 162–3).

love-object is an excellent opportunity for the ambivalence in love-relationships to make itself effective.' 'Melancholia contains something more than normal mourning . . . the relation to the object is no simple one; it is complicated by the conflict due to ambivalence' (*SE* 14, pp. 250 and 256).

In Chapter 6 it is shown that evidence derived from studies of the mourning of ordinary adults does not support that view: ambivalence towards the person lost characterizes many cases in which mourning follows a healthy course, although it is admittedly both more intense and more persistent in those that develop pathologically.

There can in fact be no doubt that in normal mourning anger expressed towards one target or another is the rule. Outbursts during mourning have been reported as being frequent by sociologists, e.g. Eliot (1955), Marris (1958) and Hobson (1964), while anthropological literature presents evidence either of the direct expression of anger, for example by the Australian aboriginals (Durkheim 1915), or of special social sanctions against expressing it. Shand (1920) in his picture of grieving gives anger a central place: 'The tendency of sorrow to arouse anger under certain conditions appears to be part of the fundamental constitution of the mind' (p. 347). Thus, neither the occurrence nor the frequency of anger can be regarded any longer as at issue.

Furthermore, there are good grounds for believing that even in healthy mourning a person's anger is often directed towards the person lost, though it may equally often be directed towards other persons, including the self. Among the many problems requiring study, therefore, are the causes of these various expressions of anger, the functions they may serve (if any), the targets towards which they may be directed, and the vicissitudes, many of them pathological, that angry impulses may undergo.

(vi) Ever since Freud's early contributions to the clinical problems of mourning, *the process of identification with the lost object* has been a cornerstone of every psychoanalytic theory. Although at first Freud believed the process to occur only in pathological mourning, subsequently (1923) he came to regard it as a principal feature of all mourning. In reaching that conclusion he was much influenced by the theory, which he was advancing at about the same time (*Group Psychology*, 1921), that 'identification is the original form of emotional tie with an object [and that] in a regressive way it becomes a substitute for a libidinal tie' (*SE* 18, pp. 107–8). A large edifice of psychoanalytic theory has been built on those propositions.

To question the grounds on which identification has been given such a key role is thus to break with a long and influential tradition. Yet it is questioned on several grounds. In the first place there is little support beyond the weight of tradition for supposing that identification is the original form of emotional tie. In the second, no systematic data have ever been offered to support the idea that identification with the person lost is central to the mourning process, whilst much of the evidence at present explained in these terms (e.g. Smith 1971) can, it is believed, be understood far better in terms of a persistent, though disguised, striving to recover the lost person (see Chapter 6). Finally, the theoretical superstructure built by Freud and others on top of his original suggestion is replaced in the paradigm adopted here by other forms of theory. Thus, in the upshot, the role given to identificatory processes in the theory advanced here is a subordinate one: they are regarded as occurring only sporadically and, when prominent, to be indicative of pathology.

(vii) This brings us to our seventh theme, that of *the differences between healthy and pathological mourning*. In 'Mourning and Melancholia' Freud suggested three criteria, each of which has been influential on clinical theorizing but none of which is adopted in this work. His first criterion, that the presence of hatred for the lost object (expressed either directly or, indirectly, through self-reproach) betokens pathology has already been referred to, and discarded as out of keeping with the evidence. His second, that identification with the lost object is present only in pathological mourning, he abandoned a few years after he had proposed it (*The Ego and the Id*, 1923), more perhaps because of a new emphasis on identification in his theory of object relations than because of new observations of how mourning proceeds. His third suggestion is cast in terms of libido theory and is therefore unrelated to the present paradigm. (It is that one form of pathological mourning, namely melancholia, differs from healthy mourning in the disposition of the libido; in healthy mourning the libido that is withdrawn from the lost object is regarded as transferred to a new one, whereas in melancholia it is withdrawn into the ego and gives rise to secondary narcissism.)

The approach adopted here is the same as that of Lindemann who, in relating to their healthy counterparts the various morbid processes of mourning that he describes, regards them as exaggerations or distortions of the normal processes. The more detailed the picture we obtain of healthy mourning the more clearly are we able to identify the pathological variants as being the result of defensive processes having interfered with and diverted its course.

(viii) This raises our eighth and final problem: *at what stage of development and by means of what processes does an individual arrive at a state which enables him thereafter to respond to loss in a favourable manner?*

Traditionally this question has been raised in the context of trying to understand the fixation point to which melancholics regress during their illness. Many psychoanalytic formulations postulate the phase as occurring in earliest infancy and carry with them the corollary that the capacity to respond to loss in a favourable manner should, if all goes well with development, be attained during that very early period. By Klein and her followers this critical phase of psychic development is known as the 'depressive position'. An account of how these and related ideas have developed is given in the next section.

An early dating of this phase of development is in fact open to much doubt. For the evidence, reviewed in later chapters, suggests that the capacity to react to loss in such a way that in course of time a resumption of personal relationships can take place is one that develops very slowly during childhood and adolescence and may perhaps never be as fully attained as we should like to believe.

This completes our brief review of some of the main themes needing consideration in any discussion of mourning. What is impressive about mourning is not only the number and variety of response systems that are engaged but the way in which they tend to conflict with one another. Loss of a loved person gives rise not only to an intense desire for reunion but to anger at his departure and, later, usually to some degree of detachment; it gives rise not only to a cry for help, but sometimes also to a rejection of those who respond. No wonder it is painful to experience and difficult to understand. As Shand rightly concludes: 'The nature of sorrow is so complex, its effects in different characters so various, that it is rare, if not impossible, for any writer to show an insight into all of them' (Shand 1920, p. 361).

Ideas to account for individual differences in response to loss

In their attempts to account for individual differences in the responses of adults to loss, most clinicians have adopted a form of theory that attributes importance to events and responses of childhood. Yet, beyond this, their opinions have been deeply divided: in regard to the nature of the relevant events, to the phases of development during which they are thought to have greatest impact, and to the way that events and responses are best conceptualized.

The classical school of psychoanalytic thought, we find, attributes great aetiological significance to childhood experiences of a kind which, it is held here, can without difficulty be construed in terms of loss or threat of loss but which in that tradition are conceived in quite different terms. Accordingly, when conceptualizing the psychological processes set in train by the experiences in question, members of the classical school have not used concepts related to loss and mourning but have, instead, elaborated a different set. Because the resulting tradition began early and has been influential it is useful to start by reviewing the work and concepts of these pioneers and thence to consider, first, the way that the clinical data to which they draw attention are relevant to our interests and, secondly, how these same data can be understood and reformulated within the concepts of separation, loss and mourning advocated here. As a separate step we consider ideas of a competing school of thought, the Kleinian. Whereas members of that school invoke, as I do, experiences of loss during early childhood as aetiological agents and conceptualize the psychological processes which they set in train in terms of mourning, the nature of the losses and also the phase of life they implicate differ greatly from those I believe important. Furthermore, the theoretical paradigm they adopt is far removed from the one adopted here.

Soon after the publication of Freud's 'Mourning and Melancholia', Abraham (1924a) advanced an hypothesis that has influenced all later workers with a psychoanalytic orientation. As a result of treating several melancholic patients he came to the conclusion that 'in the last resort melancholic depression is derived from disagree-

able experiences in the childhood of the patient'. He therefore postulated that, during their childhood, melancholics have suffered
from what he termed a 'primal parathymia'. In these passages,
however, Abraham never uses the words 'grief' and 'mourning',
despite his having already espoused the view that melancholia is to
be understood as a pathological variant of mourning. Nor is it clear
that he recognized that for a young child the experience of losing
mother, or of losing her love, is in very truth a bereavement.

Since then, a number of other psychoanalysts in trying to trace
the childhood roots of depressive illness and of personalities prone
to develop it have drawn attention to unhappy experiences in the
early years of their patients' lives. Except for Melanie Klein and
her associates, however, few have conceptualized the experiences in
terms of loss, or threat of loss, and of childhood mourning. Nevertheless, when we come to study the experiences referred to in the
light of what is now known about the development of a child's
attachment to his mother-figure, it seems evident that this is a frame
of reference that fits them well. Let us consider as examples three
patients described in the literature.

In 1936 Gerö reported on two patients suffering from depression.
One of them, he concluded, had been 'starved of love' as a child;
the other had been sent to a residential nursery and had only
returned home when he was three years old. Each showed intense
ambivalence towards any person who was loved, a condition which,
Gerö believed, could be traced to the early experience. In the
second case, he speaks of both a fixation on the mother and an
inability to forgive her for the separation.

Jacobson, in her extensive writing on the psychopathology of
depression, draws regularly on a female patient, Peggy, whose
analysis she describes in two papers (1943, 1946). On referral Peggy,
aged 24, was in a state of severe depression with suicidal impulses
and depersonalization; these symptoms had been precipitated by a
loss, actually the loss of her lover. The childhood experience to
which Jacobson attributes major significance occurred when Peggy
was $3\frac{1}{2}$ years old. Her mother went to hospital to have a new baby,
whilst she and her father stayed with the maternal grandmother.
Quarrels developed and father departed. 'The child was left alone,
disappointed by her father and eagerly awaiting her mother's return.
However, when the mother did return it was with the baby.' Peggy
recalled feeling 'This was not my mother, it was a different person'

(an experience not uncommon in young children who have been separated from their mothers for a few weeks). It was soon after this, Jacobson believes, that 'the little girl broke down in her first deep depression'.

Now it may be questioned both whether the experiences of these patients' early childhoods were accurately recalled and also whether the analysts were right in attributing to them aetiological significance. But if we accept, as I am inclined to do, both the validity of the experiences and their significance, the concept of childhood mourning is found to be well fitted not only to describe how the patient responded at the time but also to relate the experience of childhood to the psychiatric illness of later life. Neither author utilizes that concept, however. Instead, both use words such as 'disappointment' and 'disillusionment' which carry very different meanings.

Several other analysts, whilst in greater or less degree alive to the pathogenic role of such experiences in childhood, also do not conceptualize a child's response to loss in terms of grief or mourning. One is Fairbairn (1952). A second is Stengel who, in his studies of compulsive wandering (1939, 1941, 1943), draws special attention to the urge to recover a lost loved figure. A third is the present writer in his earlier work (1944, 1951). Others are Anna Freud (1960) and Rene Spitz (1946b) both of whom, by rejecting the notion that young children mourn, exclude from consideration the hypothesis that neurotic and psychotic character might in some cases be the result of mourning processes evoked during childhood having taken an unfavourable course and thereby left the person prone to respond to later losses in a pathological way.

A major reason why a child's response to loss is so often not regarded as a form of mourning is, as we have seen, the tradition that confines the concept to processes that have a healthy outcome. The difficulties consequent on that restricted usage are illustrated in an important paper, 'Absence of Grief', by Helene Deutsch (1937). In her discussion of four patients there is firm recognition both of the central place of childhood loss in the production of symptoms and character deviations, and also of a defence mechanism that, following loss, may lead to an absence of affect. Nevertheless, although she relates this mechanism to mourning, it is represented more as an alternative to, than as a pathological variant of, mourning. This distinction is not trivial. For to regard the defensive

34

process following childhood loss as an alternative to mourning is to miss both that defensive processes of similar kinds but of lesser degree and later onset enter also into healthy mourning, and also that what is pathological is not so much the defensive processes themselves as their scope, intensity and tendency to persist.

Similarly, although Freud was on the one hand deeply interested in the pathogenic role of mourning and on the other, especially in his later years, was also aware of the pathogenic role of childhood loss, he seems, none the less, never to have put his finger on childhood mourning and its disposition to take a pathological course as concepts which link these two sets of ideas together. This is well illustrated in his discussion of the 'splitting of the ego in the defensive process', to which he was giving special attention at the end of his life (1938).

In one of his papers (1927) Freud describes two patients in whom an ego split had followed loss of father.

In the analysis of two young men, I learnt that each of them—one in his second and the other in his tenth year—had refused to acknowledge the death of his father . . . and yet neither of them had developed a psychosis. A very important piece of reality had thus been denied by the ego . . . [But] it was only one current of their mental processes that had not acknowledged the father's death; there was another that was fully aware of the fact; the one which was consistent with reality [namely that the father was dead] stood alongside the one which accorded with a wish [namely that the father should still be living] (*SE* 21, pp. 155–6).

In this and related papers, however, Freud does not relate his discovery of such splits to the pathology of mourning in general nor to childhood mourning in particular. He did recognize them, nevertheless, as the not uncommon sequelae of bereavements in early life. 'I suspect', he remarks when discussing his findings, 'that similar occurrences are by no means rare in childhood.' Later studies show that his suspicion was well founded.

Thus a reading of the literature shows that, despite attributing much pathogenic significance to loss of a parent and to loss of love, in the main tradition of psychoanalytic theorizing the origins of pathological mourning in adults (or, as some might insist, of pathological alternatives to mourning) and of the consequent psychiatric illnesses to which they lead are connected neither with childhood mourning nor with the tendency for processes of mourning when evoked during infancy and childhood to take a pathological course.

A major contribution of Melanie Klein's (1935, 1940) is to have made that connection. Infants and young children mourn and go through phases of depression, she maintains, and their modes of responding at such times are determinants of the way that in later life they will respond to further loss. Certain modes of defence, she believes, are to be understood as 'directed against the "pining" for the lost object'. In these respects my approach not only resembles hers but has been influenced by it. Nevertheless, there are many and far-reaching differences between our respective positions. They concern the nature of the experiences of loss that are thought to be of aetiological significance, the age-span during which such losses having this significance are thought to occur, the nature and origin of anxiety and anger, and also the role of contemporary and subsequent conditions that are thought to influence the way a child responds to loss. Whereas, as will be seen in Part III, there is evidence that a child's responses are greatly influenced by conditions obtaining in his family at the time of and after the loss, Klein not only fails to raise that possibility but, by putting the emphasis elsewhere, conveys the impression that such conditions would be of little account.

The experiences of loss that Klein suggests are pathogenic all belong to the first year of life and are mostly connected with feeding and weaning. Aggression is treated as an expression of a death instinct, and anxiety as a result of its projection. None of this is convincing. In the first place the evidence she advances regarding the overwhelming importance of the first year and of weaning is, on scrutiny, far from impressive (Bowlby 1960b). In the second, her hypotheses regarding aggression and anxiety, together with her overall paradigm, cannot be reconciled with any biological thinking. Because so much of her theorizing is implausible it would be easy to reject her useful ideas along with the rest. That would be a pity.

The position adopted here is that, although the paradigm that Klein adopts is rejected, and also the hypotheses she advances to account for individual differences in response to loss, her ideas are held, none the less, to contain the seeds of a productive way of ordering the data. The alternative elaborations which, it is claimed, the evidence favours are that the most significant object that can be lost is not the breast but the mother herself (and sometimes the father), that the vulnerable period is not confined to the first year but extends over a number of years of childhood (as Freud always held) and on into adolescence as well, and that loss of a parent gives rise not only to separation anxiety and grief but to processes of mourning in which aggression, the function of which is to achieve reunion, plays a major part. Whilst sticking closely to the data, this formulation has the additional merit of fitting readily into biological theory.

A fuller account of how responses to loss during childhood have been treated in the psychoanalytic literature will be found in an earlier paper (Bowlby 1960b).

CHAPTER 3

Conceptual Framework

According to our times and to our experience we represent the natural and the human world by a great set of images. To this set of images we apply, as a template, a system of hypotheses which seems to us coherent. The difficulty in scientific advance arises when some new experience necessitates a reassembling of the pattern of our images.

C. F. A. PANTIN, *The Relation between the Sciences*

Attachment theory: an outline

Since the conceptual framework I bring to the study of mourning differs from those traditionally applied, it may be useful to review some of its principal features and to elaborate on those that are of special relevance.

When I began my studies of the effects on young children of their being placed away from mother in a strange place with strange people, my theoretical framework was that of psychoanalysis. Finding its metapsychological superstructure unsatisfactory, however, I have been developing a paradigm that, whilst incorporating much psychoanalytic thinking, differs from the traditional one in adopting a number of principles that derive from the relatively new disciplines of ethology and control theory. By so doing, the new paradigm is enabled to dispense with many abstract concepts, including those of psychic energy and drive, and to forge links with cognitive psychology. Merits claimed for it are that, whilst its concepts are psychological and well suited to the clinical data of interest to psychoanalysts, they are compatible with those of neurophysiology and developmental psychology, and also that they are capable of meeting the ordinary requirements of a scientific discipline.[1]

[1] For a fuller exposition of the paradigm see Chapters 3 to 10 of the first volume of this work. In addition, the reader is referred to the monograph by Emanuel Peterfreund (1971), referred to in the Preface, especially his critiques of the concepts of psychic energy and ego (Chapters 3 and 4) and his lucid exposition of the basic concepts of biological order, organization, information and control (Chapters 7 to 12). See also his recent article 'On Information and System Models for Psychoanalysis' (Peterfreund, in press).

A special advantage claimed for the paradigm is that it facilitates a new and illuminating way of conceptualizing the propensity of human beings to make strong affectional bonds to particular others and of explaining the many forms of emotional distress and personality disturbance, including anxiety, anger, depression and emotional detachment, to which unwilling separation and loss give rise. The body of theory resulting, which for convenience I term attachment theory, deals with the same phenomena that hitherto have been dealt with in terms of 'dependency need' or of 'object relations' or of 'symbiosis and individuation'. In contrast to those theories, however, attachment theory generalizes as follows:

(a) Attachment behaviour is conceived as any form of behaviour that results in a person attaining or retaining proximity to some other differentiated and preferred individual. So long as the attachment figure remains accessible and responsive the behaviour may consist of little more than checking by eye or ear on the whereabouts of the figure and exchanging occasional glances and greetings. In certain circumstances, however, following or clinging to the attachment figure may occur and also calling or crying, which are likely to elicit his or her caregiving.

(b) As a class of behaviour with its own dynamic, attachment behaviour is conceived as distinct from feeding behaviour and sexual behaviour and of at least an equal significance in human life.

(c) During the course of healthy development attachment behaviour leads to the development of affectional bonds or attachments, initially between child and parent and later between adult and adult. The forms of behaviour and the bonds to which they lead are present and active throughout the life cycle (and by no means confined to childhood as other theories assume).

(d) Attachment behaviour, like other forms of instinctive behaviour, is mediated by behavioural systems which early in development become goal-corrected. Homeostatic systems of this type are so structured that, by means of feedback, continuous account is taken of any discrepancies there may be between initial instruction and current performance so that behaviour becomes modified accordingly. In planning and guiding goal-corrected behaviour use is made of representational models both of the self's capabilities and of relevant features of the environment. The goal of attachment behaviour is to maintain certain degrees of proximity to, or of communication with, the discriminated attachment figure(s).

(e) Whereas an attachment bond endures, the various forms of attachment behaviour that contribute to it are active only when required. Thus the systems mediating attachment behaviour are activated only by certain conditions, for example strangeness, fatigue, anything frightening, and unavailability or unresponsiveness of attachment figure, and are terminated only by certain other conditions, for example a familiar environment and the ready availability and responsiveness of an attachment figure. When attachment behaviour is strongly aroused, however, termination may require touching, or clinging, or the actively reassuring behaviour of the attachment figure.

(f) Many of the most intense emotions arise during the formation, the maintenance, the disruption and the renewal of attachment relationships. The formation of a bond is described as falling in love, maintaining a bond as loving someone, and losing a partner as grieving over someone. Similarly, threat of loss arouses anxiety and actual loss gives rise to sorrow; while each of these situations is likely to arouse anger. The unchallenged maintenance of a bond is experienced as a source of security and the renewal of a bond as a source of joy. Because such emotions are usually a reflection of the state of a person's affectional bonds, the psychology and psychopathology of emotion is found to be in large part the psychology and psychopathology of affectional bonds.

(g) Attachment behaviour has become a characteristic of many species during the course of their evolution because it contributes to the individual's survival by keeping him in touch with his caregiver(s), thereby reducing the risk of his coming to harm, for example from cold, hunger or drowning and, in man's environment of evolutionary adaptedness, especially from predators.

(h) Behaviour complementary to attachment behaviour and serving a complementary function, that of protecting the attached individual, is caregiving. This is commonly shown by a parent, or other adult, towards a child or adolescent, but is also shown by one adult towards another, especially in times of ill health, stress or old age.

(i) In view of attachment behaviour being potentially active throughout life and also of its having the vital biological function proposed, it is held a grave error to suppose that, when active in an adult, attachment behaviour is indicative either of pathology or of regression to immature behaviour. The latter view, which is characteristic of almost all other versions of psychoanalytic theory, results from conceptualizations derived from theories of orality and dependency which are rejected here as out of keeping with the evidence.

(j) Psychopathology is regarded as due to a person's psychological development having followed a deviant pathway, and not as due to his suffering a fixation at, or a regression to, some early stage of development.

(k) Disturbed patterns of attachment behaviour can be present at any age due to development having followed a deviant pathway. One of the commonest forms of disturbance is the over-ready elicitation of attachment behaviour, resulting in anxious attachment. Another, to which special attention is given in this volume, is a partial or complete deactivation of attachment behaviour.

(l) Principal determinants of the pathway along which an individual's attachment behaviour develops, and of the pattern in which it becomes organized, are the experiences he has with his attachment figures during his years of immaturity—infancy, childhood and adolescence.

(m) On the way in which an individual's attachment behaviour becomes organized within his personality turns the pattern of affectional bonds he makes during his life.

Within this framework it is not difficult to indicate how the effects of loss, and the states of stress and distress to which they lead, can be conceived.

Stressors and states of stress and distress

A characteristic of any homeostatic system is that it is capable of effective operation only when the environmental conditions relevant to its operation remain within certain limits. When they do not the system becomes overstretched and eventually fails. An example, taken from physiology, is the system responsible for keeping body temperature close to the norm. So long as the ambient temperature remains within certain upper and lower limits it operates effectively. But when ambient temperature stays either above or below these limits for sufficiently long the system is unable to achieve its goal. As a result body temperature rises or falls and the organism suffers from hyper- or hypothermia. The environmental conditions that produce these physiological states are termed stressors, the states themselves states of stress. The personal experience is one of distress.

Since the goal of attachment behaviour is to maintain an affectional bond, any situation that seems to be endangering the bond elicits action designed to preserve it; and the greater the danger of loss appears to be the more intense and varied are the actions elicited to prevent it. In such circumstances all the most powerful forms of attachment behaviour become activated—clinging, crying and perhaps angry coercion. This is the phase of protest and one of acute physiological stress and emotional distress. When these actions are successful the bond is restored, the activities cease and the states of stress and distress are alleviated.

When, however, the effort to restore the bond is not successful sooner or later the effort wanes. But usually it does not cease. On the contrary, evidence shows that, at perhaps increasingly long intervals, the effort to restore the bond is renewed: the pangs of grief and perhaps an urge to search are then experienced afresh. This means that the person's attachment behaviour is remaining constantly primed and that, in conditions still to be defined, it becomes activated anew. The condition of the organism is then one of chronic stress and is experienced as one of chronic distress. At intervals, moreover, both stress and distress are likely again to become acute.

This brief outline is greatly extended in the chapters to follow. Meanwhile, it is necessary to indicate how the terms 'healthy' and 'pathological' are being applied. Following a lead from Freud (1926), Engel (1961) has provided a valuable analogy. Loss of a loved person, he insists, is as traumatic psychologically as being severely wounded or burned is physiologically. Invoking homeostatic principles he proceeds: 'The experience of uncomplicated grief represents a manifest and gross departure from the dynamic state considered representative of health and well-being . . . It involves suffering and an impairment of the capacity to function, which may last for days, weeks, or even months.' The processes of mourning can thus be likened to the processes of healing that follow a severe wound or burn. Such healing processes, we know, may take a course which in time leads to full, or nearly full, function being restored; or they may, on the contrary, take one of many courses each of which has as its outcome an impairment of function of greater or less degree. In the same way processes of mourning may take a course that leads in time to more or less complete restoration of function, namely, to a renewal of the capacity to make and maintain love relationships; or they may take a course that leaves this function impaired in greater or less degree. Just as the terms healthy and pathological are applicable to the different courses taken by physiological healing processes, so may they be applied to the different courses taken by mourning processes. Nevertheless, it must be recognized that in matters of health and pathology no clear lines can be drawn, and that what appears as restoration of function can often hide an increased sensitivity to further trauma.

Engel's way of approaching the problem is a productive one. Once the mourner is seen as being in a state of biological disequilibrium brought about by a sudden change in the environment the processes at work and the conditions that influence their course can be made the subject of systematic study in the same way that they have been for wounds, burns and infections.

In order to deal with the range of responses, healthy and pathological, that follow loss the conceptual framework so far outlined must be amplified. In no direction is this more necessary than in regard to concepts of defence.

CHAPTER 4

An Information Processing Approach to Defence

> We see only what we know.
> GOETHE

A new approach

No understanding of responses to loss, whether they be healthy or pathological, is possible without constantly invoking concepts of defensive process, defensive belief and defensive activity—the three categories, I argue, into which defences are best grouped. In this chapter a sketch is given of how the phenomena observed and the processes postulated can be understood within the conceptual framework adopted. Although here and there comparisons are made between the present theory and certain of Freud's concepts of defence and mental structure, for reasons of space no systematic attempt is made to relate the two models.

The conceptual tools on which I draw have been made available by students of human information processing. These tools enable us to examine defensive phenomena from a new point of view, to collect data more systematically and to formulate hypotheses in a language shared by other behavioural scientists. These are great advantages. Nevertheless, there is clearly a long way to go before the theory sketched is within sight of doing justice to the wide range of defensive phenomena met with clinically. Until more work has been done, therefore, it will remain uncertain how successful the new approach is going to be.

Exclusion of information from further processing

In the first volume of this work, at the end of Chapter 6 and throughout Chapter 7, I have drawn attention to current work in neurophysiology and cognitive psychology that points to the central control of sensory inflow. Whether inflow derives from the environment through exteroceptors or from the organism itself through interoceptors, sensory inflow goes through many stages of selection, interpretation and appraisal before it can have any influence on behaviour, either immediately or later. This processing occurs in a succession of stages, all but the most preliminary of which require that the inflow be related to matching information already stored in long-term memory. All such processing is influenced by central control and is done at extraordinary speeds; and all but the most complex is done outside awareness.

For most purposes the inflow of interest to psychologists and the common man alike is that which, having been selected, interpreted and appraised, goes forward to influence mood and behaviour and/or to be stored in long-term memory. The fact that in the course of its being processed the vast proportion of initial inflow is routinely excluded, for one of several reasons, is ignored. For the understanding of pathological conditions, by contrast, the interest lies in the opposite direction, namely in what is being excluded, by what means it is excluded, and perhaps above all why it should be excluded.

In the ordinary course of a person's life most of the information reaching him is being routinely excluded from further processing in order that his capacities are not overloaded and his attention not constantly distracted. Most selective exclusion, therefore, is both necessary and adaptive. Like other physiological and psychological processes, however, in certain circumstances selective exclusion can have consequences that are of doubtful or varying adaptive value. For example, given certain adverse circumstances during childhood, the selective exclusion of information of certain sorts may be adaptive. Yet, when during adolescence and adult life the situation changes, the persistent exclusion of the same sorts of information may become maladaptive. The defensive processes postulated by psychoanalysts, I believe, belong in this category. To distinguish these unusual instances of selective exclusion, of only temporary adaptive value, from the overwhelming majority of adaptive instances it is convenient to refer to 'defensive exclusion'.

The basic concept in the theory of defence proposed is that of the exclusion from further processing of information of certain specific types for relatively long periods or even permanently. Some of this information is already stored in long-term memory, in which case defensive exclusion results in some degree of amnesia. Other information is arriving via sense organs, in which case defensive exclusion results in some degree of perceptual blocking. As is made clear later in this volume, the many other phenomena described by clinicians as defensive, notably certain types of belief and certain patterns either of activity or inactivity together with their associated feeling, can be understood within this framework as being the profound consequences of certain significant information having been excluded. Correspondingly, analytic therapies can be understood as procedures aimed at enabling a person to accept for processing information that hitherto he has been excluding, in the hope that the consequences of his doing so will be equally profound.

In presenting the theory, attention is given first to the basic questions of how information, of any sort, can first be selected and then deliberately excluded. Next we consider briefly the nature of the specific information that is liable to be selected for prolonged and defensive exclusion. Only after that do we broach the two further questions: what are the causal conditions that lead certain information to be excluded for long periods of time? and what are the advantages and disadvantages of doing so? In proceeding thus we move from the less controversial questions to the most.

As regards findings from experimental work, it happens that, up to date, more light has been shed on the selective exclusion of information during the processing of sensory inflow than has been shed on the selective exclusion of information already in store. For that reason prior attention is given to studies of subliminal perception and perceptual defence. Since, however, no perception is possible without the interpretation of sensory inflow in terms of matching information already in store, it is plausible to suppose that the mechanisms employed for preventing certain information from being retrieved from store bear some resemblance to the mechanisms employed for excluding from further processing information of similar or related import arriving through the sense organs. Given this, what is known about subliminal perception and perceptual defence can be taken as a paradigm.[1]

Subliminal perception and perceptual defence

The notion that information of certain meaning could be selectively

[1] In what follows I am indebted to Dixon's *Subliminal Perception* (1971), to Norman's introduction to human information processing (1976) and to a paper by Erdelyi (1974) on perceptual defence and vigilance.

excluded from perception met with considerable scepticism when first proposed around 1950. How, it was asked, can a person selectively exclude a particular stimulus unless he first perceives the stimulus which he wishes to exclude? At first sight this might seem a conclusive argument, especially if it is assumed that perception is some sort of singular event which either happens or fails to happen. But, as Erdelyi points out, the objection ceases to have any force once perception is conceived as a multi-stage process. For during processing through a sequence of stages it would be at least possible for certain information to be excluded before it reaches some final stage associated with consciousness. There is now abundant evidence that this can happen.

After some decades of controversy and steadily improving experimental techniques a multi-stage theory of perception is now widely accepted. Some features of it relevant to a theory of defence can be summarized.

The recognition of pattern as it occurs during perception proceeds in two directions simultaneously. On the one hand, the arrival of a sensory stimulus triggers an automatic series of analyses that start at the sense organs and continue centrally far up the chain of processing stages. On the other hand and simultaneously, the situation in which the sensory events are occurring triggers expectations based on past experience and general knowledge. These expectations produce conceptually driven processing in which guesses are made about what the input probably means. As the two forms of processing merge the guesses are checked against the data and the task completed.

By proceeding in both directions simultaneously the process of recognition is greatly accelerated. Yet by relying so much on expectations derived from past experience and knowledge the possibility of error is much increased. For example, because it lies outside experience a black three of diamonds when seen briefly is commonly misperceived as a three of spades. Findings of this type cast light on several characteristics common in responses to loss.

A second feature of a modern theory of perception is that sensory inflow can be processed outside a person's awareness to a stage sufficient for much of its meaning to be determined. Thereafter it can influence his subsequent behaviour, including his verbal responses, without his being aware of it. Experiments using the technique of dichotic listening illustrate these points.

In this type of experiment two different messages are transmitted to a person, one message being received in one ear and the other in the other. The person is then told to attend to one of these messages only, say the one being received by the right ear. To ensure he gives it continuous attention he is required to 'shadow' that message by repeating it word for word as he is hearing it. Keeping the two messages distinct is found to be fairly easy, especially when they are spoken by different voices. At the end of the session the subject is usually totally unaware of the content of the unattended message. There are, however, certain exceptions. For example, if his own name or some other personally significant word occurs in the unattended message, he may well notice and remember it. This shows at once that, even though unattended, fairly advanced processing of the unattended message must be taking place.

The results of two experiments that used this technique illustrate how information derived from the unattended message can influence thought and/or autonomic responses even though the message never reaches consciousness.[2]

In one such experiment subjects were required to attend to and to shadow ambiguous messages of which the following is an example:

they threw stones towards the bank yesterday

Simultaneously with this message either the word 'river' was presented in the unattended ear or else the word 'money'. Later, subjects were presented with a recognition test for the meaning of the sentence in which they were asked to choose between the following:

(a) they threw stones towards the side of the river yesterday;
(b) they threw stones towards the savings and loan association yesterday.

Subjects who had had the word 'river' presented to the unattended ear tended to select (a) as the meaning, whereas subjects who had had 'money' in the unattended ear tended to select (b). None of the subjects remembered what word had been presented to the unattended ear and were unaware also that their subsequent judgement of meaning had been influenced.

Clearly, in order for the word presented to the unattended ear to have the effect it did in this experiment, it must have undergone

[2] The accounts given here are derived from those given in Norman (1976, pp. 31–2).

sufficient processing for its meaning to have been recognized. A similar conclusion emerges from another experiment that also used the technique of dichotic listening.

Before the experiment proper the subjects went through a few training sessions during which they were exposed to an electric shock when any one of a set of selected words was spoken to them. As a result subjects became conditioned to the word-shock combination so that whenever one of the selected words was heard it was responded to by a change in the GSR (a measure of sweating). In the experiment proper the subjects were required to attend to and shadow a message in one ear while a list of words was presented to the other, unattended, ear. Words in that list were of three kinds: neutral words, some of the words that had been conditioned to shock, and both synonyms and homonyms of those words. Despite the fact that no shocks were given during the experiment itself there was an appreciable rise in the GSR whenever a conditioned word was presented in the unattended ear. Of even greater interest is that there was also a substantial, though lesser, rise when the homonyms and synonyms were presented. Here again the findings indicate that every word presented in the unattended ear must have undergone considerable processing and its meaning established.

From these findings it is but a short step to infer that, just as a person's judgement and his autonomic responses can be influenced by cognitive processing outside awareness, so also can his mood. Once that is assumed, a mechanism becomes available in terms of which certain changes of mood otherwise inexplicable can be explained.

On the basis of findings such as those described cognitive psychologists propose that an analytical mechanism exists that performs a series of tests outside awareness on all incoming messages. As a result of these tests information can undergo one of several fates amongst which the following are easily specified:

– it can be excluded without leaving trace
– it can be retained long enough outside consciousness in a temporary buffer store for it to influence judgement, autonomic responses and, I believe, mood
– it can reach the stage of advanced processing associated with consciousness, and in so doing influence the highest levels of decision making and also become eligible for long-term storage.

The criteria by which during the series of tests information is judged for allocation are clearly numerous and range from broad and simple to specific and complex. Furthermore, many of these criteria, perhaps all, can be changed by central control. Some such changes, we know well, are a result of conscious and voluntary control as for example when, after receiving a new instruction, attention is shifted from one ear to another or from one voice to another. Other changes, we also know, occur involuntarily and outside awareness as for example when a person's attention shifts to the other voice when he hears his own name mentioned by it.

Once the possibility of subliminal perception is accepted, theoretical objections to the idea of perceptual defence and its counterpart, perceptual vigilance, drop away. For what the findings from the many hundreds of experiments undertaken in this field show is that, in addition to its being able to influence judgement and autonomic responses, the processing of sensory inflow for meaning outside awareness can influence also the further inflow of that very information itself. Either the inflow may be reduced, as in perceptual defence, or it may be enhanced, as in perceptual vigilance. Examples of these findings are drawn from Dixon's (1971) detailed examination of the evidence.

Many experiments have been done using a tachistoscope which enables words or pictures to be shown either at different speeds or else at different light levels. Since these speeds and light levels include those that are either too fast or too dim for perception to be possible, a common procedure is to start by showing a word or a picture at a speed or light level known to be impossible, and then gradually to reduce speed or increase light until the subject becomes able to identify the stimulus. A well-attested finding from experiments using this technique is that, when words or pictures known to be emotionally arousing or anxiety provoking are presented, the time taken before they are correctly identified differs significantly from that taken to identify neutral words or pictures. To demonstrate that these results are due to changes in the sensory channels and not in the response channels, other experiments have been done. In some of these a significant change of sensitivity for the sensory inflow being received through one sense modality, say sight, is found to occur when the stimulus being presented through another modality, say hearing, is changed from an emotionally arousing one to a neutral one, or vice versa.

The direction in which a change of this sort occurs differs for different individuals. In some sensitivity to emotionally arousing words is found to be habitually increased, whereas in others it is habitually decreased.

In the experiments so far described the changes being effected in sensory inflow are being effected solely by involuntary means. In certain other experiments, however, it is found that subjects may also be regulating inflow by means of eye movements or eye fixations. In so doing the subjects are employing their voluntary musculature although without being aware they are doing so and, as in all these experiments, without their being aware either of the nature of the stimulus being presented to them. In thus utilizing both involuntary and voluntary effectors, Dixon points out, the systems regulating sensory inflow resemble the systems maintaining body temperature, regulation of which can be achieved either by involuntary means, e.g. reducing peripheral circulation by capillary restriction, or by voluntary means, e.g. putting on extra clothes.

Physiological Mechanisms

It is not without significance for the scientific status of theories of subliminal perception and perceptual defence advanced by cognitive psychologists that these theories are fully compatible with theories of sensory processing advanced by neurophysiologists. There are in fact many physiological mechanisms that in principle could play the required part.

One possibility, described by Horn (1965, 1976) and for which evidence is accumulating, is that temporary reductions can be effected in the responsiveness of neurones in the sensory pathways. The means to do so are thought to be reductions in the level of a special priming input which these neurones require. Another possibility, different to though fully compatible with the first, is described by Dixon (1971)[3] whose review of the neurophysiological literature was guided by Dr R. B. Livingston.

[3] Evidence suggests that conscious perception may require that inflows of two different sorts, each of adequate intensity, should be received at a higher centre. One sort carries specific information and is routed via the classical afferent system. The other sort carries non-specific stimulation and is routed via the reticular activating system. Because the conduction rate through the classical system is faster than it is through the reticular system there would be time enough both for (a) the sensory

Whether perceptual defence and vigilance are mediated by mechanisms of these sorts or by others is of no great consequence to us. What matters is that we now have good experimental grounds for believing, as every clinician does, that sensory inflow can be processed outside awareness and that, depending on the meaning assigned to it, further inflow can either be enhanced or reduced. That being so, it becomes reasonable to consider whether perhaps there may be other stages of out-of-awareness processing at which it may be possible for analogous processes of defensive exclusion to operate.

Stages at which processes of defensive exclusion may operate

In an attempt to clarify the processes underlying perceptual defence and vigilance Erdelyi (1974) has proposed a flow diagram I find attractive and that is compatible, at least in principle, with ideas advanced by Norman (1976), MacKay (1972), Mandler (1975) and Hilgard (1974) on whose work I am also drawing. Amongst their other merits Erdelyi's proposals suggest a way to understand the role of that small but important part of information processing that occurs within consciousness.

The mental apparatus can be thought of as made up of a very large number of complex control systems, organized in a loosely hierarchical way and with an enormous network of two-way communications between them. At the top of this hierarchy we postulate one or more principal evaluators and controllers, closely linked to long-term memory and comprising a very large number of evaluation (appraisal) scales ranged in some order of precedence. This system, or possibly federation of systems, I shall call the Principal System(s), thus leaving open the question whether it is best regarded as singular or plural.

---

inflow through the classical system to be processed for meaning outside awareness and also for (b) a message, dependent on that meaning, to be sent to the reticular system before the intensity of the non-specific stimulation to be relayed forward from the reticular system had been determined. In this way it would be possible for the intensity of the non-specific stimulation relayed forward to be so regulated that it was set either above the level required for conscious perception or below it, depending on the meaning that had been assigned to the inflow during its preliminary assessment outside awareness.

On the inflow side the task of these Principal System(s) is to scan all raw data as it becomes available (for fractions of a second or at most a second or two in 'sensory register'[4]), undertake a preliminary analysis and evaluation of it in terms of stored knowledge and relevant scales, and then send commands to an encoder regarding what should be selected for further processing and what should be discarded. Not only does all this preliminary scanning and sorting take place outside awareness but information rejected at this stage is likely to be permanently lost (although, as the experimental study of hypnosis, discussed later, shows, this may not always be so). This is the stage at which perceptual defence, or vigilance, is postulated to take place.

The reason for having this preliminary scan, Erdelyi suggests, is that the channels engaged in all the more advanced processing are of limited capacity and therefore incapable of dealing with more than a small fraction of inflow. Main bottlenecks appear to be at the stages of encoding, first, for short-term storage and, later, for long-term storage.

Information selected after preliminary scan for further processing, having already been encoded for short-term storage, is then in a form likely to give rise to the conscious perception of objects in a space–time continuum. Thus, in Erdelyi's words, perception is 'the conscious terminus of a sequence of non–conscious prior processes', and occurs probably in the region of short-term storage. 'While the span of consciousness or conscious perception is small, the span of perceptual processing and analysis is probably vast.'

After the stage of short-term storage and conscious processing, some information is selected for further encoding and eventual storage in long-term memory; other information, having served its purpose, is discarded.

Consciousness

During the past decade experimental psychologists have been giving much thought to the concept of consciousness which is now

[4] Information received through sense organs is believed to be held initially in a number of extremely brief stores, each linked to a single sensory mode and capable of handling large amounts of minimally processed information. Those accepting visual and auditory data have been termed by Neisser (1967) 'iconic' and 'echoic' respectively.

accepted as being scientifically 'respectable, useful and necessary', to quote Mandler (1975) whose ideas I draw upon.[5]

Consciousness can be regarded as a state of mental structures that greatly facilitates certain distinctive types of processing to occur. Among those are the following:

(a) the ordering, categorizing and encoding of information (which is already in an advanced state of processing) in new and further ways prior to storage;

(b) the retrieving of information from long-term storage by framing simple addresses to extract it from complex memory structures;

(c) the juxtaposition of information of varying kinds, e.g. representational models, plans and sensory inflow, derived from diverse sources; this makes possible reflective thought;

(d) arising from (c) the framing of long-term plans by preparing an array of alternative plans and sub-plans and then evaluating them, thus making possible high level decisions;

(e) the inspection of certain overlearned and automated action systems, together with the representational models linked to them, that may be proving maladapted. As a result of such inspection, systems and models long out of awareness become available for reappraisal in the light of new information, and, if necessary, attempts can then be made to reorganize or, perhaps, to replace them.

Inspecting, Reappraising and Modifying Automated Systems

The relevance and value of this fifth and last function of conscious processing for the practice of psychotherapy will at once be evident; for it is conceived as enabling certain structures (or programmes) basic to personality to be reappraised and, if necessary, in some degree modified. Let us consider two such basic structures, (a) that which mediates attachment behaviour and (b) that which applics all those rules for appraising action, thought and feeling that together are usually referred to as constituting the super-ego. Both these programmes are conceived as being stored in long-term memory

[5] All workers recognize the formidable problem of relating the phenomenal world of consciousness to concepts of information processing. Shallice (1972) argues that the problem bears some resemblance to that of relating two neighbouring fields of science.

and as being ready to be drawn upon to participate in processing and planning action as inflow from exteroceptors and interoceptors seems to indicate.

Both the nature of the representational models a person builds of his attachment figures and also the form in which his attachment behaviour becomes organized are regarded in this work as being the results of learning experiences that start during the first year of life and are repeated almost daily throughout childhood and adolescence. On the analogy of a physical skill that has been acquired in the same kind of way, both the cognitive and the action components of attachment are thought to become so engrained (in technical terms overlearned) that they come to operate automatically and outside awareness. Similarly, the rules for appraising action, thought and feeling, and the precedence given to each, associated with the concept of super-ego are thought also to become overlearned during the course of childhood and adolescence. As a result they also come to be applied automatically and outside awareness.

Plainly this arrangement has both advantages and disadvantages. On the one hand, it economizes effort and, in particular, makes no demands on the limited capacity channels mediating advanced processing. On the other is the disadvantage that, once cognition and action have been automated, they are not readily accessible to conscious processing and so are difficult to change. The psychological state may then be likened to that of a computer that, once programmed, produces its results automatically whenever activated. Provided the programme is the one required, all is well. Should an error have crept in, however, its correction not only demands skilled attention but may prove troublesome and slow to achieve.

The upshot is that, provided these representational models and programmes are well adapted, the fact that they are drawn on automatically and without awareness is a great advantage. When, however, they are not well adapted, for whatever reason, the disadvantages of the arrangement become serious. As anyone who has developed a bad style in some physical skill knows well, to review the cognitive and action components of a system that has long been automated and to change it is arduous and often frustrating; moreover, it is not always very successful. Hence some of the difficulties encountered during psychotherapy.

This, however, is neither the only problem nor the greatest. For the task of changing an overlearned programme of action and/or of appraisal is enormously exacerbated when rules long implemented by the evaluative system forbid its being reviewed. An example of this, highly germane to what follows, is when a person finds himself unable to review the representational model(s) he has built of his attachment figure(s) because to do so would infringe a long-learned rule that it is against one or both his parents' wishes that he study them, and their behaviour towards him, objectively. A psychological state of this kind in which a ban on reviewing models and action systems is effected outside awareness is one encountered frequently during psychotherapy. It indicates the existence of another stage of processing at which defensive exclusion can also take place, different to the stage at which perceptual defence occurs.

Information Processing under Hypnosis

Yet further evidence of the part played by information processing outside awareness, and of the power of selective exclusion in keeping it so, derives from studies of hypnosis.

As a result of a long experimental programme Hilgard (1973) concludes that during hypnosis, and as the result of the hypnotist's suggestion, what he calls the Executive Ego, which I shall call Principal System A, assigns control to a Subordinate System, which I shall call Principal System B. Following System A's assignment of control, the hypnotist's orders are received, processed and acted upon by System B without System A being in any way aware of what is being processed. Furthermore, these orders are being continuously scanned, still outside System A's awareness, by an evaluative system. This becomes plain whenever System B receives an order that would be unethical to obey and refuses to comply with it. To criticisms that the Executive Ego is only pretending to be unaware of what orders are being received, Hilgard replies effectively by pointing to the genuine surprise expressed by his subjects when, subsequently, they see or hear taped recordings of their sessions.

Many of Hilgard's experiments were concerned with hypnotic analgesia. Pain was produced by placing the subject's hand and forearm in circulating ice water for 45 seconds. Ordinarily this causes him to show many signs of discomfort, e.g. grimacing and restlessness, and to report that he is experiencing great pain and distress. In addition, changes are found to occur in his heart rate, blood pressure and other physiological measures, of most of which he is also well aware. When the suggestion is made under hypnosis

56

that his hand will be analgesic to the pain of the circulating ice water, by contrast, the same situation produces no visible signs of discomfort, whilst System B reports neither feeling pain nor being aware of autonomic changes.[6] Yet the changes are occurring just as in the unhypnotized subject.

From these findings Hilgard concludes that in the hypnotic condition System B is able to exclude, selectively, sensory inflow from two types of interoceptor, namely the pain-endings and those reporting autonomic activity. The mechanism that he postulates thus appears to be a counterpart to the mechanism responsible for perceptual defence, which excludes inflow from the exteroceptors.

It is interesting to learn how the subjects themselves experience the session, which can be done if, before hypnosis is ended, they are instructed to recall what their experiences have been. Some report concentrating on imagining that their arm is numb. Others use what Hilgard refers to as a 'dissociative technique' in which, for example, the subject might concentrate on the separation between his arm and his head, or on imagining himself going away to the country where all is quiet.

In discussing his findings Hilgard (1974) notes that, while some are compatible with Freud's theory of repression but not with Janet's theory of dissociation, others are more compatible with dissociation theory than with psychoanalytic. Thus Hilgard's findings show that the exclusion of information that would normally be

[6] Casey (1973) has discussed the neural mechanisms mediating awareness of pain and the means by which awareness may be suppressed, as it is in conditions of great excitement, e.g. battle, strenuous sport, and under hypnosis. As in the case of visual and auditory perception, there is evidence that conscious awareness of pain requires that inflows mediated by two different systems should be received at a higher centre. One is a rapidly acting system that provides information relating to the location of a disturbance, the other, which acts more slowly, provides for the aversive and emotional components. Evidence suggests that, as in the case of visual and auditory perception, a mechanism may exist whereby neural excitation in the slower acting system can be blocked from reaching the higher centre so that the aversive and emotional components would be excluded and no pain be experienced. Even so, there would often be limited awareness that in some part of the body all is not well. Another means for the physiological suppression of pain is suggested by the discovery of substances secreted by the pituitary and the brain (endorphins and enkephalins) which have an analgesic action comparable to opiates (Jeffcoate and others 1978).

accepted is an active process requiring effort, which is a point integral to Freud's theory but missing from dissociation theory. On the other hand, the findings show that the dissociative process segregates organized systems from one another, as Janet and other advocates of dissociation theories emphasize and in contrast to Freud's notion of an unorganized, chaotic id. Because the position Hilgard adopts resembles dissociation theory but yet differs from it in certain critical respects, he describes his position as neo-dissociative.

Further information about what is going on in hypnotic states is available from those few subjects who are capable whilst under hypnosis of enabling yet a further system to communicate by means of automatic writing and automatic talking.[7] Hilgard refers to this third system as the 'hidden observer'; I shall call it System C.

When these subjects took part in an experiment in which hypnotic analgesia is induced so that System B is unaware either of pain or of autonomic changes, System C reports, by contrast, being aware of both (though the pain may be at an intensity a little less than in the normal non-hypnotic state) (Knox *et al.* 1974). Here again it is of great interest to learn how the subject himself experiences the session.

The account following was given by one who had taken part in a session during which System C had reported, by means of automatic talking, whenever the subject had felt the experimenter's hand on his shoulder. (In accordance with instructions the subject refers to System C as the 'hidden observer'.)

In hypnosis I kept my mind and body separate, and my mind was wandering to other places—not aware of the pain in my arm. When the hidden observer was called up, the hypnotized part had to step back for a minute and let the hidden part tell the truth. The hidden observer is concerned primarily with how my body feels. It doesn't have a mind to wander and so it hurt quite a bit. When you took your hand off my

[7] Hilgard (1974) describes the procedure for inducing automatic writing: while the left hand and forearm were kept in the ice water without any discomfort, the right hand was placed in a box arranged for automatic writing or for reporting pain on a numerical scale through key pressing. The hypnotized subject was then told that 'the hand would tell us what we ought to know, but that the subject would pay no attention to this hand and would not know what it was communicating or even that it was doing anything at all'. Procedure for automatic talking is described in detail in Knox *et al.* (1974).

shoulder, I went back to the separation, and it didn't hurt any more, but this separation became more and more difficult to achieve.

The experimenter comments that it was very apparent from the subject's grimaces and movements that he was feeling intense pain whenever her hand was on his shoulder. When, however, her hand was removed his face gradually relaxed and he appeared comfortable again. Yet after the session was over the subject made plain that effecting the dissociation required constant effort and that he found it difficult to maintain.

A further point emphasized by Hilgard is that the interruption to communication between systems that occurs in the hypnotic state is rarely complete. Often one system has some knowledge of what is going on in the other, even if the second has no knowledge of what is going on in the first. The existence of partially permeable barriers may provide a lead for understanding the phenomena that clinicians refer to, paradoxically, as 'unconscious feelings'.

In recounting these experiments I recognize that only a small minority of individuals are susceptible to being hypnotized and that an even smaller proportion are capable also of automatic writing. (Of the student population tested by Hilgard, no more than one or two per cent proved suitable.) Yet the findings made it clear that, at least in some persons, the mental apparatus is such that not only is a dominant system capable of excluding selectively much sensory inflow that would normally reach consciousness but also that the processing of this excluded inflow may reach a state of consciousness within another system parallel to but segregated from the first.

Self or selves

Experimental findings of this sort, together with comparable findings by clinicians, raise difficult questions of how best to conceive of the self. In the case of Hilgard's experiments, it may be asked, is Principal System A to be regarded as the self and, if so, what do we make of Principal Systems B and C? Or should all three be regarded as selves? And, in the clinical field, how can we most usefully conceptualize what Winnicott calls a false self and how contrast it with what he calls a true self?

In approaching these problems it is useful to start with Hilgard's proposal that what he terms the Executive Ego is the system that, being capable of self-perception, becomes capable also of conceiving of the self as an agent; and, further, that the integrity of that system is provided through its constant access to a more or less continuous store of personal memories. Questions that then arise are, first, whether we can conceive of more than one system becoming capable of self-perception and, second, whether there is evidence that the memory store may be sectionalized; and, if so whether it is plausible to postulate that in some individuals barriers to communication are set up between two or more major sections of it.

Within the conceptual framework advanced neither of these proposals raise problems of principle.

As regards the first, MacKay (1972) in his discussion of how we may suppose conflict to be regulated postulates a hierarchy of evaluating and organizing systems, in which the higher systems can be described as meta-systems, meta-meta-systems, and so on with indefinite extension. Whereas in a hierarchy of this sort it is customary to think of the arrangement as moving steadily upward from a large array of lower systems to a single system at the top, other configurations are possible. For example, it is possible to consider two or more systems at the top working in greater or less collaboration with each other. Whereas such an arrangement might be less efficient than one in which the chain of command is unified, it might nevertheless be more flexible. The point I wish to make is simply that a plural arrangement of this kind is well within the bounds of possibility and cannot be ruled out on *a priori* grounds. It is for this reason that earlier in this chapter I speak of Principal System(s), thereby leaving open the issue singular or plural.

The question whether it is reasonable to suppose that the processing of information can reach the phase of consciousness within more than one Principal System is also not to be ruled out on *a priori* grounds, especially as we still remain totally ignorant of what the special conditions are that determine whether or not processing ever reaches this phase.

The second question posed earlier concerns the possibility of the personal memory store being sectionalized and communication between sections being impeded or blocked. Here again there are no *a priori* difficulties, whilst such evidence as we have is entirely compatible with such notions.

In his discussion of long-term memory, Norman (1976) emphasizes that there is more than one way in which information can be encoded for storage and that the same information can be encoded, and can coexist in storage, in several different forms, and can also be accessible by any of several different routes. For example, a mental representation can encode information about the world in an analogue form, which mirrors certain selected properties of the world as in a map or a mechanical model, or it can encode information in a propositional form, which comprises a set of interpreted abstract statements about perceptual events as in a prose description. The design of the human cognitive system, Norman believes, allows flexibility in the way it represents information. Not only can it employ whichever system of encoding best suits its purposes but it appears able also to transform one form of representation into another. For example, analogical representation appears to be well suited for the storage of operations and action programmes, whereas propositional representation appears well suited for the storage of the meaning and interpretation of events. A compromise in which different forms of encoding are used in combination to represent different aspects of the world is probably available also. The information conveyed in diagrams, Norman points out, is often partly in analogue form and partly in propositional.

Episodic and Semantic Storage

Norman also draws attention to the distinction, introduced by Tulving (1972),[8] between storing information according to personal experiences, autobiographically, and storing it according to its meaning, its contribution to personal knowledge. Since I suspect this distinction may have very significant implications for psychopathology, it is worth examining further.

In the episodic type of storage, information is stored sequentially in terms of temporally dated episodes or events and of temporo-spatial relations between events. It commonly retains its perceptual properties and each item has its own distinctive place in a person's life history. 'Thus, an integral part of the representation of a remembered experience in episodic memory is its reference to the rememberer's knowledge of his personal identity' (Tulving, p. 389). An

---

[8] In a review chapter, Tulving notes that experimental work on memory falls naturally into these two classes and concludes, therefore, that the distinction may prove to have heuristic value. He compares the two memory systems in terms of the nature of the information selected for storage, the networks within which it is stored, and the means whereby it is retrieved.

example would be a person's lively recollections of the events that occurred during a particular holiday. In the semantic type of storage, by contrast, information exists as generalized propositions about the world, derived either from a person's own experience or from what he has learned from others, or from some combination of the two. Inflows into the semantic memory system, therefore, are always referred to an existing cognitive structure. Examples would be any views the person might form about holidays in general and how any particular holiday might compare with others.

A corollary of the distinction between episodic and semantic storage, and one likely to be of much clinical relevance, is that the storage of images of parents and of self is almost certain to be of at least two distinct types. Whereas memories of behaviour engaged in and of words spoken on each particular occasion will be stored episodically, the generalizations about mother, father and self enshrined in what I am terming working models or representational models will be stored semantically (in either analogical, propositional or some combined format). Given these distinct types of storage a fertile ground exists for the genesis of conflict. For information stored semantically need not always be consistent with what is stored episodically; and it might be that in some individuals information in one store is greatly at variance with that in the other.

My reason for calling attention to the different types of storage and the consequent opportunities for cognitive and emotional conflict is that during therapeutic work it is not uncommon to uncover gross inconsistencies between the generalizations a patient makes about his parents and what is implied by some of the episodes he recalls of how they actually behaved and what they said on particular occasions. Sometimes a generalization refers in broad and glowing terms to a parent's admirable qualities, some or all of which are called sharply in question when episodes of how he or she had actually behaved and/or spoken are recalled and appraised. At other times the position is reversed, with the generalization being uniformly adverse and what is recalled from episodes being appraised more favourably. Similarly, it is not unusual to uncover gross inconsistencies between the generalized judgements a patient makes about himself and the picture we build up of how he commonly thinks, feels and behaves on particular occasions. For these reasons it is often very helpful for a patient to be encouraged to recall actual events in as much detail as he can, so that he can then appraise afresh, with all the appropriate feeling, both what his own desires, feeling and behaviour may have been on each particular occasion and also what his parents' behaviour may have been. In so doing he has an opportunity to correct or modify images in semantic store that are found to be out of keeping with the evidence, historical and current.

One reason for discrepancies arising between the information in one type of storage and that in another lies in all likelihood in there being a difference in the source from which each derives the dominant portion of its information. Whereas for information going into episodic storage the dominant part seems likely to derive from what the person himself perceives and a subordinate part only from what he may be told about the episode, for what goes into semantic storage the emphasis may well be reversed, with what he is told being dominant over what he himself might think. An everyday example of a large discrepancy between information in episodic storage and what is in semantic storage is found in the images we have of the earth we live on. In our daily round we experience the earth as flat and for most purposes we treat it as though it were so. Yet most educated Westerners, having learned that it is spherical, would claim that their model of it is indeed spherical. In this case, of course, although the discrepancy exists, no conflict of emotional consequence is nowadays experienced. In the case of information about parents and self, however, on which so much of emotional consequence does turn, major discrepancies are likely to produce a disturbing sense of unease.

Let us return now to the questions posed at the beginning of this section, namely how within the framework proposed we can best conceive the self and how it may be possible also to conceive of a person having more than one self. In most individuals, we may suppose, there is a unified Principal System that is not only capable of self-reflection but has more or less ready access to all information in long-term store, irrespective of its source, of how it is encoded and in which type of storage it may be held. We may also suppose that there are other individuals in whom Principal Systems are not unified so that, whilst one such System might have ready access to information held in one type of storage but little or no access to information held in another, the information to which another Principal System has, or has not got, access might be in many respects complementary. The two systems would then differ in regard to what each perceived and how each interpreted and appraised events, which is exactly what we seem sometimes to meet with clinically. In so far as communication between systems is restricted, they can be described as segregated.

When during therapy a patient compares the discrepant images he has both of his parents and of himself that derive from stores of different types, the images from episodic storage are, I suspect, those he most often judges to have the greater validity and to be the ones with which he most closely identifies. If that is so it would be the self that has the readier access to those images that he would experience as his real self.

This is as far as it is useful to take these rather speculative ideas at this stage. In later chapters, e.g. 12, 13, 20 and 21, they are drawn on to provide possible ways to understand certain not uncommon responses to loss.

Some consequences of defensive exclusion

Whenever information that would normally be accepted for further processing because of its significance to the individual is subjected to defensive exclusion for prolonged periods the consequences are far-reaching. Among them, I believe, are most, perhaps all, of the very diverse array of phenomena that at one time or another have been described in the psychoanalytic literature as being defences.[9]

Of the many possible consequences there are two major ones, each with certain contingent consequences, to which at this point I wish to draw attention:

(a) One or more behavioural systems within a person may be deactivated, partially or completely. When that occurs one or more other activities may come to monopolize the person's time and attention, acting apparently as diversions.

---

[9] In the comprehensive list of defences compiled by Sperling (1958) all the following appear: disease entities, character, symptom complexes, affects, physiological states and processes, psychological states and processes, art forms, and behaviour both of social and anti-social kinds. From among that array I am confining attention to those phenomena which, together, appear to be central to the concept, namely defensive process, defensive behaviour and defensive belief. The position adopted is in all important respects the same as Peterfreund's (1971).

(b) One or a set of responses a person is making may become disconnected cognitively from the interpersonal situation that is eliciting it, leaving him unaware of why he is responding as he is. When that occurs the person may do one or more of several things, each of which is likely to divert his attention away from whoever, or whatever, may be responsible for his reactions:

He may mistakenly identify some other person (or situation) as the one who (which) is eliciting his responses.

He may divert his responses away from someone who is in some degree responsible for arousing them and towards some irrelevant figure, including himself.

He may dwell so insistently on the details of his own reactions and sufferings that he has no time to consider what the interpersonal situation responsible for his reactions may really be.

The Deactivation[10] of a System: Repression

A behavioural system becomes active only when the necessary combination of inflows, from exteroceptors and/or interoceptors and/or memory stores reaches it. Should such inflows be systematically excluded, it follows that the system must be immobilized, together with the thoughts and feelings to which such inflows give rise, and that it must remain so until such time as the necessary inflow is received. In traditional terms the system thus deactivated is said to be repressed. Or, put the other way about, the effects of repression are regarded as being due to certain information of significance to the individual being systematically excluded from further processing. Like repression, defensive exclusion is regarded as being at the heart of psychopathology. Only in their theoretical overtones is it necessary to make any distinction between the two concepts.

The exclusion of significant information, with the resulting deactivation of a behavioural system, may of course be less than complete. When that is so there are times when fragments of the information defensively excluded seep through so that fragments of the behaviour defensively deactivated become visible; or else feeling

[10] Whereas the term 'inactivation' would be grammatically correct, I follow Peterfreund (1971) in using 'deactivation'. The advantage of the latter term is that it keeps the condition distinct from that of a behavioural system which merely happens at a given moment to be inactive but which remains accessible, in the usual way, to all potentially activating inflow.

and other products of processing related to the behaviour reach consciousness, for example in the form of moods, memories, day dreams or night dreams, and can be reported. These psychological phenomena have given rise in traditional psychoanalytic theory to concepts such as the dynamic unconscious and the return of the repressed.

The magnitude of effect on personality functioning of a behavioural system being deactivated will clearly depend on the status of the system within the personality. Should the system be of only marginal importance, the absence of the behaviour from the person's repertoire may be of no great consequence. Should, however, it be a behavioural system, or set of behavioural systems, as central for personality functioning as, for example, is the set controlling attachment behaviour, the effects are likely to be extensive. For, on the one hand, certain forms of behaviour, thought and feeling, will cease to occur or be experienced and, on the other, forms of behaviour, thought and feeling of some other kind will take their place. For, as Peterfreund (1971) emphasizes, within a network of control systems a major change in one part will have repercussions throughout the whole.

The diversionary role of defensive activity. Many of the patterns of behaviour, thought and feeling judged by clinicians to be defensive can be understood as alternatives to the behaviour, thought and feeling that have disappeared following deactivation. In judging them to be defensive what is usually in mind is that they give the impression, on the one hand, of being carried out under pressure and of absorbing an undue proportion of a person's attention, time and energy, perhaps in the form of overwork, and, on the other, of being undertaken by him in some way at the expense of his giving his attention, time and energy to something else. They seem thus to be not merely alternatives but also to be playing a diversionary role; and this is probably what they do. For the more completely a person's attention, time and energy are concentrated on one activity and on the information concerning it the more completely can information concerning another activity be excluded.

Experience suggests that there is no activity, mental or physical, that cannot be undertaken as a diversion. Whether it is work or play, of great social value or none, provided the activity is all-absorbing it meets the psychological requirement. This means that

66

the effects of defensive activity must be judged on a number of distinct scales. For example we can ask:

- what are its effects, beneficial or otherwise, on the personality concerned?
- what are its effects, beneficial or otherwise, on the members of the person's family?
- what are its effects, beneficial or otherwise, on the community at large?

The answers to these questions may differ greatly.

Cognitive Disconnection of Response from Situation

We are so used to regarding our thoughts, feeling and behaviour as being linked more or less directly to the circumstances in which we find ourselves that it may seem strange that the link may sometimes be missing, or the wrong link be made. Yet at a trivial level this occurs not infrequently. A man comes home from work and finds fault with his son. Subsequently he may, or may not, be aware that his irritation was aroused initially by events at work and that his son's behaviour was of only marginal relevance. Another man wakes up feeling worried and depressed and may only subsequently identify the situation that is making him feel so. In both examples certain information relevant to his mood and behaviour is being excluded from conscious processing. When exclusion is only partial or temporary, no great harm results. When, however, exclusion is systematic and persistent ill effects may be grave.

This cognitive disconnection of a response from the interpersonal situation that elicited it I believe to play an enormous role in psychopathology. Sometimes the disconnection is complete, in which case the response may appear wholly inexplicable in terms of a psychological reaction and is consequently readily attributed to something quite different, e.g. indigestion or disturbed metabolism. At other times the disconnection is only partial, inasmuch as the person is unaware only of certain aspects of the situation whilst being well aware of other aspects. In such cases it is the intensity and persistence of the response that pose the problems.

Since in the chapters to follow, notably numbers 9 to 13 and 19 to 24, very many examples of pathological responses to loss are attributed to complete or partial disconnection of response from situation, no more need be said about the process here.

Misidentification of the interpersonal situation eliciting a response. Just as defensive activities may serve in part to ensure that attention is not given to inflow that is being defensively excluded, so may the attribution of a response to some insignificant situation serve to direct attention away from the situation truly responsible. Several examples of this are given in Volume II in the discussion of phobias (Chapters 18 and 19). A child afraid to leave home for fear his mother might desert or commit suicide during his absence claims, or is persuaded, that what he is really afraid of is being criticized by the teacher; or an adult, similarly afraid of what might happen at home during his or her absence, claims that what he or she is really afraid of is to go alone into public places.

Redirection of responses away from the person arousing them. To direct anger away from the person who elicited it and towards some more or less irrelevant person is so well known that little need be said about it. In traditional theory it is termed displacement. The term 'splitting' is also used in this connection when an ambivalent reaction is aroused, with the loving component being directed towards one person and the angry component redirected towards another.

Not infrequently anger is redirected away from an attachment figure who aroused it and aimed instead at the self. Inappropriate self-criticism results.

Preoccupation with personal reactions and sufferings. It not infrequently happens that when a set of responses has become disconnected from the interpersonal situation that elicited them the person focuses his attention, not on any person or situation relevant or even irrelevant to his state of mind, but solely on himself. In such cases he may dwell at length on the details of his reactions, both psychological and physiological, and especially on the extent of his sufferings. He may then be described as morbidly introspective and/or hypochondriacal. Examples of patients whose introspective preoccupations are effectively diverting their attention away from a difficult and painful situation are described by Wolff and others (1946b) and by Sacher and others (1968) and are referred to further in Chapters 9 and 13.

There are in fact many other consequences of the defensive exclusion of relevant information in addition to those noted above, including the conditions traditionally described as denial or disavowal. Since, however, they occur frequently as responses to loss and since, moreover, their classification as defences needs examination, discussion of them is left to later chapters.

Conditions that promote defensive exclusion

At the beginning of this chapter it is pointed out that in the ordinary course of a person's life most of the information reaching him is being routinely excluded from conscious processing in order that his capacities are not overloaded and his attention not constantly distracted; and also that where defensive exclusion differs from the usual forms of exclusion the difference lies not in the mechanisms responsible for it but in the nature of the information that is excluded. In examining the conditions that promote defensive exclusion, therefore, the focus of attention is on the nature of the information being excluded.

The theory that I believe best fits the evidence is one proposed by Peterfreund (1971), namely that the information likely to be defensively excluded is of a kind that, when accepted for processing in the past, has led the person concerned to suffer more or less severely. Whether this formula embraces all cases cannot be known until it has been tried and tested. Meanwhile I adopt it since it appears sufficient for the understanding of the responses with which this volume is concerned.

There are a number of possible reasons why incoming information of certain kinds could, if accepted, lead the person concerned to suffer. One example, long recognized in clinical literature, is when the incoming information might, if accepted, arouse feelings and/or elicit actions that would be evaluated adversely by the person's own evaluating systems, thereby creating conflict and guilt. Another, closely related to the first, is when the incoming information might, if accepted, result in a serious conflict with parents, with the acute distress that that is likely to bring. There are two situations of that kind that are especially germane to my thesis.

The first is when a child's attachment behaviour is strongly aroused and when, for any reason, it is not responded to and terminated. In these circumstances the child protests more or less violently and is much distressed. Should the situation recur frequently and for long periods, not only is distress prolonged but it seems that the systems controlling the behaviour ultimately become deactivated. This, the evidence indicates, is more likely to occur should lack of termination be accompanied by active rejection and, perhaps especially, when the child is punished or threatened with punishment for reacting as he is likely to do, for example by crying strongly and persistently, by demanding his mother's presence or by being generally contrary and difficult.

The deactivation of systems mediating attachment behaviour, thought and feeling, appears to be achieved by the defensive exclusion, more or less complete, of sensory inflow of any and every kind that might activate attachment behaviour and feeling. The resulting state is one of emotional detachment which can be either partial or complete.

Deactivation of attachment behaviour is especially liable to be initiated during the early years, though it can undoubtedly be increased and consolidated during later childhood and adolescence. One reason why a young child is especially prone to react in this way is that it is during the second half of the first year of life and the subsequent two years or so that attachment behaviour is elicited most readily and continues to be so at high intensity and for long periods, leading to great suffering should no one be available to comfort him. As a result it is during these years that he is especially vulnerable to periods of separation, and also to being rejected or threatened with rejection. Another and quite different reason seems likely to be that selective exclusion occurs more readily in children than in adults. An example of this to which Hilgard (1964) draws attention is the ease with which post-hypnotic amnesia is induced in children when compared to adults.

Since there is evidence that the deactivation of attachment behaviour is a key feature of certain common variants of pathological mourning, and also of personalities prone to respond in those ways, the condition is referred to repeatedly in later chapters.

A second class of conflict with parents, and one that I believe accounts for a great many instances of defensive exclusion, arises when a child is in course of observing features of a parent's behaviour that that parent wishes strongly he should not know about. Most of the data that can be explained by this hypothesis are well known, though the explanations adopted have usually been very different.

In therapeutic work it is not uncommon to find that a person (child, adolescent or adult) maintains, consciously, a wholly favourable image of a parent, but that at a less conscious level he nurses a contrasting image in which his parent is represented as neglectful, or rejecting, or as ill-treating him. In such persons the two images are kept apart, out of communication with each other; and any information that may be at variance with the established image is excluded.

Various views have been advanced to account for this state of affairs. One view, prominent in traditional psychoanalytic theorizing, postulates that a young child is unable to accommodate within a single image the parent's kindly treatment of him as well as any less favourable treatment he may receive or, much emphasized by some theorists, is disposed to imagine. A second view is that a young child, being totally dependent on his parents' care, is strongly biased to see them in a favourable light and so to exclude contrary information. A third view, to which clinicians interested in family interaction call attention, and already described, with references, in Volume II (Chapter 20), emphasizes how insistent some parents are that their children regard them in a favourable light and what pressures they put on them to comply. On threat of not being loved or even of being abandoned a child is led to understand that he is not supposed to notice his parents' adverse treatment of him or, if he does, that he should regard it as being no more than the justifiable reaction of a wronged parent to his (the child's) bad behaviour.

Since these explanations are not mutually exclusive, it is possible that each of the factors postulated makes some contribution. In evaluating the probable role of each, however, I believe such evidence as there is strongly favours the last, namely the role of parental pressure, and gives least support to the traditional view. Since examples of that evidence are presented in many later chapters (e.g. Chapters 12 and 18 onwards), it is unnecessary to pursue the matter further here.

Finally, let us consider a related matter, namely whether defensive exclusion originates only during earliest childhood, as has been widely assumed by psychoanalysts, or may be initiated also during later childhood and, perhaps, during adolescence and adult life as well. This is an important though difficult question since the evidence is far from clear. A principal problem lies in distinguishing between the conditions that may be necessary for initiating defensive exclusion and those capable of maintaining or increasing it.

The following tentative propositions are, I believe, reasonable interpretations of the evidence:

(a) There is reason to suspect that vulnerability to conditions initiating defensive exclusion is at a maximum during the early years of life, perhaps the first three in particular (some reasons why this should be so are already referred to and others are examined in Chapter 24).

(b) Although vulnerability diminishes during later childhood and early adolescence, it probably does so only slowly and remains comparatively high throughout most of these years.

(c) There is probably no age at which human beings cease to be vulnerable to factors that maintain or increase any defensive exclusion already established.

A corollary of this position is that in examining the conditions that initiate defensive exclusion it is as necessary to consider those that may affect older children and young adolescents as it is those to which infants and very young children may be vulnerable.

Defensive exclusion: adaptive or maladaptive

In considering whether defensive exclusion is biologically adaptive the relevant criterion is whether it contributes in any way to the individual's surviving and leaving viable offspring.[11] Since this is not an easy criterion to apply, it is necessary to weigh arguments.

First, there can be little doubt that those persons in whom defensive exclusion plays a prominent part are handicapped in their dealing with other human beings when compared to those in whom it plays only a minor part. Furthermore, they are more prone to suffer breakdowns in functioning when, for periods lasting weeks, months or years, they may be unable to deal effectively with their environment. Thus, whatever the benefits of defensive exclusion may possibly be, the personality which adopts it pays a penalty, sometimes severe. The question therefore arises whether there are any

[11] This, of course, is a very different criterion to those traditionally adopted by psychoanalysts which are concerned either with the distribution of psychic energy or else with the degree of mental pain experienced.

circumstances in which such benefits as it may confer outweigh these undoubted penalties. This brings us back to the conditions that promote the process.

In the last section it was proposed that much of the information liable to be defensively excluded, because when accepted previously it has led to suffering, falls under two main heads: (a) information that leads a child's attachment behaviour and feeling to be aroused intensely but to remain unassuaged, and perhaps even to be punished, and (b) information that he knows his parent(s) do not wish him to know about and would punish him for accepting as true. The question arises, therefore, whether, in the conditions that make these types of information unacceptable, the behaviour to which its exclusion leads may, at least in some cases, confer benefits that outweigh the penalties.

Let us consider each of these cases.

Main (1977) describes observations of infants aged twelve to eighteen months with their mothers and reports finding that those who fail to show attachment behaviour in circumstances in which it would be expected, e.g. after a separation lasting a few minutes in a strange setting, are highly likely to be the infants of mothers who habitually reject their advances. In the conditions described an infant of this sort, instead of showing attachment behaviour as infants of responsive mothers do, turns away from his mother and busies himself with a toy. In so doing he is effectively excluding any sensory inflow that would elicit his attachment behaviour and is thus avoiding any risk of being rebuffed and becoming distressed and disorganized; in addition he is avoiding any risk of eliciting hostile behaviour from his mother. Yet he remains in her vicinity. This type of response, Main suggests, may represent a strategy for survival alternative to seeking close proximity to mother. Its advantages are that the child avoids becoming disorganized but yet remains moderately close to and on fair terms with his mother, the chances being that, should risk of danger become high, she would then protect him.

Nevertheless, even should this suggestion prove valid, Main emphasizes, there is much evidence that the strategy is no more than second best and to be adopted only when a mother's attitude is adverse. This is shown by the readiness with which the response is replaced by attachment behaviour once a child has become confident that his mother will respond to him kindly.

The same argument can be applied in the second case, that in which information that a child knows his parents do not wish him to know about is subjected to defensive exclusion. Here again, it is suggested, the advantages of conforming to the parent's demands may outweigh the disadvantages. For, as children know in their bones, when mother is prone to be rejecting it may be better to placate her than to risk alienating her altogether.

If this reasoning is correct, there must none the less come a point at which the advantages of conforming to a parent's requirements may be outweighed by the disadvantages. This is the case in those adolescents and adults who, having for long adopted the strategy of placating a parent, now find themselves unable to do anything else.

In this chapter I have tried to indicate the lines along which it may be possible to develop a theory of defence using concepts derived from recent studies of human information processing. In the chapters to follow I attempt to use these ideas to shed light on responses to loss.

CHAPTER 5

Plan of Work

Since a principal aim of this volume is to compare, and if necessary to contrast, the responses to loss of young children with those of adults, it is necessary to decide at which end of the age-range to start. Advantage lies, I believe, in starting with what we know of the responses of adults, and thence to work down the age-scale, first to the responses of adolescents and children and, finally, to those of children during their earliest years of life. The merit of proceeding thus is that we ensure that before considering the controversial issues of children's responses to loss our picture of the responses of adults is both accurate and comprehensive. This, fortunately, is now made possible thanks to several well-planned and systematic studies of adults having been completed during the past two decades.

With one or two notable exceptions these studies of adults' responses have been directed to losses due to death. Moreover, a great majority of the clinical reports, both of adults and of children, that implicate loss have also been concerned with losses due to death. For that reason the cause of the losses with which the greater part of this volume is concerned is also death. Paradoxically, it is only in regard to the young children whose responses provide the starting-point for this work that loss due to circumstances other than death is involved.

To some readers it may seem a pity to confine most of the discussion to the effects of loss due to the single cause of death, since a great number, probably a majority, of losses that occur in our society are due to causes other than death. Familiar examples are losses caused by divorce or desertion and also losses of a temporary kind which can be caused by a host of different circumstances and can be either long or short. There are, however, also advantages in restricting the study in this way. Even limiting ourselves to this single cause of loss entails considering the effects of an awesome array of variables that influence the way a loss is responded to; and to have included losses due to other causes as well would have increased this array still further. There is therefore merit, as a beginning, in concentrating attention on responses to losses that have a single cause; and to select for that beginning the cause of loss the responses to which are best described. The more successful we are in this enquiry, I believe, the better prepared we shall be to examine the responses to losses of other kinds. For there can be little doubt that, whatever the cause of a loss may be, certain basic patterns of response are present and that such variations of response as may result from losses having one or another of many different causes are best regarded as variations on a single theme.

To present a picture of the range of responses to a major loss seen in adults several chapters are necessary. In the first three we describe the responses shown by a majority, or at least a substantial minority, of married people in several different cultures after suffering the loss of a spouse or a child, and the usual progression of mourning through a number of phases. In Chapter 9, keeping still at a descriptive level, we consider responses that occur in only a minority of bereaved people. This leads to a discussion of individual variations in the course of mourning with special reference to features evident during the early months which correlate with an unfavourable outcome later. That done, we proceed, in Chapters 10 to 12, to consider the many factors that are believed to influence the course taken by mourning in different individuals, especially those that play a part in determining whether outcome is healthy or pathological. Certain of these factors, relatively neglected in the past but given increasing attention in recent studies, concern experiences that a bereaved person has at the time of the loss and during the months and years after it. Others, always the subject of intense debate in the psychoanalytic literature, concern a set of interrelated variables active prior to the loss. These include (a) the personality of the bereaved prior to his loss, (b) the pattern of the relationship he had with the person lost, and (c) the many variables that have been postulated by psychoanalytic theorists to account for the development of different types of personality and different patterns of relationship, and hence also for differences in the courses that mourning can take. This leads to a central theme of the volume, namely, the influence on responses to loss of the experiences which a bereaved person has had with attachment figures during the whole course of his life, and especially during his infancy, childhood and adolescence. These experiences are held to account for a large proportion of the variance observed in the course taken by mourning in adults.

At that point in our study it becomes fruitful to examine afresh what is known regarding the course taken by responses to loss when the loss is sustained during the years of immaturity and also the factors responsible for differences in how individual children respond. These are the subjects of Part III.

Part II: The Mourning of Adults

CHAPTER 6

Loss of Spouse

Eva was experiencing grief for the first time. When Keir had first broken the news to her of John's illness she had experienced shock, but that had been different—almost the opposite. For that had been an inability to feel, whereas this was an inability not to feel—an ugly, uncontrollable glut of emotion that distended her until she felt she might burst and be a splatter of guts on the floor . . . She wanted to smash something, howl. She wanted to throw herself on the floor, roll about, kick, scream.

BRYAN MAGEE, *Facing Death*

Sources

There is now a good deal of reliable information about how adults respond to a major bereavement. In addition to data reported by early students of the subject, already referred to in previous chapters and in Appendices I and II of Volume II, observations are now available deriving from later and more carefully designed projects. Those most useful for our present purposes are studies in which observations are begun shortly after a bereavement, and in some cases before it has occurred, and are then continued for a year or more afterwards. In this chapter and those following we draw extensively on the findings of such projects. They fall into two main classes. The first, described in this chapter, comprises studies which aim to describe typical patterns of response to the loss of a spouse during the first year of bereavement and, further, to identify features which may predict whether the state of health, physical and mental, of the mourner at the end of the first year will be favourable or unfavourable. The second group comprises studies of the course of mourning in the parents of fatally-ill children and are described in the chapter following.

It is evident that to be ethical all such studies must be conducted with sensitivity and sympathy and only with those who are willing to participate. Experience shows that, when so conducted, a majority of the subjects co-operate actively and, moreover, are usually grateful for the opportunity to express their sorrow to an understanding person.

Table 1 lists the principal studies drawn on in this chapter and in Chapters 9 to 12 giving certain basic information about each. Each sought to be as representative of the population studied as was possible: thus members of all socio-economic classes were approached. In the degree to which they were successful in tracing and in obtaining the co-operation of those approached, however, studies varied greatly—from over 90 per cent success in some to no more than 25 per cent in others.

In almost every study interviews were held in the bereaved's home, by prior arrangement, and lasted at least an hour, sometimes as long as three hours. In most studies interviews were semi-structured, aimed both to give the bereaved an opportunity to talk freely about his or her experiences and also to ensure that certain fields were covered adequately.

The studies to which I am especially indebted are those by my colleague Colin Murray Parkes, one of which he conducted in London (Parkes 1970a) and the other, in association with Ira O. Glick and Robert S. Weiss, in Boston, Mass. (Glick, Weiss and Parkes 1974, second volume in preparation).

Readers wishing to have further information regarding the samples of subjects studied, the procedures employed, and the publications in which results are given are referred to the note at the end of this chapter.

Limitations of Samples Studied

Taken together we find that the number of widows and widowers included in these samples total several hundred; and we find also that with few exceptions the degree of agreement between the findings is impressive. Yet we must ask ourselves how representative of all bereaved spouses the samples studied are.

First it will be noted that in the studies described there are many more widows than widowers. This is not surprising since, because of their higher relative age and lower life expectancy, husbands die relatively far more frequently than wives. Thus, we find ourselves better informed of the course of mourning in women than in men, so that there is danger that generalizations may reflect this imbalance. In what follows, therefore, we describe first the course taken by mourning in widows and at the end of the chapter discuss what is known regarding differences in the course taken by mourning in widowers. In general the pattern of emotional response to loss of a

TABLE I *Loss of spouse: particulars of studies drawn upon*

Author	Subjects				Place	Method	Period elapsed since bereavement
	Widows	Widowers	Ages	% of those approached			
Parkes	22	—	26–65	over 90	London	Interviews: repeated	at 1, 3, 6, 9 and 12½ months
Glick, Weiss & Parkes	49	19	under 45	25	Boston, U.S.A.	Interviews: repeated	at 3 and 6 weeks, 13 months and 2–4 years
Clayton *et al.*	70	35	20–90 (mean 61)	50	St Louis Missouri	Interviews: repeated	at 1, 4 and 13 months
Maddison Viola	132	—	40–60	50	Boston, U.S.A.	i Questionnaire	at 13 months
Walker	243	—	under 60	50	Sydney Australia	ii single interviews of sub-samples	after 13 months
Raphael	194	—	under 60	not known	Sydney Australia	i long interview ii questionnaire	within 8 weeks at 13 months
Marris	72	—	25–56	70	London	Interview: single	1–3 years
Hobson	40	—	25–58	over 90	English market town	Interview: single	6 months to 4 years
Rees	227	66	40–80	over 90	rural Wales	Interview: single	some years
Gorer	20	9	45–80	not known	throughout the U.K.	Interview: single	within 5 years

spouse appears to be similar in the two sexes. Such differences as there are can be regarded as variations in the ways that men and women, of Western cultures, deal with their emotional responses and with the ensuing disruption of their way of life.

Secondly, most of the samples are biased towards the younger age groups. The Harvard study excludes all subjects over the age of forty-five; Marris excludes almost all those over fifty; Hobson, and also Maddison and his colleagues, those over sixty. Only in the case of the studies by Clayton and her colleagues, by Rees and by Gorer are there included any widows or widowers over the age of sixty-five. This bias has been deliberate because many of the workers engaged have been concerned to study subjects whom it was thought were at relatively high risk of suffering serious or prolonged emotional disturbance, and such evidence as there was suggested that intensity of reaction, and perhaps also difficulty in recovering, tend to be greater in younger subjects than in older ones. The reason for this, recent evidence suggests, is that the age at which a person suffers loss of a spouse or of a child is correlated with the degree to which the death is felt to have been untimely, to have cut short a life before its fulfilment. For it is evident that the younger the widow or widower, the younger is the husband or wife who has died likely to have been, and the more likely therefore is the death to be felt by the bereaved as having been untimely.

Next, we have to consider how findings may be affected by most of the samples having comprised volunteers drawn from larger populations of bereaved people. To what extent are the responses of these volunteers typical of those that would be seen in the larger population? There is no easy way to answer this, but such evidence as is available, especially that from the comprehensive studies of Hobson (1964) and Rees (1971), does not suggest that responses of volunteers are biased in any systematic way. The same conclusion is reached by Marris (1958) in regard to his London sample and also by Glick et al. (1974) in regard to their Boston sample. In both cases those who participated differed little from the non-participators in regard to demographic variables. In addition, in the Boston study a telephone call to a sample of the non-participators about two years after the first (abortive) contact suggested that their emotional and other experiences after bereavement had not been dissimilar to the experiences of those who had participated in the study.

84

Finally, it must be recognized that the subjects of these studies come exclusively from the Western world. Would similar findings obtain elsewhere? Though evidence to answer this question is inadequate, such as there is suggests that overall patterns are indeed similar. A few examples of this evidence are presented in Chapter 8.

Four phases of mourning

Observations of how individuals respond to the loss of a close relative show that over the course of weeks and months their responses usually move through a succession of phases. Admittedly these phases are not clear cut, and any one individual may oscillate for a time back and forth between any two of them. Yet an overall sequence can be discerned.

The four[1] phases are as follows:

1. Phase of numbing that usually lasts from a few hours to a week and may be interrupted by outbursts of extremely intense distress and/or anger.
2. Phase of yearning and searching for the lost figure lasting some months and sometimes for years.
3. Phase of disorganization and despair.
4. Phase of greater or less degree of reorganization.

In what follows we concentrate especially on the psychological responses to loss, with special reference to the way the original relationship continues to fill a central role in a bereaved person's emotional life yet also, as a rule, undergoes a slow change of form as the months and years pass.[2] This continuing relationship explains the yearning and searching, and also the anger, prevalent in the

[1] In an earlier paper (Bowlby 1961b) it was suggested that the course of mourning could be divided into three main phases, but this numbering omitted an important first phase which is usually fairly brief. What were formerly numbered phases 1, 2 and 3 have therefore been renumbered phases 2, 3 and 4.

[2] In concentrating on these aspects of mourning we are able to give only limited attention to the social and economic consequences of a bereavement, which are often also of great importance and perhaps especially so in the case of widows in Western cultures. Readers concerned with these aspects are referred to the accounts of Marris (1958) and Parkes (1972) for the experiences of London widows and to that of Glick et al. (1974) for those of Boston widows.

second phase, and the despair and subsequent acceptance of loss as irreversible that occur when phases three and four are passed through successfully. It explains, too, many, and perhaps all, of the features characteristic of pathological outcomes.

In the descriptions of responses typical of the first two phases we draw especially on Parkes's study of London widows. In descriptions of the second two phases we draw increasingly on the findings of the Harvard and other studies.

Phase of Numbing

The immediate reaction to news of a husband's death varies greatly from individual to individual and also from time to time in any one widow. Most feel stunned and in varying degrees unable to accept the news. Remarks such as 'I just couldn't take it all in', 'I couldn't believe it', 'I was in a dream', 'It didn't seem real' are the rule. For a time a widow may carry on her usual life almost automatically. Nevertheless, she is likely to feel tense and apprehensive; and this unwonted calm may at any moment be broken by an outburst of intense emotion. Some describe overwhelming attacks of panic in which they may seek refuge with friends. Others break into anger. Occasionally a widow may feel sudden elation in an experience of union with her dead husband.

Phase of Yearning and Searching for the Lost Figure: Anger

Within a few hours or, perhaps, a few days of her loss a change occurs and she begins, though only episodically, to register the reality of the loss: this leads to pangs of intense pining and to spasms of distress and tearful sobbing. Yet, almost at the same time, there is great restlessness, insomnia, preoccupation with thoughts of the lost husband combined often with a sense of his actual presence, and a marked tendency to interpret signals or sounds as indicating that he is now returned. For example, hearing a door latch lifted at five o'clock is interpreted as husband returning from work, or a man in the street is misperceived as the missing husband. Vivid dreams of the husband still alive and well are not uncommon, with corresponding desolation on waking.

Since some or all of these features are now known to occur in a majority of widows, there can no longer be doubt that they are a regular feature of grief and in no way abnormal.

Another common feature of the second phase of mourning is

anger. Its frequency as part of normal mourning has, we believe, habitually been underestimated, at least by clinicians, to whom it seems to have appeared out of place and irrational. Yet, as remarked in Chapter 2, it has been reported by every behavioural scientist, of whatever discipline, who has made grieving the centre of his research.

When such evidence as was then available was examined some years ago (Bowlby 1960b, 1961b) I was struck by the resemblance of these responses to a child's initial protest at losing his mother and his efforts to recover her and also by Shand's suggestion that searching for the lost person is an integral part of the mourning of adults. The view I advanced, therefore, was that during this early phase of mourning it is usual for a bereaved person to alternate between two states of mind. On the one hand is belief that death has occurred with the pain and hopeless yearning that that entails. On the other is disbelief[3] that it has occurred, accompanied both by hope that all may yet be well and by an urge to search for and to recover the lost person. Anger is aroused, it seems, both by those held responsible for the loss and also by frustrations met with during fruitless search.

Exploring this view further, I suggested that in bereaved people whose mourning runs a healthy course the urge to search and to recover, often intense in the early weeks and months, diminishes gradually over time, and that how it is experienced varies greatly from person to person. Whereas some bereaved people are conscious of their urge to search, others are not. Whereas some willingly fall in with it, others seek to stifle it as irrational and absurd. Whatever attitude a bereaved person takes towards the urge, I suggested, he none the less finds himself impelled to search and, if possible, to recover the person who has gone. In a subsequent paper (Bowlby 1963) I pointed out that many of the features characteristic of pathological forms of mourning can be understood as resulting from the active persistence of this urge which tends to be expressed in a variety of disguised and distorted ways.

Such were the views advanced in the early sixties. They have since been endorsed and elaborated by Parkes, who has given

[3] Traditionally the term 'denial' has been used to denote disbelief that death has occurred; but 'denial' always carries with it a sense of active contradiction. Disbelief is more neutral and better suited for general use, especially since the cause of disbelief is often inadequate information.

special attention to these issues. In one of his papers (Parkes 1970b) he has set out evidence from his own studies which he believes supports the search hypothesis. Since this hypothesis is central to all that follows, his evidence is given below.

Introducing the thesis he writes: 'Although we tend to think of searching in terms of the motor act of restless movement towards possible locations of the lost object, [searching] also has perceptual and ideational components . . . Signs of the object can be identified only by reference to memories of the object as it was. Searching the external world for signs of the object therefore includes the establishment of an internal perceptual "set" derived from previous experiences of the object.' He gives as example a woman searching for her small son who is missing; she moves restlessly about the likely parts of the house scanning with her eyes and thinking of the boy; she hears a creak and immediately identifies it as the sound of her son's footfall on the stair; she calls out, 'John, is that you?' The components of this sequence are:

– restless moving about and scanning the environment
– thinking intensely about the lost person
– developing a perceptual set for the person, namely a disposition to perceive and to pay attention to any stimuli that suggest the presence of the person and to ignore all those that are not relevant to this aim
– directing attention towards those parts of the environment in which the person is likely to be found
– calling for the lost person.

'Each of these components,' Parkes emphasizes, 'is to be found in bereaved men and women: in addition some grievers are consciously aware of an urge to search.'

Presenting his findings on the 22 London widows under these five heads Parkes reports that:

(a) All but two widows said they felt restless during the first month of bereavement, a restlessness that was also evident during interview. In summarizing his own findings Parkes quotes Lindemann's classical description of the early weeks of bereavement: 'There is no retardation of action and speech; quite to the contrary, there is a rush of speech especially when talking about the deceased. There is restlessness, inability to sit still, moving about in aimless fashion, continually searching for something to do' (Lindemann 1944).

Nevertheless, Parkes believes the searching is by no means aimless. Only because it is inhibited or else expressed in fragmentary fashion does it appear so.

(b) During the first month of bereavement 19 of the widows were preoccupied with thoughts of their dead husband, and a year later 12 continued to spend much time thinking of him. So clear was the visual picture that often it was spoken of as if it were a perception: 'I can see him sitting in the chair.'

(c) The likelihood that this clear visual picture is part of a general perceptual set that scans sensory input for evidence of the missing person is supported by the frequency with which widows misidentify sensory data. Nine of those interviewed described how during the first month of bereavement they had frequently construed sounds or sights as indicative of their husband. One supposed she heard him cough at night, another heard him moving about the house, a third repeatedly misidentified men in the street.

(d) Not only is a widow's perceptual set biased to give precedence to sensory data that may give evidence of her husband, but her motor behaviour is biased in a comparable way. Half the widows Parkes interviewed described how they felt drawn towards places or objects which they associated with him. Six kept visiting old haunts they had frequented together, two felt drawn towards the hospital where their husband had died, in one case to the point of actually entering its doors, three were unable to leave home without experiencing a strong impulse to return there, others felt drawn towards the cemetery where he was buried. All but three treasured possessions associated with their husband and several found themselves returning repeatedly to such objects.

(e) Whenever a widow recalls the lost person or speaks about him tears are likely, and sometimes they lead to uncontrollable sobbing. Although it may come as a surprise that such tears and sobs are to be regarded as attempts to recover the lost person, there is good reason to think that that is what they are.

The facial expressions typical of adult grief, Darwin concluded (1872), are a resultant, on the one hand, of a tendency to scream like a child when he feels abandoned and, on the other, of an inhibition of such screaming. Both crying and screaming are, of course, ways by means of which a child commonly attracts and recovers his missing mother, or some other person who may help him find her; and they occur in grief, we postulate, with the same objective in mind— either consciously or unconsciously. In keeping with this view is the finding that occasionally a bereaved person will call out for the lost person to return. 'Oh, Fred, I do need you,' shouted one widow during the course of an interview before she burst into tears.

Finally, at least four of these 22 widows were aware that they were searching. 'I walk around searching,' said one, 'I go to the grave . . . but he's not there,' said another. One of them had ideas of attending a spiritualist seance in the hope of communicating with her husband; several thought of killing themselves as a means of rejoining theirs.[4]

Turning now to the incidence of anger amongst these widows, Parkes found it to be evident in all but four and to be very marked in seven, namely one-third of them, at the time of the first interview. For some, anger took the form of general irritability or bitterness. For others it had a target—in four cases a relative, in five clergy, doctors or officials, and in four the dead husband himself. In most such cases the reason given for the anger was that the person in question was held either to have been in some part responsible for the death or to have been negligent in connection with it, either towards the dead man or to the widow. Similarly, husbands had incurred their widows' anger either because they had not cared for

---

[4] Behaviour influenced by an expectation of ultimate reunion is observed in many women with a husband who has deserted or whose marriage has ended in divorce. Marsden (1969) studied eighty such women, all with children, and dependent on the State for support, a great number of whom had not lived with their husband for five years or more. Remarking on the striking resemblance of the responses shown by some of them to responses seen after a bereavement, Marsden writes (p. 140): 'The mother's emotional bonds with the father did not snap cleanly with the parting. Almost half the mothers, many of whom had completely lost touch with the father, had a sense of longing for him . . . It was evident that a sizable minority of women persisted, in spite of evidence to the contrary and sometimes for many years, in thinking they would somehow be reunited with their children's father.' After having moved into a new house three years earlier one of them had still not unpacked her belongings, unable to believe the move was permanent.

themselves better or because they were thought to have contributed to their own death.[5]

Although some degree of self-reproach was also common, it was never so prominent a feature as was anger. In most of these widows self-reproach centred on some minor act of omission or commission associated with the last illness or death. Although in one or two of the London widows there were times when this self-reproach was fairly severe, in none of them was it as intense and unrelenting as it is in subjects whose self-reproachful grieving persists until finally it becomes diagnosed as depressive illness (see Chapter 9).

Within the context of the search hypothesis the prevalence of anger during the early weeks of mourning receives ready explanation. In several earlier publications (see Volume II, Chapter 17) it has been emphasized that anger is both usual and useful when separation is only temporary. It then helps overcome obstacles to reunion with the lost person; and, after reunion is achieved, to express reproach towards whomever seemed responsible for the separation makes it less likely that a separation will occur again. Only when separation is permanent is the anger and reproach out of place. 'There are therefore good biological reasons for every separation to be responded to in an automatic instinctive way with aggressive behaviour; irretrievable loss is statistically so unusual that it is not taken into account. In the course of our evolution, it appears, our instinctual equipment has come to be so fashioned that all losses are assumed to be retrievable and are responded to accordingly' (Bowlby 1961b). Thus anger is seen as an intelligible constituent of the urgent though fruitless effort a bereaved person is making to restore the bond that has been severed. So long as anger continues, it seems, loss is not being accepted as permanent and hope is still lingering on. As Marris (1958) comments when a widow described to him how, after her husband's death, she had given her

[5] There is some evidence that the incidence of anger varies with the sex of the bereaved and also with the phase of life during which a death occurs. For example, findings of the Harvard study, which show an even higher incidence of anger among widows, show a lower incidence among widowers (see p. 43); and Gorer (1965) believes it to occur less frequently after the death of an elderly person—a timely death—than after that of someone whose life is uncompleted. The low incidence of anger reported by Clayton et al. (1972) may perhaps be a result of their sample being both elderly and also made up of one-third widowers.

doctor a good hiding, it was 'as if her rage while it lasted had given her courage'.

Sudden outbursts of rage are fairly common soon after a loss, especially ones that are sudden and/or felt to be untimely, and they carry no adverse prognosis. Should anger and resentment persist beyond the early weeks, however, there are grounds for concern, as we see in Chapter 9.

Hostility to comforters is to be understood in the same way. Whereas the comforter who takes no side in the conflict between a striving for reunion and an acceptance of loss may be of great value to the bereaved, one who at an early stage seems to favour acceptance of loss is as keenly resented as if he had been the agent of it. Often it is not comfort in loss that is wanted but assistance towards reunion.

Anger and ingratitude towards comforters, indeed, have been notorious since the time of Job. Overwhelmed by the blow he has received, one of the first impulses of the bereaved is to appeal to others for their help—help to regain the person lost. The would-be comforter who responds to this appeal may, however, see the situation differently. To him it may be clear that hope of reunion is a chimera and that to encourage it would be unrealistic, even dishonest. And so, instead of behaving as is wished, he seems to the bereaved to do the opposite and is resented accordingly. No wonder his role is a thankless one.

Thus, we see, restless searching, intermittent hope, repeated disappointment, weeping, anger, accusation, and ingratitude are all features of the second phase of mourning, and are to be understood as expressions of the strong urge to find and recover the lost person. Nevertheless, underlying these strong emotions, which erupt episodically and seem so perplexing, there is likely to coexist deep and pervasive sadness, a response to recognition that reunion is at best improbable. Moreover, because fruitless search is painful, there may also be times when a bereaved person may attempt to be rid of reminders of the dead. He or she may then oscillate between treasuring such reminders and throwing them out, between welcoming the opportunity to speak of the dead and dreading such occasions, between seeking out places where they have been together and avoiding them. One of the widows interviewed by Parkes described how she had tried sleeping in the back bedroom to get away from her memories and how she had then missed her husband so much that she had returned to the main bedroom in order to be near him.

Finding a way to reconcile these two incompatible urges, we believe, constitutes a central task of the third and fourth phases of mourning. Light on how successfully the task is being solved, Gorer (1965) believes, is thrown by the way a bereaved person responds to spoken condolences; grateful acceptance is one of the most reliable signs that the bereaved is working through his or her mourning satisfactorily. Conversely, as we see in Chapter 9, an injunction never to refer to the loss bodes ill.

It is in the extent to which they help a mourner in this task that mourning customs are to be evaluated. In recent times both Gorer (1965) and Marris (1974) have considered them in this light. At first, Marris points out, acts of mourning attenuate the leave taking. They enable the bereaved, for a while, to give the dead person as central a place in her life as he had before, yet at the same time they emphasize death as a crucial event whose implications must be acknowledged. Subsequently, such customs mark the stages of reintegration. In Gorer's phrase, mourning customs are 'time-limited', both guiding and sanctioning the stages of recovery. Although at first sight it may seem false to impose customs on so intense and private an emotion as grief, the very loneliness of the crisis and the intense conflict of feeling cries out for a supportive structure. In Chapter 8 the mourning customs of other cultures are considered and attention drawn to certain features that are common to a large majority of them, including those of the West.

Phase of Disorganization and Despair and Phase of Reorganization

For mourning to have a favourable outcome it appears to be necessary for a bereaved person to endure this buffeting of emotion. Only if he can tolerate the pining, the more or less conscious searching, the seemingly endless examination of how and why the loss occurred, and anger at anyone who might have been responsible, not sparing even the dead person, can he come gradually to recognize and accept that the loss is in truth permanent and that his life must be shaped anew. In this way only does it seem possible for him fully to register that his old patterns of behaviour have become redundant and have therefore to be dismantled. C. S. Lewis (1961) has described the frustrations not only of feeling but of thought and action that grieving entails. In a diary entry after the loss of his wife,

H, he writes: 'I think I am beginning to understand why grief feels like suspense. It comes from the frustration of so many impulses that had become habitual. Thought after thought, feeling after feeling, action after action, had H for their object. Now their target is gone. I keep on, through habit, fitting an arrow to the string; then I remember and I have to lay the bow down. So many roads lead through to H. I set out on one of them. But now there's an impassable frontier-post across it. So many roads once; now so many culs-de-sac' (p. 59).

Because it is necessary to discard old patterns of thinking, feeling and acting before new ones can be fashioned, it is almost inevitable that a bereaved person should at times despair that anything can be salvaged and, as a result, fall into depression and apathy. Nevertheless, if all goes well this phase may soon begin to alternate with a phase during which he starts to examine the new situation in which he finds himself and to consider ways of meeting it. This entails a redefinition of himself as well as of his situation. No longer is he a husband but a widower. No longer is he one of a pair with complementary roles but a singleton. This redefinition of self and situation is as painful as it is crucial, if only because it means relinquishing finally all hope that the lost person can be recovered and the old situation re-established. Yet until redefinition is achieved no plans for the future can be made.

It is important here to note that, suffused though it be by the strongest emotion, redefinition of self and situation is no mere release of affect but a cognitive act on which all else turns. It is a process of 'realization' (Parkes 1972), of reshaping internal representational models so as to align them with the changes that have occurred in the bereaved's life situation. Much is said of this in later chapters.

Once this corner is turned a bereaved person recognizes that an attempt must be made to fill unaccustomed roles and to acquire new skills. A widower may have to become cook and housekeeper, a widow to become the family wage-earner and house decorator. If there are children, the remaining parent has so far as possible to do duty for both. The more successful the survivor is in achieving these new roles and skills the more confident and independent he or she begins to feel. The shift is well described by one of the London widows, interviewed a year after her bereavement, who remarked: 'I think I'm beginning to wake up now. I'm starting living instead of just existing . . . I feel I ought to plan to do something.' As initiative and, with it, independence returns so a widow or widower may become jealous of that independence and may perhaps break off rather abruptly a supportive relationship that had earlier been welcomed. Yet, however successfully a widow or widower may adopt new roles and learn new skills, the changed situation is likely to be felt as a constant strain and is bound to be lonely. An acute sense of loneliness, most pronounced at night time, was reported by almost all the widows interviewed whether by Marris, by Hobson or by Parkes in England or by Glick or Clayton and their respective teams in the U.S.A.

To resume social life even at a superficial level is often a great difficulty, at least in Western cultures. There is more than one reason for this. On the one hand, convention often dictates that the sexes be present in equal number so that those who enjoy the company of the other sex find themselves left out. On the other are those who find social occasions in which the sexes are mixed too painful to attend because of their being reminded too forcefully of their loss of partner. As a consequence we find that both widowers and widows most often join gatherings of members of their own sex. For men this is usually easier because a work group or sports group may be ready to hand. For women a church group or Women's Institute may prove invaluable.

Few widows remarry. This is partly because suitable partners are scarce but at least equally because of a reluctance of many widows to consider remarriage. Plainly, the remarriage rate for each sample will depend not only on the widows' ages at bereavement but on the number of years later that information is gathered. In the studies reviewed here the highest rate reported is about one in four of the Boston widows; at the end of some three years fourteen had either remarried or appeared likely to do so. All of them, it should be remembered, were under 45 years when widowed. In the Marris study one in five of the 33 widowed before age forty had remarried. For older widows the proportions are much lower. By contrast, the proportion of widowers who remarry is relatively high, a difference considered further at the end of the chapter.

Many widows refuse to consider remarriage. Others consider it but decide against it. Fear of friction between stepfather and children is given as a reason by many. Some regard the risk of suffering the pain of a second loss too great. Others believe they could never

95

love another man in the way they had loved their husband and that invidious comparisons would result. In response to questions, about half the Boston widows expressed themselves uninterested in any further sexual relationship. Whilst half of the total acknowledged some sense of sexual deprivation, others felt numbed. It is probably common for sexual feelings to continue to be linked to the husband; and they may be expressed in masturbation fantasies or enacted in dreams.

A year after bereavement, continued loyalty to the husband was judged by Glick to be the main stumbling-block to remarriage in the case of the Boston widows. Parkes remarks that many of the London widows 'still seemed to regard themselves as married to their dead husbands' (Parkes, 1972, p. 99). This raises afresh the issue of a bereaved person's continuing relationship with the person who has died.

Persistence of Relationship

As the first year of mourning draws on most mourners find it becomes possible to make a distinction between patterns of thought, feeling and behaviour that are clearly no longer appropriate and others which can with good reason be retained. In the former class are those, such as performing certain household duties, which only make sense if the lost person is physically present; in the latter maintaining values and pursuing goals which, having been developed in association with the lost person, remain linked with him and can without falsification continue to be maintained and pursued in reference to memory of him. Perhaps it is through processes of this kind that half or more of widows and widowers reach a state of mind in which they retain a strong sense of the continuing presence of their partner without the turmoils of hope and disappointment, search and frustration, anger and blame that are present earlier.

It will be remembered that a year after losing their husbands twelve of the twenty-two London widows reported that they still spent much time thinking of their husband and sometimes had a sense of his actual presence. This they found comforting. Glick *et al.* (1974) report very similar findings for the Boston widows. Although a sense of the continuing presence of the dead person may take a few weeks to become firmly established, they found it tends thereafter to persist at its original intensity, instead of waning slowly as most of the other components of the early phases of mourning do. Twelve months after their loss two out of three of the Boston widows continued to spend much time thinking of their husband and one in four of the 49 described how there were still occasions when they forgot he was dead. So comforting did widows find the sense of the dead husband's presence that some deliberately evoked it whenever they felt unsure of themselves or depressed.

Similar findings to those for the London and the Boston widows are reported also by Rees (1971), who surveyed nearly three hundred widows and widowers in Wales, nearly half of whom had been widowed for ten years or longer. Of 227 widows and 66 widowers 47 per cent described having had such experiences and a majority were continuing to do so. Incidence in widowers was almost the same as in widows and the incidence varied little with either social class or cultural background. The incidence tended to be higher the longer the marriage had lasted, which may account for its being higher also in those who were over the age of forty when widowed. More than one in ten of widows and widowers reported having held conversations with the dead spouse; and here again the incidence was higher in older widows and widowers than in younger ones. Two-thirds of those who reported experiences of their dead spouse's presence, either with or without some form of sensory illusion or occasionally hallucination, described their experiences as being comforting and helpful. Most of the remainder were neutral about them, and only eight of the total of 137 subjects who had such experiences disliked having them.

Dreams of the spouse still being alive share many of the characteristic features of the sense of presence: they occur in about half of widows and widowers, they are extremely vivid and realistic and in a majority of cases are experienced as comforting. 'It was just like everyday life', one of the London widows reported, 'my husband coming in and getting his dinner. Very vivid so that when I woke up I was very annoyed.' Several of Gorer's informants described how they sought to hold the image in their minds after waking and how sad it was when it faded. Not infrequently a widow or widower would weep after recounting the dream.

Gorer (1965) emphasizes that in these typical comforting dreams the dead person is envisaged as young and healthy, and as engaging in happy everyday activities. But, as Parkes (1972) notes, as a rule there is something in the dream to indicate that all is not well. As one widow put it after describing how in the dream her husband was

97

trying to comfort her and how happy it made her: 'even in the dream I know he's dead'.[6]

Not all bereaved people who dream find the dream comforting. In some dreams traumatic aspects of the last illness or death are re-enacted; in others distressing aspects of the previous relationship. Whether on balance a bereaved person finds his dreams comforting seems likely to be a reliable indicator of whether or not mourning is taking a favourable course.

Let us return now to a widow's or widower's daytime sense of the dead spouse's presence. In many cases, it seems, the dead spouse is experienced as a companion who accompanies the bereaved everywhere. In many others the spouse is experienced as located somewhere specific and appropriate. Common examples are a particular chair or room which he occupied, or perhaps the garden, or the grave. As remarked already, there is no reason to regard any of these experiences as either unusual or unfavourable, rather the contrary. For example, in regard to the Boston widows Glick *et al.* (1974) report: 'Often the widow's progress toward recovery was facilitated by inner conversations with her husband's presence . . . this continued sense of attachment was not incompatible with increasing capacity for independent action' (p. 154). Although Glick regards this finding as paradoxical, those familiar with the evidence regarding the relation of secure attachment to the growth of self-reliance (Volume II, Chapter 21) will not find it so. On the contrary, it seems likely that for many widows and widowers it is precisely because they are willing for their feelings of attachment to the dead spouse to persist that their sense of identity is preserved and they become able to reorganize their lives along lines they find meaningful.

That for many bereaved people this is the preferred solution to their dilemma has for too long gone unrecognized.

Closely related to this sense of the dead person's presence are certain experiences in which a widow may feel either that she has

[6] Early in his work Freud (1916) had remarked on the way a dream can express incompatible truths: 'When anyone has lost someone near and dear to him, he produces dreams of a special sort for some time afterwards, in which knowledge of the death arrives at the strangest compromises with the need to bring the dead person to life again. In some of these dreams the person who has died is dead and at the same time still alive . . . In others he is half dead and half alive' (*SE* 15, p. 187).

become more like her husband since his death or even that he is somehow within her. For example, one of the London widows, on being asked whether she had felt her husband was near at hand, replied: 'It's not a sense of his presence, he's here inside me. That's why I'm happy all the time. It's as if two people are one . . . although I'm alone, we're sort of together if you see what I mean . . . I don't think I've got the will power to carry on on my own, so he must be' (Parkes 1972, p. 104).

In accordance with such feelings bereaved people may find themselves doing things in the same way that the person lost did them; and some may undertake activities typical of the dead person despite their never having done them before. When the activities are well suited to the capabilities and interests of the bereaved, no conflict results and he or she may obtain much satisfaction from doing them. Perhaps such behaviour is best regarded as an example, in special circumstances, of the well-known tendency to emulate those whom we hold in high regard. Nevertheless, Parkes (1972, p. 105) emphasizes that in his series of London widows it was only a minority who at any time during the first year of bereavement were conscious either of coming to resemble the husband or of 'containing' him. Moreover, in these widows the sense of having him 'inside' tended to alternate with periods when he was experienced as a companion. Since these widows progressed neither more nor less favourably than others, such experiences when only short-lived are evidently compatible with healthy mourning.

Many symptoms of disordered mourning can, however, be understood as due to some unfavourable development of these processes. One form of maldevelopment is when a bereaved person feels a continuing compulsion to imitate the dead person despite having neither the competence nor the desire to do so. Another is when the bereaved's continuing sense of 'containing' the person lost gives rise to an elated state of mind (as seems to have been present in the example quoted), or leads the bereaved to develop the symptoms of the deceased's last illness. Yet another form of unfavourable development occurs when the bereaved, instead of experiencing the dead person as a companion and/or as located somewhere appropriate such as in the grave or in his, or her, familiar chair, locates him within another person, or even within an animal or a physical object. Such mislocations as I shall call them, which include mislocations within the self, can if persistent easily lead to behaviour

99

that is not in the best interests of the bereaved and that may appear bizarre. It may also be damaging to another person; for example, to regard a child as the incarnation of a dead person and to treat him so is likely to have an extremely adverse effect upon him (see Chapter 16). For all these reasons I am inclined to regard mislocations of any of these kinds if more than transitory as signs of pathology.

Failure to recognize that a continuing sense of the dead person's presence, either as a constant companion or in some specific and appropriate location, is a common feature of healthy mourning has led to much confused theorizing. Very frequently the concept of identification, instead of being limited to cases in which the dead person is located within the self, is extended to cover also every case in which there is a continuing sense of the dead person's presence, irrespective of location. By so doing a distinction that recent empirical studies show is vital for an understanding of the differences between healthy and pathological mourning becomes blurred. Indeed, findings in regard both to the high prevalence of a continuing sense of the presence of the dead person and to its compatibility with a favourable outcome give no support to Freud's well-known and already quoted passage: 'Mourning has a quite precise psychical task to perform: its function is to detach the survivor's memories and hopes from the dead' (*SE* 13, p. 65).

Duration of Grieving: Ill-Health

All the studies available suggest that most women take a long time to get over the death of a husband and that, by whatever psychiatric standard they are judged, less than half are themselves again at the end of the first year. Almost always health suffers. Insomnia is near universal; headaches, anxiety, tension and fatigue extremely common. In any one mourner there is increased likelihood that any of a host of other symptoms will develop; even fatal illness is more common than it is in non-bereaved people of the same age and sex (Rees and Lutkins 1967; Parkes *et al.* 1969; Ward 1976). To do justice to the important issue of the impaired physical health of bereaved people would require a chapter to itself and would take us too far from the topics of this volume. The reader is therefore referred to the above papers and also to the following: Parkes (1970c); Parkes and Brown (1972); Maddison and Viola (1968).

As regards duration of mourning, when Parkes interviewed the twenty-two London widows at the end of their first year of bereavement, three were judged still to be grieving a great deal and nine more were intermittently disturbed and depressed. At that time only four seemed to be making a good adjustment.

Findings of the Harvard study (Glick *et al.* 1974) were rather more favourable. Even though a majority of the 49 Boston widows were still not feeling wholly themselves again at the end of the first year, four out of five seemed to be doing reasonably well. Several described how at a particular moment during the year they had asserted themselves in some way and had thereafter found themselves on a path to recovery. Deciding to sort through husband's clothes and possessions, itself an intensely painful task, had for some been the turning-point. For others it had followed a sudden and prolonged fit of crying. Although consulting husband's wishes continued to influence decisions, by the end of the year his wishes were less likely to be the dominant consideration. During the second and third years the pattern that a widow's reorganized life would take, in particular whether she would remarry, seemed firmly established. Except for those on the road to remarriage, however, loneliness continued a persistent problem.

In contrast to the majority of Boston widows who were making progress, there was a minority who were not. Two became seriously ill, one dying; and six continued disturbed and disorganized. The impression was gained that if recovery was not in progress by the end of the first year prognosis was not good.

From these and other findings it must be concluded that a substantial minority of widows never fully recover their former state of health and well-being. A majority of those who do, or at least come near to it, are more likely to take two or three years to do so than a mere one. As one widow in her mid-sixties put it five years after her husband's death: 'Mourning never ends: only as time goes on it erupts less frequently.' Indeed, an occasional recurrence of active grieving, especially when some event reminds the bereaved of her loss, is the rule. I emphasize these findings, distressing though they are, because I believe that clinicians sometimes have unrealistic expectations of the speed and completeness with which someone can be expected to get over a major bereavement. Research findings, moreover, can be very misleading unless interpreted with care. For at one interview a widow may report that at last she is progressing favourably yet had she been interviewed a few months later, after she had met with some disappointment, she might have presented a very different picture.

Emotional Loneliness

Reference has been made more than once to the deep and persisting sense of loneliness that the bereaved so commonly suffer and which remains largely unalleviated by friendships. Although for long noted at an empirical level, for example by Marris (1958), this persistent loneliness has tended to be neglected at a theoretical level, largely perhaps because social and behavioral scientists have been unable to accommodate it within their theorizing. Recently, however, thanks largely to the work of Robert S. Weiss of Harvard, it is receiving more attention.

Weiss, a sociologist who participated in the Harvard bereavement study (with Glick and Parkes), has carried out another study, this time into the experiences of marital partners after they had become separated or divorced (Weiss 1975b). In order better to understand the problems of such people he worked in a research role with an organization, Parents without Partners, designed to give them a meeting-place. Friendly interaction with others in the same plight would, it had been expected, compensate them in their loss, at least in some degree. But it proved otherwise: '. . . although many members, particularly among the women, specifically mentioned friendship as a major contribution of the organization to their well-being, and although these friendships often became very close and very important to the participants, they did not especially diminish their loneliness. They made the loneliness easier to manage, by providing reassurance that it was not the individual's fault, but rather was common to all those in the individual's situation. And they provided the support of friends who could understand' (Weiss 1975a, pp. 19–20).

As a result of these and similar findings Weiss draws a sharp distinction between the loneliness of *social* isolation, for mitigating which the organization proved useful, and the loneliness of *emotional* isolation, which went untouched. Each form of loneliness, he believes, is of great importance but what acts as remedy for one does not remedy the other. Couching his thinking in terms of the theory of attachment outlined in these volumes, he defines emotional loneliness as loneliness that can be remedied only by involvement in a mutually committed relationship, without which he found there was no feeling of security. Such potentially long-term relationships are distinct from ordinary friendships and, in adults of Western societies, take only a few forms: 'Attachment is provided by marriage, by other cross-sex committed relationships; among some women by relationships with a close friend, a sister or mother; among some men by relationships with "buddies" ' (Weiss 1975a, p. 23).

Once the nature of emotional loneliness is understood its prevalence among widows and widowers who do not marry again, and also among some who do, is hardly surprising. For them, we now know, loneliness does not fade with time.

Differences between widows and widowers

Of the various studies drawn upon in this chapter only one, the Harvard study, gives sufficient data for tentative conclusions to be drawn between the course of mourning in widows and in widowers (Glick et al. 1974). Two other studies, by Rees (1971) and Gorer (1965), provide additional data which, so far as they go, support those conclusions.

The initial size of the Harvard sample was 22 widowers; of these 19 were available at the end of the first year and 17 at the end of about three years. Despite small numbers all levels of socio-economic life were represented and so were the major religious and ethnic groups. Like the Boston widows, all widowers were under the age of 45 at the time of bereavement.

Comparing the responses of the widowers with those of the widows the researchers conclude that, although the emotional and psychological responses to loss of a spouse are very similar, there are differences in the freedom with which emotion is expressed and differences also in the way in which attempts are made to deal with a disrupted social and working life. Many of these differences are not large but they appear consistent.

Let us start with the similarities. There were no differences of consequence in the percentages of widows and widowers who, during the first interviews, described pain and yearning and who were tearful. The same was true of their experiencing strong visual images of the spouse and a sense of his or her presence. At the end of the first year, although rather fewer widowers described themselves as being at times very unhappy or depressed, the difference was still small, namely widows 51 per cent and widowers 42 per cent. The proportions who claimed that, after a year, they were beginning to feel themselves again was, similarly, tilted only slightly in favour of the widowers, namely widows 58 per cent and widowers 71 per cent. When at a year the condition of widowers was compared to that of a control group of married men, a larger proportion of them than of the widows seemed to have been adversely affected by the bereavement, the widows being judged, similarly, by comparing their condition with that of members of a control group of married women.[7] The widowers at that stage seemed to suffer especially from tension and restlessness. Fully as many widowers as widows reported feeling lonely.

In expressing their sense of loss widowers were more likely to speak of having lost a part of themselves; in contrast, widows were more likely to refer to themselves as having been abandoned. Yet both forms of expression were used by members of both sexes and it remains uncertain whether or not such difference as was noted is of psychological significance.

Turning now to the differences, it was found that, at least in the short term and during interviews, widowers tended to be more matter-of-fact than widows. For example, eight weeks after bereavement, whereas all but two of the widowers gave the impression of having accepted the reality of the loss, only half the widows gave that impression: the other half were not only on occasion acting as though their husbands were still alive but also were sometimes feeling he might actually return. In addition a larger proportion of widows than widowers were fearing they might have a nervous breakdown (50 per cent of widows and 20 per cent of widowers) and were likely still to be rehearsing the events leading to their spouse's death (53 per cent of widows and 30 per cent of widowers).

In keeping with their matter-of-fact attitude fewer widowers admitted to feeling angry. During the first two interviews the proportion of widows clearly expressing anger varied between 38 and 52 per cent, the proportion of widowers between 15 and 21 per cent. Taking the year as a whole 42 per cent of the widows were rated as having shown moderate or severe anger compared with 30 per cent of the widowers. In regard to feelings of guilt, however, the picture

[7] This finding is difficult to interpret, however, because the married women controls were found to be appreciably more depressed than their male counterparts.

was equivocal. Initially self-reproach was evident in a higher proportion of widowers than widows; but subsequently the proportions reversed.

It is likely that some of these differences stem from a greater reluctance of widowers than widows to report their feelings. Whether this was so or not, there was no doubt that many of the widowers regarded tears as unmanly, and that more of them therefore attempted to control expression of feeling. In contrast to the widows, a majority of widowers disliked the idea of some sympathetic person encouraging them to express feeling more freely. Similarly, a greater proportion of widowers tried deliberately to regulate the occasions when they allowed themselves to grieve. This they did by choosing the occasions when they would look at old letters and photographs and avoiding reminders at other times. In keeping perhaps with this tendency to exert control over feeling was the dismay expressed by some of the widowers that their energy and competence at work should have become as reduced as it often was.

Most widowers welcomed any assistance given by their female relatives in caring for house and children, and were relieved at the chance to carry on with their work much as before.

A sense of sexual deprivation was much more likely to be reported by widowers than widows; and, in contrast to the marked reluctance of about one-third of the widows even to consider remarriage, a majority of widowers moved quickly to think of it. By the end of a year half of them had either already remarried or appeared likely to do so soon (in comparison with only 18 per cent of widows). At the time of the final interview half had in fact remarried (in comparison with a quarter of the widows). A majority of these second marriages appeared to be satisfactory. In some it was a tribute to the second wife who was willing not only for her husband to remain a good deal preoccupied with thoughts of his first wife but to engage with him often in talking about her.

Although after two or three years a majority of widowers had reshaped their lives reasonably successfully, there was a minority who had failed to do so. For example, there were then not less than four widowers who were either markedly depressed or alcoholic or both. One had made an impulsive remarriage which had ended as soon as it had begun. Another, who had had a breakdown before marriage and who had lost his wife very suddenly from a heart attack, remained deeply depressed and unable to organize his life. All four had had no forewarning of their wife's death.

Note: details of sources

The purpose of this note is to describe the various studies listed in Table 1 in rather more detail than is convenient in the text of the chapter. Because of my indebtedness to the studies undertaken in London and Boston by my colleague, Colin Murray Parkes, we start with some particulars of those.

In the first of his two studies Parkes set out to obtain a series of descriptive pictures of how a sample of ordinary women respond to the death of a husband. To this end he interviewed, personally, a fairly representative sample of 22 London widows, aged between 26 and 65, during the year following bereavement. The sample was obtained through general practitioners who introduced the research worker to the subjects. Each widow was interviewed on at least five occasions—the first at one month after bereavement and the others at three, six, nine and twelve-and-a-half months after. Interviews, held in the widow's own home in all but three cases, lasted from one to four hours. At the start of each, general questions were put to encourage the widow to describe her experiences. Only when she had finished did the interviewer ask additional questions either to cover areas she had not mentioned or to enable ratings to be made on scales designed in the light of previous work. By proceeding in this way good rapport was established so that information was given frankly and intense feeling often expressed. Most of the widows regarded their participation in these interviews as having been help-ful to themselves, and some of them welcomed the suggestion of additional interviews.

Details of the sample, the ground covered in the interviews and the probable reliability of assessments are given in Parkes (1970a). Subjects were drawn fairly evenly from the various social classes, and ranged in age for 26 to 65 years (average 49 years). All but three had children. The commonest causes of the husband's death were cancer (ten cases) and cardiovascular disease (eight). Most of the husbands had died in hospital and without their wife being present; eight had died at home. Nineteen widows had been warned of the seriousness of their husband's condition, thirteen of them at least one month before the end. The final deterioration and death was foreseeable for at least a week in nine cases, for some hours in three but had come suddenly in nine.

The second study was initiated at the Harvard Laboratory of Community Psychiatry in Boston by Gerald Caplan. Subsequently, Parkes was invited to join the team and later took over responsibility for the study which came to be known as the Harvard Bereavement Project. Its aim was to devise methods for identifying, soon after bereavement, those subjects who are likely to be at higher than average risk of responding to loss in a way unfavourable to their mental and physical health.

Because it was believed that bereaved subjects under the age of 45 years are more likely than older subjects to have an adverse outcome to their mourning the sample studied were all under that age. Those who completed all interviews numbered 49 widows and 19 widowers and represented 25 per cent of the 274 men and women of appropriate age in the community selected who had lost a spouse during the relevant period and who could be contacted. (40 per cent refused to participate and 16 per cent proved unsuitable because of language, distance or other problems. A further 15 per cent dropped out of the study during the first year of bereavement, a major reason being their unwillingness to review painful memories.)[8]

Three weeks after bereavement and again six weeks later widows and widowers were interviewed in their homes by experienced social workers. Each interview lasted between one and two hours and was tape-recorded. The next interviews were not until thirteen months

[8] As a proportion of all those conforming to the sampling criteria, the final sample was derived as follows:

conforming to criteria	349	
unable to be contacted	75	
actually contacted	274	
		% of those contacted
refused to participate	116	40
found to be ineligible	43	16
refused later interviews	42	15
completed all interviews	68	26
total contacted	269	97

The proportions of widowers and widowers respectively affected by these reductions are similar. (These figures, derived from Table One in Glick *et al.* (1974), leave five cases unaccounted for.)

after bereavement when two further interviews were conducted. In the first of these, which proceeded on lines similar to the earlier ones, a detailed account of the events of the preceding year and of the respondent's present condition was obtained. In the second a fresh interviewer, who was unknown to the respondent and who himself had no knowledge of the previous course of events, administered a questionnaire; this, constructed in terms of forced-choice questions, was aimed to give independent and clear-cut measures of the respondent's current state of health. By relating these measures of outcome at thirteen months to information obtained at three and six weeks, it was hoped to discover what features present during the early weeks of bereavement are indicative of favourable or unfavourable outcome later. As a final step a follow-up interview was conducted by a social worker between one and three years later, namely between two and four years after the death. All but six widows and two widowers were able to participate at this stage, giving a sample of 43 widows and 17 widowers.

Details of the sampling, of the methods of coding the interview material and of devising outcome measures, and estimates of the reliability of such measures, can be found in the two volumes in which the findings are published (Glick, Weiss and Parkes 1974, second volume in preparation). In nearly half the cases death had been sudden, due to accident or heart, or else had occurred without much warning. In most of the remainder deaths followed illnesses of obvious severity ranging in duration from several weeks to years. How much forewarning a bereaved person is given is found to be related in considerable degree both to the capacity of the bereaved to recover from the loss and also to the form recovery takes, matters to which much more attention will have to be paid in future than has been given hitherto.

In addition to these studies we draw on the findings of several other studies of widows and of some which included widowers also. All of them differ from the London and Harvard studies in a number of ways and, by so doing, complement their findings in certain respects. For example, two of them, by Hobson (1964) and by Rees (1971), were conducted outside urban settings; and in both cases the researcher managed to interview almost every one of the bereaved subjects who fell within the initial sampling. In all but one of these additional studies interviewing was done at least six months, and usually a year or more after the loss had occurred, thus giving good coverage of later phases of mourning at the price of poor coverage of the earlier ones.

The first of these additional studies is the pioneer study by Marris (1958), a social psychologist. His aim was to interview all women who had been widowed during a certain two-and-a-quarter-year period whilst living with their husbands in a working-class district of London and whose husbands had been 50 years old or under at death. Of the total of 104 such widows, 2 had died, 7 were untraceable, 7 had moved away and 16 refused, leaving a total of 72 who were interviewed. Their bereavement had occurred from one to three years earlier, in the main about two years. Their ages ranged from 25 to 56 years with an average of 42 years, and the duration of their marriages ranged from one to thirty years, with an average of sixteen years. All but eleven had children living, the children being of school age or less in the case of 47. Interviews covered not only a widow's emotional experiences but also her current financial and social situation.

A rather similar study was conducted by Hobson (1964), a social-work student, who interviewed all but one of the widows in a small English market-town who were under the age of sixty and who had lost their husband not less than six months and not more than four years earlier. Her interview method was similar to Marris's, though briefer. The number interviewed was forty; their ages ranged from 25 to 58 years (the majority being over 45 years). All but seven had been married for ten years or longer; and the husbands of all but five had been working class, either skilled or unskilled.

In an attempt to learn more of the health problems of widows Maddison and Viola (1968) studied 132 widows in Boston, U.S.A., and 243 in Sydney, Australia. The main studies were conducted by questionnaire. In Boston the age of husbands at death lay between 45 and 60; in Sydney the lower age-limit was abandoned. Since in both cities refusal rates were about 25 per cent and another 20 per cent proved untraceable, those questioned reached only about 50 per cent of the total aimed for. The questionnaire was designed to give basic demographic data and the widows' responses to 57 items which reviewed her physical and mental health over the preceding 13 months, with special reference to complaints and symptoms which were either new or substantially more troublesome during the period. In each city a control group of non-bereaved women was also studied.

Maddison's studies, both in Boston and in Sydney, have a second part. In each city a sub-sample of widows whose health reports showed they were doing badly and a sub-sample of those doing well, matched as closely as possible on socio-economic variables, were interviewed. The aims were, first, to check on the validity of the questionnaire, which proved satisfactory, and secondly to cast light on factors associated with a favourable or an unfavourable outcome. Findings, which are drawn on in Chapter 10, are reported in Maddison and Walker (1967) and Maddison (1968) for Boston, and in Maddison, Viola and Walker (1969) for Sydney. The work in Sydney has been extended by Raphael (1974, 1975; Raphael and Maddison 1976); particulars are given in Chapter 10.

Another study, also with a focus on health, was conducted by a team in St Louis, Missouri (Clayton *et al.* 1972, 1973; Bornstein *et al.* 1973). The sample comprised 70 widows and 33 widowers, who represented just over half those approached. Ages ranged very widely from 20 to 90 years, with a mean of 61 years. Interviews were conducted about thirty days after bereavement and again at four months and at about thirteen months. In a quarter of the cases death had been sudden, namely five days of forewarning or less. In 46 forewarning was six months or less and in the remaining 35 more than six months. Whenever forewarning was sufficient spouses were interviewed also before the death had occurred. A serious limitation of this study was that interviews were restricted to an hour's duration.

Another study including widowers as well as widows, but with a different focus, was conducted by Rees (1971), a general practitioner, who interviewed all the men and women who had lost a spouse and were resident in a defined area of mid-Wales, omitting only those who were suffering from incapacitating illness and a mere handful of others. The total numbers interviewed were 227 widows and 66 widowers, who ranged widely in age with most between forty and eighty. In this study interviews were concerned especially to determine whether the widowed person had experience of illusions (visual, auditory or tactile, or a sense of presence) or hallucinations of the dead spouse.[9] He found them to be far more common than might formerly have been supposed.

[9] Contrary to Rees's own account the great majority of the experiences reported by him appear to have been illusions, namely misinterpretations of sensory stimuli; and not hallucinations.

There is at least one other study which reports on responses to loss of spouse, although here widows and widowers make up only a minority of the sample. This is by Gorer (1965, 1973), a social anthropologist who interviewed eighty bereaved people selected to cover persons of all ages over 16 years and both sexes who had lost a first-degree relative within the previous five years and to cover also a wide range of social and religious groups throughout the United Kingdom. Since some of those interviewed had lost more than one relative and tables are incomplete exact numbers are not available. Included are some twenty widows, of ages varying from 45 to over 80, and nine widowers, of ages from 48 to 71. (Of others interviewed, thirty or more had lost a mother or father during adult life, a dozen had lost a sibling, and others had lost a son or daughter.) Gorer's principal interest is the social context in which death and mourning take place and the social customs or lack of them obtaining in twentieth-century Britain. Because in regard to any one class of bereaved people samples are small, it is not possible to know how representative his findings are. Nevertheless, his book, which contains many vivid transcripts of how bereaved people describe their experience, is of great psychological interest.

CHAPTER 7

Loss of Child

I dreamed one night that dear More was alive again and that after throwing my arms round his neck and finding beyond all doubt that I had my living son in my embrace—we went thoroughly into the subject, and found that the death and funeral at Abinger had been fictitious. For a second after waking the joy remained—then came the knell that wakes me every morning—More is dead! More is dead!

SAMUEL PALMER[1]

Introduction

In order to broaden the perspective, I review in this chapter what is known of the responses of fathers and mothers to the loss of a child; and, in the next, consider briefly how loss affects parents, and also spouses, in cultures other than our own. Despite variations both in relationship to the dead and in culture we find essentially the same patterns of response as those already described.

In regard to loss of child the principal sources drawn upon are studies of the parents of children who are fatally ill, mainly with leukaemia. Not only are there several such studies but some of them present data that are unusually systematic and detailed. It has of course to be asked how representative of the mourning of other parents these findings are. Not only is the death delayed for many months after the diagnosis is reached but the age-range of the children whose parents have been studied is restricted, the great majority being between eighteen months and ten years. Nevertheless, in so far as information from other sources and in regard to other age groups is available, it appears to be highly consistent. That relating to stillbirth and the deaths of young babies is referred to at the end of the chapter.

Naturally, in carrying out these studies all the same professional sensitivity and ethical safeguards are necessary as in the studies of widows and widowers.

[1] In a letter to a friend (Cecil 1969).

Parents of fatally ill children

Sources

With the parents of a fatally ill child it is possible to begin the study immediately after the diagnosis has been conveyed to them, and therefore some months before the child dies, and to continue it afterwards. There are several such studies published: the first reports only on the mother's responses before the child's death; the others report responses of both mothers and fathers and both before and after the death.

In the first study the sample comprised 20 mothers, aged between 22 and 39 years. Their children, ranging in age from $1\frac{1}{2}$ to $6\frac{1}{2}$ years, were in hospital undergoing palliative treatment. Interviews were conducted by a psychiatric social worker and varied between two and five in number depending on the length of time between the diagnosis being communicated to parents and the child's death, when the observations ceased. In addition to interview data, casual remarks made by the mothers were noted and also the ways that they behaved to their children and to doctors and nurses. Nine mothers also agreed to take part in a Thematic Apperception Test. (Details of the study are given in Bozeman, Orbach and Sutherland 1955; and Orbach, Sutherland and Bozeman 1955.)

Further studies of parents of fatally ill children were initiated jointly by David A. Hamburg of the U.S. National Institute of Mental Health, Bethesda, Maryland, and John W. Mason of the Walter Reed Army Medical Center, Washington D.C. The results have been reported in a series of multi-authored papers starting in 1963. The principal aim of these studies was to investigate the effects on a person's endocrine secretion rates of his undergoing a prolonged stressful experience. Two sets of observations were therefore made. One comprised information regarding the parent's behaviour and psychological experience during the time his child was fatally ill and after the child's death; the other comprised information about endocrine function by measuring urinary excretion rates of certain adrenocortical steroids.

Parents who came from a distance, the majority, lived in the hospital in a special ward with other parents and with healthy volunteers taking part in various related research projects. Parents who lived in the vicinity took part in certain of the studies when they visited their children during liberal visiting hours.

113

In the first of these N.I.M.H. studies all but one pair of parents were willing to co-operate, though the parents of a further seven children were insufficiently available to be included in all phases of the study. There remained 26 mothers and 20 fathers, of ages ranging from 23 to 49 years, willing and available to take part. Parents living in the hospital were interviewed by a psychiatrist at least once a week and were also seen briefly by him almost daily. In addition, nurses recorded observations daily. Parents living locally were studied less intensively, especially during periods when a child was well enough to be at home; none the less they took part in fairly regular interviews. Interviews were concerned with how a parent perceived the child's illness and coped with the distressing prospect ahead and how he or she approached the many emotional and practical problems that arise when caring for a seriously ill child who is not expected to live. The age-range of the children was from $1\frac{1}{2}$ to 16 years with a median of five years. Six months after the child's death nearly half the parents were willing to take part in further interviews and endocrine estimates. Particulars of the sample of parents and of the psychological and behavioural methods used are in Friedman, Chodoff, Mason and Hamburg (1963) and, in briefer form, in Chodoff, Friedman and Hamburg (1964). A related paper by Friedman, Mason and Hamburg (1963) gives information on the endocrine investigations and findings.

A second study in the N.I.M.H. series, designed to test certain hypotheses that emerged from the first, followed rather similar lines. Further groups of parents of fatally ill children were observed. In the first part, which concentrated on psychological and physio-logical observations prior to the child's death, a total of nineteen mothers and twelve fathers in an age-range from 20 to 49 years agreed to take part. In the second part, which concentrated on responses after the child's death, 21 mothers and 15 fathers took part. Whilst their child was ill all these parents were living in the special hospital ward. Some six months after the child's death (the interval varying between 19 and 42 weeks) they agreed to return there for a period of four days. Three more psychiatric interviews, each lasting from one to two hours, were held and physiological studies made. After a further interval, varying from a minimum of one year to over two, about two-thirds of these parents (twenty mothers and one father) were willing to return to the hospital for a second time to take part in the study.

An account of the findings prior to the child's death is given in a pair of papers by Wolff *et al.* (1964a & b) and an account of findings subsequent to it in a pair by Hofer *et al.* (1972). The findings of both parts throw light not only on the usual courses taken by the mourning of healthy parents but more especially on defensive responses, which differ markedly from individual to individual. Because many of the findings of this second N.I.M.H. study refer to individual variations in response, including the correlation of psychological response and endocrine response, detailed discussion is postponed to Chapter 9.

Certain other studies have been concerned with the impact on the family as a whole of a child dying from leukaemia. In one, reported by Binger *et al.* (1969), the families of children who had died were invited to return to the hospital to give an account of their experiences both before and after their child had died; from that information the pediatric staff hoped to be able to improve their ways of dealing with such families. Of 23 families invited, 20 came for interviews which lasted two to three hours. In another study, reported by Kaplan *et al.* (1973), the aim was to identify 'adaptive and maladaptive coping responses . . . as early as possible after diagnosis' with a view to developing methods of therapeutic intervention suitable for families judged likely to fail. Of the many families studied, forty agreed to a follow-up interview three months after the sick child had died.

Limitations of Samples

In three respects the limitations of the samples of parents mainly drawn upon (namely those of the Bozeman study and the two N.I.M.H. studies) resemble those of samples of bereaved spouses: all the parents are relatively young (under fifty); all are from Western cultures; and there is a preponderance of women (roughly twice as many mothers as fathers). The reason for the latter is that mothers were more willing, and also probably more available, to participate than were fathers.

How representative of all parents the parents of children fatally ill with leukaemia may be in terms of their personalities is unknown. Caution in generalizing from the findings is therefore necessary.

Phases of Mourning

For parents of fatally ill children the mourning process starts at the moment that the diagnosis is conveyed to them. As in the case of widows and widowers, it begins with a phase of numbing, often punctuated by outbursts of anger. Because the child is still alive, however, the second phase differs. Instead of a widow's or widower's disbelief that the spouse has died, a parent disbelieves the accuracy of the diagnosis and especially the prognosis; and, instead of a widow or widower searching for the lost partner, a parent attempts to retain the child by proving the doctors wrong. In the studies drawn upon these two phases are graphically described and fully documented. By contrast, the later phases of mourning, despair and disorganization and subsequent reorganization, are usually described only briefly.

Phase of Numbing

In the first N.I.M.H. study every parent described later how, when told that their child's illness was likely to prove fatal, they had felt stunned and nothing had seemed real. Whereas on the surface a majority had appeared to accept the diagnosis and its implications, they admitted afterwards that it had taken some days to sink in. Meanwhile, feeling is sealed off and a parent may behave in a detached way as though he 'were dealing with the tragedy of another family', even giving the impression that he or she is unconcerned.

Nevertheless, anger is apt to break through. This is likely to be directed at the physician who conveys the diagnosis. One of the mothers in the Bozeman study likened her response to that of the Greeks who murdered messengers bearing bad tidings: 'I could have killed him,' she said.

Phase of Disbelief and Attempts to Reverse Outcome

During this phase the physician's message has been received but is vehemently disputed. Disbelief can be directed at either or both of two main points. First, the diagnosis is challenged: 'I know that this has happened to others, but it cannot happen to my child.' Secondly, the high probability of a fatal outcome is questioned, especially its relevance to the child affected: 'I knew of course that leukaemia is fatal but I didn't connect that with my child.'

Both the Bozeman study, from which the above quotations are taken, and the N.I.M.H. study report that every parent interviewed responded with one or another version of disbelief. In some parents, it seemed, turning away from the painful news was conscious and deliberate; in others conscious effort was not apparent. Not infrequently friends or relatives encouraged disbelief in the medical opinion and promoted unrealistic hope. When disbelief is only partial it holds painful affect in check and often seems helpful. When it is strongly asserted, however, a parent may be unable to grasp the nature of the therapeutic programme proposed and thus fail to participate usefully in it. Whether disbelief is advantageous or the reverse thus turns not on its mere presence but on its dominance and its persistence despite contrary evidence.

Closely linked to disbelief in the accuracy of the diagnosis and prognosis is anger at those responsible for making or accepting them—notably the doctors and nurses. In most parents anger recedes as disbelief gives way to recognition that the doctors may be right. In a minority of parents a strongly held disbelief, and with it anger, may persist for weeks or months. Mourning is then taking an unfavourable course (see Chapter 9).

As well as anger, bouts of intense activity are also closely linked to disbelief. These may take the form of a frantic search for medical information about the disease, often designed more to find loopholes that would prove his or her child to be an exception than for other purposes. Or they may take the form of a parent keeping excessively busy, not only caring for and amusing the child in a useful way but sometimes doing so to the point of obtruding on his other interests. The Bozeman group speak of visiting mothers insisting on close physical contact and clinging frantically to their child 'as though [they] believed that they could prevent the feared loss by an intensified unity'. A variant of the anxious care directed at a mother's own child is intense caring for other children. Whether these caring activities are beneficial or not turns, of course, on the degree to which a parent can regulate them to suit the child or is driven compulsively irrespective of the child's interests. The more compulsive the activity the more likely is it to be associated with a determined effort to exclude distressing ideas and feeling.

Coupled with intense activity directed towards the sick child is a tendency to neglect all else. Housework, care of other children, recreation are scamped. Insomnia and loss of appetite are common. Bozeman speaks especially of the mothers' inability to think about the future: 'Life stood still for many of them, and no new matters could be considered until the illness had terminated in one way or another.'

In addition to feeling angry at doctors and nurses, the great majority of parents blamed themselves for not having paid sufficient attention to early signs of the disease. Although in a majority of the parents studied such self-reproach was not intense and they could be reassured, there was a minority in each study who showed persistent self-blame. For example, the child's illness might be interpreted as God's punishment; or a mother, feeling that someone must be to blame and, reluctant to blame her husband, blames herself.

It is all too easy for conflicts to develop between the parents of a fatally ill child. Kaplan *et al.* (1973) describe a number of families in which one parent is more willing than the other to consider the prognosis seriously. For example, in one family mother recognized the seriousness of the illness and felt frightened and depressed. When she wept and sought consolation from her husband, however, he became angry: 'What in hell are you crying about?' he demanded, refusing to accept the diagnosis. As a result of his failure to consider the problem and to support her, mother became angry in return and rows were frequent.

Disagreements between parents are likely also to lead to disputes about whether, at an appropriate moment, to tell the sick child that he is very seriously ill and whether to tell his brothers and sisters. As a result, instead of the true prospects being communicated honestly and sympathetically at some suitable time, which promotes understanding and trust, contradictory and confused information is given leading to a widening gulf of distrust between all members of the family. Binger and his colleagues (1969) describe the tragic isolation of the dying child who knows he is dying but knows also that his parents do not wish him to know.

Belief or disbelief in the accuracy of the prognosis varies not only between parents but also within each of them over time. Bozeman and her colleagues describe how disbelief may vary according to the progress of the disease. Discharge from hospital during a remission can be an occasion for uncontrolled elation, as though it signalled recovery. At such times parents may talk of the college and business career which they were planning for their son 'as though the disease were only a passing episode'. Conversely, when a child suffers a setback or another child dies a parent may suddenly recognize the true outlook. Then he or she will be consumed by pangs of grief, sighing and sobbing and experiencing all the weakness and somatic symptoms that make grieving so painful. Yet, a little later, the same parent may revert to a previous disbelief and its associated intense activity.

After a child has been ill for many months and rising hopes have repeatedly been dashed a parent may move some way towards recognizing the accuracy of the doctor's prognosis. Some degree of anticipatory mourning follows. In the case of loss of spouse there is reason to believe that anticipatory mourning is rarely complete and that the actual death is still likely to be felt as a shock. In the case of parents of fatally ill children anticipatory mourning may proceed further. For example, in a report on the first N.I.M.H. study, Chodoff et al. (1964) state that 'the gradual detachment of emotional investment in the child was noted in most cases in which the course of illness was longer than three or four months, and resulted in a muting of the grief reaction so that the terminal phase and death of the child was often received with an attitude of "philosophical resignation"'. The researchers note by contrast that parents who show a strongly held disbelief in the prognosis do not engage in anticipatory mourning.

For many parents, it is clear, some degree of disbelief persists for many months after the child's death. In the first N.I.M.H. study 23 parents were invited to return to the hospital between three and eight months after their child had died. Eighteen of them, including eight couples, accepted. In doing so, they reported that their feelings had been mixed. On the one hand was a dread of returning; on the other, a feeling that they would have been drawn back even if they had not been invited. Both feelings arose, it seems likely, from their lingering belief that their child was still a patient in hospital. This was described explicitly by a few of them who went on to say that return had been less painful than they had expected and that it had helped them to accept that their child was no longer alive. In fact all but two of the eighteen parents who returned described the experience as having been helpful. The exceptions were two parents who, at the end of six months, appeared still not to have accepted their loss to any significant degree. In addition there was evidence that some at least of those who refused the invitation to return did so because they dreaded what they might have to confront.

In the second N.I.M.H. study (Hofer et al. 1972), which concentrated on individual differences, of 51 parents who had participated before their child's death 36 (21 mothers and 15 fathers) were willing to return for interviews and physiological observations about six months after the death had occurred. The responses shown in these interviews and the accounts given by parents of how they had been during the interval varied between two poles. At one pole were those who during the interview expressed their grief freely and were eager to communicate both thoughts and feelings. They showed intense affect, described both guilt and anger and, when free to do so, talked almost exclusively of the dead child. From their account of how they had been since their child's death it was clear that they had re-experienced the loss repeatedly and painfully, and had kept visible reminders of the child about them; and they confessed that they had occasionally caught themselves thinking of the child as still alive. Three of them were conscious of thinking that they might find him still in hospital.

At the other pole were parents who expressed no sadness during the interviews. Some were bland and cheerful, others cool and impersonal, or perhaps guarded and overcontrolled; some 'seemed intent upon giving the impression of great strength and self-control'. Their accounts of how they had been since their child's death suggested they had engaged in little active grieving. Reminders of the child had been put away and both thoughts and talk about him avoided.

Further discussion of these diverse patterns of response is postponed to Chapter 9. Meanwhile, it is worth remarking that the effects that these two classes of bereaved parent had on the interviewer were very different. The grieving parents, he found, drew him into their lives and made him feel sympathetic; but those who did not grieve made him feel excluded.

Phases of Disorganization and Reorganization

As the illness progresses and a child gets worse, hope ebbs. Yet it is only very few parents who despair completely whilst their child is still alive and, as we have seen, it is usual for some disbelief that the child has died to be present during the months afterwards. By parents in whom mourning is proceeding favourably the true facts are gradually recognized and accepted. Slowly but steadily representational models of the self and of the world are aligned to the new situation.

How well or badly mourning proceeds, every study shows, turns in great degree on the parents' own relationship. When they can mourn together, keeping in step from one phase to the next, each derives comfort and support from the other and the outcome of their mourning is favourable. When, by contrast, the parents are in conflict and mutual support absent the family may break up and/or individual members become psychiatric casualties.

In the studies drawn upon, the casualty rates either for marriages or for individuals or for both were appallingly high. Of the forty families studied by Kaplan and his colleagues (1973) three months after the child's death, a majority presented problems which either had not been evident previously or had been exacerbated by the loss (David M. Kaplan, personal communication). In 28 of these families there were marital problems, including two divorces and seven separations (all of which led to divorce subsequently). In 30 of the families one or both parents suffered from psychiatric or psychosomatic symptoms or were drinking heavily; and in 25 there were problems with the surviving children. Of the twenty families studied by the Binger group eleven reported emotional disturbances severe enough to require psychiatric help in members who had never required such help before. Amongst the parents were several cases of severe depression or of psychosomatic symptoms, one of hysterical aphonia and one divorce. In about half the families one or more previously well siblings of the patient developed symptoms, which included school refusal, depression and severe separation anxiety. Thus few families escaped damage altogether.

There can be little doubt that much of the disturbance reported in the surviving children is a result more of the changed behaviour of the parents towards them than of any direct effect the death may have had on the children themselves. Breakup of the marriage, mother's depression, explanations that God had taken the child who died can lead readily to anxiety about separation and refusal to leave home, and to angry behaviour. Blaming a surviving child for the death is not unknown and very damaging, but is probably more likely to occur when the death is sudden.

Among the conclusions drawn from these studies is that the pattern of parent's response to a child's fatal illness tends to be shaped during the first few weeks after the diagnosis is made and changes very little thereafter.

When parents are still young it is not unusual for them to decide to replace the lost child by having another. In the first N.I.M.H.

study it was known that, of 24 couples, five mothers became pregnant either during or immediately following their child's illness; and in two of them it was known that conception had been deliberate. A few months later a sixth mother was hoping to become pregnant, and a seventh couple were planning to adopt a child (Friedman *et al.* 1963).

There are reasons for doubting the wisdom of these very early replacements, since there is danger that mourning for the lost child may not be completed and that the new baby is seen not only as the replacement he is but as a return of the one who has died. This can lead to a distorted and pathogenic relationship between parent and new baby (see Chapter 9). A better plan is for parents to wait a year or more before starting afresh to enable them to reorganize their image of the lost child and so retain it as a living memory distinct from that of any new child they may have.

Parents of infants who are stillborn or die early

During recent years increasing attention has been given to the grieving of parents of infants who are stillborn or who die within days or months of birth. Principal findings are that, despite the bond between parent and child being of such recent growth, the overall patterns of response are little different to what they are in those who are widowed (Klaus and Kennell 1976). Numbing, followed by somatic distress, yearning, anger and subsequent irritability and depression, are all common. So also are preoccupations with the image of the dead baby and dreams about him. One mother described how she would dream about the baby and then wake up: 'I wouldn't know where the baby was, but I'd want to hold her . . .'

Many mothers express the strongest desire to hold the dead baby, a desire often frustrated by hospital practice. Lewis (1976) describes how the mother of a very premature baby who died after ten days in an incubator was encouraged to touch him. With great excitement she stripped off his clothes, kissed him all over and then walked him on the floor. Soon afterwards she calmed down and handed the dead baby back to the nurse.

Both Klaus and Kennell in the U.S. and Lewis in the U.K. have expressed concern at the ways in which stillbirths and the deaths of prematures are apt to be dealt with by hospital personnel. Supposing it to be for the best, the staff quickly remove all evidence of the dead baby and dispose of the body without funeral in a common grave. Often little information is given the parents and the whole episode veiled in silence.

All the authors emphasize how procedures of these sorts greatly increase the emotional problems parents are faced with and strongly recommend changes. Parents, they believe, should be allowed to visit a sick infant, to participate in his care, and to be with him when he dies. After the death they should be encouraged to see him, touch him and hold him. He should be given a simple funeral, a grave and, when possible, a name. Without such provision the parents are faced, as Lewis remarks, with a non-event and with no one to mourn.

Even with insightful care parents, especially mothers, may be burdened by a sense of shame at not having been able to give birth to a healthy infant and/or of guilt at having failed to care successfully for one who died. For these and other reasons Klaus and Kennell recommend that both parents should be given counselling interviews together, the first one immediately after the death, and the next one two or three days later by which time the parents will be less stunned and more able both to express their feelings, worries and doubts and also to make use of the information conveyed to them. In addition, the authors recommend a third interview some months later to check whether mourning is following a healthy course, and, if not, to arrange further aid. They emphasize especially the value of helping the parents to grieve together.

Unfortunately there is no lack of evidence that loss of a baby can give rise to serious problems later, both for the parents themselves, especially mothers, and for surviving children. Of fifty-six Swedish mothers, studied by Cullberg[2] one to two years after the deaths of their neonates, nineteen were found to have developed severe psychiatric disorders (anxiety attacks, phobias, obsessional thoughts, deep depressions).

Inevitably disturbance of this degree in a mother can have very adverse effects should she have other children. Her failure to respond to the surviving children and sometimes her outright rejection of them are reported. Moreover, when a baby dies suddenly and inexplicably at home, as in 'crib-death', a distraught mother may impulsively accuse an older child of being responsible. Both Halpern (1972) and Tooley (1975) report cases in which a bereaved mother not only accused an older child (in the age-range three to

[2] Quoted by Klaus and Kennell (1976).

five) but punished him or her severely. Subsequently these children came to psychiatric attention on account of being moody, spiteful or destructive.[3] Not unexpectedly these mothers had had difficult childhoods and/or unhappy marriages themselves.

In addition to the risk that a stillbirth or early death may affect a mother's relationship with an older child is the risk that it may affect also her feelings about having a new baby. Wolff *et al.* (1970) report that a large proportion of women who had had a stillbirth were later insistent on having no more children. Lewis and Page (1978) describe a mother who became depressed after the birth of another baby, a girl, turned against her and was afraid she might batter her. Although initially both parents kept silent about the previous stillbirth, once persuaded to talk about it both expressed deep feelings of grief about their loss and anger with the hospital. These interviews brought relief and an improvement in mother's condition and in her relationship with the new baby. Once again, these parents had had earlier experiences that had made them especially vulnerable to a loss.

Affectional bonds of different types: a note

In this chapter I have emphasized that the pattern of response to the death of a child or to a stillbirth has a great deal in common with the pattern of response to the loss of a spouse. In regard to the aftermath, however, there is a difference of importance. Whereas loneliness is a principal feature after the death of a spouse, it seems not to be prevalent after the death of a child. Correspondingly, the sense of loneliness after the death of a spouse is usually not assuaged by the presence of a child.

These observations are of great significance for the theory of affectional bonding. They show that, whatever the different types of affectional bond may have in common, they cannot be regarded as identical.[4] Thus to make progress it will be necessary to study

---

[3] In Volume II of this work, at the end of Chapter 18, an account is given (derived from Moss 1960) of a woman of forty-five who since her childhood had suffered an intense fear of dogs. During therapy this was traced to her mother having blamed her for the death of a younger sister to which, it seemed, the family dog had in fact contributed.

[4] I am indebted to Robert Weiss for having drawn my attention to these findings and to their implications.

not only the many characteristics that different types of bond have in common but also their differences. In view of the number of types of bond—child to parent, parent to child, spouse to spouse, and sibling to sibling with the many sub-types due to sex differences —this represents a formidable undertaking.

CHAPTER 8

Mourning in Other Cultures

Even among the most primitive peoples the attitude at death is infinitely more complex and, I may add, more akin to our own than is usually assumed . . . The nearest relatives and friends are disturbed to the depth of their emotional life.

BRONISLAW MALINOWSKI, *Magic, Science and Religion*

Beliefs and customs common to many cultures

In their extensive writings on the mourning customs of other peoples social anthropologists have been more interested in the variety of rituals prescribed than in the emotional responses of the bereaved. Yet there is evidence enough to show that these responses resemble in broad outline, and often in great detail, those familiar to us in the West. Social custom differs enormously. Human response stays much the same.[1]

First, a word about social custom. 'There are very few universal traits or practices found in all human societies,' writes Gorer (1973, pp. 423–4). 'All recorded human societies speak a language, conserve fire, and have some sort of cutting implement; all recorded societies elaborate the biological bonds of bearer, begetter, and offspring into kinship systems; all societies have some division of labour based on age and sex; all societies have incest prohibitions and rules regulating sexual behaviour, designating appropriate marriage partners, and legitimizing offspring; and all societies have rules and ritual concerning the disposal of the dead and the appropriate behaviour of mourners.' In some societies a funeral is the most important of all social ceremonies in terms of numbers present and duration (Mandelbaum 1959; Palgi 1973).

[1] In making the generalizations that follow I have drawn on the work of a number of anthropologists who have written on the subject in recent years, Raymond Firth, Geoffrey Gorer, David Mandelbaum, Phyllis Palgi and Paul C. Rosenblatt, as well as on the classic texts of Durkheim, Frazer and Malinowski. I am also indebted to a review of cross-cultural studies undertaken jointly by a psychoanalyst and a rabbi, George Krupp and Bernard Kligfeld.

Anthropologists have discussed why a funeral rite should play so large a part in the social life of a people. 'Its ostensible object is the dead person,' writes Firth (1961), 'but it benefits not the dead but the living . . . it is those who are left behind . . . for whom the ritual is really performed.' He then postulates that a funeral has three major functions.

The first is in the help it gives to the bereaved, for example, by aiding them to deal with their uncertainty through bringing home that the loss has in fact occurred, by providing them with an opportunity for the public expression of their grief, and, through defining the period during which mourning is appropriate, by setting a term to it. Through these rituals, moreover, the bereaved are inducted into the new social role which they are henceforward required to fill.

The second function is that the funeral allows other members of the community to take public note of their loss and, in a prescribed way, not only to say farewell to one of their number but to express the powerful emotions of fear and anger that are often engendered. By fulfilling a social sequence and directing emotional behaviour into acceptable channels funeral rites serve to maintain the integrity of the continuing society.

The third function postulated by Firth, which he terms economic, is that it provides the occasion for a complex interchange of goods and services between families and groups. In addition to such material benefits as may accrue, these exchanges may perhaps be regarded also as a demonstration of reciprocal altruism (Trivers 1971). When calamity strikes at one family or group every other family and group expresses its willingness to help, if only in a symbolic way. Thereby each lays claim, by implication and tradition, to the assistance of all the others should adversity later strike it too.

Reflection on the frame of mind in which close friends and relatives attend a funeral suggests that it functions also in ways additional to those mentioned by Firth. One is that it provides opportunity for the living to express gratitude to the deceased; another that it provides them opportunity to take some further action felt to be for the benefit of the person who has gone. These motives are expressed both in a ceremonial and burial believed to be in keeping with the dead person's wishes and in prayers for his future welfare.

Returning now to the anthropological literature, we find that in most societies it is taken for granted that a bereaved person will be personally shocked and socially disoriented. Furthermore, there are certain specific types of response and belief, that, even if not universal, are very nearly so. Three stand out.

Almost all societies, it seems, believe that, despite a bodily death, the person not only lives on but continues his relationships with the living, at least for a time. In many cultures these relationships are conceived as wholly beneficial; in which case rules and rituals obtain for preserving them. In other cultures, especially the more primitive, the persisting relationships are conceived as in some degree adverse; in which case rules and rituals obtain for protecting the living and despatching the dead (see especially Frazer 1933-4). Nevertheless, according to Malinowski (1925) every society conceives such relationships as more beneficial than harmful: 'never do the negative elements appear alone or even dominant', he asserts.

To examine why these persisting relationships should be conceived in such diverse ways would take us too far from our theme. Cursory consideration suggests that each culture selects as a stereotype one only from the broad range of personal experiences reported by individuals who are mourning a lost relative; these, as we have seen in Chapter 6, range from a sense of the presence of the dead person being experienced as that of a comforting companion to his being experienced as damaged and potentially hostile. What matters in the present context is that, no matter in what light a culture may conceive these continuing relationships, in all of them a sense of the persisting presence of the dead person is socially sanctioned and appropriate behaviour prescribed.

A second feature common to a great majority of cultures is that anyone bereaved is expected to feel angry with whoever is held responsible for the death. This ubiquity of anger becomes readily intelligible if we bear in mind that, in most communities outside the West, death comes more often to children, adolescents and adults in the prime of life than to the old. As a result most deaths are untimely; and the more untimely a death is felt to be the more likely is someone to be held to blame and anger with him to be felt.

As we saw in earlier chapters, those potentially responsible comprise third parties, the self and the dead person. Most cultures define who amongst these can properly be blamed and, by implication, who may not. Because each culture has its own beliefs and rules, the forms prescribed for the angry behaviour of mourners differ greatly from society to society. In some, active expression of anger is an established part of the funeral rites; in others, funeral customs lay down strong sanctions against the expression of violence and, instead, direct hostile feelings towards people *not* present at the ceremony. People who live a little distance away, for example members of a neighbouring village or tribe, are particularly common as targets for blame. According to Durkheim (1915, p. 400) blood revenge and headhunting may well have originated in this way.[2]

Nevertheless, even though it is common for anger at loss to be directed outside the group, there are many societies in which it is accepted that blame be laid and anger be directed either at the self or, and less commonly, at the person who has died. Complaints against the dead for having deserted the living are known and sanctioned in many societies. 'Oh, why did you leave us?' is a widespread lament. Actual attacks on the dead, either verbal or physical, are perhaps less rare than might be supposed. Among the Hopi Indians of Arizona, Mandelbaum (1959) reports, tradition prescribes that as little importance as possible should attach to death and funerals. 'Their funeral rites are small private affairs, quickly over and best forgotten. Those who are bereaved may well feel the pain of loss as deeply as do mourners in any society' (p. 201) but overt expressions of grief are discouraged. Yet during a field study of these people, Kennard (1937) found that private responses failed to conform to public prescription, especially when someone young or middle-aged dies. In searching for a possible cause for such a death it may be decided that the dead person has died deliberately in order to spite the living, in which case he has earned their just anger. Kennard describes one woman who 'slapped the face of a corpse and cried "You are mean to do this to me" '.

At an opposite pole are the numerous other societies in which to express anger towards the dead is strictly forbidden. In some, perhaps many, of those societies, to direct it against the self instead is not only permitted but prescribed. For example, among Moroccan Jews it has been an old-established custom for women mourners to

[2] A study of the development of Hitler's fanatical anti-semitism strongly suggests that it began after his mother's death from cancer in 1907 when Hitler was eighteen. During her illness she had been treated by a Jewish doctor. The treatment he gave her, which may well have been mistaken, seems to have caused great pain and perhaps made her worse. In any event Hitler held him responsible for his mother's death and thereafter regarded all Jews as enemies (Binion, 1973).

tear their flesh with their finger nails until the blood flows. Palgi (1973) describes how this ritual can create social conflict when practised in Israel by Moroccan immigrants.

A third feature common to mourning rituals is that they usually prescribe a time when mourning should end. Although the length of time prescribed differs enormously from culture to culture, the calendar year of traditional Jewry, at the end of which the bereaved are expected to find ways of returning to a more normal social life,[3] is not atypical. In a number of societies special rites of mourning and commemoration are performed at this time.

In illustration of several of these themes we draw on an account by Mandelbaum (1959) of the two distinct funeral ceremonies prescribed by the Kota, one of the remnant tribal peoples who live in a remote area of India and whose funeral rites (at least until the early nineteen-fifties) still followed much of their ancient form.

The Kotas hold two funeral ceremonies, called respectively the Green and the Dry. The Green takes place soon after the death and at it the body is cremated. Only close relatives and friends attend. The Dry is a communal occasion held at intervals of a year or two to commemorate all the deaths that have occurred since the last Dry funeral. To these ceremonies come all the Kota peoples of the area.

During the period of many months between the Green funeral and the Dry one the dead person is deemed still to play a social role. In particular, a widow is held still to be her late husband's wife so that, should she become pregnant, the child is regarded as his with all the social rights that that confers. Not until the Dry funeral does the dead person's spirit depart and his social status disappear.

The Dry funeral lasts eleven days and is highly ritualized. During the first week the year's dead are remembered one by one and the bereaved are seized by renewed grieving. At the first sound of the funeral lament with which the ceremony begins, all the bereaved women stop in their tracks, suffused with sorrow. They sit down, cover their heads, and wail and sob through that day and the next. Men of a bereaved household, busy with duties preparing for the ceremony, stop to weep only at intervals. Most grief-stricken of all are the widows and widowers who must observe the most stringent

---

[3] Discussing the several stages of mourning prescribed by the Jewish religion, Pollock (1972) suggests that they can each be related to one of the psychological phases through which healthy mourning progresses.

mourning taboos and undergo the most extensive purificatory ritual. The siblings and children of a dead person have less extensive but nevertheless important roles to play. Curiously enough, no provision is made for parents to mourn a son or daughter although, Mandelbaum reports, 'they may be personally as grief-stricken as bereaved parents can be in any society' (pp. 193–4).

On the eighth day a second cremation is held at which a piece of skull bone, taken from the first cremation and kept reverently since, is set on a pyre together with the goods and personal ornaments of the widow or widower. Afterwards the bereaved and some others spend the whole night at the cremation ground.

Next day at dawn the mood changes abruptly. There is dancing and feasting during which widows and widowers perform rituals designed to bring them progressively closer to normal social life. At nightfall the climax is reached. A pot is smashed which signals that the spirits of the dead are now making their final departure from this world. The living return to the village without looking back. That night the widows and widowers have sexual relations, preferably with a sibling of the dead spouse. Finally there are two days of singing and dancing.

In commenting on the Kota ceremonies Mandelbaum endorses fully Firth's views regarding the social functions of funeral customs. The cohesion of the family is demonstrated and kin relationships beyond the family reaffirmed. Every participant is given 'a renewed sense of belonging to a social whole, to the entire community of Kotas'. At the same time the personal and emotional responses of the bereaved are recognized and sanctioned, and in due course help and encouragement given to them to return to a normal social life.

In promoting the latter Rosenblatt (1975) notes that many societies prescribe customs which, whatever their ostensible rationale, seem to have the effect of facilitating the remarriage and resumption of apparently normal married life by widows. Most of these customs entail the elimination of reminders of the dead. They include practising a taboo on the name of the deceased, destroying or disposing of his property, and changing residence. As a rule these customs are embedded in a set of beliefs that are unrelated to the effect noted by Rosenblatt. Some, for example, relate to fear of ghosts, or of contamination, or of contagious sorcery; others are prescribed to honour the deceased. Yet Rosenblatt may well be right in believing that a main reason for their existence is that they impel a widow through the transition from widowhood to a new married life. The extent to which this might help a widow is likely to be determined by many factors, not least the timing of the ritual.

Thus perusal of the anthropological literature shows that, although cultural patterns differ enormously in what they encourage and what they forbid and in the extent to which ceremony is elaborated or curtailed, in virtually all of them rules and rituals of at least three kinds obtain: those for determining how a continuing relationship with the dead person should be conducted, those that prescribe how blame should be allocated and anger expressed, and those that lay down how long mourning should last. In these ways a culture channels the psychological responses of individuals and in some degree ritualizes them. The origins of the responses themselves lie, however, at a deeper level. This becomes evident when we consider the psychological experiences of individuals who participate in the ceremonies.

The two illustrative accounts that follow are drawn from cultures of strongly contrasting kinds, the one from a small remote community in the Pacific, the other from modern Japan.

Mourning a grown son in Tikopia

Tikopia is a small Pacific island 100 miles south-east of the Solomons. When studied during the nineteen-twenties by Firth[4] the community of some 1,300 people was still extremely isolated and visited from the outside world on average only once a year. Apart from a few tools bought or bartered from European vessels, the people depended on their own local materials and technology. Food came from fishing and agriculture, but margins were small so that drought or hurricane could bring famine. Despite its small size, the social structure of the community was complex: it imposed limits on behaviour and also conferred advantages on those who conformed. Formalized relations between kin, with varying emphasis on freedom and on obligations to protect, assist and support, not only defined an individual's duties and privileges but mitigated tensions and served in powerful fashion as factors of social integration. As an illustration of how the community dealt with loss, Firth

[4] The account given here is derived from Firth's *Elements of Social Organization* (1961), in which references are given to the various books and articles in which he has described and analysed Tikopia society.

recounts the events that followed the loss at sea of a local chief's elder son (Firth 1961, pp. 61–72).

The boy, on the threshold of manhood, had returned home in a bad humour and had had a minor row with his father who had scolded him for unbecoming behaviour. Thereat the boy had flung out of the house, taken his canoe to sea and had not been heard of again. As the months went by it became increasingly certain that he had been drowned. In circumstances such as these, which are not uncommon, tradition prescribes a simulated burial in which the usual mats and bark-cloth clothes are buried but in an empty grave. This is called 'spreading the grave clothes to make the lost one dry'.

After about a year of mourning for the boy, which entailed keeping food taboos and abstaining from public affairs, his father decided it was time for the funeral to be held. But this proposal conflicted with plans already afoot to hold a ritual dance festival in another connection. Friction between the chief and his own father and brothers about which ceremony should take place first led to an unexpected outbreak of anger by the chief who, tearful and incoherent, kept bursting out with wild remarks. Everyone was deeply concerned. After some time and the intervention of intermediaries family peace was restored. The funeral was then tacitly agreed to.

Next day Firth, who already knew the chief well, was able to talk with him. Soon the chief brought up the topic of his dead son, Noakena, and said, rather bitterly, 'He abandoned me and went off to sea.' Then he described two dreams he had had during the night before he had quarrelled with his father and brothers. In both of them the spirit of his son had come to him for the first time since the boy's disappearance.[5]

In the first dream father and son were picking coconuts and there was some friction between them over whether Noakena should hand a nut down, as his father wanted, or just throw it down. After the boy had moved away some distance to another tree father called out to him by name several times, but there was no reply. 'Again, I called, "Noakena, curse you! Why don't you answer me?" And then I heard him grunt at me in a high tone, and then he was gone away. I then returned to my house . . .'

In the second dream two women appeared, one of whom was the chief's sister who had died, but who took the form of a girl living

[5] Descriptions of the dreams are slightly condensed from Firth's account. Quotations are father's statements as translated by Firth.

in a near-by house. After giving some other details father proceeded, illustrating his account by dramatic action: 'Then Noakena came to me . . . He came to my side, and I looked on his face and body. He crawled to where I lay, and leant over and said to me, "Have you said that I shall be made dry?" Then I stirred. I stretched out my arms to embrace him, and called out, "Oh! alas! my baby!" And then my hand hit this box [which stood by his bed mat] . . . I awoke, I sat up and grasped the bark-cloth . . . I unfolded it and laid it out saying, "Thy making dry is there." And then I sat down and wept for him . . .' As father recounted his dream, Firth records, 'His face showed his emotion, and his voice was husky and broken, and near to tears. His cry as he opened his arms to demonstrate how he tried to hug his son to him and struck only the wooden box was poignant . . .'

During next morning father had been in a highly emotional state and had reacted violently at such opposition as there had been to holding the funeral forthwith. 'My belly was like as if a fire had entered into it', he remarked in explanation.

Only brief comment is called for. First, the feeling and behaviour depicted in the dream—anger at being deserted, desire for reunion, remorse—differ not one whit from the feeling and behaviour depicted in the mourning dreams of Western peoples. Secondly, even though, as in this case, there is no body to be disposed of, a society requires that a funeral take place. It was indeed reflection on this Tikopian ceremony that led Firth to insist that the principal function of funeral ritual is not disposal of the body but the psycho-social benefit it brings to the bereaved and to the society as a whole.

Mourning a husband in Japan

In Japan, in both Buddhist and Shinto religions, there is a deep-seated regard for ancestors. They are normally referred to by terms which are used also to designate divine beings; and their spirits, it is believed, can be called back to this world. Mourning rituals are prescribed which encourage a continuing relationship with any person who has died; and accordingly each family erects an altar in their living room on which is a photograph of the deceased, the urn of ashes, flowers, water, rice and other offerings.

When a woman loses her husband, therefore, a first duty is for her to build an altar to him. This she visits at least once a day to offer incense. In addition, tradition encourages her to visit it at other times as well in order, perhaps, to seek his advice about a current problem, to share happy events with him, or to shed tears in his presence. In company with other members of the family who share her grief, the dead man can then be cherished, fed, berated or idealized. In this way the relationship with him is maintained unbroken through his transformation from living man to revered ancestor.

Recognizing how different these beliefs and customs are to those of the West, a group of Japanese psychiatrists made a small but systematic study of widows in Tokyo with a view to comparing the experiences reported there with those of London widows, as described by Marris (1958) and Parkes (1965). The resulting report by Yamomoto *et al.* (1969), from which the above description of beliefs and customs is taken, is of much interest.

Twenty widows in the age-range 24 to 52 years were interviewed in their own homes some six weeks after the death of their husband in a road accident.[6] Most were working class and had been on foot or motor-bicycle on their way to or from work. The length of time they had been married ranged from one to 26 years (average 14 years). All but one had children, in the great majority of cases one or two. Fourteen widows had definite religious affiliations (thirteen Buddhist and one Shinto); six had none.

The experiences of grieving that the Tokyo widows described are extremely similar to those reported by widows in London. Twelve of them described difficulty in believing their husband was dead; for example, one would go to the tramway stop at the hour her husband used to return from work, and another would go to the door when she heard a motor bike, supposing it to be her husband's. Of the twenty, all but two had followed tradition by building an altar. There they experienced a strong sense of their husband's presence, and, as with Western widows, the majority found it comforting. The ambiguity of the situation was vividly conveyed by one: 'When I look at his smiling face I feel he is alive, but then I look at the urn and know he is dead.'

Since every husband had been killed in a road accident, it is not

[6] Initially 55 had been written to; of these 23 had agreed to interview, 7 had refused and the remainder had either not been traced or had not replied. Of the 23 who had agreed, three had either been ill or absent at the time of interview.

135

surprising to find that twelve of the widows blamed the other driver and felt angry with him. There was little self-reproach. In regard to anger felt against the husband, the report is almost silent and the reader may wonder whether the necessary enquiries were made. One widow, however, volunteered how she was angry with her husband and intended to scold him when he returned. (We are not told why she would scold him but, if Western experience is a guide, we might expect it to be for not having taken sufficient precautions.)

The proportions of widows who reported anxiety, depression or insomnia differ hardly at all between Tokyo and London. There is, however, a large difference in the proportions who describe attempts to escape reminders of their husband's death, a proportion three times as large in Tokyo as in London. As possible explanations of this high incidence Yamomoto and his colleagues draw attention to the fact that their interviews were held during the widows' period of acute grieving, that in all cases death had been sudden and that in some the widow had been exposed to a gory and distressing scene. The likelihood of the latter being of special importance in the Tokyo findings is indicated by the findings of Maddison and his colleagues which are reported in Chapter 10. It is also possible that the constant presence in their living rooms of the altar to the dead spouse may have played some part in provoking their desire to escape reminders.

It is not without interest that four of the six Tokyo widows who disclaimed any religious affiliation none the less followed the tradition of building an altar, and one of the other two was also planning to do so. This is further illustration of the strong urge to maintain the relationship with the dead person which seizes the bereaved whether it is in keeping with consciously held beliefs or at variance with them. A comparable example is reported by Palgi (1973) from Israel: 'Soon after the Six-day War there was a sudden upsurge of interest in spiritualism among some of the younger educated groups of Western origin. There were even incidents in some of the secular left-wing Kibbutzim of young soldiers participating in seances in an attempt to establish contact with their fallen comrades.'

CHAPTER 9

Disordered Variants

Sorrow concealed, like an oven stopp'd,
Doth burn the heart to cinders where it is.

SHAKESPEARE, *Titus Andronicus*

Two main variants

A great deal of the literature on disordered mourning derives from the work of psychoanalysts and other psychotherapists who have traced the emotional disturbances of some of their patients to a bereavement suffered at some earlier time. Not only has an enormous amount been learned from these studies about the psychopathology of mourning but it was these findings that first drew attention to the field and led on to the more systematic studies of recent years. In this chapter we start by drawing on the findings of these recent studies because, based as they are on fairly representative samples, they present a broader and more reliable perspective in which to view the problems than can findings drawn exclusively from psychiatric casualties. Once the scene is set, however, the therapeutic findings become an invaluable source for deepening our understanding of the processes, cognitive and emotional, that are at work.

Disordered variants of mourning lead to many forms of physical ill health[1] as well as of mental ill health. Psychologically they result in a bereaved person's capacity to make and to maintain love relationships becoming more or less seriously impaired or, if already impaired, being left more impaired than it was before. Often they affect also a bereaved person's ability to organize the rest of his life. Disordered variants can be of every degree of severity from quite slight to extremely severe. In their lesser degrees they are not easily distinguished from healthy mourning. For purposes of exposition, however, they are described here mainly in their more extreme versions.

In one of the two disordered variants the emotional responses to

[1] For the literature on physical ill health, see Parkes (1970c).

loss are unusually intense and prolonged, in many cases with anger or self-reproach dominant and persistent, and sorrow notably absent. So long as these responses continue the mourner is unable to replan his life, which commonly becomes and remains sadly disorganized. Depression is a principal symptom, often combined or alternating with anxiety, 'agoraphobia' (see Volume II, Chapter 19), hypochondria or alcoholism. This variant can be termed *chronic mourning*. At first sight the other variant appears to be exactly the opposite, in that there is a more or less *prolonged absence of conscious grieving* and the bereaved's life continues to be organized much as before. Nevertheless, he is apt to be afflicted with a variety of psychological or physiological ills; and he may suddenly, and it seems inexplicably, become acutely depressed. During psychotherapy with such people, which is sometimes undertaken for ill-defined symptoms and/or interpersonal difficulties which have developed without any breakdown having occurred, and sometimes after breakdown, the disturbances are found to be derivatives of normal mourning though strangely disconnected, both cognitively and emotionally, from the loss that led to them.

Opposite in many respects though these two variants are they none the less have features in common. In both, it may be found, the loss is believed, consciously or unconsciously, still to be reversible. The urge to search may therefore continue to possess the bereaved, either unceasingly or episodically, anger and/or self-reproach to be readily aroused, sorrow and sadness to be absent. In both variants the course of mourning remains uncompleted. Because the representational models he has of himself and of the world about him remain unchanged his life is either planned on a false basis or else falls into unplanned disarray.

Once it is realized that the two main variants of disordered mourning have much in common the existence of clinical conditions with features that partake of both, or that represent an oscillation between them, gives no cause for surprise. A common combination is one in which, after a loss, a person for a few weeks or months shows an absence of conscious grieving and then, perhaps abruptly, is overwhelmed by intense emotions and progresses to a state of chronic mourning. In terms of the four phases of mourning described in Chapter 6 absence of conscious grieving can be regarded as a pathologically prolonged extension of the phase of numbing, whereas the various forms of chronic mourning can be regarded as extended and distorted versions of the phases of yearning and searching, disorganization and despair.

Because the two variants have elements in common not all the terms used to describe them are distinctive. In fact a variety are in use. For the first variant Lindemann (1944) introduced the term 'distorted' and Anderson (1949) 'chronic'; for the second, terms such as absent (Deutsch 1937), delayed, inhibited and suppressed are used.

In addition to these two main variants of disordered mourning there is a third, less common one—euphoria. In some individuals this may be of such severity that it presents as a manic episode.

Before describing these variants further it may be useful to look afresh at the painful dilemma facing every mourner in order to see at what points in the course of mourning the pathological variants diverge from the healthy ones. So long as he does not believe that his loss is irretrievable a mourner is given hope and feels impelled to action; yet that leads to all the anxiety and pain of frustrated effort. The alternative, that he believes his loss is permanent, may be more realistic; yet at first it is altogether too painful, and perhaps too terrifying, to dwell on for long. It may be merciful, therefore, that a human being is so constructed that mental processes and ways of behaving that give respite are part of his nature. Yet such respite can only be limited and the task of resolving the dilemma remains. On how he achieves this turns the outcome of his mourning—either progress towards a recognition of his changed circumstances, a revision of his representational models, and a redefinition of his goals in life, or else a state of suspended growth in which he is held prisoner by a dilemma he cannot solve.

Traditionally the mental processes and also the ways of behaving that mitigate the painfulness of mourning are known as defences and are referred to by terms such as repression, splitting, denial, dissociation, projection, displacement, identification and reaction formation. An extensive literature, which seeks to distinguish different processes and to explain them in terms of one or another model of the mental apparatus and of one or another fixation point, has grown up; but there is no agreed usage of terms and much overlap of meaning. In this volume a new approach is adopted. As already described in Chapter 4, the model of the mental apparatus drawn upon is one based on current work on human information processing. In keeping with this new approach and in order to avoid the many theoretical implications that every traditional term has accreted, terms that are less theory laden and that keep closer to the observed phenomena are used.

My thesis is that the traditionally termed defensive processes can all be understood as examples of the defensive exclusion of unwelcome information; and that most of them differ from each other only in regard to the completeness and/or the persistence of the exclusion. Many are found in both healthy and disordered variants of mourning, but a few are confined to the disordered. In a first step towards sorting them out, let us consider first those that in a majority of cases are fully compatible with a healthy outcome.

Arising from his study of London widows Parkes (1970a) lists a number of such processes. One or more of them, he inferred, were active in every subject of his series. Each widow, he found, presented her own idiosyncratic pattern and no correlation between one process and another emerged. He lists the following:

(a) processes that result in a bereaved person feeling numbed and unable to think about what has happened;
(b) processes that direct attention and activity away from painful thoughts and reminders and towards neutral or pleasant ones;
(c) processes that maintain a belief that loss is not permanent and that reunion is still possible;
(d) processes that result in recognition that loss has in fact occurred combined with a feeling that links with the dead none the less persist, manifested often in a comforting sense of the continuing presence of the lost person.

Since there are good reasons to think that processes of the fourth type, so far from contributing to pathology, are an integral part of healthy mourning, they are excluded from further consideration in this chapter. Processes of each of the other types may, however, take pathological forms.

The criteria that most clearly distinguish healthy forms of defensive process from pathological ones are the length of time during which they persist and the extent to which they influence a part only of mental functioning or come to dominate it completely. Consider, for example, the processes that direct attention and activity away from painful thoughts and reminders and towards neutral or pleasant ones. When such processes take control only episodically they are likely to be fully compatible with health. When, by contrast, they become rigidly established they lead to a prolonged inhibition of all the usual responses to loss.

The extent to which processes of defensive exclusion are under voluntary control is often difficult to determine. There is in fact a continuum ranging from what seem clearly to be involuntary processes, such as the numbing which is a common immediate reaction to bereavement, to the deliberate avoidance of people and places likely to evoke painful pangs of pining and weeping. As regards the subject's awareness, the processes listed under heading (c) are particularly variable. On one dimension they range from a clear and conscious belief that loss is not permanent to a belief that is so ill-defined and remote from consciousness that it may require much therapeutic work to make it manifest, with examples occurring of every intervening gradation of which the human mind is capable. On another dimension such beliefs range from being open to new information, and therefore to revision, to their being shut away and resistant to any information that might call them in question.

In addition to these various types and forms of defensive process there are at least two other types that occur during mourning which, unless present only fleetingly, appear never to be compatible with a healthy outcome. They comprise:

(e) processes that redirect anger away from the person who elicited it and towards someone else, a process usually referred to in the psychoanalytic literature as displacement;

(f) processes whereby all the emotional responses to loss become cognitively disconnected from the situation that elicited them, processes that in traditional terminology may be referred to as repression, splitting or dissociation.

Almost any combination of the processes described may be active in any one person, either simultaneously or successively. This presents a problem for theorists and accounts, it seems likely, for many of the disagreements that occur.

In the descriptions of disordered variants that follow I am deeply indebted to the various studies already described in Chapters 6 and 7.

Chronic mourning

Amongst the eighty bereaved people interviewed by Gorer (1965, for particulars see Chapter 6), there were nine whom he found in a state of chronic despair, despite at least 12 months having passed since their loss. 'Despair is almost palpable to the lay interviewer; the toneless voice, the flaccid face muscles, the halting speech in short sentences. Three out of the nine . . . were sitting alone in the dark.' Of the nine, five had lost a spouse (3 widows and 2 widowers), two had lost a mother (both of them middle-aged men), and two had lost grown-up sons (one a married woman and the other a widower). Thus both sexes and several types of loss are represented.

Gorer expresses himself surprised that the proportion of depressed people in his sample (about ten per cent) should have been so large. Other studies of more or less representative samples of bereaved people, however, report no less high an incidence. For example, of the 22 London widows studied by Parkes (1970a) for at least a year, three were in a state at year-end not unlike that described by Gorer. Of the 68 Boston widows and widowers studied by Glick et al. (1974), the majority for two or more years, two widows became alcoholic with depression and two others severely depressed (with one of them repeatedly attempting suicide); and one of the widowers remained deeply depressed and disorganized.[2]

Although in his account of his findings Gorer avoids using terms such as depression and melancholia (on the grounds that they should be reserved for psychiatric diagnosis), he nevertheless believes those terms to be applicable to the conditions he describes. Probably a majority of psychiatrists would agree with him: one of the three widows whom he had found in a despairing state committed suicide a few months after he had seen her. Yet there is a school of psychiatric thought that holds an opposite view. For example, Clayton and her colleagues (1974), despite having demonstrated that the sixteen bereaved people they describe as depressed were showing

[2] Other studies report an even higher incidence of depressive conditions present a year or so after bereavement. Thus of 132 widows in Boston, U.S.A., and 243 in Sydney, Australia, studied by Maddison and Viola (1968) by means of a questionnaire given thirteen months after bereavement, 22 per cent were suffering from depression, over half of whom were thought to be in need of medical treatment. Of 92 elderly widows and widowers, of mean age 61 years, studied in St Louis, Missouri and interviewed thirteen months after bereavement, 16 were showing many depressive symptoms, of whom twelve had been depressed continuously throughout the year (Bornstein et al. 1973).

features that in all respects conform to criteria they had already adopted for diagnosing a primary affective disorder,[3] none the less contend that they should not be so diagnosed. Their reasons are that the condition is reactive to loss and that, in contrast to similar patients in psychiatric care who experience their condition as a 'change', the bereaved regard it as 'normal'. Since the studies of Brown and Harris (1978a)[4] show that a majority of all cases of depressive disorder are reactive to a loss, I believe (with them) that such a distinction is untenable. The view taken here is that the great majority of depressive conditions are best looked upon as a graded series, with the more serious forms having morbid features resembling those found in the less serious forms, though perhaps more intense, and with certain other features added.

In the case of chronic mourning it seems clear that depression can be of very varying degree. The following account of a thirty-year-old mother who took part in the second of the two N.I.M.H. studies of parents of fatally ill children (particulars of which are given in Chapter 7) describes a condition lying towards the less severe end of the scale.

Like other parents taking part in this study, Mrs QQ was interviewed twice by a psychiatrist some time after her child's diagnosis had been conveyed to her. During the interviews, which were closely spaced in time and together lasted from two to four hours, a parent was asked to describe as fully as possible what the experience of being the parent of a fatally ill child was like. In addition to the parent's report, notes were made of his manner and how he behaved during the interview. Although the interviewer was asking the parents to go through the experience all over again, it was found not only that they were willing to do so but that most of them became

[3] The criteria for diagnosis of depression that they adopted were as follows: at the time of the interview the subject admitted to low mood characterized by feeling depressed, sad, despondent, discouraged, blue, etc., plus four of the following eight symptoms: (i) loss of appetite or weight, (ii) sleep difficulties, (iii) fatigue, (iv) agitation (feeling restless) or retardation, (v) loss of interest, (vi) difficulty in concentrating, (vii) feelings of guilt, (viii) wishing to be dead or thoughts of suicide.

[4] Brown and Harris cite the failure of Clayton and her colleagues to classify these states as cases of clinical affective disorder as a startling example of the logical confusion that results whenever aetiological assumptions are built into diagnostic definitions instead of being examined independently.

deeply engaged and provided information that was neither stereo-typed nor superficial. This was because the interviews provided them with an opportunity, first, to confide some of their deepest feelings to someone not personally involved in the crisis and, secondly, by contributing to the research project, to feel that they were able to do something useful in a situation that otherwise made them feel helpless and useless.[5]

During the final six weeks of her son's life Mrs QQ always appeared tense and frequently seemed anxious, agitated and tearful. She was con-stantly preoccupied with how she felt and spoke of being 'unable to stand it any longer'. During interview it was extremely difficult to get her to focus on the realistic evidence of her son's steady deterioration. To every attempt to get her to do so she reacted not only by becoming upset but by dwelling on her own sufferings to the exclusion of all else, including discussion of her son's condition. The physicians and nurses as well as her husband became so anxious and concerned about her condition that they began protecting her from the true facts about her son.

During the two days when her son was dying, however, Mrs QQ's state of mind changed abruptly. She became much less emotional and agitated and, instead, stayed quietly with her son, tenderly caring for him. For the first time she stated that she knew he was going to die and, when asked about herself, replied quietly that she would be all right. At a follow-up interview later Mrs QQ described these last two days. Inwardly, she said, she had felt just as unhappy and upset as before but all her previous concerns had now seemed unimportant. She realized her son was dying and had wanted to help him to be unafraid; also she had wanted to apologize to him for whatever she had done to make him unhappy. Most of all she had wanted to say goodbye and to caress him in order to express some of the tender feelings for which she could not find words.

In their commentary on the case Wolff and his colleagues note how Mrs QQ's emotional condition changed in parallel with the direction of her concern. Initially she had avoided thinking about her son and his impending fate, had concentrated all her attention on her own suffering, and had been tense, anxious and agitated. Later, she had shifted her attention towards the boy and began caring tenderly for him; and at the same time had ceased to be preoccupied with her own sufferings and had become relatively calm.

[5] This abbreviated account is taken from Wolff et al. (1964b) who refer to this mother as Mrs Q. Here she is referred to as Mrs QQ to differentiate her from another mother referred to already in this work as Mrs Q.

From observations of this kind together with measurements of certain physiological variables,[6] Wolff and his colleagues draw a most important conclusion. The level of overt expression of affect is a most misleading guide to how a person is responding to a stressful situation. For, as in Mrs QQ's case, a high level of overt affect may be part of a response which is largely disconnected from the situation that elicited it. Indeed the very intensity of the affect may play a leading part in helping divert the attention, both of the near-bereaved herself and also of her companions, away from the distressing situation. Conversely, when the situation is recognized and attended to, as happens during healthy mourning, overt expression of affect may be reduced. The principal change, however, is in the quality of affect. Instead of unfocused anxiety, agitation and despair, there is sadness and longing, combined perhaps with fond memories which, although sad, are none the less intensely pleasurable. The distinction drawn by Wolff is one to which I shall constantly be returning.

Let us turn now to an example of a bereaved person whose mourning became far more firmly established and chronic than Mrs QQ's and who, as a consequence, was admitted to a mental hospital.[7]

Mr M was 68 when his wife died. They had been married for forty-one years and according to a member of the family he had 'coaxed and coddled her' throughout their married life. She died, unexpectedly, after a brief

[6] In this study as well as in other ones (e.g. Sachar *et al.* 1967, 1968) the rate of excretion of certain steroids is found to vary closely with the extent to which a person is attending to the stressful situation or, instead, is diverting his attention away from it. Though absolute levels vary much from person to person, the more effort a person is giving to dealing with the distressing situation the more likely is his excretion rate to be raised. By contrast, rates show no correlation with level of overt affect: thus they remain low *both* during chronic mourning, when overt affect tends to be high, and also during prolonged absence of grieving when there is little or no overt expression of affect. In keeping with these findings, Mrs QQ had a low excretion rate for these steroids during the period when her attention was directed away from her son and towards her own troubles but showed a marked rise during the final two days when her attitude changed and she became deeply concerned for him.

[7] This patient was seen during an earlier study by Parkes (1965) in which he interviewed patients admitted to a psychiatric hospital for a condition, usually depressive, that had developed within six months of a bereavement. The account is taken, unaltered, from Parkes (1972, pp. 112–13).

illness. For several days he was 'stunned'. He made all the funeral arrangements, then shut himself up at home and refused to see anyone. He slept badly, ate little, and lost interest in all his customary pursuits. He was preoccupied with self-reproachful thoughts and had fits of crying during which he blamed himself for failing her. He blamed himself for sending his wife into hospital (fearing that she had picked up a cross-infection on the ward) and was filled with remorse for not having been a better husband and for having caused his wife anxiety by himself becoming ill. At the same time he was generally irritable, blaming his children for hurting their mother in the past and blaming the hospital for his wife's death. When he went to meetings of a local committee he lost his temper and upset his fellow-members.

His son took him on a trip abroad in the hope of getting him out of his depression but he became more disturbed than ever and broke off the holiday to return to the home which he had cared for fastidiously since his wife's death.

Ten months after bereavement he was admitted to a psychiatric hospital where, after spending some time in psychotherapy talking about his loss, he improved considerably. It was at this time that I saw him and I was struck by the way in which he talked of the deficiencies of his wife while denying any feeling of resentment. 'I looked forward so much to when I retired—that was one of the things that cracked it. I wanted to go on holiday abroad but I couldn't get her to see eye to eye with that. She had been brought up to believe that to go without was essential. I never cured her of that.' He had bought her a home but 'she regarded it as a millstone'—nevertheless she became very attached to her home, 'happier there than anywhere'. Her timorous attitude was reflected in numerous fears. 'She was afraid of the sea—I never pressed her to go abroad. The children would ask her to do things and automatically she'd say "No". No man could have wished for a better wife.'

In addition to many features typical of such conditions, we note the combination of ruminating self-reproach with, on the one hand, blame directed at third parties (his children and the hospital) and, on the other, a total absence of criticism or resentment directed towards his wife. Despite his account of the many ways in which she had frustrated and disappointed him, he insists on regarding her as having been a perfect wife. The case illustrates vividly Freud's contention that the criticisms that a depressed person is directing towards himself often apply not so much to the bereaved as to the lost person. It illustrates also how, whenever persistent anger or self-reproach occur, they are apt to be found together—an association reported by Parkes (1965) as statistically significant in his series of cases.

Although much self-reproach is found to be reproach elicited by the lost person and redirected towards the self and third parties, there are also conditions in which the self-reproach is, at least in some degree, appropriately directed at the self but fastens on some trifling deficiency instead of on one or more real events wherein the bereaved may have been genuinely at fault.

Whereas self-reproach, as often as not associated with reproachful anger directed at third paries, is a feature of all the more severe cases of chronic mourning, there are also cases in which neither is prominent. For example, amongst the sixteen chronically depressed widows and widowers described by Clayton and her colleagues, guilt was said to be present in only two, a feeling of worthlessness in only six, and a tendency to blame someone for the death in only eight (Bornstein et al. 1973). It is, however, not improbable that those findings are due in part to these researchers having relied on a single interview of only one hour's duration and that longer or repeated interviews would have yielded a higher incidence of cases showing anger, guilt or a sense of worthlessness.

Features of Response Predictive of Chronic Mourning

As already stated, Parkes (1970a) found that a few individuals who subsequently develop chronic mourning show little or no response during the weeks immediately after their loss. In some this lull is an extension of the phase of numbing beyond a few days; others seem not even to experience numbing. When mourning starts, which it is likely to do within a month or two, it may be abrupt. It is also likely to be more intense and disrupting than in healthy mourning.

An example of this sequence, given by Parkes, is that of a London widow, Mrs X, who described how, on being told of her husband's death, she had remained calm and had 'felt nothing at all'—and how she had therefore been surprised later to find herself crying. She had consciously avoided her feelings, she said, because she feared she would be overcome or go insane. For three weeks she continued controlled and relatively composed, until finally she broke down in the street and wept. Reflecting on those three weeks, she later described them as having been like 'walking on the edge of a black pit'.

In the Harvard study it was found that those widows and widowers who were doing badly at follow-up two or three years after the loss were likely, during the interviews at three and six weeks, already to have been showing acute disturbance in the form of one or more of the following: unusually intense and continuous yearning, unusually deep despair expressed as welcoming the prospect of death, persistent anger and bitterness, pronounced guilt and self-reproach (Parkes 1975b). Instead of improving during the course of the first year, moreover, as did those who made a reasonably good recovery, these widows and widowers continued to be depressed and disorganized. As a result of their study, Glick and his colleagues (1974) conclude that if recovery has not started by the end of the first year the outlook is not good.

Clayton's findings regarding despair are comparable. Of the 16 widows and widowers judged depressed at thirteen months, twelve were amongst the 38 who were found markedly depressed one month after their loss; and, in addition to those twelve, a further three were found to be depressed at interview four months after loss. Although depression one month after loss proved to be statistically the most powerful predictor they could find of depression at thirteen months, it should not be overlooked that two-thirds of those who had been judged depressed at one month were none the less doing reasonably well a year later (Bornstein et al. 1973).

A further finding of the St Louis study was that a significantly higher proportion of those found to be depressed at thirteen months than of the remainder reported that they had experienced a severe reaction on the anniversary of their spouses' death, a finding also reported by Parkes (1972).

Yet another feature predictive of chronic mourning is anger and resentment persisting long after the early weeks. This, Parkes (1972) found, was correlated with the persistence of tension, restlessness, and intense yearning. The latter was illustrated by Mrs J, a widow of 60 whom he interviewed nine months after she had lost her husband, who had died of lung cancer at the age of 78. When reminded that her husband really was dead, she burst out angrily: 'Oh, Fred, why did you leave me? If you had known what it was like, you'd never have left me.' Later, she denied she was angry and remarked, 'It's wicked to be angry.' Three months later, on the anniversary of her loss, she recalled every moment of the unhappy day her husband died.

'A year ago today was Princess Alexandra's wedding day. I said to him, "Don't forget the wedding." When I got in I said, "Did you watch the wedding?" He said, "No, I forgot." We watched it together in the even-

ing except he had his eyes shut. He wrote a card to his sister and I can
see him so vividly. I could tell you every mortal thing that was done on
all those days. I said, "You haven't watched anything." He said, "No,
I haven't." '

Thereafter for several years she remained mourning chronically,
apparently prepared to continue mourning her dead husband for
ever and repeatedly expressing her anguish and disappointment.[8]

Discussion of the way in which persistence of anger and resentment after a loss can be related both to the patterns of personality
found of those who are prone to disordered mourning and to the
childhood experiences of such people will be found in Chapters 11
and 12.

The following account of a forty-two-year-old London widow[9]
illustrates a fairly typical sequence of events:

After her husband's death Mrs Y had shown very little emotion, a
reaction she explained as due to her having been brought up always to
bottle up her feelings. When she was a child her home had been unstable.
Later, she had made what she described as 'a marriage of companion-
ship' which had clearly been unsatisfactory in many respects. Nevertheless she insisted that the last four years had been 'terribly happy'.

Her husband had died, unexpectedly, on the day on which he was due
to leave hospital after being thought to have recovered from a coronary
thrombosis. She had been unable to cry and for three weeks had 'carried
on as if nothing had happened'. During the fourth week, however, she
was filled with 'terrible feelings of desolation', began sleeping badly and
had vivid nightmares in which she tried to rouse her sleeping husband.
During the day she had panicky feelings; and vivid memories of her husband's corpse kept coming into her mind. Headaches, from which she
had suffered for years, became worse; and she quarrelled with both her
mother and her employers. She remained depressed and restless.

Nine months after bereavement she emigrated to Australia. Four
months later, in reply to enquiry, she wrote at length describing herself
as 'very depressed' and 'missing my husband dreadfully'. She had no
friends in Australia, felt insecure, and was worried about her future.

Features described here which occur repeatedly in accounts of
people whose mourning is progressing unfavourably are: the death
having been sudden, a delayed response, nightmares connected

[8] Information about Mrs J is given in Parkes (1972, pp. 48, 81, 89 and
125), and in a personal communication. Further reference to the case
will be found in Chapter 11.
[9] This account is a rewritten version of one given by Parkes (1970a).

with the death, quarrels with relatives and others, an attempt to escape the scene; and, prior to the bereavement, a history of an unsettled childhood and of having been brought up to bottle up feelings.

Another feature predictive of an unfavourable outcome to mourning is the report that a bereaved person gives after a few weeks about the degree to which he finds relatives, friends and others to be helpful to him in his mourning, or to be unhelpful. This is a variable to which Maddison has drawn attention (Maddison and Walker 1967; Maddison, Viola and Walker 1969) and one discussed further in the next chapter.

Mummification

During the course of his study Gorer (1965) found six people, four widowers and two widows, who were proud to show him how they had preserved their houses exactly as they had been before the spouse's death. A widower of 58, whose wife had died fifteen months previously, explained (p. 80):

> She had her certain places for different things and I haven't shifted them at all. Everything is in the same place where she left it . . . Things run just the same as when she was here . . . everything seems, well as a matter of fact, normal . . .

Two other widowers had been buying flowers for their wives at Christmas and on their birthdays for the past four and five years respectively. Queen Victoria, who lost her husband very suddenly when she was only 42, not only preserved every object as Prince Albert had arranged them but continued for the rest of her life to have his clothes laid out and his shaving water brought (Longford 1964).[10]

To describe this form of response to a loss Gorer introduces the term 'mummification'. It is an apt metaphor because, by embalming the body and burying it with a quantity of personal and household

[10] Gardner and Pritchard (1977) describe six cases in which the bereaved kept the deceased's body in the house for periods ranging from one week to ten years. Of these individuals, two were manifestly psychotic and one was an elderly and eccentric widow who lived as a recluse. The other three, however, were single men whose mother, with whom each had always lived, had died. One of them, who had kept the body for two years before it was noticed by a window cleaner, had made his mother's bedroom into a shrine and explained, 'I couldn't accept that she had died, I wanted things to go on the same.'

equipment, the Egyptians were making provision for the dead person's afterlife. In the form in which it is seen in Western cultures today it may represent the bereaved's more or less conscious belief that the dead person will return and a desire to ensure that he will be properly welcome when he does so. This hypothesis stems from information given me by a patient, the mother of a young child, whom I was treating because of acute anxiety and depression. After losing her elderly father very suddenly (during an operation for cataract) she had insisted for a year or more that neither her mother's flat nor her own should be redecorated. In explanation, she told how she believed that the hospital had mistaken the identity of the man who had died, how she held to the belief that her father was still alive, and how important it was that he should find everything unchanged when at length he returned. Although fully conscious, she was keeping this belief to herself because her mother and others might laugh at it.[11]

Thus mummification is, at least initially, a logical corollary of the belief that the dead person will return. Yet, it may outlive its origins and be continued because to abandon it would set a seal on the loss which the bereaved cannot quite bring himself to do. The widower, whose account (quoted above) of how he kept everything in the house just as it was when his wife was alive and who claimed that 'everything seems . . . normal', ended by remarking pathetically: 'It's just that it's my feeling that everything seems empty. When you walk in the room and there's nobody there, that's the worst part of it.'

Suicide

Ideas of suicide, conceived especially as a means of rejoining the dead person, are common during the early months of bereavement. For example, when interviewed three weeks after their loss one in five of the Boston widows said they would welcome death were it not for the children. Similar ideas were expressed by a number of the London widows, one of whom went as far as to make a half-hearted gesture of suicide.

More serious suicidal attempts and completed suicides, however, are less common. Even so, among the 60 Boston subjects who were followed up between two and four years after loss, one severely

[11] A fuller account is given in Bowlby (1963). Other findings from this case of a mother and son, referred to as Mrs Q and Stephen, are to be found in the second volume of this work, Chapters 15 and 20.

depressed widow had repeatedly attempted suicide; whilst among the widows interviewed by Gorer, one committed suicide a few months after he saw her.

Much internal evidence, including the commonly expressed desire to rejoin the lost person, points in most cases to there having been a direct causal link between the completed suicide and a preceding bereavement. This likelihood is strongly supported by an epidemiological study conducted in the south of England by Bunch (1972).

Bunch compared the incidence of a recent bereavement in the histories of 75 cases of completed suicide, 40 of them male and 35 female and aged from twenty-one years upwards, with that of a control group matched for age, sex and marital status. In the group of suicides the incidence of the loss of a parent or a spouse by death during the preceding two years was five times higher than it was for the controls (24 per cent and 4·7 per cent respectively), a highly significant difference. Differences between the groups for loss of mother and for loss of spouse considered separately also reached statistical significance. An especially high risk group was unmarried men who had lost their mother.

Prolonged absence of conscious grieving

Helene Deutsch was first to draw attention to this condition. In a brief paper published in 1937 she described four adult patients who from early years had suffered severe personality difficulties and episodic depressions. During the course of psychoanalytic treatment, she found, these troubles could be traced to a loss the patients had experienced during childhood but had never mourned: in each case the patient's feeling life had in some way become disconnected from the event. Since then the condition has become well recognized, and a large number of case reports, most of them referring to losses that occurred during childhood or adolescence, are in the literature, together with much theorizing. Examples are papers by Root (1957), Krupp (1965), Fleming and Altschul (1963), Lipson (1963), Jacobson (1965), and Volkan (1970, 1972, 1975). Nevertheless, the condition can also follow a loss during adult life. For example, Corney and Horton (1974) have described a typical syndrome in a young married woman whose episodes of crying and irritability were found during brief therapy to be related to, but disconnected from, a miscarriage (at $4\frac{1}{2}$ months) which had occurred a few months earlier. Only brief references are made to this body of work, however, since all of it is based on the retrospective method. Here we rely on prospective observations of the condition that have been recorded by those who have studied the course of mourning in representative groups of widows and widowers or of parents who have lost a child.

A brief phase of numbing we now know to be very common following a bereavement; but we do not expect it to last more than a few days or perhaps a week. When it lasts for longer there is reason for unease; for example, we have seen how delay of a few weeks or months may presage chronic mourning. Abundant evidence now shows that delay, partial or complete, can last far longer than that, certainly for years or decades, and presumably in some cases for the rest of a person's life.

At this point a sceptic might ask how it is that we know that a person's state of mind is one of disordered mourning and not simply that he is unaffected by the loss and therefore has no cause to grieve. The answer is that in many cases there are tell-tale signs that the bereaved person has in fact been affected and that his mental equilibrium is disturbed. No doubt such signs are more evident in some people than in others; and were they to be totally absent admittedly we should be left guessing. We know enough about them, however, to be able to describe at least some of them.

Adults who show prolonged absence of conscious grieving are commonly self-sufficient people, proud of their independence and self-control, scornful of sentiment; tears they regard as weakness. After the loss they take a pride in carrying on as though nothing had happened, are busy and efficient, and may appear to be coping splendidly. But a sensitive observer notes that they are tense and often short-tempered. No references to the loss are volunteered, reminders are avoided and well-wishers allowed neither to sympathize nor to refer to the event. Physical symptoms may supervene: headaches, palpitations, aches and pains. Insomnia is common, dreams unpleasant.

Naturally there are many variants of the condition and it is impossible to do justice to them all. In some persons cheerfulness seems a little forced; others appear wooden and too formal. Some are more sociable than formerly, others withdrawn; in either case there may be excessive drinking. Bouts of tears or depression may come from what appears a clear sky. Certain topics are carefully avoided. Fear of emotional breakdown may be evident, whether admitted as it sometimes is or not. Grown-up children become protective of a widowed parent, fearing lest reference to the loss by a thoughtless friend or visitor should disturb a precarious balance. Consolation is neither sought nor welcomed.

In illustration of some of these features we describe the responses during her son's illness of a forty-year-old mother who was taking part in the second of the N.I.M.H. studies of parents of fatally ill children, particulars of which are given in Chapter 7.[12]

Mrs. I. was an intelligent, sensitive and warm woman, strong-minded and inclined to be controlling. As a mother she devoted much energy to providing for her children and protecting them; but she did so in a martyred way and seemed to have many unmet needs of her own.

During the interview she appeared subdued and somewhat sad and anxious. She expressed no guilt. At times she seemed fairly open with the interviewer, at others guarded and defensive. Throughout she took control of what was discussed and, rather obviously, avoided reference to anything that might be painful, such as thoughts of the future. When asked how she viewed the probable outcome of her son's illness, she thought there was no need to consider it. Although she gave the impression of finding the interview unpleasant, she also seemed to convey that, because she was being useful, she was willing 'as usual' to sacrifice her own interests.

In describing her experiences whilst her son had been ill it seemed to the interviewer that she was adopting a Pollyana attitude. She should be feeling optimistic, she remarked, because her son was doing well; yet to her surprise she was feeling blue and frightened of the future. Much of the time she was keeping feverishly busy making sure that her son was happy by providing for his every need. The truth about his illness she was keeping from him, and she disputed the possibility that he might already be aware of the facts. She made a point always of controlling her own behaviour so that he would not know she was unhappy. In spite of her constant activity and apparent optimism, she admitted she often felt worried that perhaps the drugs her son was taking would not work. She was not sleeping very well and her appetite had diminished; although on occasion she found herself eating compulsively. From her references to her childhood it became evident that there had been considerable unhappiness and emotional deprivation, though she denied feeling any anger towards her parents. From an early age she had become self-sufficient and had taken responsibility for others; and she had developed a 'protective shell' for herself, she claimed.

[12] The account that follows, rewritten to avoid theory, is taken from the appendix to Wolff et al. (1964b).

Many people who react in this type of way to a loss, or an impending loss, manage like Mrs I to avoid losing control. Others are less successful and at times, and against their will, become tearful and upset. For example, Parkes (1972) describes Mrs F, a forty-five-year-old widow with three teenage children whose husband, ten years her senior, had died very suddenly.[13]

For three weeks after her loss Mrs F had felt 'shocked'; but she had experienced no other emotion and, like Mrs I, had kept herself very busy. Nevertheless, she had been tense and restless, had had headaches and little appetite. At the end of three weeks, she became anxious and depressed and, to her great annoyance, broke down on occasion into uncontrollable tears. Later, however, she took over her husband's business; and thereafter became engaged in what seemed a ceaseless battle to maintain her status and possessions. From the first she had been unable to discuss their father's death with her children; nor could she confide in her mother. Instead, she remained tense and anxious, her headaches continued and she developed chronic indigestion. Relations with one of her daughters deteriorated badly.

In commenting on Mrs F's inability to grieve, Parkes draws attention to four interrelated features of her personality: her image of herself as a poised, sophisticated woman, free of sentiment and able to control her own fate; her claim that her marriage had been one more of convenience than of love, which meant to her that her husband's death had left her nothing to grieve about; her avowed atheism with its contempt for religious consolation and ritual; and her unwillingness to share thoughts and feelings with anyone.

Perhaps the most extreme case of absence of grief yet on record is that of a parent who participated in the same research project as Mrs QQ and Mrs I.[14] This was Mr AA, the thirty-three-year-old father of a leukaemic child.

A salesman by occupation, Mr AA was jovial, responsive and overweight; and he was inclined to be excessively friendly and to work hard to impress. To the research workers, whom he tried to engage in long intellectual discussions, he was eager to be more helpful than was necessary. Yet, although he visited the hospital every day, he avoided spending time with his son. While his wife did the visiting, Mr AA socialized with other parents or watched television in the day-room. His absence from

[13] This is a rewritten version of a case described by Parkes (1972, pp. 140–1).
[14] This account, also rewritten, is from Wolff et al. (1964b).

the ward, he explained, was because he found it so distressing to see all the *other* sick children.

One weekend his wife could not visit and Mr AA was left alone with his son, with whom he spent much longer than usual. During this weekend he had a ninety-minute interview with the psychiatrist who was expecting him on this occasion to reveal at least a little anxiety or distress. That was not so, however. Mr AA seemed exactly his usual self, and proceeded to describe how he preferred to be alone with his son because when his wife was not there the boy showed more interest in him. The nurses' record of the weekend was that he had appeared in good spirits and had been as usual, pleasant and talkative. Thus to all appearances there was no evidence of any active grieving.

It will be remembered, however, that one of the aims of the project was to investigate the effects on a person's endocrine secretion rates of his undergoing a prolonged stressful experience. Accordingly, throughout the time his son was ill, readings were being taken of the excretion rates of certain of Mr AA's steroids. The results were dramatic. During the weekend when he was alone with his son the rate spiked to more than double its usual level. This finding strongly suggests that during the weekend certain physiological components of mourning were being activated even though the usual psychological and behavioural components were missing. In view of Mr AA's earlier behaviour it came as no surprise that, when at length his son's condition deteriorated and death was imminent, he found a good reason to stay away from the hospital.

Compulsive Caring for Others

Although the people I have been describing are averse to dwelling on the loss that they themselves are about to suffer or have suffered, and are thankful that they are not prone to distressing emotion like others, they are none the less apt, like Mrs I, to concern themselves deeply and often excessively with the welfare of other people. Often they select someone who has had a sad or difficult life, as a rule including a bereavement. The care they bestow may amount almost to an obsession; and it is given whether it is welcomed, which it may be, or not. It is given, also, whether the cared-for person has suffered real loss of some kind or is only believed to have done so. At its best this caring for another person may be of value to the cared-for, at least for a time. At its worst, it may result in an intensely possessive relationship which, whilst allegedly for the benefit of the cared-for, results in his becoming a prisoner. In addition, the compulsive caregiver may become jealous of the easy time the cared-for is thought to be having.

Because a compulsive caregiver seems to be attributing to the

156

cared-for all the sadness and neediness that he is unable or unwilling to recognize in himself, the cared-for person can be regarded as standing vicariously for the one giving the care. Sometimes the term 'projective identification' is given to the psychological process that leads to this kind of relationship; but it is a term not used here because, like many similar terms, it is used in more than one sense and stems from and implies a theoretical paradigm different to the one adopted here.

Since it is usual for compulsive caregiving to develop initially during childhood as a result of experiences about which a good deal is now known, further discussion of the pattern and its psychopathology is postponed to later chapters (see Chapters 12, 19 and 21).

Treatment of Reminders

In sharp contrast to the tendency for chronic mourners to retain all the possessions of the deceased in a mummified condition ready for use immediately he returns, those who avoid grieving are likely to jettison clothes and other items that might remind them of the person they have lost. In a precipitate and unselective disposal items that others would value are consigned to oblivion.

Yet there are exceptions. Volkan (1972, 1975) describes a number of patients who, despite not having grieved a relative's death, had none the less secretly retained certain items which had belonged to the relative. These items, perhaps a ring, a watch or a camera, or else a photograph or merely something that happened to be at hand at the time of the death, were kept especially safe but neither worn nor used. Either they were not looked at at all or else they were looked at only occasionally and in private. One man, who was 38 when his father died at a ripe age, kept his father's old car and spent large sums on it to keep it in good order, despite never using it. A woman, Julia, in her early thirties when her mother died, retained, unused, a luxurious red gown which she had originally bought for herself but which had subsequently been pre-empted by her mother, with whom she had lived and whom she had cared for devotedly for many years.

In the latter case there was clear evidence that Julia was expecting her mother to return. During psychotherapy, begun eight months after bereavement, she described her special retention of the gown and how she imagined her mother in some way emerging from it. She also described dreams in which her mother, undisguised and living, appeared, and from which Julia awoke in a panic feeling that perhaps her mother 'might not be gone'.[15] In the case of the man, who also developed symptoms and who during psychotherapy told about his retention of his father's car, Volkan presents no evidence of this kind. Yet, if the theory proposed is correct, we should expect to find that this man, too, was expecting that his father would return and would want to use the car.

Precipitants of Breakdown

Sooner or later some at least of those who avoid all conscious grieving break down—usually with some form of depression. That they should do so is not surprising; but the question arises why they should do so at the particular moment they do.

It is now well established that there are certain classes of event that can act as precipitants of breakdown. These include:

– an anniversary of the death that has not been mourned
– another loss, apparently of a relatively minor kind
– reaching the same age as was a parent when he or she died
– a loss suffered by a compulsively cared-for person with whose experience the failed mourner may be identifying.

Each of these four classes of event, it should be noted, is readily overlooked even by someone who is knowledgeable of these precipitants. By someone ignorant of such possibilities and/or whose theoretical expectations divert his attention elsewhere there is no chance whatever of their being noted. For these reasons we have no information about the relative frequency with which events of each of these kinds act as precipitants.

For almost anyone who grieves a death each anniversary is likely to bring recurrence of the same thoughts and feelings as were experienced earlier. Those who become chronically depressed, we know, are likely to be especially upset at such times (Bornstein *et al.* 1973). This being so, it is no surprise that some of those who have never consciously grieved their loss should suddenly, and apparently inexplicably, develop a strong emotional reaction on such an occasion, despite the loss having occurred perhaps many years earlier. The following example is described by Raphael (1975):

[15] Information about the relationship Julia had had with her mother is given in Chapter 12.

Soon after the second anniversary of her husband's death Mrs O presented in a state of psychotic depression. Prior to breakdown she had appeared, at least to her children, to be dealing well with her loss. She had neither cried nor spoken of her husband at any time since his death; but each morning she had placed his clothes out as usual, and each evening she had set his meal at the time of his expected return from work. The children described how proud they were of their mother's fortitude and how they never referred to their father because they thought the two had been so close that it would be bad for their mother to be reminded of him. After her breakdown she confessed that, unknown to her children, she had carried on long conversations with her husband every night.

During therapy Mrs O was encouraged to talk of her husband and their relationship in considerable detail, aided by family photographs, and to express her feelings in an atmosphere in which they were accepted as natural. In this setting she wept for the first time. Initially she dwelt on her husband's good qualities and insisted that he had met her every need, loved her and protected her. Only later was she able to admit how much she had always depended on him and how angry and helpless she had felt at what had seemed to her to be his desertion.

Although there is now an extensive literature on anniversary reactions, it is striking in how many of the cases reported the loss to which there is belated reaction is that of a parent during childhood or adolescence (see, for example, review by Pollock 1972).

All those who try to help people who are in psychological difficulties after a recent loss know how frequent it is for current grief to arouse, sometimes for the first time, grief for a loss sustained many years previously. Lindemann (1944) reports the case of a woman of 38 whose severe response to her mother's recent death was deeply compounded by hitherto unexpressed grief for her brother who had died in tragic circumstances twenty years earlier.

Another example (taken from the experience of an acquaintance) is of a woman in her forties who found herself weeping bitterly after the death of her parakeet which had formerly belonged to her mother. Astonished that she should grieve so deeply, she soon realized that the recent loss had aroused grief for her mother who had died at a good age a couple of years previously and whom she had not mourned deeply. In view of the quick recognition of the connection and the subsequent time-limited response we may suppose this to have been a relatively healthy reaction.[16]

[16] Not all responses to deaths of pets are healthy, however. Both Keddie (1977) and also Rynearson (1978) report cases of chronic disturbed

A probable explanation of the tendency for a recent loss to activate or reactivate grieving for a loss sustained earlier is that, when a person loses the figure to whom he is currently attached, it is natural for him to turn for comfort to an earlier attachment figure. If, however, the latter, for example a parent, is dead the pain of the earlier loss will be felt afresh (or possibly for the first time). Mourning the earlier loss therefore follows.[17]

As is the case with anniversary reactions, we find that a great deal of the literature about the way current losses can activate or reactivate grieving for an earlier loss refers to the loss of a parent, or perhaps of a sibling, sustained during childhood or adolescence. The same is true of the third and fourth classes of precipitant event. Because of that, further discussion of all these precipitants is postponed to a later chapter.

Personal Difficulties Short of Breakdown

Many people who have failed to mourn the loss of someone important to them though they suffer no actual breakdown feel none the less deeply dissatisfied with their lives. Gradually they may come to realize that their personal relations are in some way empty, especially relations with members of the opposite sex and with children. The following account by a widow, quoted by Lindemann (1944), is typical: 'I go through all the motions of living. I look after my children. I do my errands. I go to social functions, but it is like being in a play; it doesn't really concern me. I can't have any warm feelings. If I were to have any feelings at all I would be angry with everybody.' Terms such as 'depersonalization' and 'sense of unreality' are used to describe these states of mind; and, when loss has occurred during childhood and absence of conscious grieving is long entrenched, the condition may be referred to by Winnicott's term 'false self' (see Chapter 12).

It must be emphasized that the final remark of Lindemann's

---

mourning following the death of a pet. In the three cases of adult women described by Rynearson each of the patients seems to have turned to a pet during her childhood as a substitute for an extremely unhappy relationship with her mother. In each the disturbed reaction to the loss of the pet was a reflection of the intensely painful experiences each had had with her mother before she had finally despaired of that relationship and had turned instead to the pet.

[17] I am indebted to Emmy Gut for suggesting this explanation.

patient—that were she to have any feelings at all she would be angry with everybody—is a half truth only. Anger there would certainly be, directed at the person she had lost. But in addition to anger, and at least as important if she were ever to feel herself again, would be for her to discover within herself also yearning for her husband and sorrow for his loss.

Because here also many such conditions are products more of childhood experience than of adult, further discussion is once again postponed.

Mislocations of the lost person's presence

In our discussion in Chapter 6 of the common responses to loss much attention was given to the continuing sense of the dead person's presence; and it was emphasized that, whereas perhaps half of all bereaved people locate the dead person somewhere appropriate, for example in the grave or in his favourite chair, and experience him or her as a companion, a minority locate the dead person somewhere inappropriate, for example within an animal or physical object, or within another person, or within the bereaved him- or herself. Since it is only these inappropriate locations that can be regarded as pathological, the distinction is of key importance. Because the term identification has been used rather loosely to cover all these conditions and others besides, and has also accreted much complex theory, it is used here very sparingly.

Mislocations when established seem always to be associated with uncompleted mourning; most often they are part of chronic mourning. When the mislocation is within the self, a condition of hypochondria or hysteria may on occasion be diagnosed. When the mislocation is within another person a diagnosis of hysterical or psychopathic behaviour may be given. Such terms are of no great value. What matters is that the condition be recognized as one of failed mourning, and as the result of a mislocation of the lost person's presence.

Mislocations Within Other People

To regard some new person as in certain respects a substitute for someone lost is common and need not lead to any special problem (though there is always some danger that invidious comparisons will be made). To attribute to another person the complete personal identity of someone lost, however, is a very different matter because far-reaching distortions of the relationship become inevitable. This is particularly serious when the individual affected is a child; this is done, it seems likely, more frequently than within an adult, if only because it is easier to endow an infant with a ready-made identity drawn from another person than it is an adult whose own identity is already established. The ready-made identity attributed to an infant by a bereaved parent may not only be that of a dead sibling: it may be that of one of the child's grandparents or that of his dead father or mother.

An example of a widow mislocating her husband in her young child is described briefly by Prugh and Harlow (1962, p. 38).

This woman's husband, with whom she is said to have had a close relationship, died six months after she had given birth to a son who greatly resembled him. Thereafter her relationship to the boy was deeply influenced by her identification of him with her husband; for example, for several years she spent much time dressing him to look like his father. Not surprisingly difficulties developed between son and mother: later on he became rebellious, ran away and began associating with a delinquent group.

The difficulties this woman had in mourning her husband were thought to be connected with her own father having died when she was a young girl.

A 35-year-old widow whose relationship to her baby began in a similar way is reported by Raphael (1976).

At the time of her husband's death following an operation, Mrs M was seven months pregnant with her first child. Soon afterwards the baby, a boy, was born prematurely. After Mrs M's return from hospital with the baby the interviewer called. Although Mrs M cried briefly and sadly at times, all her thoughts were on the baby and it soon became evident that she saw the baby as a 'reincarnation' of her husband, a word she herself used. She insisted the baby had 'long fingers just like his father's and a face just like his father's' and that consequently her husband was still with her. Each time the interviewer sought to encourage her to express grief Mrs M insisted the baby represented a replacement of her husband.

In subsequent interviews[18] Mrs M's idealization both of her husband

[18] Mrs M, who had also lost an elder brother a few months earlier and a close friend a few days later, was one of a group of widows predicted to have a bad outcome and who were willing to receive therapeutic interviews during the early months of bereavement. Raphael's project is described in the latter half of the next chapter. The account of Mrs M given above is a rewritten version of Raphael's.

and the baby gave way to more realistic pictures of both, and also to a more realistic appreciation of her own feelings. She felt isolated and uncared for, she said, like 'a ship without a rudder', and she envied the baby for all the care and attention he was receiving. Subsequently her mourning progressed fairly favourably.

Examples of children whose psychiatric disturbances are traceable to their having been treated from conception onwards simply as replicas of dead siblings are given by Cain and Cain (1964). Deriving their data from a study of six children, four boys and two girls aged between seven and twelve years, these authors present the following history as fairly typical.

A child of latency age or early adolescence, with whom one or both parents has had an especially intense relationship, dies. His parents mourn this tragic loss and one or both develop a state of chronic mourning in which despair, bitter self-accusation, and persistent longing for and idealization of the dead child are prominent. A decision is then taken to have another child (in half the cases encouraged by their doctor in order to give the grieving parent something new to live for). In five of the six cases the parents already had other children and previously had had no intention of having more.

In none of the cases described, however, had the birth of the new child done much to ease the parents burden of chronic mourning. Indeed, the atmosphere of the homes seems to have remained funereal, with one or both parents still totally preoccupied by the child who had died and still wrestling incessantly with questions such as why had the death occurred and how would things have been had it not done so. Since the role in which the new child was cast was that of being a replica of the lost sibling, his every expression and performance was constantly compared with the parent's image, strongly idealized, of the sibling. Similarities would be noted with satisfaction, differences ignored or else deplored. The parent's insistence that the new child was a replica could persist even when he or she was of the wrong sex.

Inevitably the substitute child would be hedged around with restrictions lest he also contract an illness or incur an accident and die too. Every symptom, however trifling, would be treated as ominous, every hazard exaggerated. Occasionally a mother might enforce a restriction by threatening to kill herself were anything to happen to this child too.

The effects on these children of being treated thus had been calamitous. Never allowed an identity of their own, they had grown up knowing themselves to be in their parent's eyes merely inadequate replicas of their dead siblings. Because, moreover, the originals had died, the substitute children confidently supposed they would die too. Meanwhile they were perpetually anxious, frightened like their parents of every ailment and hazard, and strongly bound to the parent's apron-strings. Two of the children developed symptoms similar to those the sibling had had before he died: a boy whose brother had choked on a piece of bread suffered continually from a 'clogged' throat and gasped for air; a girl whose brother had died of leukaemia, during which he had experienced peculiar sensations in his arms, developed pains in her arms. Each of these children was approaching the age at which the sibling had died. The clinical states of the six are said to have ranged from 'moderately severe neuroses to (two) psychoses'.

The parents, especially the mothers, who had treated their children in these highly pathogenic ways were thought by the authors to have shown various neurotic features before they had suffered the traumatic loss. Cain and Cain refer, first, to the 'guilt-ridden, generally depressive, phobic and/or compulsive personalities' of these mothers and, secondly, to the especially intense 'narcissistic investment' each had had in the child who had died. They were struck also by the number of losses these mothers had suffered during their own childhoods. As we see in Chapters 11 and 12, all these findings are characteristic of persons prone to develop chronic mourning.[19]

[19] James Barrie, the author of *Peter Pan*, tells how, from the age of six and a half, he attempted to fill the place of a dead elder brother whose loss had prostrated his mother. The elder brother, David, was killed in a skating accident when aged eleven. The second son in a family of eight, David had always been his mother's favourite, and she had great ambitions for him. Quiet, studious and successful at school, he was destined for the ministry. After his sudden death mother took to her bed and became a permanent invalid, leaving an elder girl to act as mother to the younger children.

Barrie tells of his attempts to replace David. It began soon after the loss. His mother lay in bed holding the christening robe in which all the children had been baptized. James crept in and heard his mother enquire anxiously, 'Is that you? Is that you?' Believing her to be addressing his dead brother, James replied in a little lonely voice, 'No, it's no' him, it's just me.' Subsequently his sister told him to get his mother to talk about

In making these generalizations Cain and Cain are keenly aware that they are based on data obtained long after the relevant events. They are aware also that the sample of children, because drawn from a psychiatric clinic, is inevitably biased, and can cast no light on the proportion of parents who, grieving a lost child, engage in this sort of behaviour. They note, too, that because of the personality problems of the parents, disturbances in their relationships with their children were likely to have occurred in any case. The field is one that clearly merits further research.

Mislocations within Animals or Physical Objects

To locate a lost person's presence within an animal or physical object may be thought unusual. Yet it may well be commoner than we know: for not only do a majority of people in the world believe in some form of reincarnation, often in animal form, but according to Gorer (1965) beliefs of this kind are held by about one in ten of native-born Britons today.

David; and this she did, to the point where her preoccupation with the dead boy led James to feel totally excluded. Thereafter, in the words of his biographer, Janet Dunbar (1970, p. 22), James became 'obsessed by the intense desire to become so like David that his mother would not see the difference'.

It seems that in establishing James's role of impersonating David, his sister, his mother and he himself each played some part. For James, it is clear, the role gave him an access to his mother that he would not otherwise have had. As his mother's confidant, moreover, he acted almost like a bereavement counsellor; and he listened intently to her long accounts of her own troubled childhood. When she was eight her own mother had died and she had taken on the role of 'little mother' to her father and younger brother, who was also called David. It should be remembered that, since the information given above comes from a book about his mother written by Barrie himself, it may well be biased, either wittingly or unwittingly.

Barrie grew up to have many emotional difficulties. His marriage remained unconsummated. On the one hand, he developed strong platonic relationships with married women; on the other, he became a compulsive caregiver, notably to five boys who had been left orphans and of whom he became fiercely possessive. A friend who knew him well wrote: '... he strikes me as more than old, in fact I doubt whether he ever *was* a boy'. It is not difficult to trace themes derived either from his mother's childhood or from his own relationship with her in his plays and stories.

Mislocations of these kinds are illustrated by the case of Mrs P who at the age of 30 had been admitted to a psychiatric hospital because of a chronic emotional disturbance which had developed soon after her mother had died.[20] The sequence of events was as follows:

When her mother died Mrs P consciously directed her search towards making contact with the departed spirit. In company with her sister she improvised a planchette with which she 'received' messages which she believed came from her mother.

At a seance she noticed a toby jug which seemed to resemble her mother. She felt that her mother's spirit had entered into this jug and she persuaded her sister to give it to her. For some weeks she kept the jug near at hand and had a strong sense of the presence of her mother. However, the jug proved a mixed blessing since she found that she was both attracted and frightened by it. Her husband was exasperated by this behaviour and eventually, against her will, he smashed the jug. His wife noticed that the pieces, which she buried in the garden, 'felt hot'—presumably a sign of life.

Mrs P did not give up her search. Shortly after the jug was broken she acquired a dog. Her mother had always said that if she was ever reincarnated it would be in the form of a dog. When I interviewed Mrs P three years later she said of the dog: 'She's not like any other animal. She does anything. She'll only go for walks with me or my husband. She seems to eat all the things that mother used to eat. She doesn't like men.'

Mrs P's mother is described as having been an assertive and somewhat dominant woman, and Mrs P herself as having been a devoted daughter.

Mislocations within the Self: Identificatory Symptoms

Mislocations of the dead person within the self take several forms; each of them leading to symptoms that can accurately be termed identificatory. One form is a conscious sense of his presence within. One of the London widows who had this experience is already referred to briefly in Chapter 6. Another, Mrs D, described her experience as follows: 'At dawn, four days after my husband's death, something suddenly moved in on me—invaded me—a presence, almost pushed me out of bed—terribly overwhelming.' Thereafter she had a strong sense of her husband's presence near her but not always 'inside' her. At the end of the year she claimed to

[20] This account, unaltered, is taken from Parkes (1972, p. 60).

be seeing many things 'through his eyes'. This was a condition that may well have been felt by her as alien and which was almost certainly pathological since at the end of the year she was still socially isolated and full of self-reproach. 'I feel criminal,' she said, 'terribly guilty.' Throughout their married life, it emerged, she and her husband had been at odds and she had often regarded him as sacrificing the family's interests by irresponsible behaviour (Parkes 1972, pp. 103, 137–8).

In discussing the responses of fighter pilots to the deaths in action of comrades in arms, Bond (1953) describes a condition which may be comparable to that of Mrs D, though less conscious. Whereas the usual response to a friend's death was one of revenge, there were cases in which a pilot became convinced that he would suffer the same fate as his friend and he seemed thenceforward to court it. In describing a typical case, Bond continues: 'He now is looking at his flying from an entirely different view. No longer is he a young and happy airman about to win great victory for his country but he is a young man going out to die in the exact replica of the way that a friend has died.' After treating a number of these young men psychotherapeutically Bond concluded that the relationship between the survivor and the dead pilot had been ambivalent: 'In each one of these boys it was not hard to find the angry thought or the selfish thought that gave them satisfaction in their friend's death.' Recognition of this and expression of grief led to recovery.

Another form of mislocation within the self results in the bereaved developing symptoms of certain kinds, often but not always symptoms similar to those of the bereaved's last illness. In this form of disordered mourning the mislocation of the lost person's presence within the self, if that is how it is to be understood, is completely unconscious.

Among those to give examples are Murray (1937) and Krupp (1965); Parkes (1972, pp. 114–16) also describes a number of cases. Of eleven patients seen by him who were in a psychiatric hospital because of hypochondriacal or hysterical symptoms that had developed within six months of a bereavement, four had pains resembling those of coronary thrombosis, one a pain simulating lung cancer, one a pain similar to one believed to have been suffered by a son killed in a car accident, three showed the effects of a stroke, and there was one case of recurrent vomiting. In all cases the symptoms had developed after a close relative had died from a condition the symptoms of which the patient's own symptoms simulated.

A dramatic example described by Parkes is that of a woman who was already in psychotherapy at the time her father died, following a stroke which had paralysed the left side of his body. She had nursed him for several weeks before the end. The night after he died she had a dream (reported to her therapist next day) in which she saw her father lying in his coffin. He had reached up at her and had 'stroked' the left side of her body, whereupon she awoke to find the left side of her body paralysed. In this case the paralysis soon wore off and she had no further symptoms of that nature. As in so many other cases of disordered mourning, here too the previous relationship had not been happy; during psychotherapy she dwelt at length on how in earlier years her father had harmed her in various ways.

Disordered mourning is not confined to Western cultures. For example, Miller and Schoenfeld (1973) report that amongst the Navajo it is relatively common for depressive states, sometimes with hypochondriacal symptoms, to follow a bereavement; and, from the descriptions they give, it appears that these conditions differ in no way from the chronic mourning seen in the West. In illustration the authors give details of a 48-year-old married woman who was referred for psychiatric help because of pain in two parts of her body. First, there was a line of pain running from ear to ear across her forehead; and, secondly, there was pain running midline down her abdomen. The patient described the pains as being sharp. They had begun about three months after the death of her nephew whom she had raised and had regarded as a son. On investigation it turned out that an autopsy had been performed on the boy and that, afterwards, the patient had been the member of the family to dress the body. Her own midline abdominal pain corresponded with the midline autopsy incision, and her head pain corresponded in reverse with the routine incision used in order to examine the skull and brain.

It is to be noted that Navajo mourning customs are like those of their neighbours, the Hopi, described in Chapter 8, namely extremely brief and with expression of emotion so far as possible to be avoided. In addition, there is a taboo on touching the body, which this patient had broken. Although there is a Navajo ceremony designed to deal with such problems, she had refrained from asking for it because of her ostensible Christian beliefs. Nevertheless, she subsequently consulted a medicine man and went through the appropriate ceremonies. Thereafter she was freed of her symptoms.

Euphoria

Although euphoria is well recognized as an atypical response to loss, it does not occur commonly and there are no systematic studies of it. Such as there are show it to occur in at least two quite distinct forms.

In some cases a euphoric response to a death is associated with an emphatic refusal to believe that the death has occurred combined with a vivid sense of the dead person's continuing presence. In other cases the reverse appears to hold: the loss is not only acknowledged but is claimed to be greatly to the advantage of the bereaved. No simple theory can cover both.

An example of the first type of response is given already in Chapter 6. When asked whether she felt her husband was near at hand one of the London widows interviewed by Parkes replied, 'It's not a sense of his presence—he's here inside me. That's why I'm happy all the time. It's as if two people were one . . . Although I'm alone, we're sort of together if you see what I mean . . . I don't think I've got the will-power to carry on on my own, so he must be.' In this last remark the despair and desperation latent in her response stand out bleakly.

A euphoric response of this kind is clearly unstable, and it is apt to collapse and to be replaced by intense grieving. In a small minority of cases, by contrast, the mood may persist, or recur, and hypomanic episodes may ensue. Although no such case has been described in any of the studies so far drawn upon, an example of the sequence is given by Rickarby (1977).

Mrs A was aged 44 with two grown-up children when her estranged husband was killed in a motor accident. When informed of the event, she showed no emotion and set about arranging the funeral, at which she was said to have been 'falsely cheerful'. Six days after the bereavement she became agitated and overactive, with pressure of speech. In a euphoric state she talked much about her husband, idealizing him and their relationship, and maintained that he was listening to her.

After three weeks in a manic state during which she received drug treatment she became sad and voiced worries about the future. During therapeutic sessions she expressed much anger at her husband for having left her some eight months earlier, as well as anger and guilt about his death.

In fact the marriage had been extremely unhappy for many years, characterized by hostility and withdrawal on both sides. Mrs A was said to have found fault with everyone, to have rejected her husband and children, and to have lavished all her affection on an elderly dog. Three years earlier she had had a severe depressive illness.

In discussing this and three other patients in which there was a connection between a manic illness and a bereavement, Rickarby invokes the psychosomatic hypothesis, advanced by Bunney and others (1972), that a manic episode is a response to a stressful experience in a person genetically predisposed. In view of Mrs A's personal relations it seems not unlikely that adverse experiences during her childhood had also contributed to her vulnerability.

That childhood loss can increase vulnerability is strongly suggested by a scrutiny of the series of hypomanic adults described by MacCurdy (1925). In several of these patients a prominent feature was their strong insistence on the continuing presence of a parent or sibling who had died many years previously during their (the patients') childhood.

There are no examples in the studies drawn upon of a widow or widower claiming euphorically that the spouse's death has been wholly to his or her advantage; though this may be an artifact due to such person's having refused to participate. Useful information about such responses, however, is given by Weiss (1975b) in his study of married couples who have separated from each other, and it is useful to refer briefly to his findings (pp. 53–6). One example is of a woman in her early forties who had separated from her husband after nearly twenty years of marriage:

I found that I felt quite euphoric for about three months. I sort of did everything that I wanted to do. I hadn't gone out much, so I went to the theatre. I didn't do these things before I was married. I sat in a bar, drinking, just talking to anybody. I met just lots of different people.

After three months and having met just one or two people who were really interesting, I found it was an empty life. I realized that my family meant a great deal to me and that there was no family any more. There was just the kids and myself. And the things I had done with my husband, I could no longer do them.

So long as the euphoria lasted, Weiss observed, these individuals seemed to be unusually active and also effective, though latent tension and anxiety might also be evident. For example, an insistence that everything was fine might be belied by a rush of speech or a nervous mannerism.

In Weiss's experience a euphoric response is extremely fragile and can be shattered by some minor setback or even by merely hearing that it might not last. Once ended it was likely to be replaced by separation distress, and pining for the former spouse.

In keeping with the view that the euphoria, however effective the activity may be to which it leads, is no more than skin deep are the reflections of those who have been through it. One woman, who during the first months of her separation had described how she was feeling on top of the world, two years later referred to those same first months as having been miserable.

In explanation of his findings Weiss suggests that euphoria reflects an 'appraisal that the attachment figure is not needed after all, that one can do very well alone' (p. 54). Its collapse he sees as due to 'recognition that life without attachment is unsatisfying . . . The world appears suddenly barren, and the individual alone. The resultant distress may be the worse for following so closely a state in which the individual felt entirely self-sufficient' (p. 56).[21]

When we compare the condition described by Weiss and the condition described earlier in which there is a vivid sense of the dead person as a living companion, it is clear that, although the moods appear similar, the two conditions are quite different in psychopathology. In the one, attachment desires continue to be directed towards the original figure who is claimed still to be meeting them. In the other, by contrast, desire for attachment is disowned and the claim to self-sufficiency is paramount. In these respects the condition has much in common with prolonged absence of grieving and its related condition of compulsive self-reliance.

This completes our description of the common variants of disordered mourning as they are seen in bereaved adults. Next we consider what we know of the conditions that tend to influence mourning to take a pathological course.

[21] Weiss hazards the view that in this condition attachment feelings have become directed towards the self, and he proposes 'narcissistic attachment' as a possible description. I doubt, however, whether this is a useful formulation. He gives no clear evidence that attachment feelings are in fact directed towards the self—only that the person concerned claims to be completely free of attachment to others and acts as though he were.

CHAPTER 10

Conditions Affecting
the Course of Mourning

He oft finds med'cine who his grief imparts.
SPENCER, *The Faerie Queene*

Five categories of variable

Although, thanks to the research of the past twenty years, a great deal is now known about why the mourning of some individuals follows a pathological course whereas that of others does not, the problem remains very difficult and a great deal more is still to be learned. Variables likely to be relevant are numerous; they tend to occur in clusters so that items within each cluster are difficult to tease apart; they interact in complex ways; and many of what appear to be the most influential are among the most controversial. All that can be attempted is to present a classification of variables, give brief indications of the likely role of each and direct attention to those thought likely to prove most powerful in determining outcome.

Variables can be classified under five heads:

– the identity and role of the person lost
– the age and sex of the person bereaved
– the causes and circumstances of the loss
– the social and psychological circumstances affecting the bereaved about the time of and after the loss
– the personality of the bereaved, with special reference to his capacities for making love relationships and for responding to stressful situations.

In determining the course of mourning the most influential of these variables seems likely to be the personality of the bereaved, especially the way his attachment behaviour is organized and the modes of response he adopts to stressful situations. In thus postulating that some types of personality organization are more vulnerable to loss than are others, I am following a long-established psycho-analytic tradition; where the difference lies is in how the causes of vulnerability are conceived.

The effects which the many other variables have on the course of mourning are mediated inevitably through their interactions with the personality structures of the bereaved. Many of these other variables, the evidence suggests, exert great influence, either going far to facilitate healthy mourning or else going far in the opposite direction. Perhaps some of them, acting in conjunction, could lead even a relatively stable person to mourn pathologically; but more often, it seems, their effect on a stable personality is to lead mourning to be both more intense and more prolonged than it would otherwise be. Their effects on a vulnerable personality, by contrast, are far more serious. In such persons, it is clear, they not only influence the intensity and length of mourning for better or worse but they influence also and greatly the form that mourning takes, either towards a relatively healthy form or else towards one or other of the pathological variants.

Of these variables the first three are the most easily defined and can be dealt with briefly. We proceed thence to consider the social and psychological conditions which affect the bereaved around the time of the loss and during the months or years after it. The existence of some of these conditions may be independent, wholly or in large degree, of any influence that the bereaved himself may be exerting. Towards the production of others, by contrast, the bereaved may be playing some part; often it appears large. This sequence of exposition leaves to the last, indeed to the ensuing chapter, consideration of the bereaved's personality. Reasons for postponement are, first, that features of personality are less easily defined than are other variables and, secondly, that their consideration leads on to questions of personality development and the role that family experience during childhood plays in determining individual differences, which it is argued here is of the greatest relevance to an understanding of the psychopathology of mourning.

Identity and role of person lost

Some of the discussions of disordered mourning to be found in the literature are concerned with losses other than those of persons, for example a house, a pet, a treasured possession or something purely symbolic. Here, however, we confine ourselves to losses of persons since they, by themselves, raise more issues than can be dealt with adequately. Furthermore, when loss of a pet has led to disordered mourning there is evidence that the relationship to the pet had become of such intense emotional significance because human relationships had ended in persistent rejection or loss.[1]

Almost every example of disordered mourning following loss of a person that has been reported is the result of the loss of an immediate family member—as a rule a parent (including parent substitute), spouse or child; and occasionally a sibling or a grandparent. Loss of some more distant relative or of a friend is reported extremely rarely. There are several reasons for this restriction to close kin. Some are artificial. For example, much of the research of recent years has deliberately selected for study only those individuals who have lost close kin. Another is that during routine clinical work losses of close kin, because easily defined, are more quickly and confidently identified as being of major relevance to a clinical condition than are losses of other kinds. Nevertheless, even after discounting these artificial biases, there seem solid enough reasons for believing that an overwhelming majority of cases of disordered mourning do in fact follow the loss of an immediate family member. This is so often either taken for granted or else overlooked that it is worth emphasizing.

It is of course no surprise that when disordered mourning occurs during childhood and adolescence the loss in an overwhelming majority of cases is that of a parent or parent-substitute. Perhaps it is rather more surprising that during adult life, too, such losses continue to be of some significance. In this regard, we must note, statistics are not consistent. For example, in an early study, Parkes (1964a) reviewed 94 adult patients, 31 male and 63 female, admitted to two psychiatric hospitals in London during the years 1949–51 and whose presenting illness had come on either during the last ill-

---

[1] Keddie (1977) and Rynearson (1979) each report three cases, all of women. In one the patient when aged three years had become deeply attached to a puppy given her soon after losing both her parents due to a breakup of the marriage. In three the patient had suffered repeated rejection by her mother and had turned to a cat or a dog instead. In two the patient seems to have regarded the pet as taking the place of a child, in one of a son who died in infancy and in the other following an early hysterectomy.

174

ness or within six months of the death of a parent, a spouse, a sibling or a child. Although in no less than half the cases symptoms had followed the illness or death of a parent (in 23 loss of father and in 24 loss of mother), the incidence of such loss was found to be no greater than would have been expected in the population from which the patients were drawn. In a more recent and much larger study in north-east Scotland by Birtchnell (1975b), however, in which criteria are different, a raised incidence of parent loss is found. In a series of 846 patients aged 20 and over diagnosed as depressive (278 men and 568 women) loss of a parent by death was likely to have occurred in a significantly larger number of them during a period one to five years prior to psychiatric referral than would have been expected in the population concerned.[2] The incidence in men of loss of mother and in women of loss of father was in each case raised by about fifty per cent. Since the findings apply to married as well as to unmarried patients, Birtchnell concludes that marriage confers no protection.

It might be supposed that adults who respond to loss of a parent with disordered mourning will have had a close relationship with that parent; and that a majority of them therefore would be living either with the parent or else close by and seeing him or her frequently. Data so far published, however, give insufficient detail to test this possibility: such as are available refer only to those who have been residing in the same house as the parent and omit any that might be residing near by and having frequent contact, as occurs so often. Even so, of the patients in Parkes's study whose illnesses had followed loss of a parent, no less than half had been residing with that parent for a year or longer immediately prior to the bereavement. Since in our culture only a minority of adult children live with parents, this finding, together with others reported below, support the commonsense view that disordered mourning is more likely to follow the loss of someone with whom there has been, until the loss, a close relationship, in which lives are deeply intertwined, than of someone with whom the relationship has been less close.

[2] Whenever a comparison is made between the incidence of a potential pathogen in a group of patients and the incidence in the whole population from which the patients are drawn, it is likely that the difference between the two will be underestimated. This is because undeclared cases of the condition may be present in the comparison group.

In this connection we note that all students of disordered mourning seem to be agreed that the relationships which precede disordered mourning tend to be exceptionally close. Yet it has proved very difficult to specify in what ways they differ from other close relationships. Much confusion is caused by the ambiguity of the term 'dependent'. Often it is used to refer to the emotional quality of an attachment in which anxiety over the possibility of separation or loss, or of being held responsible for a separation or loss, are commonly dominant if covert features. Sometimes it refers merely to reliance on someone else to provide certain goods and services, or to fill certain social roles, perhaps without there being an attachment of any kind to the person in question. In many cases in which the term is used about a relationship it is referring to some complex mesh into which both of these components enter.

Naturally the more a bereaved person has relied on the deceased to provide goods and services, including extended social relationships, the greater is the damage the loss does to his life, and the greater the effort he has to make to reorganize his life afresh. Yet a relationship 'dependent' in this sense probably contributes very little to determining whether mourning takes a healthy or a pathological course. It is certainly not necessary; for example, disordered mourning can follow loss of child or loss of an elderly or invalid parent or spouse on whom the bereaved is in no way dependent in that sense of the word.

We can conclude therefore that the kind of close relationship that often precedes disordered mourning has little to do with the bereaved having had to rely on the deceased to provide goods and services or to fill social roles. As we see in the coming chapters many features of these relationships are reflections of distorted patterns of attachment and caregiving long present in both parties.

Although for reasons to be discussed shortly the number of cases reported in which disordered mourning has followed loss of child is comparatively small, students of the problem are impressed by the severity of the cases that they have seen. Lindemann (1944) remarks that 'severe reactions seem to occur in mothers who have lost young children'. Almost the same words are used by Wretmark (1959) in his report of a study of twenty-eight bereaved psychiatric patients admitted to a mental hospital in Sweden, of whom seven were mothers and one a father. Similarly, Ablon (1971), whose study of bereavement in a Samoan community is described later in this chapter, reports that the most extreme (disturbed) grief responses were seen in two women who had lost an adopted child. One woman, who had lost a grown-up son, had developed a severe depression. The other, who had lost a school-aged daughter, treated her grandson as though he were the lost daughter.

Gorer (1965) in his survey of bereaved people in the United Kingdom interviewed six who had lost a child already adolescent or adult; and from his findings was inclined to conclude that the loss of a grown child may be 'the most distressing and long-lasting of all griefs'. His samples are too small, however, for firm conclusions to be drawn; and, although the grieving of those he interviewed was unquestionably severe, it was not necessarily pathological.

Loss of a sibling during adult life is not frequently followed by disordered mourning. For example, in the series of 94 adult psychiatric patients studied by Parkes (1964a), although twelve had lost a sibling this is no greater than would be expected by chance. In any cases that might occur, it seems likely that the siblings would have had a special relationship, for example, that one had acted as a surrogate parent to the other. So far as I am aware, no systematic data are available by which that supposition can be checked.

In considering the relative importance of losing a parent, a spouse, a child or a sibling as causes of disordered mourning in adults we must distinguish between (a) the total number of individuals affected and (b) the incidence of disordered mourning that follows a loss of each of these kinds. This is because the death-rates for those in the roles of parent, of spouse, of child, and of sibling differ. Current death-rates in the West are highest for those in the role of father and decline progressively for those in the roles of mother, of husband, of wife and of child. (Rates for siblings are not available.) Thus, were the incidence of disordered mourning to be the same irrespective of the member of kin lost, the largest numbers of adults who suffer disordered mourning would inevitably be among those who had lost a father and the smallest number among those who had lost a child.

In fact we still have too little information about the differential incidence of disordered mourning in adults for losses of these different kinds, though Parkes's evidence suggests that those who lose a spouse are at greatest risk. As a result of these different factors we find that in Western cultures adults suffering from disordered mourning are drawn very largely from amongst those who have lost a husband; and on a smaller scale from those who have lost a wife, a parent, or a child, with loss of sibling being comparatively rare.

Age and sex of person bereaved

Age at Bereavement

Just as there are difficulties in determining the differential incidence of disordered mourning following losses of different kinds, so there are difficulties in determining the differential incidence by the age (and also the sex) of the bereaved. Most psychoanalysts are confident that incidence is higher for losses sustained during immaturity than in those sustained during adult life. Yet even for that difference no clear figures are available.

For losses sustained during adult life data are equally scarce: most of what there are refer to widows.

The findings of at least two studies have suggested that the younger a woman is when widowed the more intense the mourning and the more disturbed her health is likely to become. Thus Parkes (1964b), in his study of the visits that some 44 London widows made to their general practitioners during the first eighteen months after bereavement, found that, of the 29 who were under the age of 65 years, a larger proportion required help for emotional problems than of the fifteen who were over that age. Similarly, Maddison and Walker (1967) in their study of 132 Boston widows aged between 45 and 60 found a tendency for those in the younger half of the age-range to have a less favourable outcome twelve months after bereavement than those in the older half.

Other studies, however, have failed to find a relationship with age. For example, neither Maddison and Viola (1968) in their repeat of the Boston study in Sydney, Australia, nor Raphael (1977) in her later study in the same city found any correlation between age at bereavement and outcome. A possible explanation of the discordance is that the age-ranges of the widows in the various studies differ and that such tendency as there may be for younger widows to respond to loss more adversely than older ones affects only a particular part of the age-range. Whether that is so or not, evidence is clear that there is no age after which a person may not respond to a loss by disordered mourning. Both Parkes (1964a) and also Kay, Roth and Hopkins (1955), in their studies of psychiatric patients, have found a number whose illness was clearly related to a bereavement sustained late in life. Of 121 London patients of both sexes whose condition had developed soon after a bereavement, Parkes reports that twenty-one were aged sixty-five or over.

Sex of Bereaved

In terms of absolute numbers there is little doubt that there are more women who succumb to disordered mourning than there are men; but because the incidence of loss of spouse is not the same for members of the two sexes we cannot be sure that women are more vulnerable. Furthermore, it may well be that the forms taken by disordered mourning in the two sexes are different, which could lead to false conclusions. Thus it is necessary to view the following findings with caution.

There is some evidence that widows are more prone than widowers to develop conditions of anxiety and depression that lead, initially, to heavy sedation (Clayton, Desmarais and Winokur 1968) and, later, to mental hospital admission (Parkes 1964a). Yet evidence on this point from the Harvard study is equivocal (see Chapter 6). During the first year the widowers in this study seemed less affected than the widows; after two or three years, however, as great a proportion of widowers was severely disturbed as of widows. Of 17 widowers followed up, four were either markedly depressed or alcoholic or both; of 43 widows followed up, two were seriously ill and six others disturbed and disorganized.

Evidence in regard to the effects of loss of a child is equally uncertain. Whereas there is some evidence that loss of a young child is more likely to have a severe effect on a mother than on a father, in regard to loss of an older child there is reason to suspect that fathers may be just as adversely affected as mothers (e.g. Purisman and Maoz 1977).

The upshot seems to be that, whatever correlations there may be between the age and sex of the bereaved and the tendency for grief to take a pathological course, the correlations are low and probably of little importance compared to the variables yet to be considered. This perhaps is fortunate since, in our professional role of trying to understand and help bereaved people who may be in difficulty, it is their personalities and current social and psychological circumstances that we are dealing with; whereas the age and sex of the bereaved are unalterable.

Causes and circumstances of loss

The causes of a loss and the circumstances in which it occurs are enormously variable and it is no surprise that some should be of such a nature that healthy mourning is made easier and others of a kind that make it far more difficult.

First, the loss can be due to death or to desertion. Either can result in disordered mourning and it is not possible at present to say whether one is more likely to do so than the other. What follows in this chapter refers to loss by death. (Responses to loss by desertion are discussed by Marsden (1969) and Weiss (1975b).)

Next a loss can be sudden or can in some degree be predicted. There seems no doubt that a sudden unexpected death is felt as a far greater initial shock than is a predictable one (e.g. Parkes 1970a); and the Harvard study of widows and widowers under the age of 45 shows that, at least in that age group, after a sudden death not only is there a greater degree of emotional disturbance—anxiety, self-reproach, depression—but that it persists throughout the first year and on into the second and third years, and also that it leads more frequently to a pathological outcome (Glick *et al.* 1974; Parkes 1975a). This is a sequence long suspected by clinicians, e.g. Lindemann (1944), Lehrman (1956), Pollock (1961), Siggins (1966), Volkan (1970), and Levinson (1972). In the Harvard study, there were 21 widows who had clear forewarning of their husband's death and 22 who had little or none.[3] Of those who had reasonable forewarning only one developed a pathological condition; of those who suffered a sudden loss five did. The findings in regard to the widowers were similar.

A further finding of the Harvard study, and one not foreseen, is that two or three years after their loss not one of the twenty-two widows who had lost a husband suddenly showed any sign of remarrying in contrast to thirteen of the twenty followed up who had had forewarning. The authors suspect that this large difference in remarriage rate is due to those whose loss had been sudden having become terrified of ever again entering a situation in which they could risk a similar blow. They liken the state of mind they infer to the phobic reaction often developed by people who have experi-

[3] The criteria for short forewarning were less than two weeks' warning that the spouse's condition was likely to prove fatal and/or less than three days' warning that death was imminent.

enced other sudden and devastating catastrophes, such as a hurricane or fire.

Since the spouse of a widow or widower who is still under the age of forty-five is likely to have been under fifty at death, such a loss will probably be judged by the survivors to have been untimely. The extent to which this variable, to which Krupp and Kligfeld (1962), Gorer (1965) and Maddison (1968) all draw attention, may contribute to a disordered form of mourning remains uncertain, but it clearly increases the severity of the blow and the intensity of anger aroused.

There are in fact grounds for suspecting that the severe reactions after a sudden bereavement observed so frequently in the Harvard study may occur only after deaths that are both sudden and untimely. This conclusion is reached by Parkes (1975a) after he had contrasted the clear-cut Harvard findings in young widows and widowers with the failure of the St Louis group to find any correlation between sudden bereavement and an adverse outcome (as measured at thirteen months by the presence of depressive symptoms) in the elderly group they studied (Bornstein et al. 1973).

There are other circumstances connected with a death that almost certainly make bereavement either less or more difficult to cope with, though in no case are they likely to have so great an effect as that produced by a sudden and untimely death. These other circumstances include:

(i) whether the mode of death necessitates a prolonged period of nursing by the bereaved;
(ii) whether the mode of death results in distortion or mutilation of the body;
(iii) how information about the death reaches the bereaved;
(iv) what the relations between the two parties were during the weeks and days immediately prior to the death;
(v) to whom, if anyone, responsibility seems on the face of it to be assignable.

Let us consider each.

(i) Whereas a sudden death can be a great shock to a survivor and contribute to certain kinds of psychological difficulty, prolonged disabling illness can be a great burden and so contribute to other kinds of psychological difficulty. As a result of his comparison of twenty Boston widows whose mourning had progressed unfavourably with those of a matched sample of widows who had progressed well Maddison (1968) concluded that 'a protracted period of dying . . . may maximize pre-existing ambivalence and lead to pronounced feelings of guilt and inadequacy'. The situation is made especially difficult when the physical condition of the patient leads to intense pain, severe mutilation or other distressing features, and also when the brunt of the nursing falls on a single member of the family. In the latter type of case, in which the survivor has over a long period devoted time and attention to nursing a sick relative, she may find herself left without role or function after the loss has occurred.

(ii) Inevitably, the state of the body when last seen will affect the memories of a bereaved person either favourably or unfavourably. There are many records of bereaved people being haunted by memories or dreams of a lost person whose body was mutilated in some way; see for example Yamomoto and others (1969). In the Harvard study it was found that the widows and widowers interviewed were appreciative of the cosmetic efforts of the undertakers.

(iii) Knowledge of a death can reach bereaved people in a number of different ways. They may be present when death occurs or soon afterwards, or they may be informed of it by someone else and never see the body. Or news of it may be kept from them. There seems little doubt that the more direct the knowledge the less tendency is there for disbelief that death has occurred to persist. Disbelief is made much easier when death has occurred at a distance and also when information is conveyed by strangers. Finally, it is only natural that, when news of a death has been kept secret, as it often is from children, a belief that the dead person is still living and will return, either sooner or later, should be both vivid and persistent. There is abundant evidence that faulty or even false information at the time of the death is a major determinant of an absence of conscious grieving.

(iv) During the weeks and days immediately prior to a death relationships between the bereaved and the person who dies can range from intimate and affectionate to distant and hostile. The former give rise to comforting memories; the latter to distressing ones. Naturally the particular pattern that a relationship takes during this short period of time reflects in great part the pattern that the relationship has taken earlier; and this in its turn is a product of the personality of the bereaved interacting with that of the deceased. These are complex matters to be dealt with later; here emphasis is put on events that occur during only a very limited period.

For example, it is especially distressing when a death is preceded, perhaps by only hours or days, by a quarrel in which hard words were said. Raphael (1975) refers to the intense guilt felt by a woman who, a mere two days before her husband's unexpected death, had had a quarrel during which she had actively considered leaving him and had felt like murdering him. Similarly, Parkes (1972, pp. 135–6) describes the persistent and bitter resentment of a widow[4] whose husband had had a stroke some years before he died which had left him dependent on his wife's ministrations. Each had criticized the other for not doing enough and, in a fit of anger, he had expressed the wish that she have a stroke too. Shortly afterwards he died suddenly. A year later she was still angrily justifying her behaviour towards him and on occasion complained of symptoms resembling his. On a much lesser scale, the mourning of the Tikopian chief for the son with whom he had quarrelled, described by Firth and referred to in Chapter 8, will be recalled.

At the opposite end of the spectrum are those deaths in which both parties are together beforehand, are able to share with each other their feelings and thoughts about the coming separation and to pay loving farewells. This is an experience that can enrich both and which, it must be remembered, can either be greatly facilitated by the attitudes and help of professional workers or else made far more difficult by them. Measures that can give help to dying people and their relatives are discussed in a new book by Parkes (in preparation).

(v) Sometimes the circumstances of a death are such that the common tendency to blame someone for it is significantly increased. For example, a spouse or a parent may have delayed calling for medical help for much longer than was wise; conversely, response to such a call may have been tardy or inadequate in the extreme. In some cases of accident or illness the person who died may have been

[4] Parkes designates this widow as Mrs Q, but to avoid duplication of letters I am describing her as Mrs Z. A fuller account of Mrs Z's marriage is given in Chapter 11.

a major contributor to it; for example, by dangerous driving or excessive smoking or drinking, or by an adamant refusal to seek medical care. In other cases it is the bereaved who may have played a significant part, either in causing an accident or perhaps by having been the person whom the one who lost his life was attempting to rescue. In all such cases there is a feeling that the death need never have occurred, and anger at the dead person, or at the self, or at third parties is greatly exacerbated.

Death by Suicide

Death by suicide is a special case in which death is felt to be unnecessary and the tendency to apportion blame is likely to be enormously increased. On the one hand, the dead person can be blamed for having deliberately deserted the bereaved; on the other, one or other of the relatives can be held responsible for having provoked his action. Very often blame is laid on close kin, especially on the surviving spouse. Others to be implicated are parents, particularly in the case of suicide by a child or adolescent; sometimes also a child is blamed by one parent for the suicide of the other. Those who mete out such blame are likely to include both relatives and neighbours; and not infrequently the surviving spouse blames him or herself, perhaps for not having done enough to prevent the suicide or even for having encouraged it. Such self-reproach may be exacerbated by allegations made by a person before he commits suicide that he is being driven to it. This may not be fanciful. Raphael and Maddison (1976) report the case of a woman who, a few weeks before her husband's death, had separated from him telling him to go out and kill himself. This he did by using the car exhaust to gas himself.

With such high potential for blame and guilt it is hardly surprising that death by suicide may leave an appalling train of psychopathology extending not only to the immediate survivors but to their descendants as well. A number of clinicians are now alert to these pathogenic sequences and there is a growing literature, much of it brought together by Cain (1972). The articles illustrate in vivid detail the psychosocial hazards that survivors of suicide may face. Relatives and neighbours, instead of being helpful, may shun them and overtly or covertly hold them to blame. For their part the survivors, who may for long have had emotional difficulties, are tempted to challenge the verdict, to suppress or falsify what happened, to make scapegoats of others, or to devote themselves fanatically to social and political crusades in an attempt to distract themselves from what happened and to repair the damage. Alternatively, they may be beset by a nagging self-reproach and preoccupied by suicidal thoughts of their own. In the ensuing turmoil children are likely to be misinformed, enjoined to silence and blamed; in addition, they may be seen and treated as having inherited mental imbalance and so doomed to follow the suicidal parent. Further discussion of these tragic consequences is to be found in Chapter 22.

Nevertheless, as Cain is the first to realize, those seen in clinics represent only the disturbed fraction of the survivors and in order to obtain a more balanced picture we need information from a follow-up of a representative sample. A start has been made in a recent study of how the spouses of forty-four suicides fared during the five years after their bereavement undertaken by Shepherd and Barraclough (1974). Considering the number of circumstantial variables affecting direction and intensity of blame, and other factors as well, it is not surprising that those bereaved by suicide are found to be affected in extremely diverse ways.

Working in a county of southern England Shepherd and Barraclough followed up the 17 widowers and 27 widows concerned and obtained information about them all. Ages varied from eighty-one down to twenty-two, and the length of time they had been married from 49 years to a mere nine months. Almost all of them had already been interviewed once soon after the spouse's death, as part of a study of the clinical and social precursors of suicide. When followed up some five years later it was found that ten had died, two were ill (and relatives were seen instead), and one refused further interview.

The number of deaths (10) was higher than would be expected, not only when the comparison is made with married people (expected number 4·4) but also when it is made with those widowed in other ways (6·3). The latter difference (with a likelihood of occurring by chance of about 10 per cent) is such to suggest that the death rate of those widowed by suicide may well be higher than those widowed in other ways. None of the ten deaths had been from suicide; but many of the survivors reported suicidal preoccupations.

Of the survivors 31 were interviewed by social workers. Using a questionnaire, interviews averaged about an hour but varied from twenty minutes to over three hours.

When the present psychological condition of the spouse was compared with what it was judged to have been before the suicide it was found that half were rated as better and the other half as worse (14 better, 14 worse and 3 not determined). Many of those now better off had had very difficult marriages, attributed to the personality difficulties of the spouse which included alcoholism, violence and hypochondria. Once the shocks of the suicide and the inquest were over release from such a marriage had been a relief. Of these, seven had remarried, all but one of whom had been under the age of 38 at the time of bereavement. Conversely, some of those whose condition was now worse than formerly had been happily married and had been deeply distressed by the spouse's unexpected suicide, presumably the outcome of a sudden and severe depression in an otherwise effective personality. In one case of this kind the widow felt blamed by her husband's relatives and had retreated into a limited social life. Nevertheless it is interesting to note that she could still take pleasure in recalling activities in which she had engaged with her husband in earlier days. Here it is necessary to distinguish between the impoverished life that may be the outcome of a bereavement and the ill effects of mourning when it takes a pathological course.

In this series men and women had similar outcomes. Contrary to some other findings, younger spouses (average age 40) did significantly better than older ones (average age 53). Another variable found to be associated with better outcome was a favourable response to the first research interview which had been conducted soon after the suicide. Of 28 who took part in both interviews, the fifteen who reported that they had been helped by the first interview also had a better outcome. There are at least three ways in which this finding could be interpreted. One is that, as the authors note, it is possible that some, having fared well later, were disposed to look back through rosy spectacles. Another is that a favourable response to such an interview, whilst real enough, occurs only in those who are destined for a reasonably good outcome in any case. A third is that the research interview was in fact a helpful experience and in some degree influenced the course of mourning for the better. The findings of studies done in Australia, to be reported in the next section, tend to support both the second and the third of these interpretations.

Multiple Stressors

It happens on occasion that a bereaved person loses more than one close relative or friend either in the same catastrophe or within a period of a year or so. Others are confronted by the high risk of another such loss, for example by serious illness or by emigration of a grown child; or they may meet with some other incident felt to be stressful. Several workers, for example Maddison, both in his Boston study (Maddison 1968) and in Sydney (Maddison, Viola and Walker 1969) and Parkes in London (Parkes 1970a), have had the impression that widows subjected to such multiple crises fare worse than do those who are not. Nevertheless, although this finding would hardly be a surprising one, it has only recently been supported by firm evidence.

There is in fact a serious methodological difficulty in determining what should count as a stressor and what should not. Circularity of argument is easy. This is a problem tackled by Brown and Harris (1978a), who have adopted a method whereby the stressfulness of each event is evaluated independently of how the particular person subjected to it may have responded, or may claim to have responded. The findings of their study of life events that precede the onset of a depressive disorder, in which they used this method, support the view that persons subjected to multiple stressors are more likely to develop a disorder than are those not so subjected (see Chapter 14). In any further studies of this problem it is desirable that this method of evaluating life events should be adopted.

Social and psychological circumstances affecting the bereaved

There is now substantial evidence that certain of the social and psychological circumstances that affect a bereaved person during the year or so after a loss can influence the course of mourning to a considerable degree. Although some such circumstances cannot be changed others can. In that fact lies hope that, with better understanding of the issues, effective help to bereaved people can be provided.

It is convenient to consider this group of variables under the following three heads, each with a pair of sub-heads:

(i) *Living arrangements*
 – whether a bereaved person is living with other adult relatives or alone;
 – whether he or she is responsible for young or adolescent children.

187

(ii) *Socio-economic provisions and opportunities*
- whether the economic circumstances and housing arrangements make for an easier or more difficult life;
- whether or not opportunities exist which facilitate organizing a new way of social and economic life.

(iii) *Beliefs and practices facilitating or impeding healthy mourning*
- whether culturally determined beliefs and practices facilitate healthy mourning or impede it;
- whether relatives, friends and others facilitate healthy mourning or impede it.

Living Arrangements

Not surprisingly there is a tendency for widows and widowers who are living alone after bereavement to fare worse than those living with others. For example Clayton (1975) in her study of elderly people found that a year after bereavement 27 per cent of those living alone were showing symptoms of depression compared to 5 per cent of those living with others. A higher proportion also were still using hypnotics (39 per cent and 14 per cent respectively). In the case of the London widows Parkes reports trends in the same direction. He warns, however, that whilst social isolation may well contribute to depression a mourner who is depressed may also shun social exchange. Thus the causal chain may run in either direction and can readily become circular, in either a better or a worse direction.

Whereas living with close relatives who are grown up is associated with a better outcome for widows and widowers, living with younger children for whom responsibility must be taken is not. This conclusion is reached both by Parkes (1972) as a result of his London study and by Glick *et al.* (1974) from the findings of their Boston study. In the latter there were forty-three widows who had children to care for and seven who did not. No differences in outcome were found between the two groups, a result not difficult to explain.

In both studies it was found that responsibility for the care of children was both a comfort and a burden so that the advantages and disadvantages were evenly balanced. Those with children firmly believed that having children had given them something to live for, had kept them busy, and had been of substantial benefit to them during their first year of bereavement. Yet a closer examination of their lives showed the difficulties they had had in caring for the children single-handed and the extent to which it had restricted their opportunities to construct a new life for themselves. No less than half reported that the children had behaved in ways that were of major concern to them. Several described how presence of husband gives a woman a sense of security in dealing with her children and enables her to be tolerably consistent and how after becoming a widow they had found themselves uncertain and insecure. Some became unduly authoritarian, others too lax, and others again inclined to oscillate. Whether successful or not, almost all were unsure what would be best for the children and constantly worried lest they develop badly.

Presence of children to care for had the effect also of limiting a widow's opportunities for developing a new life for herself. Because widows with children wished to be at home both before the children went off to school and also when they returned, and suitable part-time work was scarce, most of them postponed starting work. Furthermore, because they did not wish to leave children at home alone and baby-sitters were expensive, they declined social invitations and also were unable to attend evening classes.

No more need be said about the problems facing the widowed mother of young children. Plainly there is here a social and mental health problem of magnitude for the solution of which much thought is needed.

Socio-economic Provisions and Opportunities

The social problem is how best to provide both for the widow's welfare and also for the children's and not to sacrifice one for the other. Adequate economic provision is obviously of importance and the same is true of accommodation. Special attention needs to be given to the provision of part-time work and also to training schemes with times consistent with caring for pre-school and school-age children.[5] By providing a widow with such opportunities, economic problems are at least reduced and her chances of reconstructing her social life improved. Yet, exceedingly desirable though these provisions are, and extremely helpful though they would be

[5] In the U.K. these problems were considered by the Royal Commission on One Parent Families whose report makes many recommendations (Finer Report, H.M.S.O. 1974).

to widows capable of responding to them, in and of themselves they would not influence greatly the incidence of disordered mourning since the most weighty determinants almost certainly lie elsewhere.

Beliefs and Practices Facilitating or Impeding Healthy Mourning

As we saw in Chapter 8, almost every society has its own beliefs and practices which regulate the behaviour of mourners. Since beliefs and practices vary in many ways from culture to culture and religion to religion, it might be expected that they would have an influence on the course of mourning, either promoting a healthy outcome or else, perhaps, contributing to a pathological one. A student of the problem who has expressed firm views on their importance is Gorer (1965) who was struck by the almost complete absence in contemporary Britain of any agreed ritual and guidance. Left without the support of sanctioned customs, bereaved people and their friends are bewildered and hardly know how to behave towards each other. That, he felt, could only contribute to unhappiness and pathology.

Another social anthropologist who in recent years has expressed a similar view is Ablon (1971), who has studied a close-knit Samoan community resident in California. In this community almost everyone lives within an extended family and a key value is reciprocity, especially of support in time of crisis. Thus, following a death, there is an immediate rallying of kin and friends who, with efficiency born of established practice, take the burdens of making decisions and arrangements from the shoulders of spouse, or parents or children, console the grieving and care for orphans. Ritual includes both Christian ceremonies and also traditional exchanges of goods and donations, in all of which family network and mutual support are emphasized and prominent. In this type of community, Ablon believes, disabling grief syndromes hardly occur. Nevertheless, although their incidence may well be reduced, her evidence shows that in certain circumstances they still do occur.

In her study Ablon made follow-up visits to a number of families whose members had suffered bereavement or major injury in a fire which had occurred during a Samoan dance five years earlier, and which had resulted in 17 deaths and many injured. Of about sixty families affected she visited 18. From the information she was able to obtain, she formed the impression that the Samoans, both as individuals and as family groups, had 'absorbed the disaster amazingly well'. She instances three young widows who had all remarried and were living full and active lives; and a fourth, in her forties and with six children, who had built up a successful business. Yet Ablon's sample was small and included, as well as those doing well, the two women who had lost adopted children and whose conditions were unmistakably those of disordered mourning. These findings call in question the theory that cultural practices alone can account for the course that mourning takes in different individuals.

Evidence from other studies raises the same issue. For example, neither in Parkes's London study nor in the Harvard study did the religious affiliation of the widows and widowers bear any clear relation to the pattern of outcome.

Reflection on the ambiguity of these findings suggests that the cultural variable is too crude a one for understanding the influence of beliefs and practices on the course of mourning. For example, although the negative findings in London and Boston may have been due to the religious sub-samples in each study having been too small to yield significant differences, it is also possible that within each religious group, and also within the non-affiliated, variations of belief and practice were as great as they were between groups. That this may be the explanation is supported by Ablon's finding that both the two Samoan women whose mourning had taken a pathological course were culturally atypical in regard to family life. Though divorce was not common among Samoans of their age, both had been divorced and were in their second marriages. Each had only one other child and neither lived in an extended family. These exceptions to Ablon's thesis may therefore point to where the rule lies.

When we turn to consider influences that are operating at an intimate personal level within the broader culture we find strong evidence that families, friends and others play a leading part either in assisting the mourning process or in hindering it. This is a variable to which clinicians have for long drawn attention (e.g. Klein 1940; Paul 1966) and on which Maddison, who worked for a time with Caplan at Harvard but whose work has been mainly in Australia, has focused attention.

Under Maddison's leadership three studies have been carried out aimed to elucidate the influence on the course of mourning of relatives, friends and other people. The first was conducted in Boston (Maddison and Walker 1967; Maddison 1968), the second and third in Sydney (Maddison, Viola and Walker 1969; Raphael 1976, 1977). The first two were retrospective, and so have deficiencies; the third which was prospective makes good many of them.

Both of the retrospective studies were carried out in the same way. The first step was to send questionnaires seeking information about physical and mental health to a large sample of widows in Boston (132) and in Sydney (243) thirteen months after their loss (see Chapter 6 for details). The 57 questions referring to health were so structured that the only scoring items were those which recorded complaints that were either new or had been substantially more troublesome since the loss. On the basis of their answers, together with a check by telephone, widows in each study were divided into three groups: those whose health record appeared favourable, those whose record indicated a substantial deterioration in health, and an intermediate group which was not further considered. The numbers and percentages of widows in each group are shown in Table 2.

TABLE 2 *Deterioration in health*

| | Numbers | | Percentages | |
	Boston	Sydney	Boston	Sydney
None	57	77	43	32
Moderate	47	88	36	36
Marked	28	78	21	32
Total	132	243	100	100

The second stage of each study began by selecting sub-samples of widows (a) with favourable outcome and (b) with unfavourable outcome, matched as closely as possible on all social and personal variables on which data were available. In the Boston study 20 pairs of widows were identified as willing to take part in further enquiry; in the Sydney study 22 good-outcome widows were matched with 19 bad-outcome.

All subjects were seen, usually in their own homes, in a long semi-structured interview which lasted on average two hours. The aims were to check on the validity of the questionnaire (which proved a good index of how a person is coping with the emotional problems of bereavement) and, more especially, to investigate who had been available to each widow during the bereavement crisis and whether she had found them helpful, unhelpful or neither. Further questions

were directed to finding out whether she had found it easy or difficult to express her feelings to each person mentioned, whether
or not he had encouraged her to dwell on the past, whether he had
been eager to direct her attention to problems of the present and
future, and whether he had offered practical help. Since the object
of the enquiry was to find out only how the widows themselves
recalled their dealings with others, no attempt was made to check
how their accounts might have tallied with those of the people with
whom they had been in contact.

First, it was found in both cities that all the widows, irrespective
of outcome, tended to report a good deal of helpful interaction. In
each city, nevertheless, there was a marked difference between
widows with a good outcome and those with a bad outcome in their
reports of unhelpful interactions. Whereas those with a good outcome reported having met with few or no unhelpful interactions,
those with a bad outcome complained that, instead of being allowed
to express their grief and anger and to talk about their dead husband
and the past, some of the people they had met had made expression
of feeling more difficult. For example, someone might have insisted
that she pull herself together and control herself, that in any case
she was not the only one to suffer, that weeping does no good and
that she would be wise to face the problems of the future rather
than dwell unproductively on the past. By contrast, a widow with a
good outcome would report how at least one person with whom she
had been in contact had made it easy for her to cry and to express
the intensity of her feelings; and would describe what a relief it had
been to be able to talk freely and at length about past days with her
husband and the circumstances of his death. Irrespective of outcome no widow had found discussion of future plans at all helpful
during the early months.[6]

The individuals with whom a widow had been in contact had

---

[6] A difference in the findings between the cities was that in Boston but
not in Sydney widows with a bad outcome felt that many of their emotional needs had gone unmet; these were especially their need for encouragement and understanding to help them express grief and anger
and their need for opportunities to talk about their bereavement at length
and in detail. By contrast, those with a good outcome expressed no such
unmet needs. (Note: In Volume I of this work, Chapter 8, it is pointed
out that the term 'need' is ambiguous and is to be avoided. In the context
in which Maddison uses the term, it is synonymous with desire.)

usually included both relatives and professionals, for example the medicals who had cared for her husband and also her own doctor, a minister of religion and a funeral director. In some cases a neighbour or shopkeeper had played a part. Some widows reported how they had received much more understanding of their feelings from such local acquaintances than they had from relatives or professionals who in some cases, they said, had been hostile to any expression of grief. In some cases the husband's mother had created substantial difficulties either by claiming or implying that the widow's loss was of less consequence than her own or else by blaming the widow for having taken insufficient care of her husband or for some comparable shortcoming.

A person of obvious importance during bereavement is a widow's own mother, should she still be alive and available. Some particulars are given for the Boston widows. Since a majority of them were middle-aged, in only twelve of the forty was the mother available. Where the relationship had long been a mutually gratifying one the mother's support seemed to have been invaluable and progress was good. Where, by contrast, relationships had been difficult mourning was impeded: all four widows who described their mothers as having been unhelpful proceeded to a bad outcome. Though the sample is small, a one-to-one correlation between a widow's relationship with her mother and the outcome of her mourning is striking and unlikely to be due to chance. Its relevance to an understanding of persons disposed towards a healthy or a pathological response to loss respectively cannot be overemphasized and is considered further in later chapters.

There is, of course, more than one way of interpreting Maddison's findings—as there was in the case of widows and widowers whose spouses had committed suicide and who referred to the first research interview as having been helpful. Here again a widow may retrospectively have distorted her experiences; or she may have attributed to relatives and others her own difficulties in expressing grief; or the behaviour of those with whom she had come into contact may indeed have contributed significantly to her problems. In any one case two or even all three of these processes might have been at work. Nevertheless Maddison himself, whilst recognizing the complexities of the data, tends to favour the third interpretation, namely, that the experiences reported are both real and influential in determining outcome. This interpretation is strongly supported by the findings of a prospective study carried out subsequently in Maddison's department in Sydney by Raphael.

Evidence from therapeutic intervention

Utilizing methods similar to those used in Maddison's earlier studies and drawing both on his findings and on some pilot work of her own, Raphael (1977) set out to test the efficacy of therapeutic intervention when given to widows whose mourning seemed likely to progress badly. Procedure was as follows:

Criteria for the sample were to include any widow under the age of sixty who had been living with her husband and who could be contacted within seven weeks of bereavement and was willing to participate. Such widows, who were first contacted when they applied for a pension, were invited by the clerk to take part in a study being conducted in the Faculty of Medicine of Sydney University and were provided with a card to post there should they be willing to do so. Altogether nearly two hundred volunteers were enlisted. For administrative reasons it proved impossible, unfortunately, to discover how many of the widows approached decided not to participate and how they might have differed from those who volunteered. The latter were visited in their own homes by an experienced social worker who first explained the project and the proposed procedure in order to obtain consent and then engaged the widow in a long interview.

Altogether 194 widows agreed to participate. Ages ranged from 21 to 59 years with a mean of 46; 119 had children aged 16 or younger. Since only those who believed themselves eligible for a pension were contacted, three-quarters or more were from the lower half of the socio-economic scale.

The purpose of the long interview was to obtain enough information about the widow, her marriage, the circumstances of her loss and her experiences since, to enable a prediction to be made as to whether her mourning was likely to proceed favourably or unfavourably. The principal criterion for predicting an unfavourable outcome was the frequent reporting by a widow of unhelpful interventions by relatives and others and of needs that had gone unmet. The following are examples of the experiences they reported:

'When I wanted to talk about the past, I was told I should forget about it, put it out of my mind.'

'I wanted to talk about how angry I was but they said I shouldn't be angry . . .'

'When I tried to say how guilty I felt, I was told not to be guilty, that I'd done everything that I should, but they did not really know.'

A widow whose normal protest and sadness had been treated with large quantities of tranquillizers remarked—

'I felt bad because I couldn't weep: it was as though I was in a strait-jacket . . .'

Among additional criteria used to predict an unfavourable outcome were exposure to multiple crises and a marriage judged to have taken a pathological form. Details are given in a footnote.[7]

[7] Assessment interviews were conducted in as spontaneous and open-ended a manner as possible and usually lasted several hours. An interview schedule was used to cover six types of information: (a) demographic, (b) a description of the causes and circumstances of the death leading to a discussion of feelings aroused by it, (c) a description of the marriage, (d) the occurrence of concurrent bereavements and other major life changes, (e) the extent to which relatives, professional personnel and others had been found supportive or not, (f) completion of a checklist of such interchanges which can be scored as having been present or absent, and, if present, whether found helpful, unhelpful or neither, and, if absent, whether an interchange of that kind had been desired or not. Since most widows were very willing to discuss their experiences, most of this information was obtained spontaneously. When it was not, the interviewer raised relevant points, remarking that there were things which other women had experienced following bereavement and querying whether they might also apply to the widow being interviewed.

Outcome was predicted as likely to be unfavourable when interview data showed that one or more of the following criteria were met:

1. ten or more examples of the widow feeling that interchanges had been unhelpful or that her needs had gone unmet;
2. six or more examples of a widow feeling that interchanges had been unhelpful combined with a mode of death judged to have been stressful to the bereaved;
3. the widow had suffered one or more additional stressors within three months, before or after, her loss;
4. there was a combination of a stressful mode of death, a marriage judged to have been pathological in form and the widow felt that at least one of her needs had gone unmet.

Criterion 1 was derived from the answers scored on the check list used during the assessment interview. The reliability of judgements made when applying criteria 2, 3 and 4 was tested and proved satisfactory for

On the basis of the information obtained, widows were allocated to one of two groups: Group A those whose outcome was predicted as good and Group B those whose outcome was predicted as bad. No differences were found between widows in the two groups in regard to age, number of children or socio-economic class. Those in Group B were then allocated at random to one of two sub-groups: B1, those who would be offered counselling and B2 those who would not. Numbers falling into the three groups were:

$$
\begin{array}{lr}
\text{Group A} & 130 \\
\text{B1} & 31 \\
\text{B2} & \underline{33} \\
\textit{Total} & 194
\end{array}
$$

Thirteen months after bereavement all widows were invited to complete the same health questionnaire that Maddison had used in his earlier studies. Scored by the same methods as formerly, it was then possible to determine what the outcome had been for widows in each of the three groups. Those whose health had deteriorated substantially were contrasted with the remainder. (In 16 cases follow-up was not practicable so that the three groups were reduced in numbers to 122, 27 and 29 respectively.) Results are summarized in Table 3.

When the outcomes of those in the two groups not given counselling (Groups A and B2) are compared it is found that the predictions

TABLE 3 *Outcome 13 months after bereavement*

Group	Prediction at assessment	Counselling	Nos. followed up	Outcome % Good	% Bad
A	Good	No	122	80	20
B1	Bad	Yes	27	78	22
B2	Bad	No	29	41	59

Comparison of Group A and Group B1	Not significant
,, ,, ,, A and Group B2	$P < \cdot 001$
,, ,, ,, B1 and Group B2	$P < \cdot 02$

judgements of the occurrence of additional stressors and also of a pathological form of marriage. (Correlations of the judgements of three independent judges for these criteria were 95 per cent.) Reliability of judgements for mode of death was not satisfactory however (correlation 65 per cent).

Rather more than half those predicted as likely to have a bad outcome were selected by applying criterion 1 were reasonably accurate and very much better than chance. In addition, when the outcomes of those in Group B1 (with an unfavourable initial prediction but given counselling) are compared with the outcomes of the other two groups it is clear, first, that the outcomes of Group B1 are virtually as good as they are for those in Group A (whose outcomes were predicted as good from the start) and, secondly, that the outcomes of Group B1 are significantly better than those of Group B2 whose predicted outcomes were also unfavourable but who received no counselling. A check on the possibility that the latter result was due to the widows in Group B1 having differed in some significant way from those in Group B2 showed that there were in fact no relevant differences between the groups.

Widows in the counselled Group B1 showed a lower incidence of depression, anxiety, excessive alcohol intake and certain psychosomatic symptoms than did widows in the non-counselled Group B2.

The conclusion that counselling is in some degree effective is strongly supported by internal evidence derived from a detailed study of the 27 widows in the counselled group, 21 of whom did well and six of whom did badly. First, it was found that those who made best use of the counselling sessions had a significantly better outcome than those of the group who did not; thus, of the six who went on to a bad outcome four had given up the sessions early. Secondly, there was a high correlation between those who were judged by an independent rater to have proceeded successfully towards healthy mourning during the weeks of counselling and a favourable outcome at thirteen months.

Although these findings point clearly to the efficacy of the techniques of counselling used, it should be borne in mind that all the subjects were volunteers. Whether or not the same techniques would have been efficacious with those who did not volunteer and who in the event went on to a bad outcome remains unknown.

A second conclusion is that the criteria used in the study for predicting outcome are valid, at least within certain limits.[8] Yet here

[8] Of the four criteria used the most highly predictive of bad outcome was criterion 1 (ten or more examples of a widow having felt either that interchanges had been unhelpful or that her needs had gone unmet). Criterion 1 was also related to the efficacy of counselling: widows whose bad outcome had been predicted on the basis of that criterion proved to be those most helped.

again qualifications are necessary. Amongst the 122 volunteers predicted to have a good outcome, one in five nevertheless progressed badly. Furthermore, it is possible that some of the others whose condition thirteen months after bereavement was reported to be good (as predicted) may have been individuals who were inhibiting grief and so would have been prone to break down later. Against this possibility, however, is Raphael's belief (personal communication) that few such individuals were likely among the volunteers, because it is in the nature of the condition that they would avoid participating in any enquiry which might endanger their defences.

Let us turn now to the techniques used by Raphael in her project. They derive from techniques pioneered by Caplan (1964) for use in any form of crisis intervention.

Within one week of a widow being interviewed and assessed as likely to have a bad outcome and having been allocated to the intervention group, the counsellor (Dr Raphael) called on the widow or made telephone contact. Linking her intervention to the problems the widow had described in the assessment interview, assistance was offered. If accepted, as it was by the majority, a further call was arranged. All further sessions took place within the first three months of bereavement and were confined, therefore, to a period of about six weeks. Almost all took place in the widow's own house and usually lasted two hours or longer. When appropriate, children, other members of the family and neighbours were included. The number and frequency of sessions varied according to need and acceptability but were never more frequent than weekly.[9] In every case the aim of a session was to facilitate the expression of active grieving—sadness, yearning, anxiety, anger and guilt.

Since the technique adopted by Raphael is similar to those now widely used in counselling the bereaved, it is described in a form that has general application.

As a first step it is useful to encourage a widow to talk freely and at length about the circumstances leading to her husband's death and her experiences after it. Later she can be encouraged to talk

[9] For the 31 widows who were offered counselling, interviews ranged from one to eight in number, with four as the most frequent. Of the 27 who were also followed up, ten had been interviewed at least once with dependent children present, and in several cases with other relatives or neighbours as well. With a further two subjects relatives or neighbours had been present on at least one occasion (personal communication).

about her husband as a person, starting perhaps from the time they first met and proceeding thence through their married life together, with all its ups and downs. Showing of photographs and other keepsakes, which is natural enough in the home setting, is welcomed. So also is the expression of feeling that has its origin in other and previous losses. During such sessions a tendency to idealize usually gives way to more realistic appraisal, situations that have aroused anger or guilt can be examined and perhaps reassessed, the pain and anxiety of loss given recognition. Whenever yearning and sadness seem to be inhibited or anger and guilt misdirected, appropriate questions may be raised. By thus giving professional help early in the mourning process it is hoped to facilitate its progress along healthy lines and to prevent either a massive inhibition or a state of chronic mourning becoming established.

The first point to be noted in considering Raphael's results is that the social interchanges encouraged by the technique adopted and that proved efficacious were exactly those that the widows had complained had not been provided or permitted by the relatives and others they had met. This finding strongly supports the view that a major variable in determining outcome is the response a widow receives from relatives, professional personnel and others when she begins to express her feeling.

The second point is a more general one. When expressed in terms of the theory of defence sketched in Chapter 4, a principal characteristic of the technique employed is to provide conditions in which the bereaved person is enabled, indeed encouraged, to process repeatedly and completely a great deal of extremely important information that hitherto was being excluded. In thus laying emphasis on information processing, I am drawing attention to an aspect of the technique that tends to be overlooked by theorists. For it is only when the detailed circumstances of the loss and the intimate particulars of the previous relationship, and of past relationships, are dwelt on in consciousness that the related emotions are not only aroused and experienced but become directed towards the persons and connected with the situations that originally aroused them.[10]

[10] A similar though more active technique, derived from the pioneer work of Paul and Grosser (1965) and applying the same principles, has been found effective in helping patients referred to a psychiatric clinic, presenting with a variety of clinical syndromes, whose illness had developed after a bereavement (Lieberman 1978). In this series as in many

With these findings in mind it becomes possible to consider afresh the question of what types of personality are prone to develop a disordered form of mourning. It becomes possible, too, to propose hypotheses regarding the family experiences they are likely to have had during childhood and adolescence and, thence, to frame a theory of the processes that underlie disordered mourning.

---

similar cases the symptoms had not usually been connected to the loss either by the referrer or by the initial psychiatric interviewer. See also the therapeutic technique used by Sachar *et al.* (1968) with a small group of depressed patients.

Personalities Prone to Disordered Mourning

Limitations of evidence

Thus far in our exposition conclusions have been underpinned by a considerable array of first-hand data, the fruits of systematic studies begun soon after a death had occurred. In this chapter, by contrast, we have no first-hand data and are dependent, instead, on second-hand reports that refer to earlier times. Furthermore these second-hand reports not only deal with extremely complex interactions between a person who, subsequently, has become bereaved and members of his immediate family but come mostly from the parties themselves. Since such reports, as we know (see Volume II, Chapter 20), are notoriously subject to omission, suppression and falsification, they must be treated with reserve. Despite these difficulties, however, it seems that certain patterns can be discerned and that, when examined and construed in terms of the theory sketched in earlier volumes, a set of plausible, interlocking and testable hypotheses emerge.

Evidence at present available strongly suggests that adults whose mourning takes a pathological course are likely before their bereavement to have been prone to make affectional relationships of certain special, albeit contrasting, kinds. In one such group affectional relationships tend to be marked by a high degree of anxious attachment, suffused with overt or covert ambivalence. In a second and related group there is a strong disposition to engage in compulsive caregiving. People in these groups are likely to be described as nervous, overdependent, clinging or temperamental, or else as neurotic. Some of them report having had a previous breakdown in which symptoms of anxiety or depression were prominent. In a third and contrasting group there are strenuous attempts to claim emotional self-sufficiency and independence of all affectional ties; though the very intensity with which the claims are made often reveals their precarious basis.

In this chapter we describe personalities of these three kinds, noting before we start that the features of personality to which we draw attention are different to those that most clinical instruments are designed to measure (e.g. introversion–extraversion, obsessional, depressive, hysterical) and not necessarily correlated with them. We note also how limited the data are on which our generalizations rest and the many qualifications that have to be made. Consideration both of the hypotheses that have been advanced, by psychoanalysts and others, to account for the development of personalities having these characteristics, and also of the childhood experiences that presently available evidence and present theory suggest are likely to play a major part, is deferred to the next chapter.

Disposition to make anxious and ambivalent relationships

From Freud onwards psychoanalysts have emphasized the tendency for persons who have developed a depressive disorder following a loss to have been disposed since childhood to make anxious and ambivalent relationships with those they are fond of. Freud describes such persons as combining 'a strong fixation to the love object' with little power of resistance to frustration and disappointment (*SE* 14, p. 249). Abraham (1924a) emphasizes the potential for anger: in someone prone to melancholia 'a "frustration", a disappointment from the side of the loved object, may at any time let loose a mighty wave of hatred which will sweep away his all too weakly rooted feelings of love' (p. 442). 'Even during his free intervals', Abraham notes, the potential melancholic is ready to feel 'disappointed, betrayed or abandoned by his love objects' (pp. 469–70). Rado (1928ab), Fenichel (1945), Anderson (1949), and Jacobson (1943) are among many others to write in the same vein.

The studies of Parkes, both in London (Parkes 1972) and in Boston (Parkes *et al.* in preparation), and also of Maddison (1968) give support to these views, though both authors emphasize how seriously inadequate their data are because obtained second hand and retrospectively.

In his second meeting (at three months) with the London widows whom he interviewed, Parkes asked each of them to rate the frequency with which quarrels had occurred between them and their husbands, using a four-point scale (never, occasionally, frequently and usually). Those who reported the most quarrelling were found likely, during their first year of bereavement, to be more tense at interview, more given to guilt and self-reproach and to report more physical symptoms, and at the end of the year to be more isolated, than those who reported little or no quarrelling. They were also less likely, during the weeks after their loss, to have experienced a comforting sense of their husband's presence. In addition Parkes found, not surprisingly, that there was a tendency for those who were most disturbed after the loss of their husband to describe having been severely disturbed by losses they had suffered earlier in their lives.

Findings of the Harvard study are comparable. In an attempt to assess the extent to which ambivalence had been present in their marriage, each widow and widower was asked a number of questions dealing with issues about which husbands and wives are apt to disagree. Both at the end of the first year and also at the follow-up two to four years after bereavement, those reporting many disagreements were doing significantly worse than were those who reported few or none. Problems described or assessed after the longer interval in a significantly higher proportion of those reporting many disagreements included: persistent yearning, depression, anxiety, guilt and poor physical health.[1]

Maddison (1968) reports similar findings. Among the twenty widows in his Boston sample whose mourning had taken an unfavourable course and who were willing to take part in intensive interviews there were several whose 'marriage had shown unequivocal sado-masochistic aspects'. In addition, 'there were several other women who gave a lengthy, sometimes virtually lifelong, history of overt neurotic symptoms or behaviour, which seemed

[1] The table below gives the proportions of each of the two groups who showed these features at the two- to four-year follow-up:

| | Group of Widows and Widowers | | |
	Many disagreements	Few or no disagreements	Value of P
	%	%	
Yearning	63	29	<0·05
Depression	45	14	<0·05
Anxiety	82	52	<0·05
Guilt	63	33	<·005
Fair to poor physical health	39	10	<0·05
N	38	21	

clearly related to their subsequent deterioration'. (Because of the unreliability of his data Maddison refrains from giving figures.)

An example of a widow who had had frequent quarrels with her husband over many years and whose mourning followed a bitter and angry course was Mrs Z, one of the widows in the Harvard study.[2]

Mrs Z was 45 when her husband died. They had been married for twenty-six years but their relationship had never been good. Mrs Z said that she had always been very fond of her husband but felt that he had never appreciated her or expressed very much real affection. This may have been due to his jealousy of her close relationship with the children but, according to a friend who knew them both well, her 'terrible temper' may also have contributed. At all events there were frequent quarrels. As Mrs Z put it, 'We were a passionate couple.'

Several years before his death Mr Z had a stroke. He had been an energetic, meticulous, and practical man and he found it particularly frustrating to be partially paralysed and dependent on his wife. He became querulous, complaining, and resentful, 'taking it out' on her and criticizing her unjustly. She 'pushed him' to do more and made plans for their future together but 'all he gave me was criticism and abuse.' Most painful of all, he frequently said that he hoped she would have a stroke too. She worried a great deal and complained of headaches which, she feared, might indicate that she had had a stroke. He died unexpectedly one night. When told that it was useless to continue mouth-to-mouth resuscitation since he was dead, Mrs Z would not believe it: 'I just couldn't take it in.' Then she collapsed and cried profusely in an agitated state for two days.

Over the next few weeks she remained distressed and agitated and matters were made worse when the will was read and she discovered that most of his property had been left in trust. She became very bitter and resentful, saying, 'What have I done to deserve this?' and spent a great deal of time trying to persuade doctors and lawyers to contest the will on the grounds of her husband's mental incapacity. When they refused to support her in this she became angry with them and, when interviewed, recited a long list of the people who, she felt, had rejected her.

Alongside this deep anger were strong feelings of guilt, but she was unable to explain these and spent much time justifying every aspect of her conduct towards her husband. She was restless and fearful, fidgeting and going from one task to another, unable to concentrate on any.

During the course of the following year she remained agitated and inclined to panic attacks. On several occasions she complained of symptoms

[2] This record is taken unchanged from Parkes (1972, pp. 135–7). To avoid duplication of letters I am designating this widow Mrs Z (instead of Mrs Q as in the original). A brief reference to the case is in Chapter 10.

resembling those her husband had suffered. She alienated friends and professional helpers by her aggressive attitude and demands for help.

She was given a variety of drugs by a psychiatrist and these helped a little; but thirteen months after bereavement she declared that she was no better than she had been a year previously. 'If only I was an ordinary widow—it's the bitterness and the will—the dreadful words. I go over it again and again thinking there must be a loop-hole.' Yet, 'if he could come back tomorrow I'd love him just the same'.

It seems evident from this account that it would be unfair to regard Mrs Z as wholly responsible for the chronic quarrelling that went on during this long marriage: her husband plainly made her worse. Yet it is evident that her contribution was large and that she felt that if she did not constantly stand up for herself, she would go to the wall. Referring to her battles over the will she remarked, 'I feel if I ever accepted what he has done to me I'd be destroyed— trampled underfoot.' As Parkes remarks, 'Her attitude to the world betrayed her fear of just this eventuality, and because hostility pro- vokes hostility she created a situation in which she was, in fact, repeatedly rejected by others.' This, he suspects, had been a lifelong attitude.

Disposition towards compulsive caregiving

Earlier in this volume (Chapter 9) it was noted that some individuals respond to loss or threat of loss by concerning themselves intensely and to an excessive degree with the welfare of others. Instead of experiencing sadness and welcoming support for themselves, they proclaim that it is someone else who is in distress and in need of the care which they then insist on bestowing. Should this pattern become established during childhood or adolescence, as we know it can be (see Chapters 12 and 21), that person is prone, throughout life, to establish affectional relationships in this mould. Thus he is inclined, first, to select someone who is handicapped or in some other sort of trouble and thenceforward to cast himself solely in the role of that person's caregiver. Should such a person become a parent there is danger of his or her becoming excessively possessive and protective, especially as a child grows older, and also of inverting the relation- ship (see Volume II, Chapter 18).

Clinical accounts make it clear that some of those who, after a loss in adult life, develop chronic mourning have for many years pre- viously exhibited compulsive caregiving, usually to a spouse or a

child. Descriptions of bereaved parents who may well have conformed to this pattern are those (described by Cain and Cain 1964,
and referred to in Chapter 9) who, after losing a child with whom
they had had a specially intense relationship, had insisted that the
'replacement' child should grow up to be an exact replica of the one
lost.

At least three examples of bereaved spouses who seem to conform
to this pattern are described by Parkes (1972) (though he himself
does not categorize them in this way). One is the case of Mr M (see
Chapter 9), who was said by a member of his family to have 'coaxed
and coddled' an anxious neurotic wife through forty-one years of
marriage and who had responded to her death by directing intense
reproach against himself, members of his family and others whilst
simultaneously idealizing his wife. A second is the case of Mrs J
(see Chapter 9) who had married a man 18 years her senior and who,
having lost him from lung cancer, had exclaimed angrily nine
months later, 'Oh, Fred, why did you leave me?' During the previous ten years or so after he had retired this pair seemed to have
lived exclusively for each other. He for his part had become totally
bound up with his home, his garden and his wife; and he had hated
it when she went out to work. Her own role she described in the
following words: 'Ten years ago he got ill . . . and I've had to look
after him . . . I felt I could preserve him . . . I gave into his every
whim, did everything for him . . . I waited on him hand and foot.' For
the last three years during his terminal illness she had given all her
time to nursing him at home.

A third example is the case of Mrs S.[3]

Mrs S was nearly fifty years old when interviewed in a psychiatric
hospital. Her *de facto* husband, with whom she had lived for eleven years,
had died nearly ten years earlier and ever since then she had been suffering chronic mourning. All the information came from herself.

During interview she described how she had been brought up abroad,
had been a sickly child, unhappy at school, and had been tutored by her
father for much of the time. Her mother, it appeared, had dominated and
fussed over her; and she had grown up nervous, timid and with a conviction that she was incompetent at all practical tasks. After leaving school
at seventeen she had remained at home for three years with her mother
and then had lived separately though still supported by her. Before she
left home she had found great satisfaction in caring for a sick child, and

[3] This account is a rewritten version of one given in Parkes (1972,
pp. 109–10 and 125–7).

later her principal occupation had been that of professional child-minder and baby-sitter.

At the age of 28 she had met a man twenty years her senior who was separated from his wife. He had been invalided out of the Navy and was having difficulty in settling down in civilian life. They proceeded to live together and she changed her name to his by deed poll. To her great regret she did not conceive a child; but, despite this and despite their having been very poor, Mrs S described this period as the best in her life.

The picture she gives of their relationship seems likely to be much idealized: 'From the first our relationship was absolutely ideal—everything—it was so right—he was so fine.' She found, she said, she could do lots of things she had never done before: 'I never feared anything with him. I could do new dishes . . . I didn't get that feeling of incompetence . . . I'd absolutely found myself.' Nevertheless, in spite of all these good features, she described how, throughout her marriage, she had been intensely anxious about the prospect of ever being separated from her husband.

For some years before his death Mr S had had a 'smoker's cough' which had worried his wife; and she became seriously alarmed when he had a sudden lung haemorrhage, for which he was in hospital for six weeks. Shortly after returning home he had lapsed into a coma and had died soon afterwards.

In recounting her grief, Mrs S insisted that she had 'never stopped crying for months'. 'For years I could not believe it, I can hardly believe it now. Every minute of the day and night I couldn't accept it or believe it.' She had stayed in her room with the curtains drawn: 'For weeks and weeks I couldn't bear the light.' She had tried to avoid things and places that would remind her of her loss: 'Everywhere, walking along the street I couldn't look out at places where we were happy together . . . I never entered the bedroom again . . . couldn't look at animals because we both loved them so much. Couldn't listen to the wireless.' Nevertheless, even after nine years, she still retained in her mind a very clear picture of her husband which she was unable to shut out: 'It goes into everything in life —everything reminds me of him.'

For a long time, she said, she used to go over in her mind all the events leading up to his death. She would agonize over minor omissions and ways in which she had failed him. Gradually, however, these preoccupations had lessened and she had tried to make a new life for herself. Yet she had found it difficult to concentrate and hard to get on with other people: 'They've got homes, husbands, and children. I'm alone and they're not.' She had tried to escape by much listening to recorded music and reading, but this had only increased her isolation.

At some time a friendly chaplain had advised her to seek psychiatric help but she had not done so; and, although she had been treated for bowel symptoms (spastic colon) by her general practitioner, she had not divulged her real problem. Eventually she had sought help from a voluntary organization and it was the people there who had finally persuaded her to see a psychiatrist.

In this account we note many of the same features that were prominent in Mr M and Mrs J. Like them, Mrs S seems to have devoted herself exclusively to caring for her spouse who, various clues suggest, may have been a rather inadequate man. Like them, too, she responded to her spouse's death by directing all her reproaches against herself while at the same time preserving an idealized picture of her husband and of their relationship.

In the cases of Mr M and Mrs J there are no data whatever that cast light on how or why they should have developed a disposition towards compulsive caregiving. In the case of Mrs S there is a distinct hint that a family pattern typical of school refusal may have been present during her childhood, but whether or not that is a legitimate inference must be left open. In any case we have information from other sources about the kinds of family experience that lead a person to develop along these lines, and this is considered in the next chapter as well as in Chapter 21.

Meanwhile, we note that in each of these three cases the pattern of marriage conforms closely to that described by Lindemann (in Tanner 1960, pp. 15–16) as having preceded some of the most severe examples of psychosomatic illness he had seen in bereaved people. These conditions had occurred, he states, 'in individuals for whom the deceased [had] constituted the one significant person in the social orbit, a person who [had] mediated most of the satisfactions and provided the opportunity for a variety of role functions', none of which were possible without him.

Patterns of Marriage Prevalent before Disordered Mourning

Looked at from one point of view the pattern of marriage of Mrs S (and also of Mr M and Mrs J), in which the relationship is idealized, and that of Mrs Z, in which there is constant quarrelling, seem poles apart. Yet, as Mattinson and Sinclair (1979) point out, they have more in common than meets the eye.

After having studied the form of interaction in a number of disturbed marriages Mattinson and Sinclair have concluded that many of them can be arranged along a continuum between two extreme patterns, which they term respectively a 'Cat and Dog' marriage and a 'Babes in the Wood' marriage. In the former the couple continually fight but do not separate. Neither trusts the other.

Whereas each partner tends to make strong demands for the other's love and support and to be angry when they are not met, each tends also to resent the demands made by the other and often to reject them angrily. Yet the couple are kept together for long periods by an intense and shared fear of loneliness. In a Babes in the Wood marriage, by contrast, all is peaceful. Each party claims he understands the other, that they are ideally suited, and perhaps even that they have achieved a perfect unity. Each clings intensely to the other.

Although overtly these two patterns are so very different, common features are not difficult to see. In both, each partner is intensely anxious lest he lose the other and so is apt to insist, or contrive, that the other gives up friends, hobbies and other outside interests. In one pattern conflict is present from the first and leads to a succession of quarrels and passionate reconciliations. In the other the very possibility of conflict is resolutely denied and each attempts to find all his satisfactions in an exclusive relationship, either by giving care to the other or by receiving it from the other, or by some combination of the roles.

In both patterns the partners may remain together for long periods of time. Nevertheless, each pattern is inherently unstable, very obviously so in the Cat and Dog marriage. In a marriage of mutual clinging the advent of a child may prove a serious threat; or one of the partners may, apparently suddenly, find the relationship stifling and withdraw. Should disruption occur, due either to desertion or death, the remaining partner is, as we have seen, acutely vulnerable and at serious risk of chronic mourning.

They are at risk too of attempting suicide and also of committing it. This emerges from a preliminary study by Parkes (in preparation) of the relatives of patients who had died in St Christopher's Hospice.[4] During a five-year period, five suicides, all by widows, were known to have occurred, four of them within five months of bereavement and the fifth two years later. The typical picture each presented was of having been 'immature' or clinging, of having had a very close relationship with her husband but of being on bad terms with other members of the family. In three there was a history of previous depressive disorder and/or of having been under psychiatric care. Since in the light of these findings high-risk individuals can be

[4] St Christopher's Hospice, in South London, is designed to provide humane terminal care for the dying and also support for the bereaved.

identified, preventive measures can be taken. These include caution in prescribing sedatives and tranquillizers, and agreement among potential caregivers as to who should undertake regular visiting.

Disposition to assert independence of affectional ties

Although it is certain that a number of those whose mourning progresses unfavourably are people who, before their loss, have been insistent on their independence of all affectional ties, our information about them is even less adequate than it is about the types of personality already considered. There are several reasons for this. First, it is in the nature of the condition that, to an external eye, their mourning should often appear to be progressing uneventfully. As a result, in all studies except those using the most sophisticated of methods, it is easy to overlook such people and to group them with those whose mourning is progressing in a genuinely favourable way. Secondly, and a source of potential error of probably far greater importance, is that individuals disposed to assert emotional self-sufficiency are precisely those who are least likely to volunteer to participate in studies of the problem. A third difficulty is that some individuals having this disposition have made such tenuous ties with parents, or a spouse or a child that, when they suffer loss, they are truly little affected by it. Among research workers whose findings we are drawing on, Parkes, Maddison and Raphael are all keenly alive to these problems; and it is for that very reason that they are so diffident about expressing firm views.

Some of the findings from Maddison's Boston study are nevertheless of much interest. Of the twenty widows interviewed whose mourning had taken an unmistakably unfavourable course, no less than nine were believed to have had a character structure of the kind under discussion. This suggests they may form a very substantial proportion of personalities prone to pathological mourning. Yet, it must also be noted that amongst the twenty widows in the comparison group whose mourning to all appearances had proceeded favourably, there were seven such women—a proportion nearly as high as that in the bad outcome group (Maddison 1968).

Reflection on these and similar findings suggests that individuals disposed strongly to assert their self-sufficiency fall on a continuum ranging from those whose proclaimed self-sufficiency rests on a precarious basis to those in whom it is firmly organized. Examples of several patterns are already given in Chapter 9. At the more precarious end of the scale is Mrs F; at the more organized end Mr AA. Others of the cases described can be ranged at various points in the middle.

Tentative conclusions

Before outlining some tentative conclusions it is necessary to note a difficulty to which Maddison (1968) and Wear (1963) amongst others have drawn attention. Occasionally a widow or widower is found who describes how various neurotic or psychosomatic symptoms from which she or he had formerly suffered have been alleviated since the spouse died. This finding is consonant with the findings of family psychiatrists which show how certain patterns of inter-action can have a seriously adverse effect on the mental health of one or more of a family's members. Some of those who have sur-vived a spouse's suicide and are subsequently improved in health (see Chapter 10) are other likely examples.

This finding, when taken in conjunction with other findings reported in this and previous chapters, points to a basic principle. In understanding an individual's response to a loss it is necessary to take account not only of the structure of that individual's per-sonality but also of the patterns of interaction in which he was engaging with the person now lost. For a large majority of people bereavement represents a change for the worse—either to a lesser or more frequently to a greater degree. But for a minority it is a change for the better. No simple correlation between pattern of personality and form of response to loss can therefore be expected.

Tentative conclusions are as follows:

(a) A majority, probably the great majority, of those who respond to a major bereavement with disordered mourning are persons who all their lives have been prone to form affectional relationships having certain special features. Included are individuals whose attachments are insecure and anxious and also those disposed towards compulsive caregiving. Included also are individuals who, whilst protesting emotional self-sufficiency, show plainly that it is precariously based. In all such persons relationships are likely to be suffused with strong ambivalence, either overt or latent.

(b) By no means all those biased to make affectional relationships of these sorts respond to a bereavement with disordered mourning. Some of those who proclaim their self-sufficiency are in fact relatively immune to loss; whilst the course of mourning of those who make anxious attachments or who engage in compulsive caregiving is likely to be influenced in a very substantial degree by the varied conditions described in the later sections of Chapter 10.

(c) Whether or not there are also individuals prone towards disordered forms of mourning whose personalities are organized on lines different from those so far described must be left an open question.

CHAPTER 12

Childhood Experiences of Persons Prone to Disordered Mourning

None of us can help the things life has done to us. They're done before you realise it, and once they're done they make you do other things until at last everything comes between you and what you'ld like to be, and you've lost your true self for ever.

EUGENE O'NEILL, *Long Day's Journey into Night*

Traditional theories

In Chapter 2, in a discussion of the development of psychoanalytic theories of mourning, we draw attention to eight areas about which there has been and still is controversy. Of these the eighth and last concerns the stage of development and the processes whereby an individual arrives at a state which enables him thereafter to respond to loss in a healthy manner. Traditionally, because of Freud's theory of libidinal stages and his classic paper linking mourning to melancholia, or depressive disorder as it would now be called, this question has always been considered in the context of trying to understand the fixation point to which depressive patients regress. In attempting to answer it, we note, most though not all psychoanalytic formulations postulate the stage as occurring in earliest infancy, and therefore carry with them the presumption that the capacity to respond to loss in a favourable manner should, if all goes well with development, be attained in this very early period. From this theoretical position a deduction that necessarily follows is that, if a child has developed favourably during the stated period, his response to a separation occurring later will be a healthy one. Thus, since all these hypotheses hold that the period in question (whether defined as a phase of orality, symbiosis, primary narcissism or primary identification, or as the one during which the depressive position is normally reached) occurs either before the first birthday or soon after it, each in effect predicts that a child who has developed favourably during that period will respond healthily to a loss sustained in the second, third or later years. This means that, in principle, these hypotheses are capable of empirical test.

Although the data from which we start (see Chapter 1) have not been collected with the purpose of testing hypotheses of this kind, in so far as our data bear on them they do not support them. Children whose previous development appears to have been reasonably favourable may nevertheless respond to a separation from mother occurring during the second, third and fourth years of life with mourning processes that have features typical of pathology; and whether the response is a pathological one or not appears to be determined in very high degree by the way a child is treated during the period of separation and after it (see Chapters 23 and 24). In adverse conditions both yearning for and reproach against the deserting mother become redirected and cognitively disconnected from the situation that elicited them and, as a result, remain active though more or less unconscious.[1] Although it would be extraordinary were previous development to be without any influence on the course of mourning at these ages, there is no evidence that it is as crucial as is required by each of the hypotheses in question. Furthermore, in later chapters evidence is presented that shows that events of later years, notably loss of mother before the tenth or eleventh birthday, when combined with certain other conditions can play a causal role in the development of depressive disorder.

Whether these conclusions are confirmed or not, traditional theory remains open to questioning on at least two other grounds. The first is the assumption that an hypothesis that is valid for depressive disorder is necessarily valid also for disordered mourning. The second and more serious point at which traditional theory is vulnerable concerns both the evidence and the reasoning which have led to the belief that depressive disorder is due always to a fixation having occurred during the first year. When these propositions are examined it is found that evidence for them is weak (Bowlby 1960b). As a result the belief, derived from them, that the main determinants of disordered mourning are operative during earliest development is ill-based.

It is of much interest, therefore, that within the central tradition of psychoanalytic thinking various alternative theories regarding

[1] In traditional terminology it would be said that yearning and reproach become displaced and repressed.

the developmental roots of depressive disorder, and by implication of disordered mourning also, are already implicit or explicit, for example in the work of Abraham (1924a), Gero (1936), Deutsch (1937), and Jacobson (1943).[2] In these studies loss of mother or of mother's love during childhood have been implicated. Furthermore, later studies of the childhood experiences of those who, during adult life, are prone to depression draw attention to a number of other forms of serious disturbance in a child's relation to his parents (usually but by no means always his mother).

The position adopted

It is time to make plain the position adopted in this work. It stems from an examination of several more or less independent sets of data, most of which are already reviewed in this volume or else in Volume II. These are as follows:

(a) evidence regarding the patterns of affectional relationships that persons prone to disordered mourning are biased to make (Chapter 11);

(b) evidence, derived from broader studies (reviewed in Volume II, Chapters 15–19), regarding the childhood experiences of persons whose affectional relationships tend to take the forms referred to in (a):

(c) evidence regarding the types of psychosocial conditions acting at the time of or after a loss that are found to influence the course of mourning either for better or for worse (this volume, Chapter 10);

(d) evidence regarding the psychological features that are found to characterize disordered mourning itself (this volume, Chapter 9);

(e) and, finally, such fragmentary evidence as we have regarding the childhood experiences of persons whose mourning has taken a pathological course (who overlap but are not identical with persons who have developed a depressive disorder). Again and again reports of those suffering disordered mourning refer to them as having been unwanted as children, to their having been subjected to separation from or loss of parent, or to their having

[2] For a comprehensive review of psychoanalytic thinking about depressive disorders, see Mendelson (1974).

had an unhappy or stressful childhood for some other reason.[3] Not infrequently details of these experiences are missing; yet, by making use of such information as we have and viewing it in the light of information from other sources, it is not difficult to propose what their nature may have been.

The hypotheses advanced here regarding the childhood experiences that predispose an individual towards a pathological response to loss are, it is held, both consistent with such evidence as we have from all these different fields and also capable of empirical test.

Before detailing hypotheses, however, it may be useful to remind the reader of the overall theoretical position adopted in this work (set out in earlier volumes, notably the final chapter of Volume II, 'Pathways for the Growth of Personality'), and to indicate how it applies to our problem:

(a) Disturbances of personality, which include a bias to respond to loss with disordered mourning, are seen as the outcome of one or more deviations in development that can originate or grow worse during any of the years of infancy, childhood and adolescence.

(b) Deviations result from adverse experiences a child has in his family of origin (or during substitute care), notably discontinuities in his relationships and certain ways in which parent-figures may respond, or fail to respond, to his desire for love and care.

(c) Deviations consist of disturbances in the way the attachment behaviour of the individual concerned becomes organized, usually in the direction either of anxious and insecure attachment or else of a vehement assertion of self-sufficiency.

(d) Although deviations, once established, tend to persist, they remain sensitive in some degree to later experience and, as a result,

---

[3] A recent study of the responses of analysands to the death of their analysts, by Lord, Ritvo and Solnit (1978), shows a strong association between a history of loss and deprivation during early childhood and disordered mourning. Of 27 patients studied, ten responded with 'complicated and prolonged mourning' and eleven with 'normal' mourning. All ten of the former group 'had been exposed to significant emotional deprivation, which included either actual or psychological abandonment, or both'. This contrasted with a much lower incidence of such experiences in those responding with normal mourning.

can change either in a more favourable direction or in an even less favourable one.

(e) Amongst types of later experience that can affect development favourably are any opportunities that arise that give the individual —child, adolescent or adult—a chance to make a relatively secure attachment, though whether he can make use of such opportunities turns both on the way his attachment behaviour is already organized and on the nature of the relationship that is currently offered.

We turn now to the relevant childhood experiences found as antecedents of the three patterns of vulnerable personality described in the previous chapter: personalities exhibiting anxious and ambivalent attachments; personalities disposed towards compulsive caregiving; and personalities assertive of independence of all affectional ties.

Experiences disposing towards anxious and ambivalent attachment

The childhood experiences of persons prone to make anxious and ambivalent attachments are considered at length in Chapters 15 to 19 of Volume II. Evidence is presented that individuals of this sort are far more likely than are those who grow up secure to have had parents who, for reasons stemming from their own childhoods and/ or from difficulties in the marriage, found their children's desire for love and care a burden and responded to them irritably—by ignoring, scolding or moralizing. In addition, anxious persons are more likely than others to have had further upsetting experiences as well. For example, some will have received daily care from a succession of different people; some will have experienced limited periods of residential care in which they received little or no substitute mothering; some will have had parents who separated or were divorced;[4]

[4] In the Harvard bereavement study, Parkes *et al.* (in preparation) report that those with a high score for ambivalence (see Chapter 11) were significantly more likely to have had parents who had been separated or divorced than were those with a low score; the incidence was 27 per cent and 0 per cent respectively. There was also a significant difference for loss of mother by death, the incidence of that being 33 per cent and 17 per cent respectively. By contrast the incident of loss of father by death was reversed: namely, 7 per cent and 30 per cent respectively.

yet others will have suffered a childhood bereavement (see Chapter 17).

Nevertheless, although those who make anxious and ambivalent attachments are likely to have experienced discontinuities in parenting and/or often to have been rejected by their parents, the rejection is more likely to have been intermittent and partial than complete. As a result the children, still hoping for love and care yet deeply anxious lest they be neglected or deserted, increase their demands for attention and affection, refuse to be left alone and protest more or less angrily when they are.

This is a picture of childhood experience and development which is the exact opposite of the one of overindulgence and spoiling which has not only been widespread as a popular belief but which, most unfortunately, became incorporated early into psychoanalytic theory. Amongst the many undesirable results of this is that childhood experiences that, it is now clear, play an influential part in predisposing a person towards responding to loss by disordered mourning have either been overlooked or given but scant attention.

An adult patient suffering disordered mourning who described a relationship with her mother which I believe is not atypical is Julia, who (as described in Chapter 9), after her mother died, had retained, unused, a red gown from which she had pictured her mother emerging.[5]

Julia, an educated black secretary, was first seen eight months after her mother died. Amongst her symptoms were loss of interest, extreme preoccupation with her mother's image, insomnia and disturbing dreams about her mother from which she awoke in a panic feeling her mother 'might not be gone'. Although Julia had maintained a cheerful façade toward others, it seems likely that her condition would have progressed to one of chronic mourning.

During therapy Julia gave the following account of her life. She was the youngest child in a family which seems to have had many difficulties. For example, when she was six months old her mother had been bedridden for a year because of severe burns and her father had taken to drink; Julia herself had been cared for by her elder siblings. After leaving school she had remained at home to look after her mother who was by then a widow crippled with diabetes. To do so had entailed Julia's surrendering college scholarships and also offers of marriage and, instead, becoming something of a martyr. Constantly anxious about her mother's health, she had slept at the foot of her mother's bed so that during the

---

[5] This account, rewritten, is taken from Volkan (1975, pp. 340–4).

night she could frequently check that her mother was still alive. During the day she had made similar checks by means of the telephone.

Julia seems always to have been 'picked on' by her mother, who is described as having been 'extremely demanding, domineering, critical and often disparaging and humiliating' and for whom the elder children had had little time. Not surprisingly Julia, as she confessed later, had often wished her mother dead; amongst the dreams she had and recounted during therapy was one in which she had pushed her mother in her wheelchair over a cliff.

In this record, as occurs so often in clinical literature, although we are told of the tyrannical ways of Julia's mother, no content is given of what she actually said. What, we wonder, were the words and phrases in which mother expressed her demands and criticisms? In what terms and tones did she disparage and humiliate Julia? Using clinical experience as a guide, we should expect that, at the least, mother would have belittled Julia's efforts to help, complained that she was being neglected, and have blamed Julia for every setback in her condition. If my hypotheses are valid, informed enquiry would probably have revealed much else in a similar vein.

In earlier discussion of the childhood experiences that lead to the most intense anxiety, especial emphasis is laid on a parent's threats to abandon a child or commit suicide. When exposed to such threats, which are often made deliberately by an exasperated mother in an attempt to control him, a child becomes extremely anxious lest he lose her for ever. He is likely also to become angry with her, though until adolescence he is unlikely to express it overtly and directly. Whether the resulting behaviour is one of anxious conformity or of angry rebellion, with a veneer of not caring, turns partly on whether there is genuine parental affection in addition to the threats and partly on the sex, age and temperament of the child. In either case the individual has been brought up to believe unquestioningly that, if his mother disappears, the blame lies firmly on his own shoulders. Small wonder therefore if, when his mother does die, or in later life his spouse, he should blame himself for its having happened.

In addition to the children who are exposed to these crude and frightening threats are others whose parents use more subtle pressure. A threat not to love a child unless he conforms to requirements is one such. To this can be added insistence that the child is intrinsically unlovable and no one but a dedicated and self-sacrificing parent would put up with his presence.

A special case of an intensely 'dependent' relationship is one in which a parent has been using techniques of these kinds to coerce a child to care for her (for reasons that are easy to understand once the parent's own childhood experiences are known, see Volume II, Chapter 18). The following account of a 45-year-old bachelor who became severely depressed after his mother's death illustrates how this type of relationship can develop and also how it leads to a pathological response to loss. In this case information came from the patient himself during the course of therapy, which began two years after his bereavement.[6]

As an only child whose father had departed while he was still an infant, Mr D had been brought up solely by his mother; and the two had lived alone together until her death. Initially during therapy he spoke of her as though she were an other-worldly and superior being. Later, however, it became evident that behind this idealized picture there was a woman who in a tyrannical way had demanded his absolute obedience whilst simultaneously ridiculing any attempt he might make at an independent existence. Mr D had grown up to believe he was a burden on his mother, was undeserving of her love and attention, and could only be accepted by her if he exerted his every effort. After reaching adult life he had remained living with her 'in a near-servile capacity' and had supported her financially until her death.

After she died he had despaired of his future, had given up his job and had only gone out either to buy food or else to visit doctors for a variety of somatic complaints. When his savings were gone he sold his belongings and moved into a shabby furnished room.

In commenting on the case, Bemporad notes how Mr D had accepted both his mother's valuation of himself and the role she had demanded he take. Viewed in the perspective adopted here we note in addition how he had also accepted his mother's valuation of herself and how she had bound him to her by a number of interlocking techniques. On the one hand she had made her love and approval turn on his conforming to her every requirement, especially that he care constantly for her; on the other she had led him to believe that he was intrinsically unlovable and would therefore never win the love of anyone else.

In the case neither of Mr D nor of Julia does the therapist discuss

[6] This account, rewritten, is taken from Bemporad (1971).

the possibility that the patient's mother may have used threats to abandon the patient as a means of achieving her ends. Yet I believe that, unless this possibility is specifically explored and no evidence for it found, it is unwise to assume that no such threats were ever made.

In addition to pressures illustrated in these cases, or discussed, there are yet others which a parent can use to ensure a child's obedience. For example, it is very easy to induce a sense of guilt by insisting to a child from his earliest years that his bad behaviour is making his mother (or father) ill and will, if continued, lead to her (or his) death. This leads to a consideration of the childhood experiences of those who grow up compulsively disposed towards caring for others.

Experiences disposing towards compulsive caregiving

No systematic study seems to have been made of the childhood experiences that contribute to this disposition. Nevertheless, clinical experience and the study of individuals diagnosed as cases of school refusal or agoraphobia (Volume II, Chapters 18 and 19) point unmistakably in certain directions.

At least two, rather different, types of childhood experience are found in the histories of those who become compulsive caregivers.

One is intermittent and inadequate mothering during early childhood which may culminate in total loss. Since this is discussed in later chapters (21 and 23) it is unnecessary to go further here.

Another type of experience is when pressure is put on a child to care for a sick, anxious or hypochondriacal parent. In some such cases the child is made to feel that he himself is responsible for his parent's being ill and therefore has an obligation to act as caregiver. In others, whilst not held responsible for the illness, he is none the less made to feel he has a responsibility to care for his parent. Since in a majority of cases the parent is the mother, what follows is written as though that were always so.

In some cases the mother is physically ill. In one such, a woman became pregnant most unexpectedly in her mid-forties and, after a difficult pregnancy and labour, suffered chronically from high blood-pressure. The baby, a boy (who had obviously been unwanted), during his childhood was left in no doubt that it was he who had made his mother ill and that it was therefore his responsibility to care for her. This he did devotedly until she died when he was adolescent. Once he had left school and was earning he became strongly drawn to a much older woman who had herself lived a deeply troubled life; and he proceeded to shoulder the responsibility of caring for her.

In another such case the mother of a five-year-old boy had severe diabetes. One night she fell into a diabetic coma and was removed by ambulance to hospital, where she recovered. Subsequently mother came to rely on her son to help her with her insulin injections and to care for her in other ways. This he did, constantly haunted by the memory of his mother being taken from the house in what to him had seemed a dying state. Intensely anxious lest something similar should recur when he was asleep or out of the house, he stayed awake at night and began refusing to attend school; at the age of ten he was referred to the Tavistock Clinic as a 'school phobic'.

This case illustrates the similarity there is between the family experiences that lead to the form of personality now under discussion and the family experiences of individuals diagnosed as suffering from either school or agoraphobia.[7] In the backgrounds of each there is likely to be a parent who has used, and who may still be using, strong pressure to invert the relationship by requiring the son or daughter to do the caregiving. In both types of case the more that moral and other pressure has been applied to the son or daughter the more tied to the parent he or she becomes, the more anxious and guilty about leaving home and the more bitterly resentful in his heart at being treated thus. Furthermore, should the parent in fact become seriously ill, it is almost inevitable that the caregiver should become even more frightened and guilt-ridden.

[7] Since writing Chapter 19, Volume II, in which the close links between the phobic conditions of childhood and of adult life are discussed, further evidence has been published. In a follow-up study of 100 adolescents who had been treated for school phobia it was found that, after an interval averaging three years, about one-third were suffering from serious emotional disturbance, including six (five female and one male) who had developed severe and persistent agoraphobic symptoms (Berg et al. 1976). In another study it was found that, of the children aged 11 to 15 years of a group of agoraphobic women, no less than 14 per cent were reported as suffering from school phobia. The mothers of these school-phobic children were more likely than were other mothers to give a history of having themselves suffered from school phobia as children (Berg 1976). These findings strongly support the view that the two conditions share much of the same psychopathology.

Finally, should the parent die it is easy for the caregiver to take all the blame and, directing resentment against himself, to develop chronic mourning.

The evidence regarding the family experiences and patterns of affectional relationships of patients who come to be diagnosed as either school phobics or agoraphobics, and the current events that precipitate them into an emotional crisis, evidence that is set out in Chapters 18 and 19 of Volume II, is at each point consistent with the views expressed in this chapter. It is therefore of particular interest that, in a significant proportion both of children and of adults diagnosed as phobic, the acute condition has been preceded by the sudden illness or death of a parent or other close relative, usually, writes Roth (1959), of 'a parent upon whom the patient has been extremely dependent'.

Experiences disposing towards assertion of independence of affectional ties

Because no systematic studies have been undertaken of the childhood experiences of persons given to asserting their emotional self-sufficiency we are once again dependent for information on a heterogeneous collection of clinical reports. From them, however, certain patterns emerge fairly clearly.

As in the case of compulsive caregiving, two rather different types of childhood experience seem to be prevalent. One is the loss of a parent during childhood, with the child being left thereafter to fend for himself. The other is the unsympathetic and critical attitude that a parent may take towards her child's natural desires for love, attention and support. Not infrequently, it seems, a person who grows up to assert his independence of affectional ties has been exposed to a combination of experiences of these kinds.

Families differ enormously in the extent to which they take account of the role of affectional bonds and attachment behaviour in the lives of family members. In one family there may be deep respect for affectional bonds, ready response to expressions of attachment behaviour, and sympathetic understanding of the anxiety, anger and distress aroused by temporary separation from a loved figure or by permanent loss. Open expression of thought and feeling is encouraged and loving support provided when asked for. In another family, by contrast, affectional bonds are little valued, attachment behaviour is regarded as childish and weak and is rebuffed, all expression of feeling is frowned upon and contempt expressed for those who cry. Because they are condemned and despised, a child comes ultimately to inhibit his attachment behaviour and to bottle up his feelings. Furthermore he comes, like his parents, to view his yearning for love as a weakness, his anger as a sin and his grief as childish.

Some individuals who are exposed to the latter type of family experience during childhood grow up to be tough and hard. They may become competent and to all appearances self-reliant, and they may go through life without overt sign of breakdown. Yet they are likely to be difficult to live and work with, for they have little understanding either of others or of themselves and are readily aroused to smouldering jealousy and resentment. Moreover, should they develop trust enough to confess it to a therapist, their feeling of being isolated and unloved may be sad in the extreme; whilst, especially in later years, they are at risk of depression, alcoholism and suicide. Even when they do not become psychiatric casualties themselves they can often be responsible for the breakdown of others—spouse, children or employees. Winnicott (1960) has used the term 'false self' to describe the self such a person experiences and which, willingly or unwillingly, he presents to the world. This term is much to be preferred to 'narcissistic' which is another sometimes used by psychoanalysts to describe these individuals.

Not everyone exposed to this type of childhood experience develops a highly organized personality, however. In many the hardness and self-reliance are more brittle and it is from amongst these persons, it seems likely, that a substantial proportion of all those who at some time in their life develop a pathological response to loss are recruited. A prolonged absence of conscious grieving is the likely form. Examples are given in Chapter 9—see the accounts of Mrs F and Mr AA.

The following account of a young man of 23, whose efforts at self-sufficiency were fast failing, describes many features that I believe to be typical of individuals of this sort. The account is presented, not as one of disordered mourning, but because of the telling details it gives of how this young man recalled having been treated as a child and of how he had reacted.[8]

[8] This account is a much abbreviated version of a fairly full case report by Lind (1973) in which she draws on material from the referral letter,

When seen by a psychiatrist prior to being admitted to hospital Mr G was severely depressed and spoke unemotionally about the likelihood of killing himself. A year previously he had made a half-hearted attempt; next time, he remarked, he would make sure of it. When offered admission he accepted it in a flat passive way, maintaining however that his state of mind was less an illness than 'a philosophy of life'. At that time there seemed a serious possibility of schizophrenia.

He was a tall handsome young man who in hospital never showed psychotic features; but he soon made himself fairly conspicuous by combining co-operative with unconventional behaviour.

In two interviews with his psychotherapist prior to starting treatment he described what to her appeared as having been 'a lifetime of anxiously pretending to be an independent person'. Although at school he had been good at both work and sport, he had been extremely uneasy about competing and had deliberately refrained from winning; nevertheless he had got to university and had taken a degree. Although he could never tolerate being alone, to be with others created conflict. On the one hand he was eager to be recognized; on the other he was petrified lest his contributions should fall flat. Often, he said, he would become cynical and sarcastic.

For a time he had been engaged to be married; but this also produced conflict. For not only was he intensely afraid of his fiancée leaving him but he was afraid also of becoming too dependent on her. When she looked elsewhere he became extremely jealous; and he then tried to cure himself of jealousy by urging her to be unfaithful to him. When he realized she had followed his prompting he had felt extremely anxious: 'not anger,' he claimed, 'but something went out of me'.

Mr G was the eldest of a large Catholic family; and by the time he was three two siblings had already been born. His parents, he said, quarrelled both frequently and violently. When the family was young father had been working long hours away from home training for a profession. Mother was always unpredictable. Often she was so distraught by her quarrelling children that she would lock herself in her room for days on end. Several times she had left home, taking the daughters with her but leaving the sons with father.

He had been told that he had been an unhappy baby, a poor feeder and sleeper, who had often been left alone to cry for long periods. His crying, it was said, had been just an attempt to gain control of his parents and to be spoilt. On one occasion he had had appendicitis and he remembered

---

from brief notes made after each of a total of 19 twice-weekly therapeutic sessions, and from an account, written by the patient after treatment had ended, in which he describes his state of being before and after treatment. The historical material, she notes, 'was not conveyed in more than fragments until after he had changed'. From a scientific point of view a major deficiency is that all the information regarding the patient's childhood comes from the patient himself and therefore remains uncorroborated.

lying awake all night moaning; but his parents had done nothing and by next morning he was seriously ill. Later, during therapy, he recalled how disturbed he used to be at hearing his younger brothers and sisters being left to cry and how he hated his parents for it and felt like killing them.

He had always felt like a lost child and had been puzzled to understand why he had been rejected, or at least should have felt rejected. His first day at school, he said, had been the worst in his life. It had seemed a final rejection by his mother; all day he had felt desperate and had never stopped crying. After that he had gradually come to hide all desires for love and support; he had refused ever to ask for help or to have anything done for him.

Now, during therapy, he was frightened he might break down and cry and want to be mothered. This would lead his therapist, he felt sure, to regard him as a nuisance and his behaviour simply as attention-seeking; and were he to say anything personal to her, she would be offended and perhaps would lock herself in her room.

Treatment progressed unexpectedly fast. This was due probably in part to the 'false self' being not too firmly organized and in part to his therapist, following Winnicott, having a clear understanding of what his true desires and feelings were. Subsequently, in an account he gave of himself prior to treatment, he described how over many years he had been vaguely aware of there being 'two me's, the real me . . . petrified to reveal itself . . . [which] hated the other me . . . which complied with social demands'. The real me, he said, would sometimes emerge briefly, for example when he felt empathy for someone in the same situation as himself. There had been occasions, he wrote, when he felt he might be inspired 'to undertake some great mission to reform mankind from a loveless miserable world'. It remains unstated in the published account what had led to Mr G's breakdown. Evidence strongly suggests, however, that it was the end of his engagement, even if, as seems probable, he himself had played a major part in bringing it about.[9]

Returning now to our theme, we note that, already in Chapter 9 there are accounts of individuals whose mourning was progressing unfavourably and who had described how, thanks to childhood experience, they had developed a protective shell for themselves, e.g. Mrs I, or had been taught to bottle up feeling, e.g. Mrs Y. Towards the end of Chapter 10, moreover, there are accounts by bereaved people of the obstacles to grieving created by the enjoinders of relatives and friends that they pull themselves together and stop crying. Conversely, we have learned how helpful it is to a bereaved person when opportunity is given him to dwell on every

[9] Discussion of this patient's psychopathology in terms of the theory sketched in Chapter 4 will be found towards the end of the next chapter.

detail of the past, to express yearning, anger and sorrow and to weep.

In the light of these considerations, and also of reports of the effects on young children of a parent insisting they do not cry (see Chapters 1 and 23), the hypothesis is advanced that a major determinant of how a person responds to a loss is the way his attachment behaviour, and all the feeling that goes with it, was evaluated by his parents and responded to during his infancy, childhood and adolescence. Especially adverse effects are attributed to disparaging and sarcastic remarks by parents and parent-surrogates made whenever a child is distressed and seeks comfort. The injunctions 'Don't cry', 'Don't be a cry-baby', 'I won't love you if you cry', can, it is postulated, do untold harm, especially when uttered in contemptuous tones. Instead of being permitted to share occasions of fear, unhappiness and grief, an individual treated thus is driven in on himself to bear his sorrows alone. The earlier in life this starts, moreover, and the more insistent the pressure the more damage, I believe, will be done.

In this chapter it has been convenient to consider under separate headings the various types of childhood experience that evidence suggests are responsible, in large part, for the various forms of personality identified as prone to develop disordered mourning. Naturally, in real life, every combination of such experiences may occur and, stemming from them, a corresponding variety of forms of disturbed personality. In the next chapter the main features of disordered mourning and the psychological processes responsible for it are examined in the light of the theoretical position outlined in Chapter 4.

CHAPTER 13

Cognitive Processes Contributing to Variations in Response to Loss

It is impossible to think that I shall never sit with you again and hear your laugh. *That everyday for the rest of my life you will be away.* No one to talk to about my pleasures. No one to call me for walks, to go 'to the terrace'. I write in an empty book. I cry in an empty room. And there can never be any comfort again.

CARRINGTON[1]

A framework for conceptualizing cognitive processes

In the preceding chapters I have reviewed the many variables that influence the course of mourning, including certain personality characteristics of the bereaved and the types of childhood experience that evidence suggests contribute to their development. Here and there the psychological processes through which the variables appear to act have been indicated, but no systematic attention has yet been given them. This deficiency I now attempt to make good.

Every situation we meet with in life is construed in terms of the representational models we have of the world about us and of our-selves. Information reaching us through our sense organs is selected and interpreted in terms of those models, its significance for us and for those we care for is evaluated in terms of them, and plans of action conceived and executed with those models in mind. On how we interpret and evaluate each situation, moreover, turns also how we feel.

When a situation occurs which we evaluate as damaging to our interests or to those of persons we care for, our first impulse is to try to rectify the situation. In making any such attempt we analyse what seems to have caused the situation and plan our actions accordingly. Naturally, our analysis of causation is in terms of what-ever representational models we may have of the objects and per-sons who are playing a part in the situation; and our plans of action

[1] Extract from diary after death of Lytton Strachey (D. Garnett, ed., 1970).

are drawn up in terms of whatever repertoire of actions is most readily available to us.

In Chapters 14 and 20 of Volume II an account is given of how during the course of development a child constructs for himself working models of his world and of himself as an agent in it. It is noted especially that, because data for model construction are derived from multiple sources, there is always the possibility of the data being incompatible and, further, that for a minority of children such incompatibility may be regular and persistent. The example is given of a parent who insists that he loves his child when the child's first-hand experience of his parent's actions suggests the reverse. In such a case the child is in a dilemma. Is he to accept the picture as he sees it himself? or is he to accept the one his parent insists is true? Several possible outcomes are sketched, of which perhaps the commonest is an uneasy compromise whereby a child gives some credence to both sets of data and oscillates uneasily between two incompatible pairs of models, each pair consisting of a model of his parent and a complementary one of himself.

This framework of cognitive theory, which is considerably extended in Chapter 4 of this volume, provides some of the basic components for the theory of mourning to be advanced.

When information regarding a new situation reaches us it can be processed with more or less haste, more or less adequately and more or less completely. For example, the more damaging to our interests a situation appears to be or likely to become the more urgently do we proceed. By evaluating the situation quickly and acting promptly damage may be minimized or avoided altogether. Yet there is a price for speed. Perception may be inaccurate, evaluation inadequate and planning faulty. As a result, we well know, more haste can mean less speed.

There is certain information, moreover, that we find difficult to process. One example is information that is incompatible with our existing models, as is illustrated by the way that evidence in conflict with a cherished theory tends to be neglected or discounted. In general, when new information clashes with established models, it is the models which win the day—in the short run almost always, in the long run very often.

Although in the short term an existing model, if strongly held, tends to exclude new information incompatible with it, in the long term an old model may become replaced by a new one. Nevertheless, much evidence exists that we undertake such replacement only very reluctantly. Initially, we take time to become convinced that the new information is of such validity and weight that a revision of models is truly necessary. And later, when embarked on the task, we proceed only in fits and starts, and revert often to the old and familiar model even though we know it to be outdated. All in all, we find that to dismantle a model which has played and is still playing a major part in our daily life and to replace it by a new one is a slow and arduous task, even when the new situation is in principle welcome. When the new situation is by contrast unwelcome the task is not only arduous but painful and perhaps frightening as well.

Certain situations that are both new and unwelcome may, indeed, appear at first sight so appalling that we dread to recognize their very existence. As a result we postpone evaluating them in their true proportions and fail to frame plans to meet them. Such postponement is especially probable whenever preliminary evaluation suggests that the situation is irreversible. For, should it prove so, we should be faced with the task of replacing existing models with new ones in circumstances in which the change is wholly unwelcome. Small wonder, therefore, that loss of a loved person should create great psychological difficulties in addition to deep distress.

Let us describe some of the processes of healthy mourning using this frame of reference.

When an affectional bond is broken there is usually a preliminary registering of the relevant information combined with an inability to evaluate it to more than the most cursory extent—the phase of numbing. Thereafter further evaluation proceeds in bouts, plentifully interspersed with moratoria. During a bout certain of the implications of the information already received are considered or reconsidered, though others are still avoided; whilst additional information may be sought. This additional information may be concerned with disputing, or verifying, or amplifying earlier information; or it may be concerned with disputing or confirming implications already tentatively accepted; or with exploring the limitations of and the opportunities available in the situation as it now seems to be. During each moratorium, by contrast, some or all of the information regarding change already received is likely to be excluded and the old models and old beliefs partially or wholly reinstated. Hence the oscillation of feeling already documented.

In the processes of receiving and evaluating the information that stems from major change of any sort a secure person habitually seeks the help of a companion. He asks him to negate or to verify the information, to confirm or disconfirm his initial evaluations, to help him consider how and why the event should have occurred, what its further implications may be, what the future may hold, and what plans of action, if any, may be appropriate. In all these ways a helpful companion may be of very great assistance. Yet by acting also as an attachment figure and caregiver the companion may perform an even greater service. For, by his very presence, the bereaved's anxiety is reduced, his morale fortified, his evaluations made less hastily, and the actions necessary to meet a situation selected and planned more judiciously.

Not infrequently after a person has been bereaved the situation with which he has to deal is unique, for the death entails the loss of the very person in whom he has been accustomed to confide. Thus, not only is the death itself an appalling blow but the very person towards whom it is natural to turn in calamity is no longer there. For that reason, if his mourning is to follow a favourable course, it becomes essential that the bereaved be able to turn for comfort elsewhere.

Whether or not a bereaved person is able both to receive and to accept help is determined by three interlocking variables:

– whether there is any potential comforter available
– if so, whether his or her approach is helpful or unhelpful
– whether when a comforter is both available and potentially helpful the bereaved is able to trust and confide in him.

In Chapter 10 attention was given to the role of the first two of these variables. Here we consider the role of the third.

Cognitive biases affecting responses to loss

When confronted with information spelling loss each individual processes it in his own idiosyncratic way—more or less slowly, more or less completely, more or less accurately—depending on the cognitive structures through which the information passes. The overall effects on processing that these structures have can be referred to as that individual's cognitive bias.

Plainly the directions in which an individual is cognitively biased are a function of the representational models of attachment figures and of self that he has built during his childhood and adolescence, and, if the views advanced in this work prove valid, these in turn are a function of the experiences he had in his family during those years. What his actual responses prove then to be turns on the interaction of the conditions that surround and follow a loss with the cognitive biases to respond in certain ways that he brings to it (and perhaps on interactions with other variables as well). In particular, I argue that the part played by the kinds of childhood experience a person has had are critical. For, through the medium of his representational models, they are in large part responsible, first, for the patterns of affectional relationship he makes during his life and, secondly, for the cognitive biases he brings to any loss he may sustain.

As a result of these reflections we can list a number of areas in which the cognitive biases specific to each individual can exercise a far-reaching influence on the way he responds to a loss, and to the various circumstances surrounding it, and thereby determine in large part the course his mourning takes. A number of these biases concern the way in which such information as may be processed is construed; others concern the extent to which information is accepted and processed adequately or else is subjected to some degree of defensive exclusion. Biases easily identified are as follows:

(a) how the bereaved construes the part played in the loss by the dead person himself;
(b) how he construes his own part in the loss, and the way the dead person might regard it;
(c) what expectations he has of the way that anyone who might proffer assistance would treat him;
(d) how aware he is of the constructions he puts on past events and of their pervasive influence on the expectations he has in the present;
(e) the extent to which whatever constructions and expectations he may have are open to new information and so to revision, or else are closed.

Much that is referred to in this chapter in terms of cognitive bias is dealt with in more conventional psychoanalytic literature in terms of phantasy. There are a number of reasons for not using that term, however. One is that phantasy is now used very loosely to refer to almost any cognitive process. Another is that little systematic attempt is made to discover how an individual has come to think in the idiosyncratic way he does. Finally, in accounting for origins, there has for long been a strong preference for hypotheses that postulate an almost wholly autonomous origin for whatever form an individual's phantasies may take and an equally strong bias against considering hypotheses, such as those advanced here, that invoke childhood experiences within the family as major determinants.

Within this broad framework of theory an attempt is now made to account for some of the principal variations in the course of mourning and some also of the most prominent of its pathological features. Although it might seem logical to start by describing responses believed typical of those whose mourning is following a favourable course, we start instead with pathology. The reason is that healthy responses stand out in clearer relief when seen against a background of pathological ones.

Biases contributing to chronic mourning

In accordance with the (admittedly fragmentary) evidence regarding the personalities and childhood experiences of those at risk of developing chronic mourning, it can be inferred that such a person has established within himself representational models of attachment figures and of self that have certain specifiable, albeit often incompatible, features.

Almost always, I infer, he will have a model of his parents as above criticism and a complementary one of himself as a more or less worthless person. He will believe himself a being given to ingratitude and unjustifiable anger, who is fortunate to have the self-sacrificing parents he has and to be in duty bound to revere them. Coexistent with, but subordinate to, this pair of models will be another pair in which his parents are seen as grudging in their affection and attention and too often unavailable, and he himself as being more justified in his demands on his parents and in his anger when they fail him than his parents allow, and also possessed of better feelings and intentions towards them than they ever credit him with.

The first pair of models, it is inferred, are derived from what his parents have always told him,[2] and the second, subordinate, pair

[2] The view advanced has elements in common with that of Sullivan, as clarified by Mullahy (see Sullivan 1953), namely that a child's appraisal

from his own first-hand experience. Although the pairs are incompatible, both persist, stored perhaps in distinctive forms (see Chapter 4). Moreover, either one pair or the other or both are almost certain to be applied unmodified whenever he embarks on any new affectional relationship, for example marriage.

As an illustration of this way of thinking about someone suffering chronic mourning let us consider the case of Mr M (Chapter 9), who at the age of 68 became depressed and self-reproachful after the death of his wife and who insisted on regarding her as being perfect despite her many acknowledged shortcomings. On the basis of the theory I infer that he was operating with a pair of models, one of which had always biased him to see any attachment figure (first his mother, then his wife) as someone above criticism and the other of which had equally biased him to see himself as necessarily responsible for whatever in the relationship might go wrong. Furthermore, the theory postulates that the influences that had led Mr M to build such models, and as a result for his perceptions and actions to be controlled by them, came from his parents, probably mainly his mother. Throughout his childhood, we should suppose, she would have insisted that he see her as always above criticism and himself as the person responsible for any ill that might come to the family. In keeping with these inferences it would be expected that, when eventually his wife died, he would be strongly biased towards blaming himself for having failed her and towards ruminating perpetually on his inadequacies as a husband and on his sins of omission and commission.

In accounting thus for a depressed person's strong tendency to idealize his attachment figure I am breaking with tradition. Almost all theorizing hitherto has drawn on explanations that invoke the concepts of regression and/or of innate aggression. Thus one explanation is that the depressed person not only wishes to see the other as perfect but in actually doing so is regressing to a childhood

---

of himself is a reflection of the way the significant adults in his life appraise him. There is a difference, however. Whereas Sullivan holds that a child accepts such views passively, partly because he lacks experience to do otherwise and partly for fear of the consequences were he to think for himself, in the view advanced here it is postulated that a child not only passively accepts the appraisals of others but that he also actively arrives at his own, perhaps totally different, appraisals both of himself and of others.

condition in which, it is contended, a child is incapable of seeing his parents in any other light. The other is that the depressed person has to direct all criticism away from his attachment figure, perhaps towards himself, because his aggressive tendencies are excessive. When called on to account for the presence of such tendencies in certain persons and their absence in others, advocates of these hypotheses habitually invoke constitutional differences.

By contrast, I am postulating differential childhood experience: an adult is strongly biased to see his attachment figure as being above criticism because one or both of his parents have insisted he do so. Not infrequently, moreover, they have backed their insistence by threatening sanctions, mild, severe, or even terrifying, should he do otherwise. Though admittedly still a conjecture demanding much further research, this hypothesis accounts well for much clinical evidence and has the merit of being testable (by means of prospective studies).

In the case of Mr M the pair of models that lead him to see his attachment figure as above criticism and all the blame to be his own would appear to have been the dominant pair through long stretches of time, perhaps indeed throughout his life. Yet we may be mistaken in thinking so. For, whenever an individual possesses two incompatible pairs of models, the situation is unstable and whatever pair is dominant during one phase of a person's lifetime may become the subordinate pair during another. For example, an individual whose perceptions and actions are for long controlled by a pair of models in which parents are above criticism and self is always to blame may experience a change of cognitive balance such that the subordinate pair becomes the dominant pair. In such a case the individual's latent resentment breaks through and, instead of his remaining a doormat, he rebels. Whether this reversal of model dominance will continue, however, is uncertain because, so long as pairs of models profoundly incompatible with each other are established in a person's mind, the mental situation remains unstable.

Even when a pair of models is in a subordinate position, it should be noted, it is likely none the less to exert a considerable effect on a person's perceptions, feeling and actions. In the case of Mr M, for example, it seems likely that his irritability, and his tendency to blame his children for having hurt their mother, and the hospital for her death, can be attributed to this 'other side of himself'. To this 'other side' can be attributed also another well-known characteristic of depressed people, their tendency frequently to engage in behaviour that has the effect of arousing the anxious concern of those around them yet doing so in ways so indirect and unacknowledged that their purpose remains concealed. In their study of the treatment of depressed patients Cohen and her colleagues (1954) have given a vivid description of such behaviour and of the disturbing effects it had on those trying to be of help.

Additional Features Biasing Perception, Feeling and Behaviour

I have now described certain basic features of the working models of attachment figure and of self which I believe control the perceptions, feeling and actions of a great majority of those who are at risk of developing chronic mourning. To these basic features may be added one or more of several others that, like the basic ones, are potentially pathogenic. Whether or not any one feature characterizes the models of an individual depends, if the theory advanced is correct, on the childhood experiences of the individual concerned.

One such feature is when the model of the self is pictured as being under total obligation always to provide care for the attachment figure. An example of a person whose perceptions and actions, it may be inferred, were controlled by such a model was Mr D (see Chapter 12), the bachelor of 45 who had gone through life regarding his mother as a superior other-worldly figure and himself as a worthless wretch in duty bound to serve her, and incapable of earning the love of anyone else. The clinical evidence strongly suggests that that model of himself, and the complementary one of his mother, had in fact been derived from what she had always insisted he believe. Due to the persistent nature of these early-constructed models, moreover, this man's behaviour, like that of Mr M, had continued to be controlled by them long after his mother had died.

In an analogous way a person brought up to see his actions as constantly jeopardizing the health, even life, of his parents will be strongly biased to construe the death of one of them as precisely the catastrophe to which his alleged selfishness, thoughtlessness and deficient caregiving was bound to lead. In keeping with this way of construing the death, no thought is permitted that perhaps the dead person may on some occasions have been at fault. Instead, the dead person is idealized, all good features exaggerated, all failings expunged.

237

Another feature that may be present in someone at risk of developing chronic mourning is a model of the attachment figure as someone who is more or less certain to react to any shortcomings of the self by threatening to desert or to commit suicide. Any person whose perceptions are controlled by such a model will inevitably be strongly biased to construe the death of a parent or a spouse as the long-awaited realization of just such threats. In response, the bereaved is likely to feel extremely angry at what he feels to be a desertion; though whether he expresses his anger directly or redirects it elsewhere will vary from person to person. In addition, the bereaved may well suspect that, by means of coercion or supplication, the person lost can still be recovered—as may always have been the case in the past. In this way, I suspect, it may be possible to account for a great many cases in which a bereaved person continues over many years to engage in angry protest and fruitless search.

Whether a bereaved person construes the death of his attachment figure as due to a punitive desertion or to his own almost criminal negligence, he cannot help being convinced that the death was brought about by his own agency and that consequently he has only himself to blame. Furthermore, in so far as he has a sense of the dead person's continuing presence, he will construe that presence as plotting revenge; hence his acute anxiety and alarming dreams.

In this regard, again, the theory proposed breaks with tradition. For long a theory strongly favoured by many psychoanalysts to account for the anxiety and self-reproaches of chronic mourning has been that both are a consequence of the bereaved having, usually unconsciously, nursed murderous wishes against the person who has died. In certain cases, it is true, there is good evidence of a person having been seized of murderous wishes; and whenever that is so anxiety and guilt are likely to be much increased. This sequence is clearly illustrated by the case of Julia, described in Chapter 12. Yet I believe that the theory applies to a minority of cases only and that insistence on it to the exclusion of all other possible explanations is a most serious error.

Furthermore, what adherents of a generalized version of that theory commonly fail to recognize is that a person does not nurse murderous feelings for nothing. Time and again we find such feelings have been provoked repeatedly, initially during childhood but in a significant proportion of cases extended into the present day.

238

Rejection, separations, inordinate demands, alarming threats issued in varying mixtures by a child's parents (or parent-substitutes) have been the lot I believe, of all, or at least a great majority, of persons who are haunted by strong impulses to hurt those close to them. Once again the case of Julia provides an illustration. (See also Volume II, Chapter 17.)

Influence of Subordinate Models

In all the more severe cases of chronic mourning the bereaved is hardly aware that, in addition to all the responses that seem wholly to possess him (and which I attribute to the influence of the pair of models which hold his attachment figure to be above criticism and he himself to be responsible for all that goes wrong), he is possessed also of other, latent, responses of a very different kind. These comprise, first, a longing for love that has never been met and, next, bitter resentment against those who for whatever reason have not given it him.

The presence of these other responses, which usually remain in some degree inhibited and segregated within the personality, are to be attributed to the influence of the subordinate pair of models built, not from what the original figure had insisted was true, but from what the bereaved has actually experienced. Only to a non-judgemental companion who shows himself sympathetic and understanding are these latent responses likely to be expressed, at first tentatively but perhaps later at their full strength. In the course of such expression, instead of the attachment figure being seen as above criticism, his or her shortcomings become frighteningly clear. Instead of the self being seen as unlovable and ungrateful, the self is seen as having frequently been wronged and as having often been excessively grateful for what small mercies have been received.

Biases contributing to prolonged absence of grieving

Enough has been said in earlier chapters, especially the final pages of Chapter 11, to indicate what the cognitive biases that contribute to a prolonged absence of grieving are thought to be. Disparaging, perhaps sarcastic, remarks made by parents whenever a child is distressed and seeks comfort result in his learning that to cry and to seek comfort is to court rebuff and contempt. Cultivation of self-sufficiency and a self-protective shell, with as much disavowal as possible of all desire for love and support, are the natural sequelae. The more frequently a child is rejected or experiences a separation, moreover, and the more anxious and distressed he becomes the more frequent and painful are the rebuffs he is likely to receive and the thicker therefore will grow his protective shell. In some persons, indeed, the shell becomes so thick that affectional relationships are attenuated to a point at which loss ceases almost to have significance. Immune to mourning they may be; but at what a price!

A person reared in this kind of way may become proud of his self-sufficiency; or he may regret his lack of feeling; or, and perhaps rather commonly, he may oscillate between the two.

A person who claimed to be proud of his self-sufficiency is Mr G, the patient with a 'false self' described in the last chapter, about whose childhood we have a good deal of information (providing we accept Mr G's account as valid, which I am inclined to do). Having experienced countless rebuffs at his mother's hands during his early years, he had interpreted his being sent to school (presumably aged five or six) as a final rejection, and had thereafter refused ever again to ask for help or to have anything done for him. As a consequence much of his life was based on a deactivation of the systems mediating his attachment behaviour. Nevertheless, deactivation was not complete and, as a result, he found himself in appalling conflicts. For example, no sooner had he committed himself to become engaged to his girlfriend than, terrified of becoming too dependent on her, he encouraged her to defect. Whether at the time he was aware that his fear of becoming too dependent reflected a fear of putting himself at risk of a further rejection, as clearly it did, is uncertain.

Although childhood experiences are thought to play a major role in accounting for a prolonged absence of grieving following loss, experiences of later life should not be overlooked. For example, Maddison (1968) reports the case of a widow who, in attempting to stifle her grief, was evidently still much influenced by her husband who, she said, had always been strongly critical of her whenever she cried. Like the mourning of other widows in Maddison's series who tried consciously to distract themselves from grieving, this woman's mourning had an unfavourable outcome.

Biased perceptions of potential comforters

Irrespective of whether a person responds to loss with chronic mourning or with prolonged absence of grief he is likely to have difficulty in finding comfort from companions. Some deliberately avoid anyone who might be sympathetic. Others search but, for reasons within themselves, do not find. Whenever representational models of the kinds described in preceding sections are established within a person, he can have little confidence that he will receive kindness or comfort from relatives or others. Not only that, but he may well believe he will receive, instead, blame and punishment; or else that the price of comfort will be further lifelong servitude. Holding those beliefs, he is bound to be extremely hesitant in responding to offers of help; and he will be apt to misinterpret a potential comforter's approaches. Criticism and rejection, or a predatory intent, will be seen where none is meant. However false these modes of construing may be, moreover, and however clearly at times he may know them to be so, he will none the less continue to be deeply influenced by them. Models once established prove very hard to change.

In a brief narrative *A Grief Observed* (1961) the well-known writer, C. S. Lewis, has described his personal experiences during the months following his wife's death. The account strongly suggests a man whose feeling life had become to a great degree inhibited and suppressed during childhood and who had grown up, as a result, to be intensely introspective. The passages following are striking.

As a deeply religious man Lewis was seeking comfort from God but, instead of experiencing a consoling presence, he felt a door was being slammed in his face:

Meanwhile, where is God? This is one of the most disquieting symptoms. When you are happy . . . you will be—or so it feels—welcomed with open arms. But go to Him when your need is desperate, when all other help is vain, and what do you find? A door slammed in your face and a sound of bolting and double bolting on the inside. After that, silence. You may as well turn away . . . (p. 9).

Is it . . . the very intensity of the longing that draws the iron curtain, that makes us feel we are staring into a vacuum. . . ? 'Them as asks' (at any rate 'as asks too importunately') don't get. Perhaps can't (p. 58).

To anyone who approaches problems of mourning from the point of view advocated here certain inferences regarding how Lewis's parents had responded to him when, as a child, he was distressed and had sought comfort will be obvious; and some confirmation of these inferences is to be found in his autobiography.[3] Not only did his mother die of cancer when he was nine and a half but his father, always temperamental, became so distraught that he was in no state to comfort his two grieving sons. On the contrary, he alienated them: 'he spoke wildly and acted unjustly . . . With my mother's death all settled happiness, all that was tranquil and reliable, disappeared from my life' (pp. 25 and 27).

If this interpretation of C. S. Lewis's response to his wife's death is valid, his frustration can be understood in terms of the theory proposed in Chapter 4, as being due to the systems mediating his attachment behaviour having become deactivated after his mother died when he was nine.

The nature of these deep-seated expectations about the behaviour of potential comforters play a large part, I believe, in determining whether a bereaved person is sad, perhaps dreadfully sad, or becomes despairing and depressed as well.

They play a large part also in explaining why other bereaved persons shun all thought of comfort and even disavow all need of it.

Biases contributing to a healthy outcome

At this point in our exposition little perhaps need be said about the cognitive biases that help a grieving person meet the loss and achieve a favourable outcome to his mourning.

Such a person, it can be inferred, is likely to possess a representational model of attachment figure(s) as being available, responsive and helpful and a complementary model of himself as at least a potentially lovable and valuable person. Those models will have been built up as a result of happy experiences during his childhood when his desires for love, comfort and support will have been respected and met. Subsequently, influenced by those models, he is likely to have been able to make further loving and trusting relationships during his adolescence and adult life.

On being confronted with the loss of someone close to him such a person will not be spared grief; on the contrary he may grieve deeply and on occasion, perhaps, be intensely angry. But, provided the causes and circumstances of the death were not especially adverse,

[3] Lewis, *Surprised by Joy*, 1955. See also Memoir by his elder brother prefacing *Letters* (W. H. Lewis, ed., 1966).

he is likely to be spared those experiences which lead mourning to become unbearable or unproductive or both. For example, it is unlikely he will have more than a fleeting sense of having been rejected or deserted; nor is it likely he will engage in much inappropriate self-reproach. Since he will not be afraid of intense and unmet desires for love from the person lost, he will let himself be swept by pangs of grief; and tearful expression of yearning and distress will come naturally. If sympathetic friends are available, he will find comfort in recalling happier days and reflecting on the satisfactions of his lost relationship without having to obliterate all memory of its limitations. During the months and years that follow he will probably be able to organize his life afresh, fortified perhaps by an abiding sense of the lost person's continuing and benevolent presence.

In case it may be thought that too much emphasis is being placed on childhood experience as a determinant of the form taken by mourning during adult life, the reader is reminded of Maddison's finding, admittedly from a small sample, which shows a one-to-one correlation between a widow's relationship with her mother and the outcome of her mourning (Chapter 10).

Interaction of cognitive biases with other conditions affecting responses to loss

Irrespective of the particular cognitive biases that influence a person's affectional relationships, the responses that follow loss are inevitably a resultant of the interaction of those biases on the one side with the particular conditions that obtain at the time of the loss and during the weeks and months after it on the other. As a result some individuals whose biases seem to bode ill may come through to a reasonably favourable outcome, whereas the presence of favourable biases are no absolute guarantee against intense and difficult mourning.

Central though an understanding of these interactions are whenever we approach an individual recently bereaved, it is perhaps unnecessary to expand on the matter here. For any reader who has got thus far in this work should hardly have difficulty in applying the theory outlined and seeing how it is that the conditions described in Chapter 10 should be expected to have the varying influences on the course of mourning that evidence suggests they do. Indeed, it can be claimed as one of the merits of this theory that it presents a simple connection between, on the one hand, the influences on the course of mourning of conditions external to the bereaved person and, on the other, the influences on its course of the personal biases which he brings with him.

Clearly, the evidence I have been able to bring in support of the views advanced is quite insufficient and much further research is required. In particular, it will be necessary to mount prospective studies starting well before bereavement is expected and to make predictions of how each subject's mourning is likely to progress, in differing conditions, should he sustain a loss. The necessary data would be of at least two kinds. First, relevant historical material would be obtained from interviews, including interviews of relatives, and also from joint interviews. For example, were the sample to be made up of married couples, which would be sensible, information about the relationship and its history would with advantage be obtained in a few joint interviews as well as in individual ones. Secondly, an assessment would be made, independently of any historical material, of the pattern of response that each subject is disposed habitually to adopt when confronted with either a temporary separation or a permanent loss. For this purpose Hansburg's Separation Anxiety Test, suitably amplified and developed, is a promising tool (Hansburg 1972).[4]

In the meantime, pending further data, the theory advanced is claimed to be consistent with such fragmentary evidence as is already available, to have internal consistency and, above all, to lead to hypotheses capable of systematic test.

[4] An account of this test is given in Volume II, Chapter 17. The principle on which it is constructed is to present the subject with a series of pictures illustrating a variety of situations in which an individual of the same age and sex as the subject experiences a separation, a loss or the risk of loss. The subject is then asked whether he has ever experienced a situation of that kind and, if so, how he felt and acted. If he has not had the experience, he is asked to imagine the experience and to recount how he thinks he would feel and act. A version of the test suitable for five-year-old children has been devised and preliminary findings reported by Klagsbrun and Bowlby (1976).

CHAPTER 14

Sadness, Depression
and Depressive Disorder

The affect corresponding to melancholia is mourning or grief—that is, longing for something that is lost.

SIGMUND FREUD[1]

Sadness and depression

In this chapter, in which I indicate how I approach the large and controversial field of depressive disorder,[2] we broaden the canvas temporarily to take account of losses due to causes other than death.

First, let us consider in what ways a person who is sad, and perhaps temporarily depressed, differs psychologically from someone who is chronically depressed or perhaps diagnosed as suffering from a depressive disorder.

Sadness is a normal and healthy response to any misfortune. Most, if not all, more intense episodes of sadness are elicited by the loss, or expected loss, either of a loved person or else of familiar and loved places or of social roles. A sad person knows who (or what) he has lost and yearns for his (or its) return. Furthermore, he is likely to turn for help and comfort to some trusted companion and somewhere in his mind to believe that with time and assistance he will be able to re-establish himself, if only in some small measure. Despite great sadness hope may still be present. Should a sad person find no one helpful to whom he can turn, his hope will surely diminish; but it does not necessarily disappear. To re-establish

[1] From Draft G, *circa* January 1895 (S. Freud 1954).

[2] To reflect my belief that there are true differences of kind between clinical depression and a normal depressive mood, in what follows I refer to the clinical conditions, variously termed 'clinical depressions', 'clinical depressive states' or 'depressive illnesses' as 'depressive disorders'. My reasons for adopting this terminology are, first, that I believe the clinical conditions are best understood as disordered versions of what is otherwise a healthy response and, secondly, that, whilst the term disorder is compatible with medical thinking, it is not tied specifically to the medical model as are the terms 'clinical' and 'illness'.

himself entirely by his own efforts will be far more difficult; but it may not be impossible. His sense of competence and personal worth remains intact.

Even so, there may well be times when he feels depressed. In an earlier paper (Bowlby 1961b) I suggested that depression as a mood that most people experience on occasion is an inevitable accompaniment of any state in which behaviour becomes disorganized, as it is likely to do after a loss: 'So long as there is active interchange between ourselves and the external world, either in thought or action, our subjective experience is not one of depression: hope, fear, anger, satisfaction, frustration, or any combination of these may be experienced. It is when interchange has ceased that depression occurs [and it continues] until such time as new patterns of interchange have become organized towards a new object or goal...'

Such disorganization and the mood of depression that goes with it, though painful and perhaps bewildering, is none the less potentially adaptive. For until the patterns of behaviour that are organized for interactions that are no longer possible have been dismantled it is not possible for new patterns, organized for new interactions, to be built up. It is characteristic of the mentally healthy person that he can bear with this phase of depression and disorganization and emerge from it after not too long a time with behaviour, thought and feeling beginning to be reorganized for interactions of a new sort. Here again his sense of competence and personal worth remains intact.

Depressive disorder and childhood experience

What accounts then for the more or less intense degrees of hopelessness and helplessness that, as Bibring (1953) pointed out many years ago, are characteristic of depressive disorders and for the sufferers so often feeling abandoned, unwanted and unlovable, as Beck (1967) among others has emphasized? As a result of this study I suggest a number of factors any one or any combination of which may be present.

Seligman (1973) draws attention to the ways in which a person, having frequently failed to solve certain problems, thereafter feels helpless and, even when confronted with a problem that is well within his capabilities, is liable to make no attempt to tackle it. Should he then attempt it and succeed, moreover, he is still liable to discount his success as mere chance. This state of mind, which Seligman aptly terms 'learned helplessness', is responsible, he suggests, for the helplessness present in depressive disorders. The theory he proposes is highly compatible with that advanced here.

In most forms of depressive disorder, including that of chronic mourning, the principal issue about which a person feels helpless is his ability to make and to maintain affectional relationships. The feeling of being helpless in these particular regards can be attributed, I believe, to the experiences he has had in his family of origin. These experiences, which are likely to have continued well into adolescence, are postulated to have been of one, or some combination, of three interrelated kinds:

(a) He is likely to have had the bitter experience of never having attained a stable and secure relationship with his parents despite having made repeated efforts to do so, including having done his utmost to fulfil their demands and perhaps also the unrealistic expectations they may have had of him. These childhood experiences result in his developing a strong bias to interpret any loss he may later suffer as yet another of his failures to make or maintain a stable affectional relationship.

(b) He may have been told repeatedly how unlovable, and/or how inadequate, and/or how incompetent he is.[3] Were he to have had these experiences they would result in his developing a model of himself as unlovable and unwanted, and a model of attachment figures as likely to be unavailable, or rejecting, or punitive. Whenever such a person suffers adversity, therefore, so far from expecting others to be helpful he expects them to be hostile and rejecting.

[3] A common motive for a parent, usually a mother, to speak to a child or adolescent in this kind of way is to ensure that he remains at home to care for her (as described in the section 'Experiences disposing towards compulsive caregiving' in Chapter 12). Most misleadingly, pressure of this kind is often mistaken for 'overprotection'.

When this mislabelling is allowed for, the conclusions reached by Parker (1979) are seen to be consistent with the types of childhood experience postulated above. As a result of a questionnaire study of 50 depressed women patients and 50 controls he concludes that the depressed patients are significantly more likely than the controls to regard their mothers as having treated them with a *combination* of 'low care' and 'high overprotection'. The figures are 60 per cent and 24 per cent respectively.

(c) He is more likely than others to have experienced actual loss of a parent during childhood (see later this chapter) with consequences to himself that, however disagreeable they might have been, he was impotent to change. Such experiences would confirm him in the belief that any effort he might make to remedy his situation would be doomed to failure.

On this view it is predicted that the particular pattern of depressive disorder that a person develops will turn on the particular pattern of childhood experiences he has had, and also on the nature and circumstances of the adverse event he has recently experienced.

Admittedly, these views are based on fragmentary evidence and are still conjectural. Yet they provide plausible and testable explanations for why someone severely depressed should feel not only sad and lonely, as might others in similar circumstances, but also unwanted, unlovable and helpless. They provide a plausible explanation also for why such persons are so often uneasy about or unresponsive to offers of help.

Exposure to experiences of the kinds postulated during childhood would also help explain why in depressive-prone individuals there should be so strong a tendency for the sadness, yearning and perhaps anger aroused by a loss to become disconnected from the situation that aroused them. Whereas, for example, in healthy mourning a bereaved person is much occupied thinking about the person who has died and perhaps of the pain he may have suffered and the frustration of his hopes, and also about why the loss should have occurred and how it might have been prevented, a person prone to depresive disorder may quickly turn his attention elsewhere—not as a temporary relief but as a permanent diversion. Preoccupation with the sufferings of the self, to the exclusion of all else, is one such diversion and, when adopted, may become deeply entrenched. The case of Mrs QQ, the thirty-year-old mother of a leukaemic child reported by Wolff et al. (1964b) and already described in Chapter 9, provides an example. Although she was frequently anxious, agitated and tearful, she successfully avoided discussion of her son's deteriorating condition by endless talk about how upset *she* was and how she could not stand *her* feelings any longer. Other authors to draw attention to the diversionary or defensive function of self-centred ruminations in patients suffering from depressive disorders are Sachar et al. (1968) and Smith (1971).

As discussed in Chapter 4, a disconnection of response from situation can be of very varying degrees and take several different forms. One of the more intractable forms, I suspect, results from a parent implicitly or explicitly forbidding a child, perhaps under threat of sanctions, to consider any mode of construing either his parents or himself in ways other than those directed by the parent. Not only is the child, and later the adolescent and adult, unable then to reappraise or modify his representational models of parent or self, but he is forbidden also to communicate to others any information or ideas he may have that would present his parents in a less favourable light and himself in a more favourable one.

In general, it seems likely, the more persistent the disorder from which a person suffers the greater is the degree of disconnection present and the more complete is the ban he feels against reappraising his models.

Brief reference has been made to some of the empirical findings reported by Aaron Beck as a result of his extensive and systematic study of patients suffering from depression (Beck 1967; Beck and Rush 1978; Kovacs and Beck 1977). It may therefore be useful to say a word about the theory he has formulated to account for his findings and how it relates to the theory advanced here.

Instead of adopting one of the traditional views that depressive disorder is 'a primary severe disorder of mood with resultant disturbance of thought and behaviour' (to quote the definition given in the 1952 and 1968 editions of the diagnostic manual of the American Psychiatric Association), or is the consequence of aggression turned inwards as Freud proposed, Beck presents evidence that a patient's dejected mood is the natural consequence of how he thinks about himself, how he thinks about the world, and how he thinks about his future. This leads Beck to formulate a cognitive theory of depressive disorders, a theory cast in the same mould as the theory of cognitive biases proposed here. Both formulations postulate that depressive-prone individuals possess cognitive schemas having certain unusual but characteristic features which result in their construing events in their lives in the idiosyncratic ways they do.

Where the two formulations differ is that, whilst one attempts to account for the development of such schemas by postulating that those who develop them have been exposed to certain characteristic types of experience during their childhood, the other offers no explanation. Although, like many clinicians, Beck assumes that experiences of childhood play some part in the development of these schemas, he pursues the matter no further, remarking with justice that research in this field is fraught with difficulty.

In summary, it can be said that Beck's data are explicable by the theory advanced here, and also that, within the limits it sets itself, his theory is compatible with mine. Where the two theories differ is that Beck's attempts much less.

Not infrequently the state of mind of someone severely depressed is described, or explained, in terms of loss of self-esteem. This is a concept I believe inadequate to the burden placed upon it. For it fails to make manifest that the low self-evaluation referred to is the result of one or more positively adverse self-judgements, such as that the self is incapable of changing the situation for the better, and/or is responsible for the situation in question, and/or is intrinsically unlovable and thus permanently incapable of making or maintaining any affectional bonds. Since the term 'low self-esteem' carries none of these meanings, it is not employed here.

Depressive disorders and their relation to loss: George Brown's study

Ever since Freud published his 'Mourning and Melancholia' the questions of the extent to which depressive disorders are related to loss and of the proportion of cases that can properly be regarded as distorted versions of mourning have remained unanswered. Nor can they be answered by proceeding as we have so far. For to answer them requires an approach different to that adopted. Instead of proceeding prospectively as we have been doing, starting with a loss and then considering its consequences, it is necessary to start with representative groups of individuals suffering from depressive disorders and then determine, retrospectively, what we know of their causes.

As it happens, the findings of a major study of this very sort by George Brown, a British sociologist, have been published during the past decade and these go some way to providing the answers we seek. His recent book with Tirril Harris, *The Social Origins of Depression* (1978a), gives a comprehensive account of the enquiry and its findings and also particulars of earlier publications.

Brown and his colleagues set out to study the parts played by social events of emotionally significant kinds in the aetiology of depressive disorders. In doing so they took account not only of recent events and current conditions but also of certain classes of earlier events. In what follows we discuss the influence of two only of the many variables Brown took into account. These are, first, the role of recent life events and, secondly, that of childhood loss. Keenly aware that these are fields long bedevilled by difficult problems of methodology Brown designed his project with exceptional care.

Some of the problems he and his colleagues sought to solve were those of sampling. To meet them they took steps to ensure both that their sample of individuals suffering from depressive disorders was reasonably representative of all those afflicted and not confined to those in psychiatric care, and also that their comparison group of healthy individuals was free of undeclared patients.

Another problem to which they gave much attention was that of deciding what is to be counted as an event of emotional significance to the person in question. Were the decision left entirely to the person there is danger of circular argument, for any event that he claims has caused him stress will be counted as stressful; and the more readily distressed a person is prone to be the more numerous the stressful events that he will be scored. Conversely, for reasons already discussed, a disturbed person may fail to mention events that may later be found to be of high relevance to his distress and may either state that he has no idea what might have upset him or else blame for his troubles events later found to be of little consequence. Even so, it must be recognized that although the person in distress cannot be taken as the final arbiter in the matter, unless attention is paid to the detailed circumstances in which he is living the meaning that an event has for him will be missed. For example, whether the birth of a baby is an occasion for great joy, for great anxiety or for great misery depends on the parent's circumstances.

Sampling. During their enquiry, conducted in a South London borough, Brown and Harris studied two main groups of women, a patient group and a community group. The patient group comprised 114 women, aged between 18 and 65, who were diagnosed as suffering from one or another form and degree of depressive disorder of recent onset and were receiving psychiatric treatment, either as in-patients or as out-patients. The community group comprised a random sample of 458 women in the same age-range as the patients and living in the same inner-London borough. From amongst its members several sub-samples were drawn.

In their investigation of the community sample a first task was to identify those women who, though not in psychiatric care, were none the less suffering from psychiatric disorder. This was done by a sociologist, supported by a research psychiatrist, interviewing every woman using a somewhat abbreviated version of the form of clinical examination that the psychiatrist used when interviewing members of the patient group (namely, the Present State Examination devised by Wing *et al.* 1974). Drawing on the results of this examination and any other information available, a judgement was made on the mental health of each woman in the sample. Those who had symptoms of a severity sufficient to merit psychiatric attention, according to the standards generally accepted in the United Kingdom, were classified as 'cases'. Those who had symptoms but the severity of which was below criterion were classified as 'borderline cases'. Central to the judgements was the use of anchoring examples for both cases and borderline cases.

Of the 458 women in the community sample, 76 were classified as cases and 87 as borderline cases, leaving 295 as relatively symptom free. For such of the findings as are reported here the borderline cases have been pooled with the symptom free, making a sub-sample of 382 women available as a comparison group.

The next task was to identify the date of onset of symptoms in the 76 women classified as cases. In about half (39) the symptoms had been present for twelve months or longer. These are termed chronic cases. In the remaining 37, onset was judged to have been within a year of interview; these are termed onset cases.[4]

The outcome of this preliminary work was that four groups of women had been identified, the 114 in the patient group, the 39 in the chronic and the 37 in the onset case groups, and the 382 women in the community group classified as normal or borderline.

Role of Recent Life Events

For that part of the enquiry aimed to determine the role of recent

[4] Since for purposes of the research it was essential that the date of onset was recorded accurately, the investigators used a special interviewing procedure which was used also for the patient group. A test of its validity, in which the date of onset given by a patient was compared with the one given independently by a relative, proved satisfactory.

life events the group of chronic cases was excluded and the enquiry confined to the other three groups.

The events to be considered were predefined and chosen as those likely to be of considerable emotional significance to an ordinary woman. Systematic enquiries were then made of every woman in the samples regarding the occurrence of any such event in her life during the year before interview. For each event reported a number of ratings were then made, by research workers not involved in the interview, on how the event would be likely to affect a woman placed in the circumstances described. A crucial proviso was that, whilst these ratings took into account all information regarding the informant's circumstances, they were made without knowledge of how she had actually reacted. Because of the importance of the findings a fuller account of the procedure adopted is given at the end of the section.

In their analysis of findings the most important rating scale yielding positive results was that dealing with the degree of threat or unpleasantness, lasting more than a week, that an event would be likely to pose to a woman placed in the particular circumstances described. This scale, termed by Brown and Harris the long-term contextual threat scale, proved, in their opinion, to be 'the measure of crucial importance for understanding the aetiology of depression', since, once this scale had been taken into account, scales covering other dimensions of events were not found to add anything further. In giving their findings they refer to any event rated as likely to pose a moderate or severe long-term threat to a woman placed in the circumstances described as a severe event.

When the proportions of women experiencing at least one severe event during the relevant preceding period are compared for the three groups, large and significant differences are found. Among patients the proportion experiencing at least one severe event is 61 per cent, among onset cases 68 per cent, and among the comparison group 20 per cent. Furthermore, among both the patient and the onset groups a much larger proportion than of the comparison group had experienced at least two severe events during the period: here the percentages are 27, 36 and 9 respectively.

As described more fully in Chapter 17, among the patients almost as high a proportion of women diagnosed as suffering a psychotic, or so-called endogenous, depression had experienced a severe event as of women diagnosed as suffering a neurotic, or so-called reactive, depression: figures are 58 per cent and 65 per cent respectively.

After examining the interval between the occurrences of a severe event and the onset of a depressive disorder, Brown and Harris conclude that in susceptible personalities 'severe events usually lead fairly quickly to depression'. In two-thirds the period was nine weeks or less and, in almost all, onset was within six months.

Since one in five of the 382 women in the comparison group had experienced a severe event during the preceding 38 weeks without developing a depressive disorder, it remains a possibility that a severe event could have occurred by chance in the life of a patient-to-be during the period in question and have played no part in causing her depression. To allow for this contingency, Brown and Harris apply a statistical correction and conclude that in not less than 49 per cent of patients the severe event was of true causal importance, not merely the result of chance. This means that, had the patient-to-be not suffered the severe event, she would not have developed a depressive disorder at least for a long time and, more probably, not at all. This is a most important conclusion.

To this point we have said nothing about the nature of the events that were judged by the raters to constitute a severe event within the definition used. When this is examined it is found that a majority entailed loss or expected loss. In the words of Brown and Harris, 'loss and disappointment are the central features of most events bringing about clinical depression'. In fact of all the events judged, in the circumstances in which they occurred, to pose a severe or moderately severe threat, whether occurring to depressed women or women in the comparison group, almost exactly half entailed the loss or expected loss of a person with whom the woman had a close relationship, namely her husband, her boyfriend or close confidant, or her child. The causes of such loss or expected loss were death, a life-threatening illness, a child leaving for distant places, and marital breakdown, manifested in desertion, a plan or threat to separate, or the unexpected discovery of a secret liaison.

A further 20 per cent of all the severe events recorded entailed a loss or expected loss of some other kind. In a few cases the event brought home to the woman the reality or irreversibility of a distressing situation in which she already was. Examples are an estranged pair who finally decide to make their separation legal, and the birth of a child to a woman whose marriage she knew had no future. Other events entailed the loss of something other than a personal relationship. These included loss of job and enforced removal from home.[5]

When all such losses are taken into account it is found that almost exactly half of the women suffering from depression had experienced a loss (48 per cent of patients and 59 per cent of onset cases) in contrast to 14 per cent of those in the comparison group. For the proportions for whom the loss in question had been a death the same ratio between groups holds: among patients 11 per cent, among onset cases 14 per cent, among the comparison group 4 per cent.

Although it would not be permissible on the basis of these findings to claim any simple equation between depressive disorders of all kinds and states of chronic mourning, the findings make plain, nevertheless, that there is a high degree of overlap between them. Moreover, the overlap is almost certainly greater than the figures given imply. For an examination of those women who were depressed but whose recent life experiences were *not* classified as having included a loss, or even a severe event, shows that a number of them had clearly been misclassified. For example, for one woman patient relevant material discovered later had not been available to the raters: her husband had been staying out late on a flimsy pretext and she had then discovered lipstick on his handkerchief, a discovery she had not divulged to the research interviewer. For another, an event had not been classified as severe because the object lost, a pet dog, had not been listed in the original definitions. This woman, a widow living with her mother, had had the dog for ten years and, two weeks before the onset of depression, had been forced to have it put down by her landlord. The emotional

---

[5] In a comparable study by Paykel (1974) two-thirds of the events found to precede the onset of depressive illness were classified as 'exits' which are roughly the equivalent of what Brown and Harris classify as losses or expected losses.

In another study, by a group led by William Bunney (Leff, Roatch and Bunney 1970), however, the events occurring most frequently before onset are described as 'threats to sexual identity', followed in order of frequency by 'changes in the marital relationship'. Except for seven patients who had experienced the death of someone close (17 per cent), the category of loss was not used. Yet inspection of their data shows that in a number of cases, for example of divorce, separation or jilting by boyfriend, the event in question could equally well, or better, have been categorized as a loss.

significance of the dog to her was evident: 'he was our baby—our whole life was devoted to him'.

Difficulties in Obtaining Relevant Data

The work of Brown and Harris is being described at some length not only because their findings are of great importance for an understanding of depressive disorders but also because their work illustrates what care must be taken if the data necessary for the task in hand are to be obtained.

There are a number of reasons why the occurrence of an event of great emotional significance to the person concerned may be missed by a clinician or a research worker and, as a consequence, the disorder ensuing be dubbed mistakenly as endogenous. One lies in the personal nature of the events themselves and in the difficulties that some of them pose for an enquirer. The lipstick on the husband's handkerchief, taken in context of the husband's other behaviour, is one example. Others are anniversaries[6] and analogous events that suddenly bring home to the person concerned the full impact of a past event.

A second reason, or set of reasons, why events of great significance may go unrecorded lies in the propensity of a person suffering from a depressive disorder either to be unwilling to confide the relevant information to the enquirer or else to be unable to do so either because of family pressure or because of being truly ignorant of what it is that is making him depressed. Unwillingness to tell a professional worker about an event that is extremely painful, and perhaps humiliating, is relatively easy to understand. That a person should be exposed to strong family pressure not to divulge the occurrence of certain events tends, however, to be neglected. Yet there is little doubt it plays a considerable role. Goodwin,[7] for example, refers to it as having been a main problem in the study by Bunney, especially in retarded and psychotic patients. In illustration he describes a woman who had had a stillbirth four months before admission but who was unable to mention it until she had been in treatment many months. Within her family all reference to

[6] Anniversaries were not on the list of predefined events used by Brown and Harris. The reasons for their omission were the methodological difficulties of obtaining information about them systematically, not that they were thought to be of no importance (personal communication).

[7] Reported in Friedman and Katz (1974, p. 151).

it was taboo. Even more difficult to remember, perhaps, is that a person may be truly ignorant of what it is that is troubling him. Yet, as already described, such ignorance certainly occurs.

The conclusion, noted earlier, that there is very considerable overlap between depressive disorders and states of chronic mourning is strengthened by a further finding of the Brown and Harris project. Women who develop a depressive disorder in adult life are more likely than others to have suffered the loss of mother during their childhood.

Incidence of Loss of or Prolonged Separation from Parent during Childhood

For purposes of this part of the enquiry the following three groups were studied: the 114 in the patient group, the 76 in the combined groups of community cases (chronic as well as onset), and the 382 in the comparison group.

The incidence of loss of mother, due to death, desertion or a separation lasting twelve months or more,[8] before the eleventh birthday for each of the three groups is shown in Table 4, together with the figures for loss of father. In both the patient group and the group of community cases, the incidence of loss of mother is higher than it is in the comparison group, and the same is true though to a lesser extent for loss of father. Of these differences the only one to reach statistical significance is loss of mother in the group of community cases as compared to the comparison group, 22·4 per cent and 6·0 per cent respectively.

TABLE 4 *Incidence of loss of mother and of father, from all causes, before 11th birthday*

	Patients	Cases		'Normals'
	%	%		%
Loss of mother	10·5	22·4	*	6·0
Loss of father	15·8	17·1		11·5
N	114	76		382

* P = <0·01

[8] Periods of wartime evacuation were not taken into account because information was not collected on all subjects. For particulars see Brown *et al.* (1977).

The association between mother loss during childhood and depressive disorder among women in the community sample can be put another way. Among the whole sample of 458 women seen initially in the community there were 40 who had lost mother before their eleventh birthday and 418 who had not. Among the 40 who had lost mother no less than 17, or 42·5 per cent, had developed a depressive disorder; whereas among the 418 who had lived with mother in the usual way only 59, or 14·1 per cent, had done so. Thus among the whole community sample the incidence of depressive disorder was three times higher in the mother-loss sub-sample than it was in the mother-present sub-sample.

A question that arises from these findings is why the incidence of loss of or prolonged separation from mother before the eleventh birthday in the group of depressed women who were not in psychiatric care, i.e. the group of community cases, should be so much higher (22·4 per cent) than it is in those who were in psychiatric care, i.e. the group of patients (10·5 per cent). One possibility which the data gathered by Brown and Harris suggest is that the family circumstances of women who have lost or been separated from mother during their childhood are different to those of other women and that these very circumstances, for example, early marriage and several young children to care for without help, are such as to militate against their seeking medical or psychiatric treatment.

Whatever the explanation of this finding may turn out to be it is clear that future studies must no longer assume that a sample of individuals suffering from a disorder which is drawn from a psychiatric clinic is representative of all individuals suffering from that disorder.

The Role of Loss in Depressive Disorders: A Summary

The conclusions reached by Brown and Harris can now be summarized. The experience of loss can contribute causally to depressive disorders in any of three ways:

(a) as a *provoking* agent which increases risk of disorder developing and determines the time at which it does so: a majority of women in both the patient group and the onset case group had suffered a major loss from death or for other reason during the nine months prior to onset;

(b) as a *vulnerability* factor which increases an individual's sensitivity to such events: in Brown's study, and also in other studies (see Chapter 17), loss of mother before the age of eleven is of significance;

(c) as a factor that influences both the *severity* and the *form* of any depressive disorder that may develop: the findings of Brown and Harris relevant to these effects are given in Chapter 17.

Loss and related types of severe event, however, were not the only forms of personal experience found by Brown and Harris to be contributing causally to depressive disorders. Like losses, these other causal agents could be divided into those that act as determinants of onset and those that increase vulnerability. Among the former were certain sorts of family event that, although lying outside their definition of a severe event, were none the less very worrying or distressing and which had persisted for two years or more. Among the factors that seemed to have increased a woman's vulnerability were the absence in her life of any intimate personal relationship, the presence of three or more children under fourteen to be cared for, and not going out to work.

It should be noted that the findings of Brown and Harris have not gone without criticism. For example, Tennant and Bebbington (1978) question both their procedure for diagnosing the cases of depressive disorder among the community sample and some of the statistical methods they used for analysing their data. This leads them to cast doubt on the distinction drawn between provoking agents and vulnerability factors. To these criticisms, however, Brown and Harris (1978b) have replied in convincing detail.

Method used by Brown and Harris for Identifying Life Events: Further Details

In order to deal with the methodological problems of how to identify events of emotional significance to an individual in a way that enables valid comparisons between groups to be made, a three-step procedure was adopted.

The first step was to identify events of possible importance that had occurred during the period in question. To this end 38 life events likely to evoke an emotional reaction in most people were defined in advance and in detail, and those persons in the respondent's life who were to be covered specified. The interviewers had then to explore with each respondent whether or not one of these events had occurred during the relevant period and to record the facts as reported without asking any questions as to how the respondent may actually have reacted.

The period chosen for this enquiry was the year before interview. For women in both the patient and the onset case groups this covered a period averaging 38 weeks before the onset of symptoms.

Although this first step provided a reliable method of identifying the occurrence of certain sorts of event, it failed (deliberately) to take account of an individual's personal circumstances and the meaning that the event would be likely to have for someone in those particular circumstances. This was made good by the second and third steps.

Having identified the occurrence of an event conforming to the criteria used, the interviewers next covered, in as informal a way as possible, a lengthy list of questions about what had led up to and what had followed each event, and the feelings and attitudes surrounding it. In addition to questions, the interviewer encouraged each woman to talk at length and, by suitable enquiries, also sought to obtain extensive biographical material. All interviews were tape-recorded.

Since the recording of life events and their meaning was to be done for every member of the three samples on a strictly comparable basis, it was necessary next to assess the meaning that each event reported would be likely to have for a woman placed in the particular circumstances described and to do so according to some yardstick that could be applied generally and without reference to the particular way that the woman being questioned happened to have reacted. This was the third step.

For each event reported a large number of ratings were made, by research workers not involved in the interview. One rating concerned the 'independence' of the event, that is the degree to which it could be viewed as independent of the respondent's own conscious behaviour. The other scales considered how the event would be likely to affect a woman placed in the circumstances described. These ratings, made on a four-point scale, took into account all information regarding the informant's circumstances but without knowledge of how she had actually reacted. Initially, each rater, working independently, made a rating on each of the scales. Thereafter the raters discussed any discrepancies and agreed a final rating. Interrater agreement was high. Raters were helped in their task not only by their regular discussions but also by a series of anchoring examples illustrating the four points on each scale, and by certain fairly standard conventions.

By following this rather lengthy procedure the researchers aimed to close the yawning scientific gap left by the two research methods traditionally employed, namely the clinical case history with its enormously rich detail but which lacks either comparison groups or safeguards against circular reasoning, and the epidemiological approach which, though strong in safeguards, has hitherto been bare of personal meanings.

The role of neurophysiological processes

It is important to realize that to attribute a major role in the aetiology of depressive disorders to psychosocial events, and in particular to separation and loss, does not preclude attributing a significant role also to neurophysiological processes.

That there is a relationship between abnormal levels of certain neuroendocrines and neurotransmitters, on the one hand, and affective states and disorders, on the other, is now fairly certain. Controversy begins when questions are raised about their causal relatedness. One school of thought has made the simple assumption that the causal sequence is always in one direction, from the changes in neurophysiological processes to the changes in affect and cognition. Yet it is now clear that the causal sequence can equally well run in the opposite direction. Research shows that cognitive and affective states of anxiety and depression, induced in adults by events such as separation and loss, may not only be accompanied by significant changes in the levels of certain neuroendocrines but that these changes are similar to those known often to be present in adults suffering from depression. That comparable changes can occur also in children who are subjected to separation and loss seems probable.[9] Once brought about, these neuroendocrinological changes may then prolong or intensify the depressive reaction. Readers interested in this field are referred to a comprehensive review by Hamburg, Hamburg and Barchas (1975).

[9] Such changes certainly occur in infant monkeys. For example, McKinney (1977), in a review of studies of animal models of depressive disorders, reports that, in four-month-old rhesus macaques that had been separated from mother for six days, major alterations were found in both the peripheral and the central brain amine systems of the animals.

Not unexpectedly, studies show that the size and pattern of neurophysiological responses to psychological events differ greatly from person to person. Such differences are probably responsible, in part at least, for differences between individuals in their degree of vulnerability to these events. Some of the differences are likely to be of genetic origin. Yet that is not the only possibility. An alternative source of difference could be differences in childhood experience. Thus, it is conceivable that the state of the neuroendocrine system of individuals who are subjected to severely stressing conditions during childhood might be permanently changed so that it becomes thereafter either more sensitive or less so. In any case genetic influences never operate in a vacuum. During development complex interactions between genetic and environmental influences are the rule; and it is especially when organisms are under stress that genetic differences between them are likely to be of most consequence.

Part III: The Mourning of Children

CHAPTER 15

Death of Parent During
Childhood and Adolescence

... Dick ... told him about his own father's death, which had happened
when Dick was a child at Dublin, not quite five years of age. 'That was
the first sensation of grief', Dick said, 'I ever knew. I remember I went
into the room where his body lay, and my mother sat weeping beside it.
I had my battledore in my hand, and fell a-beating the coffin, and calling
papa; on which my mother caught me in her arms, and told me in a flood
of tears papa could not hear me, and would play with me no more ...
And this', said Dick kindly, 'has made me pity all children ever since;
and caused me to love thee, my poor fatherless, motherless lad.'

THACKERAY, *Henry Esmond*

Sources and plan of work

Reference is already made in the opening chapter to the controversies that still surround the question of whether children and
adolescents are capable of responding to the loss of a parent with a
healthy form of mourning and, if so, at what age they become capable
of doing so. In examining these questions our plan will be to leave
for later consideration the special problems relating to losses sustained during the first two or three years and to start by reviewing
evidence regarding responses to a loss by death sustained between
about the third birthday and late adolescence.

Since systematic current studies of the responses of reasonably
representative samples of children and adolescents who have lost a
parent by death have begun only recently,[1] we have to rely on data
of a less representative kind. Three sources are available:

– data from two pilot studies, one by Kliman (1965) and another by
  Becker and Margolin (1967)
– data from a major clinical study carried out in Cleveland, Ohio by
  a group led by Erna Furman (1974)

[1] A study of this kind was begun in 1976 by Dr Beverley Raphael in
Sydney, Australia. Findings of the pilot phase described in Raphael *et al.*
(1978), are consistent with the generalizations made in this and later
chapters.

– such data as happen to have been collected on the responses of widows' children during the various studies of bereaved adults reported in earlier chapters.

Although from none of these studies are the data as systematic as those on adult mourning already reviewed, there is enough consistency in the findings to give confidence. A principal shortcoming is that, since the number of children concerned in each study is limited and they are spread over all the years of childhood, the number available at any one developmental level is small.

The study by Gilbert and Ann Kliman, undertaken in a well-to-do suburb of New York, concerns 18 children from seven middle-class families who had been contacted through a voluntary agency following the death of a parent. In three families mother had died and in four father. The children were ranged evenly in age between 3 years 9 months and 11 years 1 month, except for one infant of under one year and one boy of 14 years 3 months. Much of the data about the children was obtained during long semi-structured interviews with the surviving parent, but subsequently the children were also seen. A main limitation of this study, apart from the small size of the sample, is that in all but one or two families contact was delayed for many months, the average being eight months. Selection of families was intended to avoid any bias towards pathology; and none of the children had been referred to a clinic because of emotional difficulty.

The study by Becker and Margolin (1967) was undertaken in Boston and concerns nine children all under the age of seven, who came from seven middle-class families. In six father had died and in one mother. In each case the surviving parent had volunteered to participate in the study, contact had been established within six months of the death (often earlier) and, following assessment, none of the children appeared in need of psychotherapy. The data reported come from weekly case-work interviews, extended over one or more years, designed to assist the surviving parent both to deal with her own loss and also to help her children with theirs. (Data from weekly psychiatric interviews with the children are not reported.)

The study by Erna Furman and her colleagues concerns 23 children all of whom had lost a parent by death. They ranged in age from ten weeks to thirteen years and 'included black and white, rich and poor, various religious denominations and cultural backgrounds'. Fourteen of the children received individual psychoanalytical treatment for five sessions weekly over periods of two to six years. The other nine, all under the age of five, attended a therapeutic nursery school, while a child analyst in weekly sessions over periods of one to three years assisted the surviving parent, or parent-substitute, to work with his child therapeutically. By these means very extensive first-hand data were collected, in a number of cases starting immediately after the parent had died, and there was unrivalled opportunity to study the extent to which the responses of each child were influenced, in one direction or another, by the responses of the surviving parent and by the sort of information or misinformation that the child had received. In so far as the clinicians influenced the course of events, which they undoubtedly did, the directions of their influence and the techniques they used are clearly stated: this enables the reader to assess for himself the status and relevance of the data obtained.

The limitations of the study stem from the way in which the main sample of children came to be included. Except for one child, none was included simply because he had lost a parent. Eight were already in psychotherapy or a parent was receiving guidance when, quite unexpectedly, a parent died. Several of the others had been referred for advice because of emotional difficulties which, only after treatment had begun, were judged by the clinicians to have been precipitated or exacerbated by a bereavement sustained earlier. Nevertheless, although the sample is biased in the direction of pathology, in several of the younger children the difficulties present before the parent's death were minimal and of common occurrence. In her discussion, moreover, Furman refers to a wide range of other observations made by herself and members of her group during their intensive study of the problem. In what follows we draw extensively on their findings.

In view of the sampling limitations of all these studies we are fortunate to have additional information on children's responses from those who have studied widows. These include Marris (1958), who gives information from 47 London widows about the 93 children under the age of fifteen for whom they had been left to care, and Glick and his colleagues (1974), whose sample of widows with children in the same age-range is of comparable size (though particulars are not given). Other reports of relevance are one by Raphael

(1973) on the responses of the children of those widows who were being given counselling because initial assessment had predicted an unfavourable outcome for their mourning, and the account by Gorer (1965) which, so far as children and adolescents are concerned, deals mainly with responses to the death of a grandparent.

From the foregoing it will be clear that we have far more information about children's responses to the death of father than of mother. The reasons are the familiar ones. First, in the age-range with which we are concerned there are several times more children who have lost father than have lost mother. Secondly, several of the studies on which we are drawing confined themselves to widows and their children. Only the study by Furman gives more than marginal data about loss of mother.

In addition to the studies mentioned there are numerous reports of patients of all ages who were receiving psychotherapy for conditions, often severe, that seemed attributable at least in part to the loss of a parent during childhood. In the case of adult patients these losses have usually occurred many years earlier and the links between the event and subsequent symptoms correspondingly difficult to be sure about. In the case of child patients, by contrast, the loss may have been comparatively recent and the links therefore much easier to trace. All these cases which include a number reported by Furman and her colleagues provide the empirical base for our discussion of pathology in subsequent chapters.[2] Meanwhile, let us consider the validity of the accounts of children's responses now to be considered.

Validity of Data

In addition to the familiar difficulties of ensuring the validity of observations of human beings responding to any real-life situation, especially distressing ones, there are special difficulties in the case of bereaved children. Almost inevitably many of the observations of children's responses recorded in the literature are derived from accounts given by the surviving parent, usually the mother. Although these accounts are often very revealing, there are several major

[2] Shortly before this volume went to press my attention was drawn to the publication of another major work by a clinician, Lora Heims Tessman (1978), on the responses of children and adolescents who have lost a parent. Although the work deals mainly with loss due to divorce, there is also a long chapter on loss due to parental death.

dangers. The first is that the surviving parent, being herself in a state of emotional disturbance, is likely to be an uncertain observer, perceptive at one moment and blind at another. Secondly, her memory of events may be more than usually selective. Thirdly, she may attribute to the child feelings and responses which are really her own. And finally it may be unclear to what extent a child is responding to the loss itself and to what extent he is responding to a distraught widowed parent behaving towards him in strange and perhaps difficult ways.

These problems are well described by Harrison and his colleagues (1967) who studied the responses of the children who happened to be patients in a children's psychiatric hospital at the time of President Kennedy's assassination, and also of members of the staff. Subsequently two types of record about the children were available: first, routine day-to-day reports written by staff members; secondly, material gathered retrospectively, much of it during staff group discussions. After noting that there were numerous and serious discrepancies between observations recorded currently and those recorded later, and also the extent to which staff were influenced by the way they thought the children ought to respond, the authors conclude: 'In our data it was impossible to distinguish between adult misperceptions and confusions, the children's reaction to the tragedy, and the children's reactions to the changes in the adults.' Thus warned, we are wise to proceed cautiously.

Plan of Work

When discussing the responses of adults it proved expedient first to present a picture of the common responses to loss, next to review the pathological variants, and only later to consider the conditions that play a part in determining the various courses that mourning may take. Here we shall proceed differently. Every recent student of the problem, we find, including Nagera (1970) whose view on children's capacity to mourn differs from that advanced here, is deeply impressed by the enormous influence on a child's responses to loss of such variables as when and what he is told, how the surviving parent herself responds, and how she wishes and expects her child to respond. Because to discuss children's responses without constant reference to these conditions would be unrealistic, throughout this series of chapters we are as much concerned with how the people in a child's immediate environment are behaving towards him as with the child himself. This of course is no more than an application to the special problems of childhood of one of the principal lessons learned about the mourning of adults, namely that the course of mourning even in an adult is deeply influenced by the way he is treated by relatives and friends during the weeks and months following the loss.

Our plan therefore is to start by considering responses of children to loss of a parent when conditions are favourable and to proceed thence to consider the wide variety of their responses when conditions are unfavourable. Before doing so, however, it is useful to examine further the nature of certain of these very influential conditions.

When and what a child is told

Adults are usually present when a near relative dies; if they are not they are likely to be given the news promptly. By contrast, children in Western societies are unlikely to be present at the time of death; not infrequently information about it reaches them only much later, and even then often in a misleading form. In view of that it is hardly surprising that children's responses are apt to be out of keeping with what has happened.

When a child's parent dies it almost always rests with the surviving parent to inform him. This is an extremely painful task. A majority do it promptly but the younger the child the more likely is the parent to delay; and in a significant minority this delay is of weeks or even months. As a stopgap the child may be told that father has gone on a trip or perhaps been transferred to another hospital. Of the Boston widows studied by Glick *et al.* (1974) some 70 per cent told the children immediately but nearly one in three delayed. Two of them asked a relative to do it for them.

The reports show that in the cultures studied the surviving parent is extremely likely to tell the child that father has gone to heaven or been taken to heaven. For those who are devout this information accords with the parent's own belief. For many others, however, it does not, so that from the start a discrepancy exists between what the child is told and what the parent believes. This creates difficulties. Unless told otherwise a young child will naturally assume that heaven is no different from other distant places and that return is merely a matter of time. A little girl of four, who like others had been told her father had gone to heaven, was angry a few months later and cried bitterly because he did not come to her birthday party (Nagera 1970). Other children persist in asking mother where heaven is, what people do there, what they wear or what they eat, all of them questions a disbeliever finds embarrassing.

Another common account, resorted to especially after the death of an old person such as a grandparent, is to say that he or she has gone to sleep. Admittedly, this is a well-known figure of speech. Yet a young child has little knowledge of figures of speech and inevitably takes most of such sayings literally. Small wonder, therefore, if falling asleep thenceforward becomes for him a dangerous activity.

The two crucial items of information which sooner or later a child needs to know are first that the dead parent will never return and secondly that his body is buried in the ground or burned to ashes. For the surviving parent to give such information is extremely difficult because of the deep concern to shield her child from awareness of death and the pain of mourning that every parent in this situation has, and also, no doubt, because to speak about these things brings home their reality too nakedly. Information regarding disposal of the body is usually postponed for longest, sometimes for a year or two (Becker and Margolin 1967). Among all the families studied only a small minority of the children attended the funeral, for example, in Marris's London study 11 out of 94. Subsequently children were either not taken to the grave or, if they were, might not be informed of the reason. In a family described by Becker and Margolin the children visited the cemetery with father, placed flowers on the grave and witnessed relatives crying without anyone mentioning their mother's death and burial. The children, moreover, refrained from asking why they and others were there.

Not only is the information given to children often tardy and misleading but every researcher notes also how eager many a surviving parent is to ensure that her child does not see how distressed she herself is. Becker and Margolin tell of one mother who avoided talking to the children about how she felt for fear she would cry and not be able to stop. This, she thought, would be too upsetting for them. By contrast, she cried a great deal during interviews and also described how she cried for long hours alone after the children were asleep at night. During the interviews she recognized that a main difficulty was that she could not bear to face the intensity of her children's feelings. Thus, so far from assisting the children to express feeling, a proportion of parents make it almost impossible for them to do so. The difficulty created is vividly illustrated in an account by Palgi (1973) of a small boy whose mother chided him for not shedding tears over his father's death. 'How can I cry', he retorted, 'when I have never seen your tears?'

Children are quick to read the signs. When a parent is afraid of feelings the children will hide their own. When a parent prefers silence the children, sooner or later, will cease their enquiries. Several observers note how eager many of the children were to learn more about how and why their parent had died and what had happened subsequently, and how their enquiries were met with evasion or silence. Two examples of parents who made their reluctance explicit are given by Kliman (1965). In the first, two boys aged seven and nine who had lost their father wanted to know more about him and also pressed their mother to show them some old movie films of him. When she found this too painful, they taught themselves to operate the projector and ran through the films repeatedly on their own. In the second a father had lost both his wife and his son in a fire and blamed himself for not having done more to save them. Unable to bear talking about the event, he made his two young daughters promise that they would never mention their mother again in his presence.

What the proportion of parents in our culture who show reluctance to share information and feeling with their children may be we have no means at present of knowing. A reading of the various reports, however, shows that it is common in both Britain and America. Not only does this finding go far to explain the frequency with which children are said to deny the reality of a parent's death but it may explain also why the theory that a child's ego is too weak and undeveloped to bear the pain of mourning should have become so widely accepted. Indeed the evidence so far presented suggests that, irrespective of what the capacity of children may be, not infrequently the adults surrounding a child are themselves unable to bear the pain of mourning—perhaps that of their own mourning, certainly that of their child's, and especially that of mourning together.

Helping the Surviving Parent to Help the Children
Those who have worked in this field and especially the clinicians

are clear that nothing but confusion and pathology results when news of a parent's death is withheld from children, or glossed over, and when expression of feeling is discouraged either implicitly or explicitly. Much effort has therefore been given to finding means to help the surviving parent to help the children.

The first task undoubtedly is to provide the surviving parent with a supportive relationship within which he or she feels free to reflect on the blow that has fallen and how and why it came about, and to express all those tempestuous urges and feelings that is so necessary if mourning is to take a healthy course. Once a parent has surmounted this hurdle herself, it becomes less hard for her to include the children in the mourning process. Modelling her behaviour, perhaps unwittingly, on that of her counsellor, she can share with the children such facts as are known and answer their questions as truthfully as she is able. Together she and they can express their shared sorrow and distress, and also their shared anger and yearning. Often in such circumstances a parent finds that a schoolchild or adolescent has a much greater capacity to face the truth both about the past and their sadly changed future than, perhaps misled by relatives or friends, she had hitherto supposed. Only, indeed, when he is given true information, and the sympathy and support to bear it, can a child or adolescent be expected to respond to his loss with any degree of realism. This raises the question of how realistic about death children of different ages are capable of being.

Children's ideas about death

There has been much controversy concerning how children of different ages think about death. Issues debated include their ideas regarding the nature of death, its causes and what happens afterwards. Since comprehensive reviews of the literature are to be found in Anthony (1971) and Furman (1974), together with their own empirical records, we need not dwell long on the controversies.

Study of the literature shows that many divergences of opinion have arisen because a number of workers have confined their attention to the special case of human death or of the even more special case of parent death. Other disagreements can be traced to some of the earlier investigators (e.g. Nagy 1948) having failed to realize the extent to which children's ideas about death are derived from the cultural traditions of their families and schoolmates. As a result, notions such that a child must be at least six years old or even adolescent before he can conceive of death as being irreversible, or that young children inevitably attribute every death to a human or quasi-human agency, gained currency. Once the cultural biases are recognized, however, and the very special problems connected with the death of a parent allowed for, the picture that emerges is radically changed.

In the ordinary course of life even very young children meet with examples of death—a dead beetle, a dead mouse, a dead bird. The phenomenon is puzzling. Contrary to all previous experience with the animal, the dead creature is immobile and fails to respond to anything done to it. As a rule this arouses curiosity. What has happened? Is the creature asleep? How can we prod it into activity? In such circumstances no child is left for long without some explanation being given him either by an adult or by another child; and it is from these explanations that he develops his own ideas.

In different families and different cultural settings the explanations given a child vary over an enormous range. At one extreme are ideas of universal reincarnation and of divine purpose, at another ideas of the irreversibility of death and the role of natural causes. Between these extremes lies a wide array of beliefs, including many in which a distinction is made between the death of what are regarded as higher forms of life and lower forms. As a result of distinctions and qualifications of varying sorts being introduced the sets of beliefs about life and death held by adults in Western societies contain as a rule many areas of uncertainty, ambiguity and inconsistency. No wonder, therefore, that the beliefs of children vary widely too. Usually they differ from those of the adults around them only by being stated more baldly, by metaphors having been construed too literally, and by ambiguities and inconsistencies being dwelt upon instead of being glossed over.

In their various publications Robert and Erna Furman present evidence to show that even a young child has no more difficulty in conceiving of death as irreversible and as due to natural causes than has an adult and that whether or not he does so turns on what he is told. If a child no more than two is told that the dead beetle or the dead bird will never come alive again and that sooner or later death comes to all living creatures he may be incredulous at first but is likely to accept his parent's word. If he is told, too, that when an animal or a person well known dies it is natural to feel sad and to wish we could bring him alive again, he will hardly be surprised since it conforms with his experience and shows that his sorrows are understood. When parents adopt such practices, the Furmans point out, the way is prepared in some degree for helping a child mourn the death of a close relative, even that of a parent, should such a tragic blow fall. Only when a surviving parent genuinely believes in religious or philosophical ideas about death and an after-life, the evidence suggests, is it useful to introduce them to children: with honest help from his surviving parent a child will be able to make something of them and so be able to share in the family mourning. In other circumstances the complexity of these ideas and the difficulty of distinguishing between bodily and spiritual death leave him puzzled and confused whilst a gulf of misunderstanding may open between him and his surviving parent.

CHAPTER 16

Children's Responses
when Conditions are Favourable

> And while that face renews my filial grief,
> Fancy shall weave a charm for my relief
> Shall steep me in Elysian reverie,
> A momentary dream, that thou art she.

WILLIAM COWPER[1]

Mourning in two four-year-olds

When we read the evidence presented by Furman (1974) and the other workers named, it seems clear that provided conditions are favourable even a young child is able to mourn a lost parent in a way that closely parallels the healthy mourning of adults. The conditions required are no different in principle to the conditions that are favourable for adult mourning. Those most significant for a child are: first, that he should have enjoyed a reasonably secure relationship with his parents prior to the loss; secondly that, as already discussed, he be given prompt and accurate information about what has happened, be allowed to ask all sorts of questions and have them answered as honestly as is possible, and be a participant in family grieving including whatever funeral rites are decided on; and, thirdly, that he has the comforting presence of his surviving parent, or if that is not possible of a known and trusted substitute, and an assurance that that relationship will continue. Admittedly, these are stringent conditions but before dwelling on the many difficulties of meeting them let us describe the way children and adolescents commonly respond when the conditions can be met.

Evidence shows that after a parent's death a child or adolescent commonly yearns as persistently as does an adult and is ready to express such yearning openly whenever a listener is sympathetic. At times he entertains hope that his lost parent will return; at others he recognizes reluctantly that that cannot be and is sad. On

---

[1] On receiving a portrait of his mother who had died when he was nearly six.

occasion he will be observed searching (though this feature is not well recorded in the literature), or will describe experiencing a vivid sense of the dead person's presence. In some circumstances he will feel angry about his loss and in others guilty. Not infrequently he will be afraid that he will also lose his surviving parent, and/or substitute-parent, or that death will claim him too. As a result of his loss and his fear of further loss he will often be anxious and clinging, and sometimes engage obstinately in behaviour that is difficult to understand until its rationale is known.

To move from generalization to individual case there follow accounts of two children both recorded in great detail by Marion J. Barnes, a member of the group headed by Robert and Erna Furman in Cleveland. The records have been selected because they are the most complete available of young children from stable homes who have been developing reasonably well and have then suddenly lost a parent.[2] One, Wendy, lost her mother when she had just turned four. The other, Kathy, lost her father when she was two months younger. The reason for examining first the responses of children at the lower end of the age-range is that the younger the child the less likely, it has been supposed, is his mourning to resemble that of an adult.

Wendy Mourns her Mother

Wendy was aged four years when her mother died in an acute exacerbation of a chronic illness. Thereafter Wendy lived with her father and her sister, Winnie, eighteen months younger. In addition, maternal grandmother made herself responsible for the children's care whilst father was at work, and a maid who had been a daily with the family since the children were infants now became resident for five days a week. Help was given at weekends by paternal grandmother and another maid.

Much information is available about Wendy's development prior to her mother's death because for eighteen months mother had been coming for weekly professional advice on account of what appear to have been, in a two-and-a-half-year-old, rather minor problems. Wendy is described as wetting her bed, to have been attached to a blanket, to have had 'some typical fantasies around penis envy', and to have been unable to express her hostility in words, particularly toward her younger sister. Six months later mother was still concerned about Wendy's attachment to the blanket,

[2] The case of Wendy is a shortened version of an account given in a paper by Barnes (1964). The case of Kathy is a shortened version of an account, also given by Barnes, in the book by Furman (1974, pp. 154–62).

her thumb sucking and her reluctance to separate from her. In other respects, however, Wendy seemed to be making good progress and began attending a nursery school.

It then transpired that Wendy's mother, now twenty-five, had had an attack of multiple sclerosis which had been in remission during the previous seven years. Apart from mother's two-hour-long daily rest periods, however, the illness made no outward difference to the family and both parents were keen to keep it dark, though not unexpectedly Wendy often resented having to keep quiet during mother's long rests. When information about the illness finally emerged the therapist felt it advisable as a precautionary measure for Wendy to be transferred to the clinic's therapeutic nursery school; but no one anticipated that tragedy was so close. For within four months of Wendy starting there, her mother had a fulminating flare-up of the illness, entered hospital suddenly and died within two weeks.

During the week or two prior to the acute attack mother was inclined to feel fatigued and had a pain in her shoulder. Wendy was worried and became reluctant to attend nursery school, especially when it meant father taking her there instead of mother. She was clearly worried about mother's being unwell; and her anxiety was increased by the paternal grandfather, whom they visited almost daily, being seriously ill also and not expected to live.

When mother's condition suddenly became worse and she was admitted to hospital, the therapist saw father daily to help him decide what to tell the children. On her advice the illness was explained to them as being very serious, so serious in fact that mother could not lift her head and arms or even talk, which helped Wendy understand why mother could not talk to her on the phone. The children were also told that the doctors were doing everything possible to help. During the last critical days, moreover, the therapist suggested to father that he not hide completely from them his sadness, concern and anxiety, as he had previously felt he must.

During the weeks prior to the flare-up of the illness, Wendy was expressing some hostility and rivalry towards mother and also expressed a fear on two occasions that mother might die. Basing her interventions on the theory that a child's fear of mother's death is commonly a result of an unconscious wish that she should die, the therapist encouraged the parents to reassure Wendy that her occasional angry thoughts would not affect mother's well-being. During the acute phase of mother's illness father was encouraged to continue giving such reassurances.[3]

On the day mother died father decided to tell the children what had

[3] In view of mother's uncertain health it seems more likely that the principal source of Wendy's fear lay in clues she had picked up from father or grandmother, or mother herself, that they were anxious about mother's condition (see Volume II, Chapter 18).

happened, and also that mother would be buried in the ground and that this was the end. This he did during a ride in the car. Mother had stopped breathing, he told them, she could not feel anything; she was gone for ever and would never come back. She would be buried in the ground, protected in a box and nothing would hurt her—not the rain nor the snow (which was falling) nor the cold. Wendy asked, 'How will she breathe and who will feed her?' Father explained that when a person is dead they don't breathe any more and don't need food. There had already been general agreement that the children were too young to attend the funeral; but father showed them the cemetery, with a near-by water tower which could be seen from their window.

That evening the children seemed relatively unaffected and for a time were busy playing 'London Bridge is falling down'. Relatives, who disagreed with father's candour and preferred to tell the children stories of heaven and angels, endeavoured to stifle their sorrow and to enter gaily into the children's games.

During the days that followed Wendy invented two games to play with her father, in both of which she would twirl around and then lie down on the floor. In one she would then quickly stand up with the remark 'You thought I was dead, didn't you?' In the other, in which she was supposed to rise when father gave the proper signal (which was her mother's first name), she remained prone. There were also occasions, for example at meals, when Wendy cheerfully enacted the part of her mother with remarks such as 'Daddy, this is such a pretty tie. Where did you get it?' or 'Anything interesting happen at the office today?'

Yet sorrow was not far away. A week after mother's death the grandmother of another child became very emotional when talking about it in the car to Wendy's grandmother. Wendy paled and fell over on the seat. Grandmother comforted her, held her and they both cried. About the same time, on a visit to relatives, cousins assured Wendy her mother was an angel in heaven and then showed her her mother's picture. Wendy cried hysterically and said her mother was in the ground.

During the third week after mother's death Wendy gave evidence that she was still hoping for mother's return. Sitting on the floor with her younger sister, she chanted, 'My mommy is coming back, my mommy is coming back, I know she's coming back.' To this Winnie retorted in an adult-like monotone, 'Mommy's dead and she's not coming back. She's in the ground by the "tower water".' 'Tsh, don't say that,' retorted Wendy.

Wendy's preoccupation with her mother was shown too in a 'snow-flake' song she had made up on the day after the funeral. At first it ran (probably influenced by the interpretations she had received): 'Snow-flakes come and they disappear. I love my mommy and she is dead. I hate my mommy and I hope she doesn't come back. I love my mommy and I want her.' A few days later she omitted 'I hate my mommy'. By the sixth day it was in the past tense, 'I loved my mommy and want her to come back.' A fortnight later on the way to school it was 'My mommy is coming back', but whispered so low that grandmother could hardly hear it.

The same preoccupation emerged from another concern of Wendy's. Almost daily on the way to school she engaged her grandmother in conversation about the ducks on the pond: 'Are they cold? Will they freeze? Who feeds them?' At times these discussions merged into more direct questions: 'Do dead people have to be fed? Do they have any feelings?' To rebut information given by grandmother that freezing temperatures result in even thicker ice, Wendy would point hopefully to a small area over a spring; 'But, Grandma, I see a little part that is not frozen even though it is so cold.' The therapist suggested to grandmother she discuss with Wendy how very hard it is to believe that a person is dead for ever and will never return.

After one such talk Wendy decided to pretend that grandmother was mother—she would call her Mommy and grandmother was to pretend that Wendy was her own little girl. At nursery school she told another child how she had a mother for pretend—her grandmother. To this the other child remarked. 'Oh, it really isn't the same, is it?' to which Wendy assented sadly, 'No, it isn't.'

On another occasion, about four weeks after mother had died, Wendy complained that no one loved her. In an attempt to reassure her, father named a long list of people who did (naming those who cared for her). On this Wendy commented aptly, 'But when my mommy wasn't dead I didn't need so many people—I needed just one.'

Four months after mother's death, when the family took a spring vacation in Florida, it was evident that Wendy's forlorn hopes of mother's return persisted. Repeating as it did an exceptionally enjoyable holiday there with mother the previous spring, Wendy was enthusiastic at the prospect and during their journey recalled with photographic accuracy every incident of the earlier one. But after arrival she was whiny, complaining and petulant. Father talked with her about the sad and happy memories the trip evoked and how very tragic it was for all of them that Mommy would never return; to which Wendy responded wistfully, 'Can't Mommy move in the grave just a little bit?'

Wendy's increasing ability to come to terms with the condition of dead people was expressed a year after mother's death when a distant relative died. In telling Wendy about it father, eager not to upset her, added that the relative would be comfortable in the ground because he would be protected by a box. Wendy replied, 'But if he's really dead, why does he have to be comfortable?'

Simultaneously with her persisting concern about her missing mother and the gradually fading hopes of her return, Wendy gave evidence of being afraid she herself might die.

The first indications were her sadness and reluctance to go to sleep during nursery school naptime. Her teacher, sensing a problem, took

Wendy on her lap and encouraged her to talk. After some days Wendy explained how, when you are asleep, 'You can't get up when you want to.' Six months later she was still occupied with the distinction between sleep and death, as became plain when a dead bird was found and the children were discussing it.

Wendy's fear of suffering the same fate as her mother manifested itself also when, during the fourth week after mother's death, she insisted that she did not want to grow up and be a big lady and that, if she had to grow up, she wished to be a boy and a daddy. She also wanted to know how old one is when one dies and how one gets ill. On the therapist's encouragement father talked with Wendy about her fear that when she grew up she would die as her mother had and also reassured her that mother's illness was very rare. A few days later Wendy enquired of her grandmother, 'Grandma, are you strong?' When grandmother assured her she was, Wendy replied, 'I'm only a baby.' This provided grandmother with further opportunity to discuss Wendy's fear of the dangers of growing up.

On another occasion when Wendy was similarly afraid, the clues were at first sight so hidden that her behaviour appeared totally unreasonable. One morning during the third week after mother's death Wendy, quite uncharacteristically, refused to put on the dress decided upon or go to school and, when the maid persisted, threw a temper tantrum. The family were puzzled, but they hit on the solution whilst discussing the incident with the therapist. Before Christmas mother had taken the children to look at the shops and in one they had seen Santa Claus attended by little angels. The angels' dresses were for sale and mother had bought one for each of the children who were delighted. It was her angel dress that Wendy had objected to wearing that morning.

A fortnight after this episode paternal grandfather died. When told, Wendy was matter-of-fact about the funeral and seemed to comprehend well the finality of death. At nursery school she was sad, and whilst sitting on the teacher's lap, she told about the death and cried a little; but then claimed she was only yawning. A little later, however, she commented, 'It's all right to cry if your mother and grandfather died.' Thereafter she recalled nostalgically how when first she came to nursery school her mother was not sick and would take her to and from school.

Shortly afterwards, hearing someone mention that grandfather's house would be sold, Wendy became apprehensive. She refused to go to school and, instead, stayed to check on the dishes and chairs at home. Only after it was explained that her house was not to be sold as well were her fears allayed and was she willing to go to school again.

There were many occasions when Wendy was afraid lest she lose other members of her family. For example, she was often upset and irritable at nursery school on Monday mornings. When asked what troubled her she replied that she was angry because her maternal grandmother and the maid had not been with her at the week-end. She did not want them to leave—ever. In the same way she was angry with her grandmother when, nine months after mother's death, she finally took a few days' break.

On two occasions father was away overnight on business trips. At school Wendy seemed sad and, when the teacher asked what she would like her to write, replied, 'I miss my mommy.' On the second occasion she did not want grandmother to leave her at nursery school, got out her old blanket and sat next to the teacher. Later she cried and agreed that she missed her father and was worried lest he not return. In a similar way she was upset when the maid was away for five weeks because of a leg injury. When at last the maid returned, Wendy wanted to stay at home with her instead of going to school.

Much else in the record shows Wendy's persistent longing for mother and her constant anxiety lest she suffer some other misfortune. When a new child arrived at school Wendy would look sad as she watched the child with her mother. On one such occasion she claimed that her mother was going to wash her face because the maid had forgotten to. Any small change of routine such as her teacher being away would be met with anxiety. On such occasions instead of playing she would sit with another teacher looking sad.

At the end of twelve months Barnes reports that Wendy was progressing well but predicted that, as in the year past, separations, illness, quarrels and the deaths of animals or people would continue to arouse in Wendy 'a surplus' of anxiety and sorrow.

In Chapter 23 an account is given of how two-and-a-half-year-old Winnie responded after her mother's death.

Kathy Mourns her Father

Kathy was aged 3 years and 10 months when her father died very suddenly of a virus infection. Thereafter she lived in the house of the maternal grandparents with her mother and two brothers, Ted aged five and Danny not quite one.

Before the tragedy the family had been known to the therapist for about eighteen months because the parents, 'a happy young couple devoted to each other and to their children', had sought advice about Ted's overactive behaviour. After a few sessions, which led to changes in the parents' handling of him, Ted's behaviour improved. A few weeks after father's death, however, mother was again worried about Ted and sought further advice.

At the time of father's illness and death all members of the family had been ill and the baby, Danny, had been admitted to hospital at the same time as father. After father died mother, shocked and distraught, immediately shared the news with Ted and Kathy and took them to stay with her own parents. After the funeral, which the children did not attend, mother sold the house and went to live with her parents, remaining at home herself to care for the children.

From babyhood onwards Kathy's development had been favourable.

She talked early, dressed herself with great pride by two years, and enjoyed helping mother in the house. Until she was two and a half she had sucked a forefinger and was also attached to a blanket, but had then lost interest. Now in her fourth year she enjoyed cooking with mother and making the beds. She was very handy with paste and scissors, could concentrate for long periods of time and took great pleasure in achievement. Soon after her birth she had become 'father's openly acknowledged favourite' and when he returned from work he had always picked her up first.[4]

After father died Kathy's life changed abruptly. Not only had she no father but mother was preoccupied and her brothers also upset. Moreover it was a new house, grandfather preferred the boys and grandmother was not very tolerant of young children. Kathy often cried and was sad; she lost her appetite, sucked her finger and resumed cuddling her blanket. At other times, however, she asserted 'I don't want to be sad' and seemed even a little euphoric.

Although mother mourned deeply, she had difficulty expressing her feelings and there was reason to think her reserve interacted with Kathy's own tendency to overcontrol. When mother, with some help, found herself able to share feeling with the children, to talk to them about father and to assure Kathy it was in order to be sad, Kathy's euphoria abated. Nevertheless, in view of her tendency to overcontrol, the therapist thought it desirable for her to be transferred to the clinic's nursery school. This was five months after father's death when Kathy was 4 years and 3 months old. Mother continued to have weekly talks with the therapist.

During the early weeks at school Kathy seemed to be in complete control. She adapted quickly to the new routines, wished to stay for longer each day and expressed few feelings of missing her mother. She did not make close relationships with other children or teachers, however, and was apt to appeal unnecessarily to the teachers instead of fighting her own battles.

From the first Kathy spoke about her father and told everyone immediately that he had died. When, on the third day of her attendance, a turtle died she insisted on removing it from the tank (into which another child had put it) and demanded it be buried. It appeared that she had a good understanding of the concrete aspects of death, even if she expressed no feeling. Yet, significantly enough, she was at this time much concerned about the welfare of another child who had also lost his father. By comforting him and amusing him she tried hard to distract him from his sorrows.

Three months after starting school Kathy for the first time visited her father's grave. She was in a conflict about going. She both wanted to go

---

[4] It seems likely that father's open favouritism of Kathy may have accounted for some of Ted's problems (J.B.).

and also cried bitterly about doing so. After placing flowers on the grave she began asking a succession of questions that mother found painful to answer: 'Are there snakes in the ground? Has the box come apart?' Mother struggled bravely to help Kathy to understand and express her feelings but sometimes found the burden too great.

During the following four months Kathy, already aged 4½ years, had a difficult time. Danny was now very active and required mother's constant vigilance. Ted, with whom Kathy had regularly played, now preferred his peers. Grandfather's preference for the boys was unmistakable. And finally Kathy, who had had a minor orthopaedic problem, now required a cast on one leg. No longer was she the happy controlled little girl. Evidently feeling left out, she became demanding of the teachers and irritable and petulant with her mother. Her play deteriorated; she refused to share her toys and became generally cranky and miserable. Either she showed off by endlessly dressing up in fancy clothes and jewellery or else withdrew into herself. Masturbation increased and so did her demand for her blanket. At night she insisted her mother reassure her that she loved her.

Throughout these later months Kathy frequently expressed intense longing for her father. Both at home and at school she talked about him and described all the activities they engaged in together; sometimes she recounted stories in which father rescued her when she was scared and alone. At Christmas when the family visited the grave Kathy was deeply sad and wished for her father's return. When asked what she wanted as a Christmas present, she replied dejectedly, 'Nothing.'

During this time Kathy was often angry and unreasonable with her mother, especially over minor disappointments. For example, on one occasion mother had promised her sledding after school but had had to cancel it because the snow had melted. Kathy, inconsolable, reproached her mother bitterly as she had on similar occasions previously: 'I can't stand people breaking their promises.' Subsequently it transpired that, on the day before his admission to hospital, father had promised to take Kathy to the candy store on the following day and inevitably had failed to keep his promise. This led on to a discussion with her mother about the frustrations father's death had brought her and how angry she felt about what had happened. Sadly Kathy described how much she missed her father both when at home and at school. 'There are only two things I want,' she asserted, 'my daddy and another balloon.' (She had recently lost one.)

During these talks, too, Kathy cast light on her ideas regarding the causes of death. Before he had been taken to hospital, she recalled, her father had looked very poorly. He had also looked sad and later she had connected this with his dying: 'I always felt if you're very happy you won't die.' For this reason she had tried to be happy following father's death.

In fact there had been many occasions following father's death when

Kathy showed she was afraid someone else in the family might die, especially when there was illness. When Kathy herself was unwell she questioned her mother whether all daddies die, would mother die, would she herself die, adding with much feeling, 'I don't want to die because I don't want to be without you.'

Some months later mother decided to move with the children into a house of their own. This was partly to avoid friction with the grandparents—for example grandmother had become increasingly critical of Kathy especially when Kathy was angry with her mother or was sadly longing for her father—and partly to be more independent. About five years later when Kathy was approaching the age of ten mother remarried and Kathy seemed to accept her stepfather without difficulty. By then things were going well for her: she was proving successful at school, in her relationships and in her various other interests.

Summing up, the therapist writes: 'Kathy's initial difficulties with excessive control of feelings and in expressing anger and sadness predated the father's death but were augmented by it. She brought out some of her own reasons for not wanting to be sad, but her mother's attitude to expressing and accepting feelings appeared to play a more prominent role. The mother's recognition of this and her attempts to work with Kathy in this area were very helpful to her, as was the support of the teachers.'

Readers may suspect too, from what we are told of grandmother, that mother's own difficulty in expressing feeling had originated during her childhood in response to her own mother's strictures.

Some Tentative Conclusions

These two records speak for themselves; and, when considered in conjunction with other observations of children whose relationships are secure and affectionate, enable us to draw a number of tentative conclusions.

When adults are observant and sympathetic and other conditions are favourable, children barely four years old are found to yearn for a lost parent, to hope and at times to believe that he (or she) may yet return, and to feel sad and angry when it becomes clear that he will never do so. Many children, it is known, insist on retaining an item of clothing or some other possession of the dead parent, and especially value photographs. So far from forgetting, children given encouragement and help have no difficulty in recalling the dead parent and, as they get older, are eager to hear more about him in order to confirm and amplify the picture they have retained, though perhaps reluctant to revise it adversely should they learn unfavourable things about him. Among the seventeen children aged between

3.9 and 14.3 studied by Kliman (1965), overt and prolonged yearning for the lost parent was recorded in ten.

As with an adult who yearns for a lost spouse, the yearning of a child for a lost parent is especially intense and painful whenever life proves more than usually hard. This was described vividly by a teenage girl who a few months earlier had lost her father suddenly from an accident: 'When I was little I remember how I used to cry for Mummy and Daddy to come, but I always had hope. Now when I want to cry for Daddy I know there isn't any hope.'

As an initial response to the news of their loss some children weep copiously, others hardly at all. Judging by the Kliman's findings, there seems a clear tendency for initial weeping to increase with age. In children under five it was little in evidence, in children over ten often prolonged. Reviewing the accounts given by widowed mothers of their children's initial reactions Marris (1958) is impressed by their extreme variety. There were children who cried hysterically for weeks, others especially some of the younger ones who seemed hardly to react. Others again became withdrawn and unsociable. Furman reports repeated and prolonged sobbing in some children who remained inconsolable, whereas for others tears brought relief. Without far more detailed studies than are yet available, however, we are in no position to evaluate these findings. Not only is it necessary to have records of a reasonable number of children at each age-level but exact particulars are necessary both of the children's family relationships and also of the circumstances of the death, including what information was given to the child and how the surviving parent responded. Such data are likely to take many years to collect.

As in the case of adults, some bereaved children have on occasion vivid images of their dead parent linked, clearly, with hopes and expectations of their returning. Kliman (1965, p. 87), for example, reports the case of a six-year-old girl who, with her sister two years older, had witnessed her mother's sudden death from an intracranial haemorrhage. Before getting up in the morning this child frequently had the experience of her mother sitting on her bed talking quietly to her, much as she had when she was alive. Other episodes described in the literature, usually given as examples of children denying the reality of death, may also be explicable in terms of a child having had such an experience. Furman (1974), for example, describes how Bess, aged three and a half, who was thought to have been 'well aware of the finality of her mother's death', announced one evening to her father, 'Mummy called and said she'd have dinner with us', evidently believing it to be true.[5] On one occasion a male cousin of twenty-two, of whom both grandmother and Wendy were fond, came to call. Without thinking, grandmother exclaimed, 'Wendy, look who's here!' Wendy looked, and then turned pale; instantly grandmother knew what Wendy was thinking.[6]

Thus the evidence so far available suggests strongly that, when conditions are favourable, the mourning of children no less than of adults is commonly characterized by persisting memories and images of the dead person and by repeated recurrences of yearning and sadness, especially at family reunions and anniversaries or when a current relationship seems to be going wrong.

This conclusion is of great practical importance, especially when a bereaved child is expected to make a new relationship. So far from its being a prerequisite for the success of the new relationship that the memory of the earlier one should fade, the evidence is that the more distinct the two relationships can be kept the better the new one is likely to prosper. This may be testing for any new parent-figure, for the inevitable comparisons may be painful. Yet only when both the surviving parent and/or the new parent-figure are sensitive to the child's persisting loyalties and to his tendency to resent any change which seems to threaten his past relationship is he likely to accommodate in a stable way to the new faces and the new ways.[7]

[5] Fortunately Bess's father knew how to respond. Gently he replied, 'When we miss Mummy so very much we'd like to think that she is not really dead. I guess it will be a sad dinner for both of us' (pp. 24–5).

[6] Wendy's misinterpretation, born of hopes and expectations, has an almost exact parallel in the experience of a middle-aged widow whose husband had died suddenly of a heart attack in the street. Seven months after his death, a police constable came to her flat and informed her that her husband had had a minor accident and had been taken to hospital. At once she thought to herself how right she had been all the time in thinking that her husband was still alive and that she had only been dreaming that he was dead. A moment later, however, as her doubts grew, she enquired of the constable whom he was looking for; it proved to be her neighbour next door.

[7] These practical problems are well discussed by Furman (1974, pp. 26 and 68).

Other features of childhood mourning which have great practical implications are the anxiety and anger which a bereavement habitually brings.

As regards anxiety, it is hardly surprising that a child who has suffered one major loss should fear lest he suffer another. This will make him especially sensitive to any separation from whoever may be mothering him and also to any event or remark that seems to him to point to another loss. As a result he is likely often to be anxious and clinging in situations that appear to an adult to be innocuous, and more prone to seek comfort by resorting to some old familiar toy or blanket than might be expected at the age he is.

Similar considerations apply to anger, for there can be no doubt that some young children who lose a parent are made extremely angry by it. An example from English literature is of Richard Steele, of *Spectator* fame, who lost his father when he was four and who recalled how he had beaten on the coffin in a blind rage. In similar vein a student teacher described how she had reacted at the age of five when told that her father had been killed in the war. 'I shouted at God all night. I just couldn't believe that he had let them kill my father. I loathed him for it.'[8] How frequent these outbursts are we have no means of knowing. Often no doubt they go unobserved and unrecorded, especially when the anger aroused is expressed in indirect ways. An example of this is the grumbling resentment shown by Kathy many months after her father's death which was channelled into her repeated complaints about people who don't keep their promises. Clearly, had Kathy not had a mother who, guided by the therapist, was attuned to the situation and was able to discover the origin of Kathy's complaints, it would have been easy to have dismissed the child as inherently unreasonable and possessed simply of a bad temper.

How prone children are spontaneously to blame themselves for a loss is difficult to know. What, however, is certain is that a child makes a ready scapegoat and it is very easy for a distraught widow or widower to lay the blame on him. In some cases, perhaps, a parent does this but once in a sudden brief outburst; in other cases it may be done in a far more systematic and persistent way. In either case it is likely that the child so blamed will take the matter to heart and

[8] This example, as well as the reference to Richard Steele, is taken from Mitchell (1966).

thereafter be prone to self-reproach and depression.[9] Such influences seem likely to be responsible for a large majority of cases in which a bereaved child develops a morbid sense of guilt; they have undoubtedly been given far too little weight in traditional theorizing.

Nevertheless, there are certain circumstances surrounding a parent's death which can lead rather easily to a child reaching the conclusion that he is himself to blame, at least in part. Examples are when a child who has been suffering from an infectious illness has infected his parent, and when a child has been in a predicament and his parent, attempting rescue, has lost his life. In such cases only open discussion between the child and his surviving parent, or an appropriate substitute, will enable him to see the event and his share in it in a proper perspective.

In earlier chapters (Chapters 2 and 6), I have questioned whether there is good evidence that identification with the lost person plays the key role in healthy mourning that traditional theorizing has given it. Much of the evidence at present explained in these terms can be understood far better, I believe, in terms of a persistent, though perhaps disguised, striving to recover the lost person. Other phenomena hitherto presented as evidence of identification can also be explained in other ways. For example, a bereaved child's fear that he may also die is found often to be a consequence of his being unclear about the causes of death and as a result supposing that whatever caused his parent's death might well cause his own too, or that, because his parent died as a young man or woman, the same fate was likely to be his also.

There are, it is true, many cases on record where a child is clearly identifying with a dead parent. Wendy at times treated her father in the same way as her mother had treated him with remarks such as, 'Anything interesting happen at the office today?' Other children play at being a teacher, or take great pains over painting, evidently influenced by the fact that the dead father was a teacher or the dead mother a painter. But these examples do little more than show that a child whose parent is dead is no less disposed to emulate him or her than he was before the death. Whereas the examples demonstrate clearly how real and important the relationship with the

[9] Examples are given in Chapters 21 and 22. See also the case of a woman suffering from a phobia of dogs reported by Moss (1960) and described at the end of Chapter 18 in Volume II.

parent continues to be even after the death, they provide no evidence of substance that after a loss identification plays either a larger part or a more profound one in a child's life than it does when the parent is alive.

Thus I believe that in regard to identificatory processes, as in so much else, what occurs during childhood mourning is no different in principle to what occurs during the mourning of adults. Furthermore, as we see in Chapter 21, the part played by identification in the disordered mourning of children seems also to be no different in principle to the part it plays in the disordered mourning of adults.

Mourning in Older Children and Adolescents

If we are right in our conclusion that young children in their fourth and fifth years mourn in ways very similar to adults, we would confidently expect that older children and adolescents would do so too; and all the evidence available supports that conclusion. Contrary opinions have arisen, I believe, only because the experience of clinicians is so often confined to children whose loss and mourning have taken place in unfavourable circumstances.

Yet there is reason to believe that there are also true differences between the mourning of children and the mourning of adults, and it is time now to consider what they may be.

Differences between children's mourning and adults'

The course taken by the mourning of adults is, we have seen, deeply influenced by the conditions that obtain at the time of the death and during the months and years after it. During childhood the power of these conditions to influence the course of mourning is probably even greater than it is in adults. We start by considering the effects of these conditions.

In earlier chapters we noted repeatedly how immensely valuable it is for a bereaved adult to have available some person on whom he can lean and who is willing to give him comfort and aid. Here as elsewhere what is important for an adult is even more important for a child. For, whereas most adults have learned that they can survive without the more or less continuous presence of an attachment figure, children have no such experience. For this reason, it is clearly more devastating still for a child than it is for an adult should he find himself alone in a strange world, a situation that can all too easily arise should a child have the misfortune to lose both parents or should his surviving parent decide for some reason that he be cared for elsewhere.

Many differences arise from the fact that a child is even less his own master than is a grown-up. For example, whereas an adult is likely either to be present at the time of a death or else to be given prompt and detailed information about it, in most cases a child is entirely dependent for his information on the decision of his surviving relatives: and he is in no position to institute enquiries as an adult would should he be kept in the dark.

In a similar way, a child is at even greater disadvantage than is an adult should his relatives or other companions prove unsympathetic to his yearning, his sorrow and his anxiety. For, whereas an adult can, if he wishes, seek further for understanding and comfort should his first exchanges prove unhelpful, a child is rarely in a position to do so. Thus some at least of the differences between the mourning of children and the mourning of adults are due to a child's life being even less within his control than is that of a grown-up.

Other problems arise from a child having even less knowledge and understanding of issues of life and death than has an adult. In consequence he is more apt to make false inferences from the information he receives and also to misunderstand the significance of events he observes and remarks he overhears. Figures of speech in particular are apt to mislead him. As a result it is necessary for the adults caring for a bereaved child to give him even more opportunity to discuss what has happened and its far-reaching implications than it is with an adult. In the great majority of cases in which children are described as having failed totally to respond to news of a parent's death, it seems more than likely that both the information given and the opportunity to discuss its significance were so inadequate that the child had failed to grasp the nature of what had happened.

Yet not all the differences between childhood and adult mourning are due to circumstances. Some stem from a child's tendency to live more in the present than does an adult and from the relative difficulty a young child has in recalling past events. Few people grieve continuously. Even an adult whose mourning is progressing healthily forgets his grief briefly when some more immediate interest catches hold of him. For a child such occasions are likely to be more frequent than for an adult, and the periods during which he is consciously occupied with his loss to be correspondingly more transient. As a result his moods are more changeable and more easily misunderstood. Furthermore, because of these same characteristics, a young child is readily distracted, at least for the moment, which makes it easy for those caring for him to deceive themselves that he is not missing his parents.

If this analysis of the differences in the circumstances and psychology of a bereaved child and of a bereaved adult is well based, it is not difficult to see how the idea has developed that a child's ego is too weak to sustain the pain of mourning.

Behaviour of surviving parents to their bereaved children

It is inevitable that when one parent dies the survivor's treatment of the children should change. Not only is the survivor likely to be in a distressed and emotional state but he or she now has sole responsibility for the children instead of sharing it, and now has to fill two roles, which in most families have been clearly differentiated, instead of the single familiar one.

The death of a child's parent is always untimely and often sudden. Not only is he or she likely to be young or in early middle-age, but the cause is much more likely to be an accident or suicide than in later life.[10] Sudden illness also is not uncommon. Thus for all the survivors, whether of the child's, the parent's or the grandparent's generation, the death is likely to come as a shock and to shatter every plan and every hope of the future. As a result just when a child needs most the patience and understanding of the adults around him those adults are likely to be least fit to give it him.

[10] In the U.K. the proportion of deaths due to accident or suicide in the younger age-groups is many times greater than it is in older ones. The table below gives the percentages for men and women who died before they had reached 45 years and for those aged between 45 and 64, for the year 1973.

Age group	% deaths due to	
	Accident	Suicide
15–44	20·6	6·5
45–64	1·9	1·3

Figures are derived from the Registrar-General's Statistical Review of England and Wales for 1973 (H.M.S.O. 1975).

Already in Chapter 10 we have considered some of the problems facing widows and widowers with young children and the limited and often very unsatisfactory arrangements from among which they have to choose, one of which is to send the children elsewhere. Here we are concerned only with the behaviour of the surviving parent when he or she continues to care for the children at home. Since the behaviour of widows and of widowers towards their children is likely to differ, and in any case we know much more about that of widows, it is useful to consider the two situations separately.

A widow caring for her children is likely to be both sad and anxious. Preoccupied with her sorrows and the practical problems confronting her, it is far from easy for her to give the children as much time as she gave them formerly and all too easy for her to become impatient and angry when they claim attention and become whiny when they do not get it. A marked tendency to feel angry with their children was reported by about one in five of the widows interviewed by Glick and his colleagues (1974). Becker and Margolin (1967) describe the mother of two small girls, of three and six, who could not bear the older one's whining and frequently hit her for it.

An opposite kind of reaction, which is also common, is for a widowed mother to seek comfort for herself from the children. In the Kliman (1965) study no less than seven of the eighteen children 'began an unprecedented custom of frequently sharing a bed with the surviving parent. This usually began quickly after the death and tended to persist' (p. 78). It is also easy for a lonely widow to burden an older child or adolescent with confidences and responsibilities which it is not easy for him to bear. In other cases she may require a child, usually a younger one, to become a replica either of his dead father or else, if an older child has died, of the dead child (see Chapter 9). Constant anxiety about the children's health and visits to the doctor as much to obtain his support as for the children's treatment occur commonly.

Not only is a widowed mother liable to be anxious about the children's health but she is likely also to worry about her own, with special reference to what would happen to the children were she to get ill or die too. Sometimes, as Glick et al. (1974) report, a mother will express such anxieties aloud and within earshot of the children. In the light of these findings it is not difficult to see why some bereaved children are apprehensive, refuse to attend school and become diagnosed as 'school phobic' (see Volume II Chapter 18).

Anxious and emotionally labile herself and without the moderating influence of a second opinion, a widow's modes of discipline are likely to be either over-strict or over-lax, and rather frequently to swing from one extreme to the other. Problems with their children were reported as being of major concern by half of the widows with children who were studied by Glick in Boston.

Our knowledge of changes in the behaviour of widowed fathers towards their bereaved children is extremely scanty. No doubt those of them who care for the children mainly themselves are prone to changes in behaviour similar to those of widows. Especially when the children are female and/or adolescent are widowed fathers apt to make excessive demands on them for company and comfort.

Should the children be young, however, their care is likely to be principally in other hands, in which case a widowed father may see much less of them than formerly. As a result he may well be unaware of how they feel or what their problems are. Bedell (1973)[11] for example, enquired of 34 widowers how they thought their children had been since they lost their mother and what changes they had noticed in them. Few of the fathers had noticed any changes and even then only small ones. In the light of what we know about children's responses to loss of mother, these replies strongly suggest that the fathers were out of touch and poorly informed.

From this brief review we conclude that a substantial proportion of the special difficulties which children experience after loss of a parent are a direct result of the effect that the loss has had on the surviving parent's behaviour towards them. Nevertheless there are, fortunately, many other surviving parents who, despite their burdens, are able to maintain relationships with their children intact and to help them mourn the dead parent in such a way that they come through undamaged. That others fail, however, can hardly surprise us.

[11] Quoted by Raphael (1973).

CHAPTER 17

Childhood Bereavement
and Psychiatric Disorder

Now I am far from saying that children universally are capable of grief like mine. But there are more than you ever heard of, who die of grief in this island of ours . . . Children torn away from mothers and sisters at that age not infrequently die. I speak of what I know.

THOMAS DE QUINCEY, *Levana and Our Ladies of Sorrow*

Increased risk of psychiatric disorder

Before describing the great variety of forms that childhood mourning can take when conditions are unfavourable, we pause to consider some of the evidence that shows that children who lose a parent by death are more likely than others to become psychiatric casualties. This view, which has for long been implicit in much psychoanalytic writing, has been advanced explicitly by a number of research workers for at least three decades. Although it has been the subject of much controversy, the more rigorous studies of recent years have shown at least some of the original claims to be valid.

The evidence derives from several sources:

– studies that show that individuals who have lost a parent by death when children are more likely than others to suffer periods of extreme emotional distress during early adult life
– studies that show an increased incidence of childhood bereavement among children and adolescents referred to a child psychiatric clinic
– studies that show an increased incidence of childhood bereavement among adults referred to a psychiatric service.

It has been found, furthermore, that loss of a parent by death during childhood influences the symptomatology of any psychiatric disorder from which a person may subsequently suffer.

Since published studies are numerous, and statistical pitfalls many, discussion is limited to a few only of the better-planned examples.

It should be borne in mind that in addition to the studies considered in this chapter and which deal with differential incidence of parent *death* during childhood in psychiatric casualties and controls, there are many more that have the related but broader aim of studying the differential incidence of loss of a parent during childhood *irrespective of the cause of loss*. Since the findings of these other studies are of no less significance for psychiatry than those considered here, their omission (for reasons of consistency) is in many ways regrettable.

Follow-up of Bereaved Children into Adult Life

So far as is known there has been only one study which has attempted to follow a group of bereaved children into their thirties and to compare them with children not bereaved. This is a study undertaken by Fulton (Bendiksen and Fulton 1975) which takes as its initial sample all the ninth-grade students in the Minnesota schools in 1954. At that time certain basic data were obtained on 11,329 fifteen-year-olds in connection with research on the Minnesota Multiphasic Personality Inventory (M.M.P.I.). Eighteen years later, in 1972 when they were aged thirty-three, three sub-samples totalling just over eight hundred individuals were selected for follow-up.

The three sub-samples were selected according to the state of the child's family in 1954, namely whether intact, broken due to death of a parent, or broken due to separation or divorce. The sexes were roughly equal. The plan was to contact all these individuals and to invite them to complete a questionnaire, which covered a fairly wide range of social and psychological information, including marital status, family relations, experience of death, personal problems and health. Despite the high overall wastage rate, discussed below, and the limitations of a postal questionnaire, certain significant differences in regard to health and emotional experiences were found.

The three groups did not differ significantly in regard to sex of subject, educational attainment, community size and similar variables, though there was a slight tendency for those from intact families to be currently married, to have a college degree and a better employment record. The main difference between the groups, however, was in their reports of having experienced extreme emotional distress and major illness, in regard to both of which subjects from intact families had fared better than had those from either of the other groups. Table 5 shows some results.

TABLE 5 *Incidence of problems reported 18 years later for three groups whose family structures differed when they were 15 years old*

Problems reported 18 years later	Family structure when aged 15			P for difference between intact and bereaved
	Intact	Bereaved	Div/Sep	
	%	%	%	
Major illness	8·8	17·1	19·6	<0·08
Extreme emotional distress	19·9	33·5	34·8	<0·05
Arrest/convictions	2·2	5·6	2·2	NS
Divorce experience	8·8	7·1	10·9	NS
Size of sub-sample	138	72	46	

In interpreting these findings it is well to bear in mind not only that the overall wastage-rate was high but that it differed markedly among the sub-samples, which is of interest in its own right. Thus, of the total of 809 in the original sample only 401 could be traced, and of them only 256 completed the questionnaire. At each stage the losses were significantly greater for those from broken families than for those whose families had been intact. The following table gives particulars:

TABLE 6 *Follow-up reaction to questionnaire*

Sub-sample	No. selected for follow-up	No. completed questionnaire	Wastage %
Intact family	324	138	57
Bereaved	264	72	73
Parents separated or divorced	221	46	79
	809	256	—

That individuals whose homes had been broken during childhood are more difficult to trace than those from intact families suggests that as a group they are more mobile; whilst the fact that even when traced fewer of them are willing to complete a questionnaire is suggestive in itself. All in all it seems likely that the differences found between the groups in respect of major illnesses and extreme emotional distress are underestimates of the true position.

Further studies with much more complete coverage are obviously desirable.

Incidence of Childhood Bereavement among Child Psychiatric Patients

In a study of over 700 children attending a clinic at the Maudsley Hospital in South London, Rutter (1966) found that 11·6 per cent had lost a parent by death. This proportion was about two and a half times greater than was to be expected among children of the same age-range in the population from which they were drawn. Bereavements were disproportionately prevalent especially during the third and fourth years of childhood. The death rates for fathers and for mothers were raised by approximately the same ratio; and the ages at which the loss had occurred were similar in the cases of those who had lost a mother and of those who had lost a father.

There was a significant correlation between the sex of the referred child and the sex of the dead parent, the girls having more often lost a mother and the boys a father.

The symptoms and problems presented by the children were equally likely to take the form of neurotic illnesses or neurotic disorders as that of anti-social or delinquent behaviour. The date of onset of these symptoms and problems, in relation to the death of the parent, also ranged widely. In some cases the onset had preceded the death, and may perhaps have been a response to the parent having been fatally ill. In other cases they had developed soon after the death. In about one-third, however, the interval had been as long as five years or more.

This long delay before the onset of symptoms leads Rutter to conclude that factors consequent upon the death were probably as important or more so than the death itself. In this connection he points to such hazards as the breakup of the home, frequent changes of caregiver, changes in family roles, the effects of bereavement on the surviving parent, and the arrival of a step-parent (which had occurred in two-fifths of the cases). As we see in the following chapters, there is good evidence that these factors are indeed of much importance in accounting for children's responses. Nevertheless, there is reason to question another of Rutter's conclusions, admittedly tentative, that pathological forms of mourning play only a minor role. For in his discussions of the problem (Rutter 1966, 1976) he does not consider the possibility of there being individuals who, though managing to carry on without overt disturbance during childhood and adolescence, are none the less made vulnerable by an early bereavement and thereby more prone than others to react to further loss with a depressive disorder. The most likely conclusion, I believe, and one to which the evidence to be presented points, is that the majority of pathological outcomes are a product of the interaction of adverse conditions following bereavement with the mourning processes set in train by it.

Incidence of Childhood Bereavement among Adult Psychiatric Patients

Several studies showing an increased incidence of childhood bereavement in the histories of psychiatric patients when compared to the general population were published between 1955 and 1965. One by Felix Brown (1961) linking childhood bereavement and depressive disorders was particularly influential. Subsequently, however, although some of the further studies confirmed the early findings others did not; and the ensuing controversy was still unsettled in the late nineteen-sixties, e.g. Granville-Grossman (1968). Nevertheless, more recent studies, notably by John Birtchnell, a psychiatrist (Birtchnell 1972), and George Brown, a sociologist (Brown et al. 1977, 1978), have not only confirmed certain, though not all, of the original findings but have also shed light on how the controversy arose.

To measure the incidence of parent loss in a group of psychiatric casualities and to compare it with the incidence of such loss in an appropriate group of mentally healthy individuals is a much more complex task than might be supposed. The biggest single problem has been to specify and find a valid comparison group. Not only have the ages of those in the patient and comparison groups to be equated, because death rates in most countries have decreased over time (except during war), but groups that happen to be easily available, for example patients attending other departments of a hospital, may contain many individuals who suffer from concealed psychiatric disorders. The same, it is now realized, may occur also in a representative sample (allowing for age and sex) drawn from the general population from which the group of patients is drawn. Failure to take these and other factors into account, it is now clear, explains why a number of studies have reported no significant differences between groups.

A study which, although it fails to ensure that the control group was free of psychiatric casualties, none the less reports differences statistically significant, though small, is one undertaken in northeast Scotland by Birtchnell (1972). In this large project the incidence

299

of childhood bereavement was measured in over five thousand
patients referred to the psychiatric services who were aged twenty
and over and were suffering from neuroses, non-organic psychoses
and addictions, and also in a control group of over three thousand
individuals drawn from the lists of general practitioners in the same
area. Since the ages of the patients in the different diagnostic categories differed, for each comparison a different control group suitably
matched for age and sex was used. Principal findings were that:

(i) it is only for parent deaths that had occurred before the
patient's tenth birthday that significant differences between the
patient and the control groups were found;
(ii) an increased incidence of childhood bereavement is found
more often among female patients than male;
(iii) an increased incidence is especially evident in depressive
conditions and in alcoholism;
(iv) when loss of each parent is considered separately it is found
that (a) the incidence of loss of mother before the tenth birthday
is significantly increased in depressed patients, both male and
female, and also in female alcoholics, (b) loss of father before the
tenth birthday is significantly increased in both depressed and
alcoholic female patients but is not significantly increased in the
case of male patients.

In none of the patient groups in this study is the incidence of
childhood bereavement greater than double what it is in the controls, and in most groups it is much less. True, in selecting his
controls Birtchnell took no steps to exclude individuals who, though
not referred to the psychiatric services, may none the less have been
in poor mental health and that, had he done so, differences are
likely to have been greater. Even so, such evidence as we have
suggests that childhood bereavement plays a causal role in only a
small minority of cases of mental illness. The value of the work
done lies, I believe, in having provided a point of entry for research
into parent–child relationships and their influence on mental health
which can be pursued in future at a much more sophisticated level.

Some disorders to which childhood bereavement contributes

In recent years it has become clear that those who have suffered a
childhood bereavement are not only rather more prone than others

to develop a psychiatric disorder but that both the form and the severity of any disorder they may develop is likely to be strongly influenced in certain special directions.

Those who have suffered a childhood bereavement and, when adult, become psychiatric casualties are more likely than others

– to express serious ideas of committing suicide
– to show high degrees of anxious attachment (or overdependency)
– to develop depressive conditions of severe degree, and classifiable as psychotic.

Since only well-attested findings are described the above list should not be regarded as exhaustive.

Suicidal Ideation and Behaviour in Students

There is now an extensive literature on the relationship of parental loss during childhood, due to losses of any kind (not only death), and attempted suicide during later life, e.g. Greer *et al.* (1966), and Koller and Castanos (1968). After reviewing this literature, some of it clinical and some statistical, Adam (1973) concludes: 'There seems general agreement . . . that of all the sequelae attributed to early childhood loss the evidence with regard to suicidal behaviour is among the strongest.' In most of these studies, however, the losses concerned are due to desertion, separation or divorce as well as to death. For this reason discussion here is restricted to a single study which distinguishes the two main causes of loss. Furthermore, this study, unlike most of the others, concentrates on the presence or absence of serious suicidal ideation as well as of attempts, instead of on attempts only. This has advantages, first, because ideas of suicide occur more commonly than do attempts and secondly because, lacking the dramatic circumstances of attempts, they are open to more rigorously controlled research.

In a project carried out within the McGill University Health Service, Adam (1973) compared the incidence and type of suicidal ideation present in three groups of students, all aged between 17 and 27 and all of whom had been referred to the Service because of psychological problems. Those in one group (35) had lost a parent by death before their sixteenth birthday; those in a second (29) had lost a parent for some reason other than death (usually separation or divorce); and those in the third, selected as matched controls (50), came from intact families. Men slightly outnumbered women in the samples.

Once selected, students were randomly assigned to an interviewer who conducted a semi-structured clinical interview covering a variety of areas, namely, general adaptation, medical history, accident-proneness, depressive trends, suicidal ideas and behaviour and attitudes towards death and dying. Key items were scored during the interview according to pre-established criteria validated in pilot studies and cross-validated by a second independent rater using a tape-recording of the interview. Only after the scoring was completed were detailed enquiries made into the student's early background and the circumstances surrounding a parental death, divorce or separation. Although every attempt was made to maintain ignorance of the family status of the subject until after the scoring had been done, this proved impossible in some cases. Subsequent statistical tests showed, however, that knowledge of status had not influenced the scoring.

During the first part of the interview a special effort was made to explore for the presence of suicidal ideas and, when these were reported, the subject was asked to give as many details as possible about their onset, frequency, intensity, duration and content. Suicidal ideas were then rated on a three-point scale in respect of their frequency, intensity and duration. Any subject whose ideas were rated as moderate or high on any two of these parameters was regarded as seriously suicidal and the others as not so. Subjects who reported a suicidal attempt of any description were also scored in the serious category. Where any doubt existed as to which category the ideation belonged it was scored conservatively as not serious.

The results, presented in Table 7, show that nearly half of the student psychiatric casualties who had lost a parent before the age of sixteen, for whatever reason, showed serious suicidal ideation whereas only 10 per cent of those who came from intact families did so. This difference is highly significant statistically. Whether parent loss was due to death or to separation or divorce made no difference: the incidence of serious suicidal ideation was high in both groups.

The incidence of suicidal attempts in the three groups follows a similar pattern. Among those who had lost a parent by death, six had attempted suicide; among those who had lost a parent for other reasons four had done so; and among those from intact families two; this gives an incidence of 17, 14 and 4 per cent respectively. Although the trend is suggestive, the differences are not significant (very possibly due to small numbers).

TABLE 7 *Incidence of serious suicidal ideation in students aged 17–27 years experiencing psychiatric problems by loss of parent before their sixteenth birthday*

Suicidal ideation	Status of student's family		
	Parent loss		Intact
	By death	By separation/divorce	
	%	%	%
Serious	48·6	41·4	10·0
Not serious	51·4	58·4	90·0
N	35	29	50

(For the difference between the two parent-loss groups and the intact family group   P<0·001)

Adam describes some of the ways in which the ideas of students who were categorized as showing serious suicidal ideation differed from the ideas of those whose ideas were judged as less serious. In the former, suicidal ideas were relatively more elaborate, more persistent and of longer duration. Often they presented in an intense way as strong urges or impulses that sometimes were frightening and difficult to control; for these reasons some students had sought help to protect themselves. The themes expressed were often those of profound isolation, hopelessness, and self hatred; and the theme of death as peace, freedom or release was sometimes reported. Such students often referred to suicide as 'making sense' and many saw it as a real possibility for them in the future, even inevitable. Many, indeed, had seriously considered killing themselves and had formulated plans to do so. A number had come close to making attempts and, of the total of 34 students whose ideas were judged to be serious, no less than twelve had actually made one. Ten of these twelve attempts had been immediately preceded by the actual or threatened loss of an important person.

In the case of seven students, all of whom belonged to the parental loss groups, the attempts they had made were judged to have been dangerous; and, of these, four also exhibited extremely reckless behaviour and/or participated in unusually hazardous sports.

That young adults who have lost a parent during childhood should be more prone than others to consider committing suicide is not surprising since many of the motives for attempting or completing a suicide can best be understood as responses to the loss of an attachment figure, either actual or threatened. Among motives that lead to a completed suicide, the clinical evidence suggests, are the following:

– a wish for reunion with a dead person
– a desire for revenge against a dead person for having deserted, which can take the form either of redirecting towards the self murderous wishes aroused by a deserting person, or else of abandoning another in retaliation
– a wish to destroy the self in order to assuage an overpowering sense of guilt for having contributed to a death
– a feeling that life is not worth living without any future prospect of a loving relationship with another person.

Among motives for making a suicidal gesture are:

– a wish to elicit a caregiving response from an attachment figure who is felt to be neglectful—the well-known cry for help
– a wish to punish an attachment figure and so to coerce him or her into being more attentive.

No doubt in any one act more than one of these motives may play a part. Such motives, moreover, can be combined in any way with motives of other kinds.

Adam describes some preliminary attempts to find differences in the histories of students who showed serious suicidal ideation that might distinguish them from students who did not. Among factors that proved *not* to be relevant was the age within the first sixteen years of a student at the time he suffered permanent parental loss. By contrast, Adam concluded that 'the presence of a consistent, stable nurturant figure of some sort seemed to be of great importance in protecting against the development of significant suicidal ideation. . . .' As is shown in the coming chapters, this conclusion is supported by much other evidence.

Anxious Attachment (Overdependency)
There is evidence that, irrespective of diagnosis, female patients who have lost mother by death during their first ten years of life are more likely than others to show a marked degree of anxious attachment, often termed overdependency. This association, to which Barry, Barry and Lindemann (1965) first drew attention, has

been explored more rigorously by Birtchnell (1975a) as part of his large study in north-east Scotland.

During the course of Birtchnell's investigation it became known that 576 of the original sample of patients had at some time completed the M.M.P.I. Of the many scales that can be derived from this, it was decided to select four as those most likely to discriminate between patients who had suffered an early parental death and those who had not. These were the scales for Dependency, Dominance, Ego Strength and Self-Sufficiency.

For making comparisons, men and women patients were kept separate, and, for each comparison, sub-samples were selected, first, of those who had lost father during the first nine years of life but whose mother had lived for at least another eleven years, and, secondly, of those who had lost mother and whose father had continued to live. A third sub-sample comprised patients both of whose parents had lived at least until the subject's twentieth birthday. For the patients in each sub-sample a mean score on each of the four M.M.P.I. scales was calculated and comparisons between them made. The numbers in some of the sub-samples were small.[1]

Of the resulting comparisons (sixteen in all) only one revealed a difference of statistical significance. The seventeen female patients who had lost mother during their first nine years of life showed a mean score for dependency significantly higher ($P < 0.01$) than the mean score of the 257 female patients who had lost neither parent. All but two of the seventeen scored above the mean of the latter group. Scrutiny of the case records showed that every one of them had depressive symptomatology and that most of them had been chronic worriers all their lives. Five had been described specifically as notably dependent.[2]

[1] Numbers of patients in each sub-sample were as follows:

Sex of patient	Number of patients who had lost			Total
	Father	Mother	Neither	
Male	9	6	157	172
Female	20	17	257	294
	29	23	414	466

[2] Although none of the other differences between mean scores reached statistical significance, it is worth noting that the six male patients who had lost mother scored relatively low on dependency and high on self-sufficiency. This suggests a response in the direction of compulsive self-reliance. Thus male patients presented a picture the converse of the females.

In a majority of these seventeen women, it emerged from the records, mother's death had been followed by distressing experiences. Substitute mothering had been makeshift and often there had been numerous changes. Quality of care had evidently left much to be desired, and most of the girls had themselves been expected to fill a maternal role from an early age. A majority reported signs of their having been nervous as children, nail-biting, enuresis, and fear of the dark being especially common.

Form and Severity of Depressive Disorder

In Chapter 14 an account is given of the study by George Brown and his colleagues of depressive disorders in women in a South London borough (Brown and Harris 1978a). For the part of the study with which we are here concerned only one of their samples was drawn upon. This is the patient sample, made up of 114 women, aged between 18 and 65, who were diagnosed as suffering from one or another form and degree of depressive disorder of recent onset and who were receiving psychiatric treatment (either as in-patients or as out-patients).

Once a patient had been identified as conforming to the research criteria laid down she was interviewed in a systematic manner, first by a research psychiatrist and, secondly and independently, by a sociologist. By these procedures both clinical and social data were obtained in a standard format.

One part of Brown's enquiry was directed to finding out whether there are differences in the life experiences of women who differ in the form and severity of the depressive disorder from which they suffer. For this purpose the patient group was divided between two diagnostic groups, those who were psychotically depressed and those neurotically depressed. This was done by a second research psychiatrist who, guided by traditional criteria, based his judgement solely on the cluster of symptoms each patient showed as determined during personal interview during which he checked on the presence or absence of some 57 symptoms, and without knowledge of any life events that may have preceded and perhaps have provoked the onset. This restriction was to enable the research group to test the long-held belief that psychotic depressions develop without being preceded by important life events, in contrast to neurotic depressions in which the incidence of such events is thought to be high.

Of the 114 patients studied, 63 were diagnosed as psychotically depressed and 49 as neurotically depressed. (Two patients were excluded from the analysis because they had also shown manic symptoms.) In general, patients classified as psychotic tended to be more retarded in movement, thought and emotion, whereas those classified as neurotic tended to be more active and to show more varied emotion. Once so classified, patients in each diagnostic group were divided into three sub-groups by the severity of their disorder—high, medium or low.

Findings of immediate interest are that in a majority of all cases a provoking life event, usually the loss by separation or death of a close relative, had occurred during the nine months preceding the onset of symptoms and that the incidence of such life events was almost as high in the psychotic group (58 per cent) as it was in the neurotic (65 per cent). Thus, Brown's findings, like those of Paykel *et al.* (1971) whose work he refers to, call sharply into question the traditional assumptions that a psychotic depression is equivalent to an endogenous depression and that only neurotic depressions are reactive.

Other findings of Brown's group concern the incidence of what he terms a *past* loss, a category that includes losses of specified types occurring mainly but not always during childhood and adolescence and that excludes any loss that had occurred during the two years before the onset of symptoms. Past losses he divided into two categories, those due to death, and those due to causes other than death. Although most such losses are of a mother or father before the patient's seventeenth birthday, for the great majority of his analyses the criteria Brown uses are more inclusive. Since the results are of great interest, the criteria are described first.

For a woman to be scored as having experienced a past loss due to death, Brown's criteria are:

- the death of her mother or her father before her seventeenth birthday
- the death of a sibling occurring between her first and her seventeenth birthday
- the death of a child (providing it had not occurred within two years of onset of symptoms)
- the death of her husband (providing it had not occurred within two years of onset of symptoms).

For her to be scored as having experienced a past loss by causes other than death, criteria are:

– desertion by her mother or her father before her seventeenth birthday
– separation from her mother or her father for one year or more before her seventeenth birthday.

When these criteria are applied to the two main diagnostic groups of patients and to the three sub-groups of each it is found:

(a) that in women who become psychotically depressed the incidence of past loss by *death* is notably high, with the incidence increasing with the severity of the condition; and, conversely, that in this group the incidence of past loss by causes other than death is low;

(b) that in women who become neurotically depressed the incidence of past loss by *causes other than death* is moderately high, with the incidence increasing with the severity of the condition; and conversely, that in this group the incidence of past loss by death is comparatively low.

Numbers and percentages are given in Table 8.

TABLE 8 *Incidence of past loss by type of loss and by form and severity of depression*

	Incidence of past loss due to	
	Death	Separation
	%	%
63 *psychotically depressed*		
12 most severe	84 ⎫	0 ⎫
41 medium severe	55 ⎬ 57%	2 ⎬ 5%
10 least severe	20 ⎭	20 ⎭
49 *neurotically depressed*		
6 most severe	0 ⎫	50 ⎫
23 medium severe	14 ⎬ 14%	22 ⎬ 22%
20 least severe	20 ⎭	16 ⎭

Differences between the two main groups in respect both of the incidence of past loss due to death and the incidence of past loss due to separations are highly significant. In both cases P is less than ·01.

Thus in Brown's series of patients several highly significant correlations were found between the type of loss a woman had suffered during her earlier life and both the form and severity of her depressive disorder. By contrast, no such correlations were found with the type or severity of any loss that she might have suffered during the year preceding the onset of her symptoms. Form and severity of disorder seem, therefore, to be determined very largely by events of earlier years.

A further finding by Brown supports this conclusion. Examination of his data showed that the loss of a parent or sibling after a patient's seventeenth birthday had played no part in determining her symptomatology.

Struck by these clear-cut and quite unexpected findings, Brown sought an opportunity to check them. Fortunately there existed at the Maudsley Hospital the records of a series of female in-patients suffering from depression who had been investigated earlier by a colleague, Robert Kendell, and about whom the necessary information was available. When these records were analysed, the results were found to be similar to those for Brown's series. Thus, not only were the original findings confirmed but they were shown to be independent of the possibly idiosyncratic judgement of the research psychiatrist.

It was remarked at the outset that most of the past losses that Brown had included in his analyses had been suffered by the patients before their seventeenth birthdays. Figures are given in Table 9.

TABLE 9 *Number of patients reporting a past loss by type of loss, age at which sustained, and form of depression*

Form of depression	Loss by death		Loss by separation	
	before 17	17 and after	before 17	17 and after
62 psychotic patients	24	13	3	I
49 neurotic patients	6	2	10	I
All patients	30	15	13	2

For purposes of the present discussion the main point to note is the relatively high proportion of women in Brown's series diagnosed as psychotically depressed who had suffered the death of a parent or a sibling before their seventeenth birthday, namely 24 out of 62, or 39 per cent. Loss of husband or child after the seventeenth birthday (but more than two years before onset of symptoms) had been sustained by a further 13 of them, or 21 per cent.

The high incidence of past loss by death in patients diagnosed as psychotically depressed is reflected in the strong association between a past loss by death and retardation. Altogether there were 45 patients (37 psychotic and 8 neurotic) who had sustained a past loss by death. Of these 34 (31 psychotic and 3 neurotic), or 75 per cent, were retarded. In searching for an explanation of this association Brown and Harris draw on ideas advanced in earlier volumes of this work and on a cognitive theory of depressive disorders. A past loss due to death, they suggest, predisposes a person to respond to any current loss as though it were another death with a consequent unrelieved hopelessness, which in turn leads to retardation. A past loss due to separation seems, by contrast, to bias a person to respond to any current loss as though it might be reversible. In consequence the resulting despair is mixed with angry, perhaps violent, protest and leads to a condition more likely to be diagnosed as a neurotic depression than as a psychotic one.

In this chapter we have considered evidence that suggests that those who have lost a parent by death during childhood or adolescence are at greater risk than others of developing psychiatric disorder and, more especially, of becoming seriously suicidal and/or psychotically depressed should they do so. Evidence of comparable though rather different effects of losses sustained during the same period of life and due to causes other than death has only been touched on but is in fact considerable. Early loss, it seems, can sensitize an individual and make him more vulnerable to setbacks experienced later, especially to loss or threat of loss. Nevertheless, by no means every child or adolescent who loses a parent becomes sensitized in this way and it is therefore necessary to determine why some should become so and others not. To this enquiry we now address ourselves.

CHAPTER 18

Conditions Responsible
for Differences in Outcome

The beauty of love has not found me
Its hands have not gripped me so tight
For the darkness of hate is upon me
I see day, not as day, but as night.

I yearn for the dear love to find me
With my heart and my soul and my might
For darkness has closed in upon me
I see day, not as day, but as night.

The children are playing and laughing
But I cannot find love in delight
There is an iron fence around me
I see day, not as day, but as night.[1]

Sources of evidence

From all that is written in earlier chapters it will already be clear
that, in my view, the variables that influence the course that mourning takes during childhood and adolescence are similar in kind to
those that influence it during adult life. They fall into three classes:

(a) the causes and circumstances of the loss, with especial reference to where and what a child is told and what opportunities are
later given him to enquire about what has happened;
(b) the family relationships after the loss, with special reference
to whether he remains with the surviving parent and, if so, how
the patterns of relationship are changed as a result of the loss;
(c) the patterns of relationship within the family prior to the loss,
with special reference to the patterns obtaining between the
parents themselves and between each of them and the bereaved
child.

Some of the evidence that supports this theoretical position has
already been referred to and more is given in this and subsequent
chapters. It derives from studies of two main types:

[1] By a girl of eleven whose parents were abroad for some years.

311

(i) studies that compare the experiences of a group of individuals who have developed well despite a childhood bereavement with those of a group who have failed to do so; information is usually obtained during a special research interview or a routine clinical one;

(ii) studies that describe the experiences of one or a few individual children or adolescents whose problems are thought to stem from the death of a parent; most of the information is obtained during therapy, though some comes from parents and others.

The strengths and weaknesses of these two types of study tend to be the opposite of one another.

Studies of the first type, which take the form of surveys, include fairly large samples of subjects and give useful information, mostly of a rather general kind, about the individual's experience after the loss but are usually weak on psychopathological detail. Studies of the latter type, the therapeutic, do much to supplement this deficiency but can be gravely misleading when treated in isolation. In the case of surveys the information is commonly obtained many years after the events; whereas in the case of therapeutic studies of children and adolescents the time interval is usually much shorter. Both types of study have the drawback that they rely heavily on information from a single source, the bereaved individual himself.

Evidence from surveys

Amongst all those who have surveyed different groups of individuals who have lost a parent during childhood there is now substantial agreement in regard to the enormous importance of a child's experience after the loss. Individuals who later develop a psychiatric disorder, it is found, are far more likely than are those who do not to have received deficient parental care following the loss. Discontinuities of care, including being cared for in unloving foster-homes or institutions and of being moved from one 'home' to another, have been the lot of many. Alternatively, should a child have remained in his home, he is likely to have had to take a parental role prematurely instead of being cared for himself. By contrast, those who have developed well despite having lost a parent during childhood are likely to have received continuous and stable parental care during the years following their loss. Amongst findings that support these conclusions are those, already cited in the previous chapter, of

Rutter (1966), of Adam (1973), and of Birtchnell (1971,[2] 1975). Amongst other studies that report closely similar findings is a well-designed one by Hilgard *et al.* (1960).

Hilgard, who had for many years been interested in the role of parent loss during the childhoods of psychiatric patients, with special reference to anniversary reactions, decided to compare the experiences to which her patients had been exposed following their loss with those of adults who had also lost a parent during childhood but were not patients. With this in view she undertook a community survey and from it identified one hundred individuals aged between 19 and 49 who had lost a parent before the age of nineteen and who were not at the time under psychiatric care. Of this initial sample, sixty-five made themselves available for structured interviews lasting one or two hours. Women outnumbered men by nearly three to one (partly because they were more numerous in the initial hundred and partly because they were more available for interview). Of the women, 29 had lost father and 19 had lost mother; of the men, 13 had lost father and 4 mother.

After interview a sub-sample was identified made up of all those who were deemed to be 'reasonably well adjusted' in terms of the following criteria: they were living in an intact home, their marriage appeared to be satisfactory, relationships with their children seemed adequate, and their scores on a brief test of social adaptation were confirmatory. Among 29 women who had lost father fourteen met these criteria.

The picture of family life before and after father's death which emerged from the accounts they gave was as follows. Before the loss the parents had provided a stable home in which each had had a well-defined role. After the loss mother had kept the home intact but had usually had to work very hard to do so. Not only was support given to the family by its social network, but mother had proved capable of making the best use of it. 'Strong', 'responsible', 'hardworking' were the adjectives most used to describe her; 'affectionate' less often.

Should a parent have died after an illness, the children were likely to have been told of the outlook and prepared in advance for what

[2] In this study Birtchnell showed that, when a sample of early bereaved psychiatric patients was compared with a sample of general population controls, they showed an over-representation of older siblings who were of the same sex as the parent lost and who also had younger siblings to be cared for.

lay in store. By these means, Hilgard writes, 'a dying parent may convey to his child an acceptance of this complete separation and in so doing may help the child to accept it also'. Furthermore, after a father had died mothers were likely to have shared their grief with the children; and it seemed as though this had been of especial help to daughters. These family patterns, in which the children had been taken into the parents' confidence, had contributed, Hilgard believes, to the striking absence of guilt about the parent's death that characterized these individuals and that contrasted sharply with what she found in her group of psychiatric patients who also had lost a parent during childhood.

In addition to Hilgard's sub-sample of individuals who were deemed to be 'reasonably well adjusted' was a complementary sub-sample of individuals who had failed to meet her criteria (a group analogous to the 'community cases' in George Brown's study but not necessarily presenting with diagnosable illness). For members of the second sub-sample the behaviour of the surviving parent had been very different to what it had been for members of the well-adjusted sub-sample. In most cases the surviving parent had made strong demands on the children for emotional support; or, to put it in the terminology used in this work, the survivor had inverted the parent–child relationship by seeking to make his or her child the caregiver. This pattern was especially common among children whose fathers had died.

In the total sample of 65 persons interviewed, there were thirteen men who had lost father. In three cases mother had remarried, leaving ten families in which the son had continued to live with his widowed mother. In no less than nine of these cases, the mothers had 'manifested an emotional dependency on their children, particularly the sons'. Some felt they had been made into substitute husbands. They had either stayed single until mother had died or else had married but later had divorced and returned to stay with mother. In one case mother had threatened to commit suicide when her son announced his plans to marry. Despite these pressures which had made satisfactory marriages extremely difficult, and possibly even because of them, a number of these sons had been very successful in their work. Some of the girls who had remained living with widowed mothers had also been put under strong emotional pressure to stay home to care for mother.

One of the women whose mother had died young described how,

because her mother had died aged twenty-five, she had confidently expected that she also would die at that age. She had therefore postponed her marriage until after the fateful year; but she had none the less chosen for her wedding day the same date as her mother's. When interviewed she was about forty-five and had been married for twenty years, apparently happily.

In reviewing her findings Hilgard expresses concern about members of the less well-adjusted sub-sample. Although living in the community and passing as mentally healthy, it was evident that for a number their lives had been restricted and their mental health impaired by the pathogenic pressures to which they had been subjected. Clearly some had suffered much more than others, and no doubt some of the sons who had postponed marriage had none the less married successfully later. Nevertheless, her study strongly supports the view that the effect that a parent's death has on a child is powerfully influenced by the pattern of family relationships to which the child is exposed after it.

Certainly all the studies which have reported the childhood experiences of those who subsequently become psychiatric casualties point to the same conclusion. An example is a study by Arthur and Kemme (1964) of 83 children and adolescents, aged between $4\frac{1}{2}$ and 17 years, who had been referred to a children's psychiatric hospital in Ann Arbor, Michigan, with a variety of emotional and behavioural problems, all of which, having either developed or become greatly exacerbated following the death of a parent, could be regarded as attributable at least in part to the loss. Sixty were boys, of whom 40 had lost father and 20 mother; 23 were girls, of whom 14 had lost father and 9 mother.

Although the details given by Arthur and Kemme are rather sparse, it is evident that the conditions affecting these children and adolescents prior to the loss and/or surrounding it and/or after it had been extremely adverse in a high proportion of cases; and in many of them it was possible to see, at least in outline, how the conditions to which the child had been, or was still being subjected, were contributing to the problems complained of. Amongst the adverse conditions prominent in this series of cases were parents who had quarrelled or separated, and parents who had threatened to abandon the children, children who had experienced several earlier separations, and children who had been made to feel responsible for making the parent ill. After the death many of the children had been given little or no information about it; and subsequently many also had experienced extremely unstable relationships. Of the 83 parental deaths, 10 had been due to suicide, an incidence discussed briefly in the opening section of Chapter 22.

In the great majority of the cases reported psychological disturbance had been present before the death, often long before it. Nevertheless, in most of them it was evident that bereavement had increased any existing disturbances. As in the case of adults, therefore, the experience of loss is found to interact with the psychological consequences of both previous and subsequent adverse experiences to produce the particular clinical picture seen.

As might be expected, some of the commonest ways in which children and adolescents respond to the loss of a parent include becoming chronically sad or anxious, or some mixture of the two; and many develop elusive somatic symptoms. In the Michigan series over a quarter appeared sad at the time of referral, 16 of the 83 were showing intense separation anxiety and 19 were experiencing acute night-terrors. About a quarter were excessively clinging during the day and/or were insisting at night on sleeping with the surviving parent, or a sibling.

Yet, although many appeared obviously sad and anxious, many others did not. On the contrary, 29 children—about one-third—were overactive and in greater or less degree aggressive. Some engaged in unprovoked violence towards peers or adults or inexplicable destruction of property.

In many of the cases an explanation of a child's sadness, anxiety or anger could be found without difficulty in the way he was construing the cause of his parent's death and/or the situation in which he now found himself. Seventeen were construing the death in terms of their having been abandoned. As one boy put it: 'My father left me and I'm very angry with him.' Double that number, namely 40 per cent, were attributing the cause of death either to themselves or to the surviving parent. Several made plain why they did so. One boy, for example, had been warned by his mother that he would be the death of her. Another supposed that his mother had committed suicide because he had been so naughty. Most of those who were blaming the surviving parent had witnessed violent quarrels between their parents in which one had attacked the other physically.

Many of the younger children disbelieved that death was final and were expecting that they would soon be reunited with their parent, either here or 'up in heaven'; some of the older children contemplated suicide with the explicit intention of joining the missing parent. Thirteen had either threatened suicide or attempted it.

In the accounts of individual children given in Chapters 19 and 21 some of these sequences are described in detail.

Evidence from therapeutic studies

Throughout the last fifty years reports have been published in the psychoanalytic journals of the treatment of adult patients whose present difficulties have been thought to be due at least in part to the loss of a parent, from death or other cause, during the patient's childhood. Since in all these cases the loss had occurred many years earlier, it is hardly surprising that the reports give little or no information about the conditions that had preceded or succeeded the loss. During the past two decades, however, accounts have multiplied of the treatment of adolescents and children whose loss had occurred comparatively recently; and in many of them a fair amount of detail is given both about the circumstances of the loss itself and about the patterns of family interaction that obtained before and after it. In the chapters to follow a number of these accounts are presented. Each has been rewritten to provide a continuous narrative shorn of extraneous theory, and with some comments of my own added.

Those sceptical of the scientific status of material obtained during the course of therapy should note that in hardly one of the cases to be described are the theoretical biases of the authors the same as my own. On the contrary, the majority subscribe more or less explicitly to the theoretical standpoint that has long been dominant amongst psychoanalysts which, until recently, has given scant weight to the influence of environmental factors and has explained almost all differences in personality development by reference to some phase of development in which the individual is thought to be fixated. When applied to differential outcome following loss this viewpoint results in the widespread assertions:

– that, owing to their psychological immaturity, children and even adolescents cannot mourn, and
– that the emotional problems that follow parental loss can be understood as due to an arrest of development either at the phase thought to have been reached at the time of the loss, e.g. Fleming and Altschul (1963), or at some earlier phase, e.g. Klein (1948).

There is an extensive literature based on these premises, some of which is referred to in Chapters 1, 2 and 12 (and see also Bowlby 1960b). Readers interested to probe further are referred to a review of the literature by Miller (1971) and another most comprehensive one by Furman in the final chapter of her book (Furman 1974, especially pp. 267–93).

I believe that the evidence at present available does not support the traditional theories. A principal difficulty with some of them is that, were they to be correct, we should expect the development of every child or adolescent who lost a parent to be impaired, which we know is not the case. It is of much significance, moreover, that the closer in time to the loss that a patient, adolescent or child, has been studied and the larger the number of cases that a clinician has seen the more likely is he not only to describe environmental factors but to implicate them when explaining outcome. Among the many who now lay emphasis on environmental factors, especially the influence of the surviving parent, are the clinicians R. A. Furman (1964), E. Furman (1974), Kliman (1965), Becker and Margolin (1967), and Anthony (1973), and also the social scientists Gorer (1965), Glick et al. (1974), and Palgi (1973). The position of other clinicians seems inconsistent with the evidence they present. An example is Wolfenstein (1966, 1969) who, despite adhering strongly to traditional theory, reports evidence that seems equally strongly to implicate family relationships.[3] Nagera (1970) avoids taking sides by embracing both viewpoints impartially. Thus, in a discussion of the

---

[3] For example, in a long paper Wolfenstein (1969) describes the case of Mary who came for treatment at the age of nineteen because of being depressed, having feelings of derealization and that the best solution for everyone would be for her to kill herself. Her father had died five years earlier. Mary's relationship to her mother had never been happy; and the mother is described as having 'depressive tendencies' and as prone to 'punish the child by long silences' (p. 444). In her comments Wolfenstein expresses the belief that Mary's problems with her mother, together with two brief hospitalizations before the age of four, had already shaken Mary's trust in her mother before father's death. In spite of this, however, she concludes her paper with the generalization that 'mourning, as a painful but adaptive process of gradually decathecting the lost object, is not an available device until after adolescence has been passed through' (p. 457). In Chapter 21 of this volume an account is given of another adolescent girl treated by Wolfenstein in which environmental factors also appeared to have played a large part in determining outcome.

origin of children's beliefs that a dead father will return, he writes: 'In some cases this happens under the direct influence of mothers who hide the truth from the child to spare it pain; *in other cases phantasies of an identical nature are the child's spontaneous production*' (italics original).

In the chapters to follow I shall repeatedly be drawing attention to the role of environmental variables, both those that the clinicians concerned refer to as having, in their opinion, been of consequence and also others that a reading of the case report has suggested to me may have been operative as well. The viewpoint adopted is, of course, consistent with the theory of developmental pathways outlined in the final chapter of Volume II and adopted throughout this work.

In judging the validity of the accounts that follow it should therefore be borne in mind that, in so far as their authors present data of a kind that support my views, it is not because of their theoretical expectations. On the contrary, I believe the reason they have done so is because in the course of their clinical work, and sometimes in spite of their theoretical bias, they have been impressed by the significance for an understanding of the children's problems of the events they describe.

CHAPTER 19

Children's Responses when Conditions are Unfavourable

> Something it is which thou hast lost,
> Some pleasure from thine early years.
> Break, thou deep vase of chilling tears
> That grief hath shaken into frost!
>
> ALFRED, LORD TENNYSON, *In Memoriam*

Four children whose mourning failed

In the opening paragraph of Chapter 16 we noted the conditions that the evidence suggests are required if childhood mourning is to follow a favourable course: first, that the child should have enjoyed a reasonably secure relationship with his parents prior to the loss; secondly, that he be given prompt and accurate information and be allowed to ask questions and participate in family grieving; thirdly, that he has the comforting presence of his surviving parent or of a known and trusted substitute. Although these conditions, as we have seen, can certainly be met, it is hardly surprising that all too often they are not. Sometimes the shortfall is in only one class of condition, sometimes in two and not infrequently in all three. On the type of shortfall, their number and, perhaps especially, their combination turns the form taken by a child's responses to his loss. Since several forms of pathology can result, and each form can occur in every degree, the field of enquiry is enormous.

Because there are as yet no studies of a representative group of bereaved children, there is no way of gauging the incidence of each of these different forms of pathological response. The best that can be done, therefore, is to describe certain patterns of response which are met with frequently in clinical practice and to indicate the conditions, present before and/or after the loss, that are playing a part, often a large part, in producing them.

We start by presenting at some length the case reports of four children who, between them, show not only a fairly representative range of pathological responses but whose experiences illustrate with adequate detail the main conditions that appear to have been responsible for the form and degree of the responses described. In some cases the causal links between the child's experiences and the responses observed seem clear; in others they are more conjectural. Of the four children, two are boys and two are girls. One of each lost a father and one a mother.

The cases selected are drawn from the reports of clinicians at work on both sides of the Atlantic. Whereas all the clinicians share an analytic approach, within that approach they differ considerably both in theoretical outlook and in the therapeutic techniques that they happen to have used in the cases selected.

Peter,[1] eleven when father died

The first account, about a boy of eleven who lost his father, is taken from a much longer clinical report by Donald Winnicott (1965, pp. 212–42), a leading British paediatrician and psychoanalyst. In addition to the picture of the boy and his mother that it presents, the account illustrates some of Winnicott's therapeutic practices.

Peter was aged 11 years and 8 months when he was first seen by Winnicott. Eight months earlier, on the day after Peter's birthday, his father had been drowned in a sailing accident; Peter himself had been involved but had been saved. For some months afterwards Peter had appeared unaffected by the event; but subsequently he had developed a variety of ill-defined ailments and, to use his mother's expression, had become 'emotional'. She had begun to worry about him and had been advised by a friend to seek Winnicott's assistance. Being already extremely busy Winnicott fitted in interviews as best he could and struggled to economize his time. Over a period of about two months he had six interviews with Peter, the first lasting two hours. Contact with mother was at first confined to several long telephone conversations, and her first interview with him was not until about three months after she had first telephoned him. There were no joint interviews.

Information about family relationships was gleaned during the therapeutic interviews with Peter and mother. In the published account no information is given about the elder brother and very little about father.

Father had been a successful professional man and together the parents had had a large circle of friends. There were two children, an elder boy at university and Peter who was a boarder at a preparatory school. The family lived in London and also had a holiday cottage by the sea. It was there that the tragedy had taken place.

[1] In the original record this boy is referred to as Patrick. Changing it to Peter is to avoid duplication with the three-year-old referred to in Chapters 1 and 23.

In the published account few details of the accident are given. Peter and his father had been out sailing together and had presumably capsized. They had then both been in the water for a long time. Peter had had a lifebelt but his father had none. At some time father had gone under but Peter had been rescued, almost by chance, when it was getting dark. Although father was already dead, Peter was told only that his father was in hospital. It is not clear when or how Peter was told the truth.

The only other information given is that during the initial telephone conversation mother had said that Peter had been to some extent responsible for the tragedy; the published account, however, says nothing more about this.

Except for the last point, all the details reported above were recounted by Peter during his first interview with Winnicott. At the start of what proved to be a very long interview Winnicott introduced Peter to the squiggle game in which, taking turns, each draws a random squiggle and the other is invited to use this as the basis for a picture. After playing this actively for a time, Peter began to talk. Soon he was describing a dream in which one person was missing though nobody knew it; there was also a church with a shadow instead of an altar. Asked by Winnicott what would be a nice dream, Peter replied: 'Bliss, being cared for. I know I want this.' Asked if he knew what depression was like, Peter said he did, especially since father's death. He loved his father but he did not see much of him. Then he began to talk about his parents and his impression of their relationship: 'My father was very kind. But the fact is mother and father were constantly under tension . . . I was the link that joined them; I tried to help . . . They were really very suited to each other, but over some little things they would begin to get across each other, and the tension would build up over and over again, and the only solution to this was for me to bring them together. Father was very much overworked . . . It was a great strain to him to come home tired and then for his wife to fail him.' In all this, Winnicott remarks, Peter showed an unusual degree of insight.

From this Peter had gone on to describe in great detail, but in a rather detached way, the accident in which his father had died and his thoughts about it. His father, he thought, might have committed suicide, or perhaps he, Peter, was at fault; it was impossible to know. 'After a long time in the water one began to fight for oneself.' Then he confided that had his father lived he believed his mother would have committed suicide. 'The tension between the two was so great it was not possible to think of them going on without one of them dying.' Peter therefore felt relief, and also indicated that he felt very guilty about doing so.

Towards the end of the interview Peter described various fears he had had since early childhood and insisted that his troubles had antedated the tragedy.

After this interview Peter had returned to his boarding school. A fortnight later, however, his mother phoned to say that he had run away and had returned home by train, laden with Latin books. He felt he was letting the school down and that he had to make a terrific effort to learn Latin. During the subsequent interview with Winnicott, Peter described how another boy had been in trouble over his Latin and had been told he was not fit to be at the school. This had made Peter feel sick and had led to his running away. It then transpired that Peter had felt like running away the previous term also. After this interview, moreover, he refused point-blank to return to school and also needed a great deal of persuasion before he would see Winnicott again.

After the interview that followed Winnicott decided that Peter was not fit to return to school and, instead, should stay at home with his mother. This was arranged. In Winnicott's words 'Peter turned into a boy of four going everywhere with his mother and holding her hand.' Much of the time was spent in the holiday cottage. This regime continued for about nine months at the end of which Peter was more himself again and Winnicott judged him fit enough to return to school. Apart from still feeling uneasy when near the sea, he progressed well.

During the months when he was away from school Peter had six further interviews with Winnicott in one of which he had recounted a long and complicated dream. In one episode there was a church and in it were three boxes that were understood to contain corpses. One of the corpses turned into a ghost and sat up. It had a waxy face and looked as if it had been drowned. In another episode school buildings were being eroded by water and 300 boys were drowned. Ultimately Peter and his mother managed to escape in his brother's sports car. In the telling of this dream Winnicott had the impression that 'Peter reached very close to the actual agony of the drowning situation'. In affective expression this interview was very different to the first one during which Peter had described the tragedy in much detail but in rather a detached way.

During these interviews it emerged also that Peter was aware that the ill-defined ailments for which he had sought the matron's care at school were really an expression of his strong desire to be cared for during the first months after the tragedy, when he was supposedly quite happy and unaffected by his father's death.

During the months when she was caring for Peter, mother had had telephone conversations with Winnicott and later had had an interview with him. During one phone talk she wanted to discuss especially how she and Peter should spend the first anniversary of father's death. One idea she had was to invite a lot of people in for a party. Believing that that would have been less than helpful, Winnicott influenced mother to spend the afternoon quietly alone with Peter. Subsequently she described to Winnicott how they had sat together all afternoon, at the end of which Peter had exclaimed, 'Oh thank goodness that's over, it wasn't half as bad as I thought it was going to be.' Immediately afterwards he had seemed a healthier boy and his face had changed.

Winnicott had had his first interview with mother a couple of months before the anniversary and he had a second interview with her eight months later about the time Peter returned to school.

Because Winnicott believed that Peter required a period during which he could be given intensive care by his mother (in the traditional terminology used by Winnicott, a period during which he could 'regress'), Winnicott had prescribed the regime he had despite knowing that mother had her own emotional difficulties and, indeed, was regarded by the school staff as being much too disturbed to be good for Peter. Nevertheless, mother proved reliable and helpful and the plan successful. Later, mother described how caring for Peter had helped her also.

Comment

This account gives all the salient features of the case from the time of the accident until about two years later. Before referring to various items of family history which are obviously relevant to an understanding of Peter's response, it may be useful to comment on some of the circumstances that surrounded the loss itself and were influencing Peter adversely during the months afterwards.

First, his father's death was both sudden and premature.

Secondly, Peter himself was the sole survivor. There was therefore no one else with knowledge of the accident with whom he could discuss how and why it should have occurred, how it might have been prevented, and how it came about that father had drowned whilst he, supported by the one lifebelt, had been saved. In such circumstances the survivor is bound to worry about what his responsibility may have been either in causing the accident or in ensuring his own survival at the expense of the other. In this connection the fact that his mother in her first telephone conversation with Winnicott had said that 'Peter was to some extent responsible for the tragedy' shows the direction that mother's ideas had taken.

Thirdly, Peter was not told the truth about his father's death immediately, despite his presumably already realizing what had happened. It is unclear what or when he was told subsequently. The impression given is that he never had an opportunity to talk freely about the event.

Fourthly, mother's initial idea that they should ask friends in for a party on the first anniversary strongly suggests that she was reluctant to accept her own grief or to share it with Peter.

Thus there is reason to think that the conditions surrounding the loss and also those affecting Peter subsequently were such as to inhibit his active grieving. Yet it is evident also that there had been difficulties in the family before father's death and that the pattern of Peter's attachment to his parents could have contributed much to his difficulties. Some further information about Peter's experiences and mother's family relationships, which support that view and which were derived from the therapeutic interviews, is given by Winnicott.

An item of family history, which had been discussed by Peter and had later been confirmed by mother, was an episode that had taken place when Peter was eighteen months old. At that time mother had had to be away for six weeks for an operation; Peter had been looked after by friends; and father had visited every day. During this period 'Peter had become over excitable, seemingly happy, and always laughing and jumping up and down . . . When his mother came back . . . suddenly all the bounce went, and he got on to her lap and went straight to sleep. It is said that he slept for twenty-four hours, and that his mother had kept him with her all that time.'[2]

In recounting this story to Winnicott, Peter claimed some memory of the episode and of how he had felt afterwards. With deep feeling, he explained to Winnicott: 'You see, I have never been able to be quite sure of mother since, and this has made me stick to her; and this meant I kept her from father; and I had not much use for father myself.'

The details of this episode were confirmed by mother during one of her interviews with Winnicott. In recounting it, moreover, she recalled a still earlier occasion when Peter had been separated from her. When he was only five days old he was admitted to hospital because of vomiting. He had remained there six weeks but his weight had continued to fall. Eventually his mother had taken him home and he had immediately begun to thrive.

In her first telephone conversation mother had described Peter as having always been devoted to her, and on some other occasion she referred to him as being in danger of becoming 'mother-fixated'. Thus it is evident that the two had for long been very close. By contrast, mother's relation to her own mother was fraught with difficulty and there were evidently difficulties also in her relationship with her husband.

During her first interview with Winnicott mother talked much about the difficult relationship she had had with her own mother since her

[2] This information, reported above in Winnicott's words, was given by Peter during his second interview with Winnicott. Much of the information had come to Peter during a talk he had had with his mother after the first interview. Mother, struck by the change in Peter after his first contact with Winnicott, had begun to think back to events in Peter's childhood and had also sought information from a friend. She had then told Peter what had happened and he had evidently been extremely interested.

earliest years. Her mother had always been demanding, she said, and had grown more so with old age and infirmity. Winnicott already knew something of this from Peter who, during one of his own interviews, had complained how impossible his grandmother was with his mother and had asked Winnicott to advise him how he might change her. In Peter's view grandmother's behaviour accounted for most of mother's difficulties. Also, grandmother's demands often led to mother being away, which always made him feel depressed.

Winnicott describes how he sought to support mother's intuitive ways of doing things. This he did especially because she felt she had got too little support from her husband in dealing with the children. Subsequently, Winnicott dealt sympathetically also with mother's rather natural resentment at his having left her 'out on a limb' during the time when he had been seeing Peter and not her.

Further Comment

In his assessment of Peter's difficulties following his father's death, Winnicott places much emphasis on Peter's six-week separation from his mother when he was eighteen months old and his subsequent uncertainty about her reliability. It seems to me, however, that he gives too little attention both to the circumstances of the loss and the conditions following it and also to the role that Peter's mother had been playing throughout his development.

A reading of the record shows that Peter and his mother present many features that are known to be typical of cases of school refusal (see Volume II, Chapter 18). An anxious boy emotionally close to his mother develops a variety of somatic symptoms and starts refusing to go to school following a family bereavement. The pattern of relationships within the three-generational family, moreover, is also typical. This leads me to believe that, though the separation at eighteen months may have played some part in making Peter more anxious than normal, and may also have affected her feeling towards him, a more weighty influence was that his mother had looked to him to support and care for her and had, probably without her being aware of it, bound him to her in a way she regretted. Characteristically, she had a close but troubled relationship with her own mother who was said to be extremely demanding and who, it may be inferred, gave her little care or support in return.

A topic about which Winnicott says little is the reference Peter makes to the possibility of one or other of his parents committing suicide. Although he states (in a footnote) that 'There is good evidence that neither parent was in fact suicidal', my experience has taught me to be doubtful of such conclusions. Peter, I believe, is unlikely to have had these ideas without one of his parents having referred to suicide. The evidence suggests to me that his mother may well have expressed some such ideas within Peter's hearing, especially perhaps when she was feeling exasperated by her mother's increasing demands. In this connection Peter's concern to get Winnicott's advice about how he could change his grandmother's treatment of his mother is suggestive.

Henry, eight when mother died

The next account, about an eight-year-old boy who lost his mother, is taken from a clinical report by Benjamin Shambaugh (1961), a child psychiatrist and psychoanalyst working in Boston, U.S.A. Since the boy's mother was known to be dying, an effort was made to help him through the experience. This meant that it was possible for the clinicians to obtain information both about the parent who was subsequently lost and also about her relationship with her son at first hand instead of second.

Henry was eight and a half when his mother died from cancer. Her death had been foreseen at least a year earlier and for that reason Henry came under psychiatric care early. Although Henry knew of his mother's illness and of the operation on her breast, he had not been told how serious the prognosis was.

Starting a year before his mother died Henry was seen weekly. He appeared as an active, open, intelligent and friendly seven-year-old who played freely with games, trucks and soldiers. After some five months, however, the sessions had to be interrupted for seven months. This was because mother disapproved of Henry (and also his younger sister) coming to the clinic and thought that they should be doing their school home-work instead. Knowing of his mother's objections, Henry refused to come. After mother's death, however, Henry was again seen regularly each week, a regime that continued for a further two years.

Henry had a sister, Dorothy, four years younger than himself, of whom he was often jealous, especially when she had father's attention. His mother gave the impression, in Shambaugh's words, of being 'a somewhat cold, stern woman, who demanded good behaviour and performance'. She was constantly prodding Henry to do better at his school work, which was said to be poor. Father, a salesman in his late thirties, was more easygoing. Towards Henry, however, he was apt to be inconsistent, at one moment emotional and indulgent and at the next angrily intolerant of Henry's boyish activities. During his wife's illness and after she died, father was said to be at a loss how to manage the children.

During the early sessions, while mother was ill, Henry usually avoided referring to his mother's condition and, whenever he did so, assured his therapist that 'she is nearly well now' or 'she'll be out of bed soon'. His feelings towards her were distinctly ambivalent. Whilst recognizing she had to be obeyed, he was often angry with her because of her constant demands that he do better at his school work. As her condition deteriorated, however, he ceased to be angry with her.

After mother died Henry and Dorothy remained at home with father. There was a succession of housekeepers about each of whom Henry spoke with unremitting abuse and criticism.

Immediately after the loss Henry clung close to father and was often jealous of Dorothy. 'At the end of each interview he would attach himself to his father who would address him in baby talk.' At about this time father seems to have talked of going with the children to Florida. Henry's idea was that he and his father should go there together and lie in the sun all day: he would not go to school and his father would not work. Nor would he worry about any of the things about which his mother had nagged him. A game he sometimes played in his sessions was of a boy and his father and a housekeeper. The boy and his father threw the housekeeper out of the house or else locked her up. The boy would then be alone with father and they would share a bed together.

At the time when the sessions were resumed after mother had died the impression Henry gave was not that of a boy who had suffered a loss. On the contrary, he came full of energy and gaiety. He said he was glad to be back, told jokes and puns he had heard at school, and showed his therapist magic tricks and new games he had invented. He also told of his exploits at school which, he claimed, led his friends to admire him. At the same time, however, he was extremely restless and distractible, and constantly moving on from one activity to another. During this period Henry made no mention of his loss and he responded angrily should the subject be broached. On one occasion when his therapist mentioned his mother Henry protested angrily and ran from the room. Later on he described his attitude: 'When she died at the hospital, I waved and said goodbye and forgot it.' Later on still, he insisted that his mother had been perfect; she had taken him to circuses and bought him candy. No one could make up for her loss.

The games he played with the toys provided by the therapist tended to end in violence and destruction. In one a family was moving from one house to another. First the removal van was demolished; next the house was blown up and everyone killed. In another somebody in the family was ill. An ambulance came, but then the house was burned down and the ambulance blew up. At these moments Henry became extremely anxious, broke off the play and turned to something else. In yet other play sequences the boy doll became destructive and then, in an effort to control himself, became Superman. Then Superman became violent and uncontrolled and various efforts were made to control Superman but none of them successful.

During these months Henry developed many ideas of being entirely self-sufficient. According to Shambaugh, Henry 'spoke of plans to take care of himself, to prepare his own meals, to get his own clothes. He spoke of getting a job and earning his own money, so that he would not need his father for support. Sometimes his fantasies were more grandiose and he thought of becoming a television star, world famous and very rich. He belittled his father as a supporter and said he did not need him. He denied he needed me or that I could do anything for him. But nevertheless, as he increasingly expressed that he had no need of me, he made innumerable demands to be given things and to be fed. He developed fantasies of omnipotence and invulnerability. On one occasion, his sister became sick and he stated that he could never become sick. Other people could get colds or pneumonia or perhaps die, but he was immune.'

Henry's behaviour towards his sister revealed some of his own conflicts and feelings. Sometimes he was protective towards her. For example, he often spoke of how sad Dorothy was and how much she missed her mother. He also described how angry she had been when children at school had teased her about her mother being dead and how she had attacked them. At these times he could be seen walking up and down the hall of the clinic with his arm around her, consoling her much as his father might do. Yet there were also occasions when he belittled her for being babyish and ridiculed her when she cried. This behaviour was of a piece with his grandiose claims to self-sufficiency.

After seven months of housekeepers, Henry heard that he was to have a new mother. At once he began disparaging his father and made fun of him for having had plans to go to Florida which he, Henry, now called silly. Four months later his father remarried.

In view of Henry's constant abuse and criticism of the housekeepers it was surprising that, initially, he accepted his stepmother enthusiastically. He told his therapist how nice she was, what a perfect mother she would be, and how much she would love him. He maintained that it was he who had proposed to her on behalf of his father and that she had accepted his proposal. He quickly referred to her as his mother and no longer as his new mother. With her, he claimed, he could have secrets which he could not share with his father or therapist.

This honeymoon period lasted throughout the engagement and for a brief time after the marriage. Father's new wife, however, soon became disillusioned with her role and felt unable to cope with the children. She resented intensely any reference to father's first wife. 'She began to complain, to have angry outbursts, and from time to time openly voiced thoughts of leaving the family. At other times, she took to her bed claiming she was sick. On these occasions Henry quickly became anxious. He started to blame his sister and then himself, telling me he had been bad at home, had spoken too loudly, or had slammed a door. The self-blame appeared intermittently but nevertheless did lead to his making efforts to be good as he had formerly tried to be good to his dying mother. He told me once he could never really love his stepmother until he was sure she would not go away. As his anxiety over her threatened departure mounted, he was again tempted to renounce her and to wish he had remained alone with his father.' Tension in the family ran high. Henry became furious with Dorothy for, as he claimed, making their stepmother ill. He was also apprehensive she might leave and was worried lest he be blamed for her doing so.

'In one interview during this time, Henry was as hyperactive, distractible, and restless as he had been following his mother's death. Then he told me that his stepmother was again very sick and in bed. Suddenly he held his hand to his chest, said he had a terrible pain, that he was having a heart attack. When I wondered what he was thinking, he told me that he had just remembered his mother's operation on her chest. Then he became sad and serious and stated that he ought not to come to the clinic and talk and play any longer; instead he should be at home doing his homework because his grades were poor.' This was the first time for many months that he had mentioned being worried about his schoolwork. Evidently he had suddenly remembered his dead mother's injunctions.

During the next few interviews Henry began, also for the first time, openly to compare his real mother and his stepmother. He described ways in which they were different; for example, they dressed differently, and whereas his real mother liked old furniture, his stepmother liked modern furniture.

A little later Henry's stepmother, intent on 'obliterating all traces in the home of the woman she had supplanted, resolved to throw out all the old furniture and have the apartment redecorated. Henry was delighted. He was again hyperactive, euphoric, and joked. He said it was good to get rid of the old furniture. Everything must be new, and the old must be forgotten.' But in the next interviews he was anxious and sad. Then he mentioned some glass animals that he claimed were worth two hundred dollars. They had been given him by his real mother and he treasured them. He was afraid his stepmother would throw them out with the old furniture and so he had locked them up so that she could not find them. Suddenly he became sad and serious and, referring again to his schoolwork, explained that it was poor and that he ought to work harder. Also he should stay at home doing homework instead of coming to the clinic to play.

Eventually he made a deal with his stepmother. He would agree to the change of furniture if she would agree to his keeping the glass animals 'for ever'.

Comment

The difficulty Henry had in mourning his mother was clearly evident long before the arrival of his stepmother multiplied the problems. Before considering some of the circumstances that are likely to have accounted for his difficulties, let us dwell briefly on the form his responses took.

Unlike Peter, who at once seized the opportunity to talk about his loss and the accident which had led to it, Henry refused to listen when his therapist referred to his mother's death and ran angrily from the room. Whilst he was in it, moreover, he was more in a mood for gaiety, jokes and restless activity than for talking about his loss. He also liked to daydream of having a happy, idle time alone with his father. Such mood and behaviour, often termed a manic defence, is clearly of a piece with the euphoric behaviour that some adults show after a loss and that is discussed at the end of Chapter 9. At both age-levels mood and behaviour seem to stem partly from relief that irksome restrictions and pressures which formerly emanated from the person lost are now lifted and partly from a frantic effort to distract attention, both their own and that of others, from the painful recognition that much that they valued has been lost.

As in the case of the adults described by Weiss, however, there is good reason to believe that this mood is no more than skin deep. The games Henry played with the toys, so far from leading to happy endings, resulted in destruction, anxiety and fruitless efforts to control further destruction.

Again contrasting Henry with Peter, we note that, whereas Peter welcomed staying close to his surviving parent, Henry was in acute conflict about doing so. On the one hand, he sought to have his father all to himself; on the other, he belittled his father and claimed he had no need of him. His claim to be able to take care of himself, to be immune from illness and to be destined for riches and fame are all typical of the compulsively self-reliant person. In keeping with that are the occasions when he ridiculed his younger sister for crying and for being, as he put it, 'babyish'.

In seeking to account for Henry's responses let us start with the pattern of relationship Henry had had with his mother before she died. She is described as having been a somewhat cold and stern woman who is known to have been constantly worried about her children's school performance despite their being aged no more than eight and four respectively. From these clues I infer that she was probably unsympathetic towards her children's natural desires for love and support and that, when Henry laughed at Dorothy for being babyish, he was doing no more than treating Dorothy in the way his mother had often treated him. As a result he had grown despairing of ever receiving love and support when he wished for them and was asserting, instead, that he had neither need nor desire for anything so babyish. Secondly, I infer that Henry had received much more criticism from his mother than ever he had received praise or encouragement from her, and that he had either taken the criticism to heart and had thought badly of himself or else had felt bitterly towards her. His picture of lying idly in the sun with his father after his mother's death makes it plain that in one part of himself he was glad to be free of her pressure and criticism.

Such guilt as these events would have engendered in Henry would have been much increased, I suspect, by his having been told either by his father or his mother, or perhaps by both, that his noisy behaviour was making his mother ill. My reasons for suspecting this are, in part, the general atmosphere in the family, including his father's angry intolerance of his son's activities, and in part the blame that Henry later directed at his sister. Dorothy, he claimed angrily, was making his stepmother ill.

The guilt engendered in Henry by experiences of these kinds accounts, I believe, for his angry refusal to discuss his mother's death when his therapist first referred to it. Guilt is likely also to lie behind the terrible pain in his chest of which he briefly complained before recalling the operation that his mother had had. Only after experiencing that, it seems, did it become possible for him to feel sad and to renew his relationship with his mother; to do so included both treasuring the 'valuable' glass animals she had given him and also taking notice afresh of her injunctions to work harder at his lessons.

It is not unlikely that Henry's responses were influenced adversely also by the experiences he had around the time of his mother's death and during the months subsequent to it. Any attempt to evaluate those influences, however, is baulked by a total lack of relevant information in the published account. Thus no information is given about what Henry was told of the causes of his mother's illness, the circumstances in which he last saw her, how or when he was informed of her death and whether he attended the funeral or visited the grave. Neither are we told how Henry's father responded to the untimely death of his wife, nor whether he was willing and able to speak about her to the children. The absence of such information, however, is at least suggestive that father neither encouraged discussion nor welcomed Henry's questions. In making these points, however, it must be remembered that at the time Shambaugh's report was published (1961) the significance of these matters had yet to be realized.

Visha, ten when father died

The account that follows, about a girl aged ten when her father died suddenly of a heart attack, is taken from the report of Elizabeth Tuters (1974), a social worker on the staff of the Tavistock Clinic, London. The case illustrates well some of the advantages of working with a child and the surviving parent in joint sessions.

Visha's mother phoned the clinic to ask for help with her ten-year-old daughter who was refusing to go to school. Father had died suddenly of a heart attack ten weeks earlier and mother was feeling too upset herself to deal with Visha. A few days later a child psychiatrist, Christopher Holland, and a social worker, Elizabeth Tuters, met Visha and her mother in order to reach a joint decision how best to proceed. The plan agreed was that mother and daughter should each have four meetings with a professional worker, Visha with Holland and mother with Tuters, after which the four would meet again to review the situation.

During these parallel interviews, held weekly, Visha and her mother presented contrasting pictures. Although the content of Visha's drawings and stories suggested she felt devastated and alone with no one to help her, to Holland she insisted that the world was filled with happy birds and gardens and endless supplies of ice-cream. Much of her talk was directed in bitter criticism at her mother because of her 'tearful carrying-on'. Visha also remarked that she missed her best friend at school and was worried about black spiders that lurk about at home.

In her interviews with Tuters mother was indeed tearful and distressed. She described how Visha had come home one day from school to find her father lying dead in bed. Earlier he had been complaining of a chest pain and was being treated for rheumatism; the cause of death was heart attack. Mother felt guilty and blamed herself for not having insisted that her husband see the doctor again. After his death, mother and Visha between them had managed all the funeral arrangements quite efficiently. Now, however, mother found herself unable to cope; she was tearful, not sleeping, dreaming of her husband's dead body stretched across her bed, drinking to excess and quarrelling with Visha. She felt she had no communication with Visha who criticized her for being weak and silly and not getting a hold of herself.

Mother painfully told of an unhappy marriage. Both she and her husband were musicians in their mid-forties and married 10 years, she for the first time, he for the second. Apparently they had married because they shared the same philosophy of classical music; but after Visha's birth all had changed. Mother had had to stay at home with the baby and had been unable to pursue her career, whereas father had become involved with all sorts of modern music and techniques. Gradually the gap between them had widened. For the past five years in fact they had lived completely separate lives, mother in her part of the house, father in his. They never even spoke. Visha went between the two.

In subsequent interviews, mother gave an account of her family of origin. She was an only child in an intellectual Ceylonese family. Her parents married late when each was well established in a career, her father as an administrator and her mother as a headmistress. When she was four her father had died of a heart attack, her mother was working and she was brought up by servants. She feared her mother whom she regarded as strict, rigid and Victorian. They had never got on together. After university mother had taught music and then had come to England where she had met and married father. He had been married previously, also unhappily; this had ended in divorce and much bitterness because he had not been given custody of the two children.

Before father died Visha's parents had been planning to go with Visha on a visit to Ceylon. Now mother and Visha intended to go there together in about two months' time.

Following these four parallel interviews Holland and Tuters felt that the best way they could help Visha and her mother in the time available was for the four of them to meet together in a series of weekly joint sessions. In Tuters's words, their reasoning was as follows: '. . . our primary focus would be on strengthening the mother–daughter relationship, as they only had each other . . . By helping them to share with us the pain of father's death we hoped to make it possible for them to share their pain with each other and thus to re-establish the contact which they seemed to have lost over the years'. When the four met in the previously arranged review meeting, Holland and Tuters proposed this plan which was accepted readily by mother and daughter.

Fifteen minutes before the first of the joint sessions was due to begin a phone message was received cancelling it. Visha had had an attack of asthma. Suspecting that this was a reaction to the prospect of a joint session, Holland and Tuters offered to arrange sessions twice weekly for the remainder of the time available; these were willingly accepted.

During the first of these sessions mother seemed worried and depressed, Visha emotionally flat. After remarking that she was afraid her mother would start to yell and scream, Visha gave a painfully cold description of her role as go-between in her parents' marriage and the responsibility she had always felt for her parents' happiness, and now for her mother's state of mind. 'I was a shuttlecock, going between the two,' she remarked; to which mother added sadly, 'She lived in fear of upsetting the peculiar balance.'

Immediately before the next session was due, mother again rang: Visha was having another and more severe asthma attack. Treating this as a crisis, Holland and Tuters visited them at home. Mother already recognized the asthma as Visha's way of coping with painful feelings. Visha, she said, had begun to have asthma at the same time that her parent's marriage had begun to deteriorate. It was noticeable that, although mother always claimed to be rather useless, in fact she was coping very effectively with Visha's attack.

During this visit Holland and Tuters were able to see for themselves the role that father still played in the lives of mother and daughter. 'His photographs, music, tapes and records were everywhere. It was as if in a shrine, complete with a tiny vase of fresh flowers by a large portrait. We became aware of memories of the past, their relationship to the present and of the ghost of father that seemed to be holding them together. The impact of this led us to suggest we continue to meet in the home.'

Thereafter Holland and Tuters visited them at home twice a week for three weeks.

At the first of these meetings Visha told how her worst fears were now coming true, how she and her mother had had a horrible fight and her mother had begun to scream and yell so that Visha could not stand it and she had run to get help from the new tenants who had moved into her father's bedroom. Visha considered her mother to be very weak. Mother appealed to Visha, admitting she was not strong. 'If you really knew what I was like then we would be better friends.' Mother's plea seemed to enable Visha to reveal how frightened she was also and how she felt she had to hold together in case her mother had a nervous breakdown. 'Why, even my grannie, the rock of Gibraltar, is shattered!' The therapists suggested that the strength Visha demonstrated might be at some cost to herself and to have resulted in her asthma. 'I am strong—I only get ill—I cannot cry,' she replied. They suggested that together they might explore her thoughts and wishes about her father's death. To this she replied, 'I never thought about it—and I couldn't believe it had come true—I never thought about it as a murder story [pause] something had to happen I guess.' This was the end of the session and mother handed Holland and Tuters a poem Visha had written for them to read outside. It was about Jimmy, a most friendly spider who lived behind their TV set, who took very good care of himself and was no trouble at all; but, the poem continued, were Jimmy to be lost and never return then all the family would 'grieve' for him.

At the next meeting Visha was in an asthmatic state. Taking their cue from her poem, Holland and Tuters tried to link Visha's feelings of loss and her inability to feel grief with her asthma—suggesting that her feelings seemed to be stuck inside her. Visha told them not to talk nonsense. Mother then began to talk about death from leucaemia and how painful it is, and she encouraged Visha to describe her views about cancer. This

335

led on to a discussion of how father had died. In Visha's opinion it would be better to be killed by a bomb because then you would not know what was happening. She reflected, 'a bomb would have been better; he was in one piece like a human being'. Mother added reflectively, 'asleep, dead asleep', echoing the words that Visha had used after she had found her father dead. Visha continued, 'I think a heart attack is better than cancer.'

There was a long silence. Then mother began, 'there were things that were left unfinished—all that he wanted to do—if one could communicate with the dead one would ask him if he'd like to finish things and the obvious answer would be, yes'; and with a voice hardly audible she added —'why did it all end this way?'

Visha's breathing had become more troubled. Mother continued, looking at her, 'Daddy would have liked to carry on and was stopped—I get angry about that!' When mother was invited to elaborate, Visha interjected sharply, 'I don't feel angry about that.' Mother described all that her husband had been doing, adding, 'Maybe it would have been simpler if I had died.' Visha retorted strongly; 'It wouldn't have been simpler—it wouldn't have been nice at all—it would have been just the same.' Her breathing became difficult as she added, 'we both miss Daddy very much —if Mummy had died I would have missed her very much'. After further talk in the same vein, Visha's asthma diminished. As the session ended all walked to the door in silence.

At the next meeting Visha seemed happy and excited, eager to talk about some psychological tests she had been doing and which she had enjoyed. Mother remarked that she had never before heard Visha laugh or be so free. She then talked sadly about her husband and their marital problems. Visha talked about the nice times she and her father had had, she as Daddy's little girl, when they had gone out to concerts and films, leaving Mummy behind. Visha admitted it had hurt her to leave Mummy at home and that she had worried about her.

Later, mother described Visha's interest in the cinema and Visha amplified with the names of her favourite stars. Mother said she thought Visha used the films to escape from the unhappiness of her home life. Visha agreed and added that her favourite song was, 'I'm Always Chasing Rainbows'. She then launched into a scathing attack on the unreality of her parents' life—how she saw them both always trying to escape from their lives by chasing rainbows—always wishing for silver linings but never doing anything effective to bring them about. She moved back through her parents' relationship to where she felt a stand could and should have been made. She revealed how, when she was five, her mother had left home and abandoned her because her father had brought another woman into the house. Visha blamed both her parents for this and told angrily how lost she had felt when she had woken one morning to find her mother gone.

The themes that emerged next and were struggled with concerned

336

anger and responsibility. Both mother and Visha vividly recalled the day of father's death, and mother told of her hysterical screams and attempts to bring her husband back to life. Visha described how angry she had felt towards her half-brother and half-sister for not being sad at the funeral. After this both mother and daughter appeared more able to tolerate painful feelings and to be angry and sad. Mother explained how she could now feel sad without feeling hysterical and that she could face the reality of her husband's death. Visha complained of feeling ill, and told how she wanted to go to Ceylon to a new life away from the dull, boring one without father. She then became angry with her mother who was trying to help her understand her feelings. In this session 'mother appeared soft and sensitive and we saw her as beginning to accept herself and her sadness'.

Visha next reported a change. She described how at school she was able to stand up for herself and could reply angrily to the children who annoyed her. This change was confirmed by the teachers. Also she no longer worried about her mother at home—her worries before were that the house might be burnt down or her mother might run away. Visha said she liked to be treated as a person, not a thing, and that the therapists were treating her like a person by listening to what she had to say.

During later sessions there was further discussion about who took responsibility. Mother felt guilty about not having been a good enough mother to Visha: she knew Visha wanted a stronger mother than she had been. Visha confirmed this but then had second thoughts; if mother were stronger she might not be able to talk to her. 'I like my Mum the way she is.' Tearfully mother confided that Visha had never said that before.

The concluding sessions were held at the clinic because mother and Visha wished to show their appreciation of the help they had received. Mother described how she had postponed dismantling father's room until the last. Now she felt ready to say goodbye both to him and to Holland and Tuters. She reflected how much she and Visha had looked forward to the sessions in their home and had tried to make the room cosy and comfortable. There were further episodes of friction between mother and Visha and some discussion of Visha's tendency in the sessions to idealize Holland at the expense of Tuters. At the final meeting Visha presented both of them with gifts. 'They assured us they would never forget us and they hoped we would not forget them.'

Comment

In view of what has been said earlier, comment is almost super-fluous. Once again father's death was sudden and premature. Because of the bad relations between Visha and her mother, Visha had no one in whom to confide. Furthermore, because of mother's

337

personal problems and the precarious marriage, Visha felt constrained to do all the caregiving herself. Her life was evidently based on the assumption that there was no one in the world from whom she could receive reliable care or comfort. As a result she was showing all the signs of developing compulsive self-reliance and perhaps also compulsive caregiving.

Much else in the family relationships is characteristic of cases that present with school refusal and failed mourning. When she was five Visha had had the experience of being abandoned by her mother and, following father's death, she was afraid mother would run away again. Mother for her part seemed to have had little mothering during her own childhood and had almost certainly sought to be mothered by Visha. As Tuters puts it in her account: 'One of the most important things we did was to re-establish mother and daughter in their appropriate roles, for when we began these roles seemed completely reversed.'

Geraldine, eight when mother died

The account that follows, that of a girl who was aged nearly eight when her mother died, is taken from the report by Marie E. McCann, a child therapist working with Erna Furman's group in Cleveland, Ohio, and republished in Furman (1974, pp. 69–87). Although there was a delay of over three years before this girl and her relatives were seen by McCann so that a great deal of the information was obtained rather late, the interest of the clinical findings offsets this disadvantage. Among much else, the account illustrates well both the patient's responses to the anniversaries of her mother's death and to interruptions of the sessions, and also the therapeutic use made of these events.

Geraldine's mother had died of cancer at the age of 48, a week before Geraldine's eighth birthday. From soon afterwards Geraldine was cared for by a neighbour, who had often looked after her earlier when her mother was working or ill. After a year there and a summer with relatives, Geraldine went to live with a maternal aunt and uncle; and she stayed with them from the time she was nine and a half years old to the time she started in analytic treatment at the age of eleven years eight months.

Nearly a year before that, at the age of 10.9, Geraldine had been found wandering in a dazed state. She did not know who she was or where she lived; she realized she was on the wrong bus and that her mother was not with her. She said she had a severe headache and asked a stranger to take her to hospital. With the help of the police she was returned to her aunt, and subsequently went to hospital for a neurological examination which proved negative. From there she was referred to a child psychiatric clinic. This led eleven months later to her being taken into psychoanalytic treatment and, simultaneously, to her being placed in a residential centre for disturbed children.

Ever since the wandering episode Geraldine had lost all memory of her mother's terminal illness and death, and also of the period of two years and nine months after her loss and before the wandering. The aunt was able to give a lucid account of events but only of course of what she knew. Father's memory was hazy and his information patchy. As treatment progressed, however, Geraldine recovered her memory and was able to fill in a great many details.

Geraldine was a negro of light-brown complexion and when treatment began was in the early stages of adolescence. Her mother had been married three times and Geraldine was the only child of the third marriage. She had a much older half-brother and half-sister, both children of the first marriage.

According to her aunt, Geraldine's mother was extremely bright and had been employed in accountancy work in government offices. 'She was portrayed as a difficult, demanding, domineering and stubborn woman... with a volatile and at times uncontrollable temper.' Father, now in his late sixties, took sporadic work as a waiter, was alcoholic and heavily in debt. Mother's pregnancy with Geraldine had been difficult owing to uterine fibroids, and birth had been by Caesarean. At first mother had cared for Geraldine herself, but to earn money she had looked after other babies as well. When Geraldine was thought old enough to enter a nursery mother had returned to full-time employment. The parents had had many quarrels, some violent, and had also separated several times. Geraldine's half-brother had left home early but her half-sister remained.

Mother's cancer was first diagnosed when Geraldine was nearly seven years old. She had had two operations and had also been in hospital for X-ray therapy. The illness progressed fast and at the end she had been admitted to an emergency ward only a day before she died.

The aunt described Geraldine as being 'strong-willed and determined with lots of grit'. Prior to the wandering and amnesia she had been withdrawn and distant from her aunt and had never cried; but afterwards, whilst she was away from school for a time, Geraldine and her aunt had become closer. When provoked, Geraldine expressed her anger in 'looks of cold fury' and never openly. She had no close friends and associated only with children she could dominate. Often she was jealous. She had a high intelligence and read widely; but, since the amnesia, she had seemed to lose almost all knowledge of maths.

At the beginning it was unclear what exactly had preceded the wandering episode. Certainly, Geraldine had been in trouble at school. She had changed her marks for music from a low grade to a high one and had been reprimanded for the deception. She had then run away for several hours and, on returning home, her father had threatened he would send her away to a school for bad girls. The next day she had gone to school, had then failed to return home to her aunt, and had later been found wandering.

When she first came for treatment eleven months later Geraldine presented herself as calm, self-assured and in command of the situation. She spoke voluminously, often in a vocabulary far in advance of her years and with apt literary references, and she avoided slang: it was evident she was keen to impress. Whilst outwardly co-operative, she remained cautious and rather stiff. In regard to her mother she remarked factually and without any feeling, 'I know my mother is dead, but I can't remember it.'

Geraldine's therapy continued for six-and-a-half years. For much of the time, especially early on, she was on her best behaviour and gave little away. But there were exceptions, related almost always either to the therapist's absences or else to one of the successive anniversaries of mother's death.

During the first four months of treatment, before the fourth anniversary came round, the therapist was away on two occasions. During the first absence Geraldine launched into a violent verbal attack on her father, blaming him for neglect. Since Geraldine had never spoken to him like that before, he was stunned: it was as though his wife had returned from the grave. During the second absence a few months later Geraldine became depressed, cried frequently, and got into serious fights with other girls where she was living. When the therapist returned, all was quiet again. Without feeling, Geraldine described what had occurred and added reproachfully, 'I don't understand it at all . . . but I'm positive that none of this would have happened if you had been here.' The therapist questioned whether something similar might have occurred in earlier years when her mother was absent. Geraldine scoffed at the idea but soon began describing what had happened during the week after her mother had died. Geraldine's half-sister, Joanne, had done her best to cheer Geraldine up by implementing mother's plans for Geraldine's eighth birthday. Then, without expressing any feeling, Geraldine described how unavailable her mother had always been: 'She did little for me as she was always working or ill.' Subsequently, in the poems and plays she wrote, loneliness and having to fend for herself were themes constantly repeated.

As the fourth anniversary of mother's death approached Geraldine talked more of her mother, how she envied mother the chocolates which she always ate leaving none for her daughter, and how beautifully mother played the piano in contrast to her own laborious performance. On the day of the anniversary Geraldine fell and injured her knee.

Before the therapist's summer holiday Geraldine denied being concerned in any way. During it, however, she became very upset and feared she would crack up. She wrote a reproachful letter to her therapist, but never posted it. When they resumed, Geraldine described the events but, as usual, without any feeling. A new quality entered the relationship, however. Geraldine read fairy stories to her therapist and sang lullabies. When her therapist suggested that her mother might have done such things with her, she disagreed flatly—her mother was always too busy.

There was a similar exchange in connection with President Kennedy's funeral. Geraldine's only affective response was when she was watching the casket being lowered into the ground. When the therapist ventured that she might have seen something similar at an earlier funeral Geraldine retorted vehemently, 'I was too young, I knew nothing of Mama's funeral, I wasn't even there.' The following week Geraldine fell in the gym and broke her left leg.

Subsequently, when the therapist referred to how Geraldine must have felt after her mother's death, Geraldine slapped her down again. Her loss was of no consequence, she insisted, her mother was never able to do much for her anyway. That night Geraldine sobbed inconsolably for hours.

On the fifth anniversary of her mother's death, Geraldine truanted from school, spent the day in a church and reported having taken forty aspirins, for which she was taken to an emergency ward.[3] These events she refused to discuss. Shortly afterwards she complained bitterly about the other girls in the centre where she was living: they hated her and were out to hurt or kill her. Ultimately, she refused to return to the centre after school and had to be brought back by one of the centre staff. She came to her session looking 'drawn, tense, mask-line. Walking in like a robot, she said, "I have taken all I can. I can stand no more."' The therapist said this must be exactly how she had felt much earlier in her life. She began sobbing. 'Yes, but it's five years now since Mama died. I should be over it but I'm not. I want more than anything for someone to hold me tight and really mean it.' She then told in detail and with tremendous feeling about her mother's final trip to the hospital, and of being told by Joanne of Mama's death. Joanne had said that her mother had gone to join Jesus and that Geraldine would join her there one day. Geraldine had replied, 'Yes, Mama is dead.' She had not cried until night-time at a neighbour's home, because she had feared she might cry for twelve hours or more, alone and without comfort.

Next Geraldine described the funeral, the hymns they had sung, the trip to the cemetery, adults discussing whether she should go to the graveside and deciding that she was too young. Thus she had sat all alone in the car. The therapist referred to her longing for reunion with her dead mother and how that was linked to her having taken the aspirins.

After this Geraldine was more able to recognize how she felt towards her therapist and expressed her wish to be the therapist's cat, to be loyal and to be loved. When the summer holidays came round Geraldine was

[3] It seems that the aspirins were taken over a period of three days.

angry and likened her therapist's trip to her mother's 'trips' to the hospital. Her mother had always deceived her; she had never spoken of cancer, had merely said she was going for an examination and then later had returned having had surgery. Geraldine seemed to voice two theories about the causes of mother's cancer. One was that it was caused by worry over father's drinking: she, by contrast, had always avoided worrying mother and, instead, had helped her at home and had got good school grades. Another idea was that her own difficult birth had been responsible for mother's illness.

Some time later Geraldine's aunt became seriously ill. Although initially Geraldine tried not to notice, she later acknowledged that she was terrified. 'Here it is again,' she thought, 'where will I go, where will they send me?' She felt like running away, but where to? These thoughts led her to recall the events that had preceded her original running-away and amnesia. At that time her aunt had had an angina attack and Geraldine was sure she would die. In addition, her father was planning to take her away to live with him in another state. He also revealed that she had been born three years before her parents were able to get married because mother was still married to her second husband. Geraldine had suddenly felt that she didn't care about anything, that her head was 'held on by strings', and she had gone off. Only after recounting this could she remember who it was with whom she had lived during the first year after her mother's death.

As the therapy proceeded Geraldine confided more about her relations with her mother and how she had felt. 'With Mama, I was scared to death to step out of line. I saw with my own eyes how she attacked, in words and actions, my dad and sister and after all, I was just a little kid—very powerless.' And, 'Mama didn't treat Dad too well at times. I remember once when I was about three, he was hospitalized with pneumonia. We moved and Mama didn't even tell him because she was mad at him.' And, in another description of her dilemma, 'How could I ever be mad at Mama—she was really the only security I had. You really have to side with the parent who looks after you.'

At the end of her treatment Geraldine was eighteen. Reflecting on her experiences she mused: 'You know, I think my treatment, or really my life, has been sort of in three phases. At first, I blotted out all feelings—things happened that were more than I could endure—I had to keep going. If I had really let things hit me, I wouldn't be here. I'd be dead or in a mental hospital. I let myself feel nothing and my thoughts were all involved with fantasies, fairy tales, science fiction. Then the second phase, my feelings took over and ruled me. I did things that were way out. And the third phase, now, is that my feelings are here. I feel them and I have control over them. One of my big assets is that I can experience things with genuine feelings. At times it hurts but the advantages, the happiness, far outweigh the pain.'

No doubt Geraldine's vivid summing-up was much influenced by what her therapist had been telling her; yet it rings true and, I believe, records true progress.

Comment

In presenting her account Geraldine's therapist, Marie E. McCann, writes: 'Geraldine had the developmental readiness for mourning . . . but she could not accomplish [it] because of characterological difficulties which predated her bereavement and because of a lack of help. She was never helped to understand the realities of the terminal illness, she lacked the assurance of her needs being met after her mother's death, and her environment failed to offer her any of the support necessary for a child to mourn.' Little more need be added. During her earlier years Geraldine seems to have had no option except to banish so far as she could all hopes and desires for love and support and to develop instead a premature and assertive self-reliance. In Chapter 21 other examples are given of children who developed in a similar way.

Striking features of Geraldine's case are her wandering from home and her associated loss of memory, symptoms typical of a fugue state. Although this condition seems to occur only rarely after a childhood bereavement, there is reason to believe that loss of a parent during childhood, due to death or other cause, is common as an antecedent in the case of those adults who present with it. In reporting on thirty-six such cases Stengel (1941, 1943) notes first that compulsive wandering with amnesia is associated commonly with pseudologia, episodic depression and impulses to commit suicide. He then draws attention to two closely connected features in the history of these patients. The first is the high frequency of serious disturbance in the patients' relationship to parents in childhood, in particular losses due to death or separation. The second is the desire to seek the lost parent that is often present during the actual episodes of wandering. 'Almost all these patients had suffered consciously from the failure of the normal child–parent relation. Many felt even in childhood that they had missed something which could never be replaced. In a number this feeling became particularly acute during their periodic depressions, i.e. at the time when the wandering compulsion arose. A few became conscious of the desire to seek for the dead or absent parent. Some imagined immediately before or in this state that the dead parent was not really dead but alive, and perhaps to be met in their wanderings' (1939).

In this connection we note that, when Geraldine was found wandering in a dazed state nearly three years after her mother's death, one of the few things reported is that 'she realized she was on the wrong bus and she knew that her mother was not with her'. Plainly this indicates, at the least, that she was preoccupied with her mother's whereabouts; it may suggest also that she thought that she had lost her mother through having boarded the wrong bus.

The four case reports presented in this chapter have, it is hoped, given the reader an introduction both to some of the features to be observed when the mourning of a child takes a pathological course and also to some of the conditions that the evidence shows are responsible for its doing so. In later chapters further evidence is presented in regard both to the pathological features to be observed and to the conditions held responsible. Meanwhile, in the next chapter we consider how Geraldine's psychological state, and the changes in it that occurred during therapy, can be described and understood in terms of the theory of defence sketched in Chapter 4.

CHAPTER 20

Deactivation and the Concept of Segregated Systems

... he who remains passive when overwhelmed with grief loses his best chance of recovering elasticity of mind.

CHARLES DARWIN, *The Expression of the Emotions in Man and Animals*

In considering the theoretical implications of Geraldine's case, a main feature to be noted is the strong contrast between the apparently composed and self-assured Geraldine of the first couple of years of therapy, a girl who expressed little emotion and gave little away, and the Geraldine of the later years who, after breaking down emotionally, described tearfully all the painful feeling she had experienced at the time of her mother's death and after it, her intense loneliness and how, more than anything else, she now wanted someone to hold her tight and 'really mean it'. Thereafter, instead of remaining aloof, she became intensely attached to her therapist, sought her love and company and was angry whenever she was away.

Of the many ways in which Geraldine's original condition might be conceptualized the one closest to the data, I believe, is to regard her as being like Mr G (Chapter 12), namely possessed of two 'selves', or Principal Systems as I am terming them. During the first two years of therapy the governing system and the one having free access to consciousness was a system from which almost every element of attachment behaviour was excluded. Not only were all forms of the behaviour itself missing but missing too were all desire and longing for love and care, all memory of her bond to her mother, and all the disappointment, the misery and the anger that any ordinary human being feels when such desires go for long unrequited. Yet there is ample evidence that, coexistent with this governing Principal System, there was another Principal System, segregated from it and unconscious, in which belonged all the missing elements, including all her personal, autobiographical, memories.[1]

[1] In Chapter 4 it is suggested that these memories are stored sequentially in a distinctive format, termed by Tulving (1972) episodic storage.

Although this segregated system was for most of the time in a state of deactivation, occasionally it found expression.

Almost always when Geraldine visited her therapist during the first two years this segregated system remained inert. There were, none the less, a few occasions when signs of its activity were to be seen. For example, there were two occasions during the early months of therapy when her therapist was away and Geraldine became angry. On the first of these occasions she directed her anger towards her father whom she accused of neglecting her, and on the second towards her schoolmates. On the second occasion, in addition, she became depressed and wept. Signs of the activity of the segregated system were to be seen also on the fourth anniversary of her mother's death and at the time of President Kennedy's funeral. Finally, on the fifth anniversary of her mother's death Geraldine truanted from school, made a suicidal gesture, and finally, during her therapeutic session, broke down in tears. Thereafter the system previously deactivated and segregated came slowly to life again.

Whenever a system that has been deactivated becomes in some degree active, such behaviour as is then shown is likely to be ill-organized and dysfunctional. Examples are the outbursts of angry behaviour exhibited by Geraldine when her therapist went away which, instead of being directed against the therapist, were directed against third parties. Another and more dramatic example, it seems probable, is to be seen in the episode of her wandering which, following Stengel's studies of fugue states, I am tentatively interpreting as having been an expression of her desire to find her dead mother.

The following account of one of Stengel's patients, to whom I refer as Miss B, given mainly in his own words and taken from his paper of 1941, illustrates the thesis.

Miss B was a girl of seventeen when 'she experienced for the first time an irresistible urge to leave the house and to stay in the open. She was always obliged to yield to this impulse unless she was locked up. This urge recurred four or five times a year for the next two years. As a rule she did not wander far, but lay down in a garden on the outskirts of the city and slept for eight to twelve hours, after which she returned home, apparently quite well. She obeyed this urge regardless of the weather, sleeping in the open in spite of snow or rain. On several occasions she entered a certain garden where she knew she would find an empty wooden trough. She would lie and sleep in this trough during the compulsive attacks, which usually occurred in the afternoon, leaving it for home just after dawn . . . The patient was of normal intelligence, and did not show any signs of organic disturbance.'

As a wealth of evidence showed, in these apparently irrational acts Miss B was still seeking her lost mother who had died 14 years earlier when she was aged 3.[2] 'Her mother has often appeared to her in stereotypical dreams at the onset of menstrual periods. In these dreams she sees her mother lying dead. The dreams occur more frequently but not invariably when she has been prevented from leaving the house in response to compulsion. This dream is a regular accompaniment of sleep in the open. When she sleeps in the open she usually feels as if she were lying on the grave of her mother. While wandering in the open she longs to be dead like her mother. She is given to daydreams in which she imagines that perhaps her mother is not dead but alive, and that she may find her some day.'

In terms of the concepts I am using, it can be said that in this girl, as in Geraldine, two Principal Systems of behaviour, thought, feeling and memory are present but segregated. On the one hand is a system, the one governing her everyday life, that takes for granted that she has neither mother nor, perhaps, any other attachment figure and that she therefore has no option but to fend for herself. On the other is a system, largely deactivated and with only marginal access to consciousness, that is organized on the assumption that her mother is still accessible and that, somehow, she can either be recovered in this world or else joined in the next. This latter system, to which it seems likely all her attachment desires, feelings and personal memories belong, provided only fragmentary evidence of its existence. Yet it was not completely inert. Not only did it influence all Miss B's day and night dreams but from time to time it influenced also her behaviour; and it did so in ways that made her appear crazy to observers ignorant of its premises.

In each of these patients, it should be noted, the system that is segregated and unconscious is an organized one and no less self-consistent than is the system with free access to action and consciousness. Furthermore, the segregated system is characterized by all those cognitive and affective elements that qualify it to be regarded as mental, namely desire, thought, feeling and memory.

[2] She had never known her father who had been killed soon after she was born: after her mother's death she is reported to have been brought up by 'various foster-parents'.

From time to time, also, when it takes control of behaviour, the segregated system shows itself to be so organized with reference to persons and objects in the environment that it is capable of framing plans and executing them, albeit in rather clumsy and ineffective ways. A main reason for this inefficiency, it is postulated, is that the system, being largely deactivated (by means of the defensive exclusion of virtually any sensory inflow that might activate it), is denied access to consciousness with the many benefits that brings.

One feature of the Principal System that was segregated in Geraldine (and probably also of the segregated system in Miss B), and a feature of the greatest importance to clinicians, is the intensity of feeling aroused once the system becomes fully active again and obtains access to consciousness. When on the fifth anniversary of her mother's death this occurred, Geraldine broke down in tears and expressed the strongest of desires for a close relationship with her therapist in which she would be held tight by someone who really meant it. To her therapist, for long kept at a distance, it must have seemed as though a dam had burst and that Geraldine was flooded with emotion.

Expressive though this type of hydraulic metaphor is when used in clinical discussion and valuable too in emphasizing the intensity of feeling aroused, it is extremely misleading when used as a basis for theory construction. On the one hand, the metaphor has encouraged theories which postulate quantities of psychic energy and quantities of affect as causal agents in mental life, and which I believe have proved scientifically unproductive; on the other, by concentrating exclusively on emotion (or affect), the metaphor has diverted attention from all the other features of the system being kept segregated, namely the specific patterns of behaviour that go to make up attachment behaviour together with the desires, thoughts, working models and personal memories integral to them. In the theory now advanced, therefore, there is no place for quantities of unstructured affect which are being kept dammed up.

It was noted that both in Geraldine and in Miss B a special feature of the segregated system is that it had virtually no access to consciousness. In other cases of disordered mourning, however, that is not so. In such people the system that continues to be oriented towards the person lost and seeks to recover him may be fully conscious and in a normal state of activation, although kept secret. An example is Mrs Q who, after her father's death in hospital, organized her thoughts, feelings and behaviour in two distinct ways. On the one hand, she believed that her father was dead and organized her life accordingly. On the other, she believed that the hospital had made a mistake and that her father was still alive; and she made secret plans to welcome him home again in due course (see Chapter 9). Thus, within a single personality there were two Principal Systems, organized on opposite premises, yet both of them active and conscious. (As previously noted it is to this condition that Freud (1927) applied the term 'split in the ego'.) As a result, in Mrs Q as in Geraldine and Miss B, any behaviour that was an appropriate expression of one Principal System was either irrelevant to or in conflict with that appropriate to the other.

At this point a reader may perhaps object that as a way of illustrating the concept of segregated mental systems I have selected special and fairly rare examples of mental illness and, therefore, that the concept is of only restricted application. I do not think this is so. On the contrary, I believe the concept to be useful for understanding many and perhaps all the examples of prolonged absence of mourning portrayed in this volume, as well as cases of compulsive self-reliance and compulsive caregiving, further examples of which will be found in the next chapter.

CHAPTER 21

Disordered Variants and
Some Conditions Contributing

When young lips have drunk deep of the bitter waters of Hate, Suspicion and Despair, all the Love in the world will not take away that knowledge.

RUDYARD KIPLING, *Baa Baa Black Sheep*

The four long accounts of children whose mourning failed, presented in Chapter 19, are intended to give an impression of some of the diverse patterns of pathological mourning seen in children and also of the ways that certain conditions can influence the form the responses take. The aim of this chapter is to examine these and other variants in more detail and the conditions that tend to promote each, and to give further illustrative examples. Once again the latter are drawn from the reports of clinicians working on both sides of the Atlantic: between them they represent almost every theoretical approach current within psychoanalysis. The fact that their empirical findings, when freed from divergent and often obscuring theory, are mutually compatible gives confidence in their validity.

It seems clear that some of the variants to be described, especially those in which self-reproach is prominent, are closely related to the chronic mourning of adults. Many others are characterized by a prolonged absence of conscious grieving. In some of the latter no psychiatric problem may be evident until many years later. In others problems of one kind or another appear fairly soon, during childhood or adolescence, and it is with these that this chapter is mainly concerned.

For purposes of exposition we consider the problems presented under a number of headings. They are chosen to reflect the great variety of symptoms and behavioural disorders that bereaved children show. The order in which they are discussed starts with those that are readily seen as responses to loss and moves on to those that, because combined with prolonged absence of mourning, may seem until examined to bear no relation whatever to loss.

What the incidence of each of these types of problem may be in a representative sample of bereaved children of different ages in a Western culture we have no means at present of knowing. Nor do we know the incidence of each relative to the others, since children with different symptoms and problems are likely to be referred to different types of agency, for example, somatic symptoms to a paediatric department, and behavioural problems to a probation service. All of what follows derives from studies concerned with small samples or with single cases.

Persisting anxiety

Fear of Further Loss

Every student of childhood bereavement has noted how common it is for children who have lost one parent to be afraid lest they lose the other also—either by death or by desertion. Nor is it difficult to see how fear of such happenings, which is natural enough in the circumstances, can be increased, often very greatly.

Fear that the surviving parent will die is likely to be exacerbated by such unavoidable events as two or more deaths occurring in the family together, or the surviving parent in fact falling ill. Among conditions that are avoidable are leaving the cause of the parent's death a mystery and discouraging a child's questions about it, and also remarks which directly or indirectly lay responsibility on the child either for the death of the dead parent or for the state of health of the surviving one. Another circumstance that can easily be overlooked is the effect on a child of his hearing his surviving parent express the view that life is no longer worth living, that she wishes she were dead, or that suicide would be the best course.

Fear that the surviving parent will desert is clearly inevitable in a child who has either had such an experience, Visha for example, or in one who has been threatened with it. It will be aroused also should the surviving parent leave the children with relatives, or even strangers, and then go elsewhere for a time.

There is, of course, nothing inherently pathological about a child entertaining such fears, nor in his responding in accordance with them. What makes for pathology is when the fact that a child is afraid of such happenings goes unrecognized or, and more serious, when the circumstances that have exacerbated his fear are either suppressed or disclaimed by the surviving parent; for that is how

351

an intelligible response becomes transformed into a mysterious symptom.

Fear He Will Die Too

For a child to believe that, if his parent has died early, he will do so too is a natural enough type of reasoning, even if mistaken. Wendy provides an example (Chapter 16). Many others are given in the sources cited in Chapter 15. Since a child is likely to identify with the parent of the same sex, it seems likely that in boys fear of an early death is more likely to be aroused by death of father, and in girls by death of mother.

Furman (1974, p. 101) describes a little girl, Jenny, who was barely three years old when her mother died of an acute haemorrhage. Although her father did his best to inform Jenny about her mother's death and what it meant, it transpired several months later that she remained worried lest her father, siblings and she herself might soon die. This became apparent when, after due preparation, she was taken to visit her mother's grave.

Jenny's visit to the grave with her father gave her an opportunity to voice her questions and her father an opportunity to answer them and so clarify the position. Too often, perhaps, such opportunities are not provided and a child's very natural fear persists unnecessarily. The following account of a child of ten and a half whose mother had died five years earlier is taken from Kliman *et al.* (1973).

Norma was ten and a half when she came to psychiatric attention because of a variety of somatic complaints, including trembling and tingling sensations, anxiety about not being loved, and inhibited behaviour at school both in her work and in her social relationships. She did not want to marry and had thoughts of becoming a nun. At this time father was having many business worries.

Norma's mother had died of cancer when Norma was five years old. At the time of her death mother had been in the first trimester of her fifth pregnancy. The illness had progressed fast and she had died only a month after cancer was first diagnosed. Father, shocked and grief-stricken, had withdrawn from the children and Norma had been placed in the care of an aunt and uncle who are described as having been harsh and inconsistent. (The account does not say how Norma's three siblings were cared for.) Fourteen months later father married a widow with six children of her own and Norma returned to live with her father, her stepmother, her three siblings and the six stepsiblings—ten children in all. About a year after the family was reunited another tragedy befell Norma: a favourite uncle was killed in a car crash.

352

Following an introductory and supportive phase lasting three months, therapeutic work with Norma and her parents began to focus on the bereavement of five years earlier. Norma herself, who was seen weekly by a woman therapist, began asking questions about her mother and uncle and described how much she missed them. She seemed sad.

During the course of treatment Norma's therapist took the opportunity to link Norma's responses to interruptions caused by vacations, and also her responses to the anniversary of her mother's death to how she may have felt soon after her mother had died.

The final sessions proved especially useful. Although Norma had been told seven months in advance that therapy was to end, she at first failed to remember it. Later she began to dread saying goodbye, a dread which her therapist linked to a previous painful goodbye when her mother had died. Norma also described a curious uneasiness about looking up at the building in which the therapist's office was located; this proved to be related to waving goodbye to her dying mother who, when in hospital, had also been on one of the upper floors. Finally, in the very last session Norma voiced a question: 'Did my mother die because she was having a baby?' Only then did it become clear why Norma had decided not to have children and to become a nun instead.

Comment

Norma's adverse experiences after her mother's death were probably sufficient to have led to the problems from which she was suffering five years later. The account suggests she received little help from her father and that her experience during the fourteen months with her aunt and uncle was unhappy. On returning home, moreover, she was one of ten children and it is hardly likely that her step-mother was able to give her the affection and help of which she was in need. Other adverse events were an uncle's sudden death and her father's preoccupation with business worries.

During all these years, it is plain, Norma had been worrying about the cause of her mother's death. The fact that she attributed it to mother having a baby is not unreasonable. Though we are not told the ages of Norma's siblings, it seems fairly likely that one at least was younger than Norma and therefore that mother being in hospital was equated in Norma's mind with the birth of a new baby. It is possible also that she had become aware of her mother's current pregnancy. All this illustrates how necessary it is to give a bereaved child ample opportunity to ask questions about the causes of his parent's death.

There is much missing from the published account, including

353

any information about the relationship Norma had had with her mother. Nothing in the details given, however, suggests anything especially unfavourable.

Hopes of reunion: desire to die

Since children have greater difficulty even than adults in believing that death is irreversible, hopes of reunion with the dead parent are common. They take one of two forms: either the parent will return home in this world, or else the child wishes to die in order to join the dead parent in the next. No doubt these hopes and wishes are greatly strengthened by certain circumstances. Promises made to a child shortly before a parent's sudden death that go unfulfilled may be the source of raised and poignant hopes. Kathy's father, it will be remembered (Chapter 16), had promised to take her to the candy store but had entered hospital and never did so. Many a parent on entering hospital as an emergency, never to return, must have promised the children to be well again and back soon.

Other circumstances which strengthen these hopes and wishes are when the child's relations with the dead parent have been good and the conditions in which he is being cared for afterwards are especially unhappy.

The following account of a boy who lost his mother when he was four years old, by Marilyn R. Machlup, is taken from Furman (1974, pp. 149–53).

Throughout Seth's babyhood his mother had suffered from lassitude and her condition became worse after the birth of a younger sister, Sally, when Seth was three and a half. A few months later mother fell out of bed and could not get up. Only then was the illness taken seriously; and it was arranged for her to be admitted to hospital for investigation. A fortnight later mother packed her bag, said goodbye to the children and was taken by car to the hospital. The next day she died. The last Seth had seen of her was when she got into the car.

Mother's death came as a great shock to father. Nevertheless he did all he could to inform Seth what had happened. His mother, he told him, had died: 'She had stopped eating, breathing, moving and feeling, and her body would be buried in the ground.' Seth was sad and cried briefly. But he made no comments and asked no questions. He did not go to the funeral nor did he see his mother's grave until a year later. When eventually father heard what the illness had been (leucaemia) an opportunity to tell Seth about it seemed never to come and there was no further discussion between them.

After mother's death father and the two children moved into his parents' home. The grandparents were warm loving people who did all they could for the children. They even sought professional help for Seth to help him talk about his feelings and memories of his mother, but this was unsuccessful. Father was of no assistance since whenever reminded of his wife he became despondent and could not bear to talk about her or about the past.

At nursery school Seth was described as a good and nice boy but lacking in spontaneity. Sometimes he asked where his mother was; but he made no other mention of her.

When Seth was six, two years after mother's death, father remarried, and the family moved into their own apartment. Contact with the grandparents ceased partly with the aim of strengthening Seth's tie to his stepmother. This relationship proved most unhappy, however, in large part due to stepmother's own emotional problems. She was extremely aggressive towards Seth; and a few months after marriage she developed an acute neurotic depression, for which she was in hospital for a month.

After the change of living arrangements Seth became disturbed and difficult. In particular he was hyperactive, ran out into the street and jumped from high places, all without any regard for safety. In addition, he threw temper tantrums, was destructive of his clothes, and both wet and soiled himself. Because of these troubles he was accepted for psychotherapy.

It was soon evident that Seth was much preoccupied with his mother and why she had died. He was also afraid he might have caused it. Amongst much else he recalled the occasion when his mother had fallen out of bed and how powerless he had been to help her. Seth's father on learning of these worries found an opportunity to explain to him about mother's illness in some detail; and later they visited the grave together.

Seth's stepmother resented his relationship with the therapist and, because of this, it was decided to end therapy prematurely. This upset Seth and he resumed behaving in a hyperactive and dangerous way . . . He wanted to get hurt, he said, then he would be taken to hospital and die. He also expressed an earnest wish to get in touch with his dead mother. He held long 'conversations' with her and strung tape 'wires' across the therapy room in order to telephone her. Often the therapist had to restrict his climbing; but one day he climbed on to a windowsill, fell and broke his elbow.

Comment

Looked at from Seth's point of view mother's increasing lassitude, alarming fall and sudden disappearance into hospital must have been a complete mystery. Although father had evidently done his best to tell him about his mother having died, it is plain that the four-year-old Seth had entirely failed to grasp the situation, either in regard to what had happened or why it had happened. It seems likely that father implicitly discouraged questions at the time; and we know that subsequently he could not bear to talk about his wife or the circumstances of her death. Inevitably Seth was left in a sea of uncertainty.

It should be noted that when Seth's mother went to hospital it was for an investigation: no one had expected her to die. Before her departure, we are told, she had said goodbye to the children. In such circumstances, it is not unlikely that she would have indicated to them that she would soon be back. Had this been so, it would greatly have encouraged Seth's continuing hope of her return. Nor is it surprising that after his father's remarriage and the loss of his grandparents, and again before the impending loss of his therapist, Seth's desire to find his mother became increasingly urgent.

More is said in the last section of this chapter about the accident he sustained shortly before ending therapy.

There are no doubt many other motives for a child wishing to be in touch with his dead parent, even to the point of dying in order to be with him or her. One such might be the desire to mend a relationship that had been damaged, perhaps by a quarrel, shortly before the parent died. The following account of a therapeutic session with a six-year-old boy who had lost his father three months earlier illustrates the point. The account is taken from a report by Martha Harris (1973), a child analyst on the staff of the Tavistock Clinic.

James's father had died in hospital after a short illness. At the time James had been staying with friends and it was some weeks before he was told what had happened. He had not attended the funeral nor had he visited the grave.

James had an elder brother, Julian aged eight. Of the two, Julian had always been the easier and had enjoyed 'a more peacefully loving relationship with his father'. James, by contrast, is described as having a more difficult temperament, and as forceful, aggressive, intelligent and passionate, and as closely attached to his mother. With his father he had not always got on well; mother thought they were too much alike. When his father had shouted at him James had shouted back.

After being told of their father's death the two boys had responded very differently. Whereas Julian had wept a good deal and had become very close to his mother, James had become angry and 'a torment'. In particular, he could not tolerate seeing his mother and brother looking sad. To his mother he would say accusingly, 'You're no good! You can't keep people alive!' Julian had asked her in bewilderment, 'What's the matter with James? Why does he always try to make me cry?' At school, which James had formerly enjoyed, he had become grumpy and inattentive and was always picking quarrels with other children. After a tantrum one day with his mother he had broken down and exclaimed, 'I'm horrible, but I don't know why.' This had led her to seek advice. In coming to see a therapist, he was told, he would be seeing a lady who would try to help him understand why he felt so horrible after his father's death.

James came readily to the therapist's room and dived immediately into an open drawer of toys made ready for him. He rummaged through it as though looking for something in particular. His therapist remarked on this and asked him whether he knew what it might be. 'Yes,' he replied, but said no more and continued rummaging. Then he stopped and looked puzzled, which led the therapist to enquire whether perhaps he was looking for Daddy. 'Yes,' he replied immediately. Thenceforward he poured out his thoughts and feelings in a way that was not always easy to follow.

He started: 'Yes, my father's dead and I'd like to see him. I don't know where he's gone. Yes. I know where he is, he's in heaven . . . I know he's in heaven and not in hell.' He wondered what heaven was like. His therapist remarked that he wanted to believe that his father was in a good place and was happy. With this he agreed intensely. When after further talk the therapist referred to his being uncertain where his father was, he retorted: 'But I know where he is . . . but I would like to see him again . . . sometimes I think I must commit suicide and go to see my father.' Asked how he thought of doing it, he replied, 'With a sharp knife, or get very ill and then die . . .'

His therapist said she thought that he was uncertain how he felt about his daddy, that he didn't want to think of his daddy being cross or of his daddy being in a bad place . . . At length James looked up and said emphatically, 'One thing I know . . . just three words, I would like to say . . . I—loved—him.' His therapist concurred but added that maybe there were times also when he did not love daddy. To this he replied, 'I wish he hadn't shouted at me . . . I shouted back at him.' When asked if he thought his shouting could have made daddy ill, he looked at his therapist intensely and asserted: 'When you're little you're very very strong and when you're old, even if you can shout loud, you get weaker and weaker and then you die.'

Later he added sadly, 'Sometimes I forget what he looks like . . . I try to think of him and he's not there.' His therapist referred to his being worried at being unable to keep a true picture in his mind of a daddy he loved. 'I've got two pictures of him in my room . . . in one of them he's not smiling . . . I don't like that . . . I like the one when he's smiling.' At the end of a long session, during which his therapist had made a number of interpretations (mainly of Kleinian origin), James reverted to the theme of suicide: 'I don't want to commit suicide . . . no, I'll commit suicide with all my family and then we can all be with daddy.'

One further theme arose just as the session was ending and the question of another one was being discussed. James got up from the floor and sat in the armchair. This led his therapist to remark that maybe he was wanting to be the daddy who made the arrangements; perhaps it was that that had led to the trouble between himself and his father which had ended in their shouting at one another. 'Yes,' said James, 'and that's the trouble with Julian now because he wants to be daddy too.'

After this first session James began to talk to his mother about his father. He asked for details of his illness and expressed the wish to visit the grave. Relationships at home became easier. Though initially he had no wish to come to the clinic again, later on he came for a further six sessions at weekly intervals.

Comment

There can be no doubting James's urgent desire to see his father again, even if it meant his dying too; nor that his main concern was to assure his father that he loved him. This suggests rather strongly that shortly before his father left for hospital the pair had quarrelled, that father, perhaps, had shouted at James and that no opportunity had subsequently arisen for James to make his peace with father. Certainly a reading of the account gives the impression that, whatever occasions of friction there had been in the past, the pair had been on reasonably good terms and that in ordinary circumstances quarrels would have been made good fairly quickly.

How and why these strained relationships should have developed between them is not clear. Obvious possibilities are that father had tended to favour his elder son at the expense of the younger and/or that he resented James's close relationship with mother.

Since it is hardly to be expected that a six-year-old would talk about committing suicide in order to see his dead father unless he had overheard someone else talking in this vein, we are left to speculate who it might have been. On the information given, the most likely person would appear to have been his mother.

Persisting blame and guilt

Nothing is easier for a child than mistakenly to blame someone, including himself, for having caused or contributed to a parent's death. There are two reasons for this: first, a child is unclear in general about how deaths are caused; and secondly, children not unnaturally put much weight on what they see, what they hear and what they are told.

In the study by Arthur and Kemme (1964) no less than 40 per cent of the children and adolescents were attributing the cause of the parent's death either to themselves or to the surviving parent and, as we have already seen, why they were doing so was often quite explicit. A child will blame himself whenever the parent who later dies, or the surviving parent, has sought to control him by reiterating that his behaviour—noisy, dirty, troublesome, naughty or however else designated—is making his parent ill, or 'will be the death' of him or her. A child will blame the surviving parent when he has seen one of them attack the other or has heard threats to do so.

The following account of a child of six whose mother had died two years earlier, by Myron W. Goldman and taken from Furman (1974, pp. 140–8), illustrates this point and several others also.

Addie was five years old when she came to psychiatric attention because of a rigidly stiff neck for which no organic cause was found. In addition, maternal grandmother was complaining that Addie was wilful and disobedient, and had difficulty in falling asleep. Although the stiff neck had subsided after the psychiatrist had talked with her about her mother's death and the anger she must feel at her father for having gone away, it was evident that Addie still had many difficulties. She was therefore admitted to the therapeutic nursery school and, when she was almost six years old, began seeing a male child-therapist five times a week.

Addie's mother had died from leucaemia two years earlier, having previously been in hospital several times. On these occasions Addie and her sisters, one year and two-and-a-half years younger, had stayed with their maternal grandparents; and since mother's death they were doing so again. These grandparents, who also had two teenaged sons of their own (Addie's uncles), are described as maintaining 'a solid decent family life, with close-knit warm relationships'. They lived in a black area of the city.

Mother had been in her mid-twenties when she died, having married young. Her husband was a handsome and charming man, two years her senior, who had turned out to drink heavily and to be abusive and delinquent. He never supported his family and had spent a year in a reformatory when Addie was a toddler. During Addie's fourth year father often was not at home but would force his way into the house and then leave again, unpredictably. After mother had died he left the city, having told grandmother that it was up to her to take care of the children.

Addie and her sisters had been told next to nothing about their mother's illness and death, nor about their father's desertion. The first Addie had heard of her mother's death was when, two weeks later, a neighbour's child had told her she had been at the funeral; and only then had the grandmother admitted it to the children. Throughout, in fact, grandmother was extremely averse to talking about her daughter's death or mourning her. One reason for this, it appeared later, was her persistent feelings of guilt for not having taken action about her daughter's illness earlier.

In view of grandmother's silence it is hardly surprising that Addie was extremely confused about her mother's illness and death. One of the ideas she expressed to her therapist was that her mother was still alive and would return. Another was that her father had killed her mother; though this she quickly corrected to saying that her mother had been sick and had died. Nevertheless, when she was anticipating her therapist's summer vacation Addie was afraid lest he be killed by her father. Subsequently during therapy Addie began to recall how her father used to hit her mother, and many other frightening details of her family life—how her father got drunk, how he ate the food leaving none for the rest of the family, how her mother had to call in the police. Later still she described how the mother of a friend had died in a fire and how the friend had failed to rescue her. This led on to Addie recalling with remorse how on one occasion she had persuaded her mother to let her father back into the house and how he had then proceeded to beat mother.

About two years after the start of therapy Addie suffered a recurrence of her stiff neck. An aunt who closely resembled Addie's mother had suddenly appeared at the house, which led Addie at first to believe that her mother had returned; and during the aunt's two months' stay Addie had become extremely attached to her. Nevertheless, when the aunt left and everyone else in the family missed her, Addie was an exception. It was then that she developed the stiff neck. Discussion of this sequence led to Addie recalling her mother's many visits to the doctor and how perplexed this had made her. Among other interpretations the therapist made about Addie's stiff neck was its resemblance to her mother's stiff body which the neighbour's child had described seeing in the funeral home.

This led on to Addie visiting her mother's grave for the first time. By enabling Addie thereafter to grapple with the concept of death, this visit proved a turning-point in the therapy.[1] Attempts to help Addie experience her sadness and longing for her mother proved difficult, however. One cause for this was that grandmother was unable to mourn her daughter's death and, whenever reminded of sad feelings, burst out in anger. Another cause lay in the family relationships that had existed before mother died. Addie's mother had been chronically depressed, whilst Addie's father had repeatedly rejected her. As a result Addie had concluded that 'if you show warmth you expose yourself to being hurt' and had therefore developed what the therapist describes as 'a hard, brittle attitude'.

---

[1] The case report does not say who took Addie to the grave. Since grandmother was strongly opposed to the idea, it seems likely to have been the therapist.

Comment

When the circumstances of Addie's family life are borne in mind, it is easy to see why she had the idea that perhaps father had killed mother, and might also, possibly, kill her therapist. It is also easy to see why she felt guilty about having played some part herself. When parents quarrel a child will often seek to protect the one attacked and will feel guilty if, unintentionally, he does anything that endangers one of his parents.

Moreover it is not difficult to see why Addie had developed compulsive self-reliance. Her mother had not only been ill and depressed but had also had two other children to care for, one of them only a year younger than Addie; whilst father's erratic and brief returns to the family only provided further occasions for Addie to feel rejected by him. In these regards the overall clinical picture of Addie resembles closely that of Geraldine (Chapters 19 and 20).

Comments about Addie's stiff neck are deferred to the section dealing with somatic symptoms.

Overactivity: aggressive and destructive outbursts

When a child is sad a surviving parent has no difficulty in recognizing it as a response to loss. When, by contrast, a child is distractible and overactive, or perhaps engages in aggressive or destructive outbursts, to recognize it as being also a response to loss is much more difficult.

There is, moreover, a vicious circle here. Children who respond in the ways described, the evidence shows, are commonly the children of parents who themselves have little understanding or sympathy for a person's desire for love and care, either their own or their children's. After a loss, therefore, these parents are extremely likely to stifle their own grief and to be especially insensitive to how their children are feeling. This interactional process is well illustrated in the case of Arnold, a boy of five, described by Furman (1974, p. 58).

Arnold's father died suddenly when Arnold was five and a half. Soon afterwards he became overactive and would not tolerate any mention of the death; nor would he stay in the house when a family member cried. This led him to absent himself from home for long periods and at unexpected times. His explanations were lengthy and involved but never to the point.

Both Arnold's parents, but especially his mother, had apparently always been blind to how their children might be feeling; and mother herself tended to avoid expressing feeling; instead she gave explanations and rationalizations. After her husband died she, like Arnold, failed to mourn him. Inevitably, therefore, she failed to understand why he behaved as he did.

In many cases, it is apparent, the angry outburst and/or withdrawal from the situation are the ways that a child who is unable to mourn responds whenever the death is mentioned. Henry, it will be remembered from Chapter 19, responded to his father's death much as Arnold did. Not only did he fail to mourn and instead became restless and distractible, but he responded angrily whenever his therapist broached the subject; and on at least one occasion he ran from the room. Adults who fail to mourn are apt to respond in much the same way. Not only do they avoid all mention of the loss themselves but they are apt to respond testily should others do so (see Chapter 9).

An example of a boy whose response to his father's death was not unlike Arnold's and whose family experiences had evidently been of the same kind, though probably even more adverse, is reported by William Halton (1973), a child psychotherapist working at the Tavistock Clinic.

Howard was aged eleven when his father died suddenly of a heart attack. He decided he did not wish to go to the funeral and, after crying briefly, announced that he would not cry again: 'You only cry once.' His mother was worried at his lack of grief.

At the time of his father's death Howard had already been in treatment for two years because of behaviour that his parents found 'wild and unmanageable'. After the loss, which happened to occur a mere two weeks before his therapist's vacation, he became particularly hostile and threatening towards his therapist.

On the first occasion that Howard came for therapy after his father's death he looked very white and seemed unnaturally cheerful. Nevertheless, he was in an irritable mood and soon picked a quarrel. In subsequent sessions among the many other hostile remarks he addressed to his therapist were the threats: 'I'll do some permanent damage to the room. Smashing you would be really worthwhile, because then no one would want to know you.' Despite these emphatically expressed sentiments, however, the therapist was able to recognize what seemed to be signs that Howard was also desiring comfort from him but was despairing of ever receiving it.

In this case, as in so many others recounted in this and the previous chapter, failure to mourn his loss and angry avoidance of the subject reflected the very impaired relationships Howard had had with both his parents over many years. In briefest outline, it appears that he had been adopted at the age of four weeks but had not been told of it until he was nine years old. Both parents had had high hopes of him but these had later turned to 'resentful disillusion'. Mother (who seems to have had major emotional difficulties of her own) 'found any physical demonstration of affection embarrassing' and was accordingly much relieved when at some point in his development Howard had no longer demanded it. When she was depressed and he was troublesome there were occasions when 'they just screamed at each other'. Howard's relationship with his father was thought to have been better during the first few years of the boy's life but father had been ill and away in hospital for several months during Howard's fourth and fifth years and, after that, father felt he had never been able to make contact with him again.

Comment

In many, perhaps all, of those who respond to a loss with over-activity and/or anger, whether they are children or adults, a feeling of guilt for having been in some degree responsible is playing a part. Although this is not commented upon by Halton, I suspect it was playing a part in Howard's case also. In the first place, father had had serious heart trouble since Howard's earliest years; in the second Howard's behaviour is described as having been wild and unmanageable. Implicitly or explicitly, it seems likely, Howard was given to understand that his behaviour was responsible for making his father worse. If that was so and he was blaming himself for his father's death, it is hardly surprising that he was unwilling to express it to an adult who, judged in terms of his past experience, he would expect to be unsympathetic or indeed hostile. Many difficult and aggressive children operate on the principle that attack is the best means of defence.

The importance of a hidden sense of guilt in accounting for a person's difficult behaviour is well illustrated by the case of a boy of ten, Walter, described by Wolfenstein (1966). Unlike Arnold and Howard described above, Walter was not seriously disturbed.

Walter was eight when his mother developed breast cancer and had an operation. Thereafter he was cared for increasingly by his maternal grandmother, whom he already knew well; and this arrangement continued after mother died two years later. Despite grandmother's devoted care, however, Walter became chronically irritable with her and on one occasion after she had rebuked him for something he retorted angrily that he was leaving home; he then stormed out of the house. Fortunately his grandmother realized that he was still upset by the loss of his mother and, after he had returned, began to talk to him about it, remarking how sad both of them were. After she had told him about all the efforts that had been made to save his mother's life, Walter confided to her how he might be partly to blame. After his mother had returned home following her operation she had been very weak. Despite that, however, she had got up every morning to give him his breakfast before school. Had she not done so, he thought, she might not have died. The discussion, which went on late into the night, cleared the air.

Walter was fortunate to have a sympathetic and insightful grandmother, who provided him also with the substitute parenting that is so necessary for a bereaved child. Within this relationship of trust, and given an opening, he was able to confess his misgivings.

Origins of an Oppressive Sense of Guilt

In advancing the view that a burdensome sense of guilt lies frequently behind hostile and aggressive behaviour I am conforming to views expressed over the years by a large number of psychoanalysts. Where my view tends to differ from theirs is in how the development of an oppressive sense of guilt is to be accounted for. Whereas traditional theory lays heavy emphasis, to the exclusion of almost all else, on the role of hostile wishes harboured by the guilty survivor against the dead person, in my judgement the evidence points more clearly to the influential part that is played by the way a child is treated within his family. Consider, for example, the effects on the way he construes events of a child's ignorance of the true causes of family misfortunes, including illness and death; especially when, in addition, he is being influenced by what his parents and others are saying to him. Thus, censorious remarks, made in unguarded moments, can readily lead a child to believe that every misfortune stems from his own 'selfish demands' or his own 'aggravating ways'. Moreover, when calamity strikes, a distraught parent can all too easily lash out in unthinking reproach against whoever may be nearest—and not infrequently this is a young child. When we add to the guilt arising from these episodes the guilt systematically induced in their children by some parents in order to control them, we find no lack of external pressures to account for the development of a child's morbid sense of guilt after a parent has died.

Analysis of the problem along these lines, moreover, shows that anyone treated by a parent in these kinds of way is not only likely to feel guilty but likely also to feel resentful, perhaps bitterly resentful, against that parent. Thus the festering presence of hostile wishes against the dead person is accounted for also. This means that the theory advanced here not only respects the data on which traditional theory is built but gives them a significant place within a more comprehensive framework.

Compulsive caregiving and self-reliance

Compulsive Caregiving Intensified

The account of Visha given in Chapter 19 illustrates how a child of ten came to feel constrained to look after her mother instead of expecting to be cared for herself. Even before her father's death Visha had had to act as the go-between in her parents' marriage and had come to feel responsible for their happiness. After his sudden death she had feared lest her mother break down and had felt therefore it was necessary for her to 'hold together' and take responsibility for her mother's state of mind. The background to this, of course, was her mother's unhappy childhood: mother's father had died when she was four and her mother had been too busy to give her time or affection. Although it is recognized that Visha resented finding herself in the caregiving role, it seems likely that, had there been no therapeutic intervention, she would nevertheless have found herself trapped irretrievably in it.

Earlier, in Chapter 12, it was remarked that in the histories of persons given to compulsive caregiving two rather different types of childhood experience are found. In the one a child is made to feel responsible for the care of a parent: this was clearly so in the case of Visha, as it was also in the case of Julia (see Chapter 12). In the other the disposition follows intermittent and inadequate mothering culminating in total loss. The persons towards whom the caregiving is directed are usually different in the two types of case. After the former type of experience, the caregiving is likely to be directed towards a parent or, in later life, a spouse. After the experience of intermittent and inadequate mothering it may be directed in a less specific way, for example towards other children, including strangers.

It is in those cases especially that a child, after having lost all effective parenting, develops a pattern in which, instead of his being sad and longing for love and support for himself, becomes intensely concerned about the sadness of others and feels impelled to do all in his power to help and support them. In this way the cared-for person comes to stand vicariously for the one giving the care (see Chapter 9). This seems to have occurred briefly with the four-year-old Kathy who, soon after her father's death, became much concerned about the welfare of another child who had also lost his father (Chapter 16).

Another example of this is the case of Patricia,[2] a nineteen-year-old girl, described by Root (1957), who had come into therapy because of recurring attacks of sickness and nausea, with general anxiety and depression. The symptoms had developed soon after she had got married, two years previously.

One evening when Patricia was ten and a half her mother had been killed instantaneously in a road accident. Her father had been driving. At first, Patricia and her brother, two years older, had been told that mother was in hospital. Next day they learned she was dead.

Patricia, we are told, had already had 'much experience of missing her mother who had all along continued her work as a teacher and had done much home tutoring'. Patricia had been mostly in the care of a maid. Mother, who was the mainstay of the family financially, is described as having been ambitious, conscientious and constantly worried about the children's behaviour and health. Emetics and enemas were in frequent use; and only when Patricia was ill did her mother show her much concern. Like mother, father demanded high standards and even when Patricia did well he criticized any deficiency there was. Both parents seem to have favoured the elder brother.

After her mother's death Patricia took over responsibility for running the home. Since her father and brother gave her no help, this became a drudgery which she keenly resented whilst continuing conscientiously to do it. Later she recalled times when she had missed her mother, for example when she started her periods and also after occasions when her father had been especially thoughtless and critical.

In these circumstances it is not surprising that during her teens Patricia was eager to get away from home. Having done well scholastically therefore, she went off to college when only sixteen. She was impatient to be grown up and to have a family of her own; and within nine months she had got married to a fellow student.

[2] In Root's account the patient is not given a pseudonym; the pseudonym used here is for convenience of exposition and reference.

Her husband's childhood had been no happier than her own. His mother had suffered from a chronic illness and had died when he was ten, the same age that Patricia had been when she lost her mother. He had the reputation of being a bitter person and Patricia had taken it upon herself to help him over it. As a result she shouldered all the responsibilities, and soon came to feel burdened by his dependence on her. Sexual relations were not happy. Soon after the marriage she became depressed, felt unable to concentrate, quit college, and spent much of her time in bed.

During treatment the first statement that Patricia made about her mother was that she was 'a wonderful woman'. Since this remark was made with emphasis but without emotion her analyst suspected that Patricia's feelings for her mother were not unmixed, which later became evident. He noted also that Patricia 'could not at first comprehend, even intellectually, that she missed her mother'. Nevertheless, she was deeply concerned about the misfortunes of others and, in Root's words, 'often displaced her sadness onto something else or felt sad for someone else'. For example, she could shed tears for an orphaned beggar girl. Later in the analysis it transpired that she had not believed that her mother had died and had never expressed grief either at the time or later. Yet it was evident that she was much preoccupied with thoughts of her mother. For example, in her dreams and fantasies her mother constantly appeared. In some of them there was a happy reunion. In others she had a picture of her mother in a sanatorium or witnessed a frightening scene of her mother with head and face injuries. As time went on she became more able to mourn her mother and described how this seemed like 'letting her mother go'. She also remembered how she had felt when, at the age of seven, a maid to whom she had been attached had left. There had been a tearful parting which in the analysis had been recalled with much emotion and weeping.

Comment

There are so many features in this case that we have met before that not much comment is called for. Patricia's childhood seems to have been rather like that of Visha's mother; each had a capable mother who was so occupied in a teaching career that neither daughter saw much of her and, instead, each was left to the care of maids. To at least one of these maids Patricia had developed a strong attachment and she had suffered commensurately when the maid had left. Thus it seems clear that already before her mother's death Patricia had suffered from her mother's frequent absences and from the loss of at least one substitute to whom she had been attached.

After her mother's death she had failed to mourn and had suppressed, so far as she was able, her sadness and yearning to be cared for. Instead, she had tried hard to be the well-behaved and

367

helpful child her mother had expected. Thus she strove to be grown up and independent, with an element of compulsive self-reliance. Yet she was drawn to those who, like herself, had been bereaved, and found herself both grieving for them and caring for them. The man she chose to marry was, she believed, in need of her care and seems hardly to have been likely to care for her.

It is uncertain why exactly Patricia broke down after her marriage, though it is clear that she had burdened herself with responsibilities which were far too great for her previous mental condition. As regards her somatic symptoms, it is not unlikely that, as Root suggests, they were related to the fact that it was only when she was unwell as a child that her mother had given her much time or care. Her sexual difficulties are likely, I believe, to have been secondary to her interpersonal ones.

Compulsive Self-reliance Intensified

Two of the cases described in Chapter 19, those of Henry and Geraldine, well illustrate how a bereavement greatly intensifies any tendency a child may already have towards abjuring his desire for love and proclaiming instead his total self-sufficiency. In both the history of unhappy relations with mother give clear indications of why each child had developed in this way. The same type of background is present in the case of Patricia, though her subsequent self-sufficiency is less in evidence than her compulsive caregiving.

In his description of the treatment of a married woman of twenty-seven with severe emotional difficulties, Mintz (1976) quotes some remarks of the patient that reveal in a dramatic and tragic way the predicament in which a child of four found herself when bereft of any attachment figure.

Mrs G came for analysis because she felt irritable, depressed and filled with hate and 'evil'. In addition she was frigid with her husband, felt emotionally detached and wondered whether she was capable of love.

When Mrs G was three her parents were divorced. Her father left home and her mother, who began working long hours, had little time for her. A year later when Mrs G was four she was placed in an orphanage and remained there for eighteen months. Thereafter, although back with her mother, family relationships continued disturbed and unhappy. Mrs G left home early; before she was twenty-one she had already been married and divorced twice. Her present husband was her third.

In the early phases of the analysis Mrs G was extremely reluctant to recall the painful events of her childhood; and when she did so she broke down into tears and sobbing. Nevertheless, her analyst encouraged her to go over them and to do so in minute detail since he believed this would help her. At the same time he paid at least equal attention to her relationship with himself in which, as would be expected, all the interpersonal difficulties that she had had in other close relationships recurred.

Amongst much else in her childhood that was painful, Mrs G recalled how sad she had felt when she parted with her pets when she was sent to the orphanage. Sometimes she dreamed about her time there with feelings of being overwhelmed. She recalled feeling very small among the many children, how there were no toys, the harsh treatment, and how she had sometimes misbehaved deliberately in order to get smacked.

Inevitably the emotional conflicts in Mrs G's relationship with her analyst became more acute when, after four years, it was decided to end the treatment after a further six months for financial reasons. Mrs G now dreamed and daydreamed more openly of her analyst. She had realized from the first that parting would be painful. Separations had always made her angry and, as she put it, 'anger makes me sad because it means the end . . . I'm afraid you'll leave me or kick me out or put me away.' The analyst reminded her of her feeling when sent to the orphanage. Struggling to think of herself as self-sufficient, Mrs G exclaimed: 'I'm clinging on to me . . . I'm taking care of me all by myself.'

A few months later as termination approached, she linked how she felt about her analyst with how she had felt earlier about her mother: 'I don't want to release my mother—I don't want to let her go—she's not going to get rid of me.' Active yearning for love and care, and anger at those who had denied it her, had returned.

Other episodes showed how, within the supportive analytic relationship, she had become able to bear the pain of longing and grieving. For example, during the early days of the analysis Mrs G's cat had died but she had felt indifferent about it. This she had explained: 'If I let it hurt me, I'd be saddened by everything. One will trigger off the rest.' Towards the end of the analysis, however, when another cat died, she wept.

Although therapy had restored this patient's feeling life and had resulted in her becoming able to make improved relationships, including that with her mother, a follow-up five years later showed that, as would be expected, she remained vulnerable to situations that arouse anxiety and sadness, such as separation and loss.

There are, of course, many similar cases on record of compulsive self-reliance having developed after a childhood bereavement, for example in the papers by Deutsch (1937) and by Fleming and Altschul (1963). In few, if any of them, however, is adequate information given about personality development and family relationships prior to the loss, about the circumstances of the loss, or about what happened after it, including what and when the child was told. The reason for these omissions is partly that most of these patients came into treatment many years after the loss had occurred, and partly that at the time they were treated the clinicians concerned were unaware how relevant these matters are.

Nevertheless some of these cases have an interest far beyond the historical. In particular some of them document with great clarity how, beneath the hard shell of an adult's proclaimed self-sufficiency, there lies dormant a strong yearning to be loved and cared for. The following is taken from the seminal paper on absence of grief published by Helene Deutsch in 1937.

The patient was in his early thirties when, without apparent neurotic difficulties, he came into analysis for non-therapeutic reasons. The clinical picture was one of a wooden and affectionless character. Deutsch describes how 'he showed complete blocking of affect without the slightest insight. In his limitless narcissism he viewed his lack of emotion as "extraordinary control". He had no love-relationships, no friendships, no real interests of any sort. To all kinds of experience he showed the same dull and apathetic reaction. There was no endeavor and no disappointment . . . There were no reactions of grief at the loss of individuals near to him, no unfriendly feelings, and no aggressive impulses.'

As regards history, we learn that his mother had died when he was five years old and that he had reacted to her death without feeling. Later he had repressed not only the memory of his mother but also everything else preceding her death.

'From the meager childhood material brought out in the slow, difficult analytic work,' Helene Deutsch continues, 'one could discover only negative and aggressive attitudes towards his mother, especially during the forgotten period, which were obviously related to the birth of a younger brother. The only reaction of longing for his dead mother betrayed itself in a fantasy, which persisted through several years of his childhood. In the fantasy he left his bedroom door open in the hope that a large dog would come to him, be very kind to him, and fulfil all his wishes. Associated with this fantasy was a vivid childhood memory of a bitch which had left her puppies alone and helpless, because she had died shortly after their birth.'

Euphoria and depersonalization

Some measure of euphoria is a not uncommon feature of children and adolescents who fail to mourn. Kathy (Chapter 16), Henry (Chapter 19), and Howard (this chapter) are all examples. An explanation of this response is not easy. Several motives appear to be playing a part.

In some cases, it seems likely, euphoria is an expression of relief that irksome restrictions imposed by the dead parent will now be lifted. This motive may have been playing a part in Henry who had been up against his disciplinarian mother, and perhaps also in Howard. It was this motive that seems to have been playing a part also in the case of the woman in her early forties who had separated from her husband after nearly twenty years of marriage whose account of her experience (reported by Weiss 1975) is quoted in Chapter 9.

In seeking other motives for a euphoric response we can take a lead from the four-year-old Kathy whose healthily progressing mourning for her father is described in Chapter 16. During the early weeks, when Kathy alternated between being sad and a little euphoric, she asserted candidly 'I don't want to be sad'. Some months later, moreover, when she was trying to understand why her father should have died, she made it plain that she had connected his looking sad with his having died: 'I always felt if you're very happy you won't die.' To be very happy, therefore, or rather to convince yourself and others that you are happy, is a safeguard against dying yourself.

It seems likely that some cases of overactivity can be explained, at least in part, in the same way. Mitchell (1966) points out, discerningly, that the most typical and also the most frightening characteristic of a dead animal or a dead person is their immobility. What more natural, therefore, for a child who is afraid he may die than for him to keep moving. Notions of preserving others of the family from dying, or even of restoring the dead to life, may also play a part in these responses.

Not infrequently euphoric responses are seen in those who experience a prolonged absence of conscious grieving; and they may also have experiences of depersonalization. Both are well illustrated in the account of an adolescent girl who had lost her mother reported by Wolfenstein (1966).

Ruth had just turned fifteen when her mother died suddenly from a cerebral haemorrhage. Shortly after the funeral Ruth found herself no longer able to cry. She felt an inner emptiness as though a glass wall separated her from what was going on around her.

At the time of her mother's death Ruth had already been in treatment for six months (for reasons that are not reported). When coming for a session during the week following her loss she remarked, 'I guess it will be pretty bad this week', implying that she was expecting to feel distressed. Yet often she seemed the reverse. For example, on one occasion she appeared in an exuberant mood and explained how she had written a successful humorous composition in which she had congratulated herself on her performance at school and had transformed various embarrassing predicaments into comic situations. Each time she was in this sort of mood she hailed it as the end of her feeling distressed.

How precarious these euphoric moods were was shown by some of the dreams she had. In one, for example, she and her father were trying to escape from a disaster-stricken city but had then turned back to try to rescue the dying and the dead.

Several months after her mother's death Ruth became depressed. She complained that nothing gave her pleasure any longer, neither being with friends, nor listening to music; everything she had formerly enjoyed had lost its savour. She felt she had nothing to look forward to, that any effort was too much, that all she wished to do was stay in bed. Often she felt like crying. For Ruth, however, none of this feeling was associated consciously in any way with her mother's death. Instead, she berated herself for the senselessness of feeling like that; or else attributed it to her inability to be at ease with her schoolmates. Although the therapist tried repeatedly to help Ruth see and feel the connection between her feeling depressed and her loss, for Ruth this remained only an intellectual exercise.

Nevertheless, there were unmistakable signs of what her feelings were. Sometimes in bed at night, she said, she felt desperate with frustration, rage and yearning. On these occasions she tore the bedclothes off the bed, rolled them into the shape of a human body and embraced them. At other times she felt, when she was talking to someone, that she was not really addressing the person before her. When asked to whom perhaps she was talking, she said it might be her mother. But this seemed no more than detached speculation.

It was not until the second year after her loss that Ruth's yearning for her mother began to emerge more clearly. Ruth had for long been overweight and her mother had repeatedly urged her to diet. Now she began to do so and after some months became surprisingly slim. On the eve of her birthday she went for a long ramble by herself and returned in a state of dreamy euphoria. But on the night of her birthday she started on an 'eating binge' which lasted many weeks. The explanation of this sequence only emerged later. Having conformed with her mother's wishes over the dieting, it appeared she had been expecting her mother to return on her birthday: it was a bargain which had not been kept.

Yet, hopes of her mother's return persisted. She felt as though she was constantly waiting for something. There should be an arrangement, she claimed, for people to be dead for five years and then come back again.

At length Ruth began to experience in full force her longing for her mother and her terror of losing her. As in other children and adolescents described in this and the preceding chapters, this experience occurred at times of separation or impending separation from her analyst. On one such occasion Ruth complained, 'If my mother were really dead, I would be all alone'; on another, 'If I would admit to myself that my mother is dead, I would be terribly scared.' Eventually, four years after her mother's death and at the time when she was going to transfer to another therapist, Ruth wrote to her therapist quoting the words of a cantata in which she was singing and in which the chorus voiced the desperate feelings of drowning children: 'Mother, dear mother, where are your arms to hold me? Where is your voice to scold the storm away? . . . Is there no one here to help me? . . . Can you hear me, mother?' This, she said, expressed exactly how she was feeling.

In her account of the case Wolfenstein gives few particulars of Ruth's family, of the personalities or activities of her parents, of family relationships, or of Ruth's experiences with her parents. Nor is it clear how Ruth was cared for after her mother's death, though it appears that she lived with her father at least until he remarried three years later. (There is no mention of siblings.)

In so far as Ruth had referred to her mother in the sessions after the loss, she had done so in idealized terms, echoing in part, we are told, 'what was being said in the family circle'. She was beginning to realize, Ruth maintained, what a remarkable woman her mother had been. She dwelt especially on an incident that had occurred during the year previously when she had been greatly distressed and her mother had been very sympathetic and understanding. In Ruth's mind this image of her mother became archetypal of their relationship, and she 'tended to gloss over the many real difficulties and frustrations in her life with her mother'. Yet of what these real difficulties and frustrations had consisted Wolfenstein says nothing.

Comment

The reasons for all these omissions are not far to seek. In presenting the clinical material Wolfenstein is intending to illustrate her thesis that, due to the primitive phase of their ego development, children and adolescents are unable to mourn. Since she is unconcerned with the alternative view which implicates adverse family experiences, no data relevant to that are given. Even the fact that Ruth had had emotional problems prior to her mother's death of a kind that had led her to receive therapy is not referred to as being of relevance.

An alternative view is that Ruth's responses are in no way typical of adolescent mourning, but are a pathological variant no different in principle to the examples of adults who experience a prolonged absence of conscious grieving described in Chapter 9. In supporting this view I would point especially to the following features of Ruth's condition:

– her prolonged inability to cry or to experience any longing for her mother
– her inappropriate bouts of euphoria
– her subsequent depression, totally disconnected in her mind from the bereavement she had suffered
– the reproaches she directed against herself for having such 'senseless' feelings
– the terror she felt at admitting that her mother was dead.

From these features, and drawing on the theories advanced in Chapters 12 and 13, I would infer a number of things about the way Ruth's mother had treated her. First, I infer that as a rule Ruth's mother had been brusquely unsympathetic towards Ruth's desire for love and care, especially towards any distress or anxiety Ruth may have expressed about her (mother's) absences. As a result of such treatment I would expect Ruth to have grown up knowing that sorrow and tears are rewarded not with comfort but with reprimands, that to be unhappy when mother is busy with everything but oneself is held to be babyish, silly or senseless, and that a bright, happy demeanour is what receives mother's approval. Furthermore, I would infer that the image of her mother that Ruth was expected to hold was that of a capable woman who gave her daughter all the care that could reasonably be expected. Brought up in this way a child will naturally come to fear responding to a loss with sorrow, yearning and tears.[3]

---

[3] The theory of adolescent development that Wolfenstein assumes in her 1966 paper is one that unwittingly tends to encourage the idea that an adolescent developing compulsive self-reliance (or a 'false self' in Winnicott's terms) is developing satisfactorily. For example, tears are identified as regressive; and it is believed that during normal development an adolescent 'is forced to give up a major love object' and that 'developmental exigencies require a radical decathexis of the parents'. This view of adolescent development as requiring a radical withdrawal of attachment from parents derives from dependency theory and is still widely held. As I show in Chapter 21 of the second volume it is not supported by the findings of empirical studies.

Depersonalization

The description Ruth gave of how she felt soon after her mother's funeral is typical of the condition variously termed a sense of unreality, of depersonalization or of derealization: she felt an inner emptiness as though a glass wall separated her from what was going on around her.

Other examples of this condition, alternating, as in Ruth, with bouts of euphoria, are described by Fast and Chethik (1976). The following account, taken from their paper, illustrates vividly certain mental states experienced by a girl whose mother committed suicide when she was seven.

At the age of ten, three years after her mother's suicide, Esther[4] began a course of intensive psychotherapy which lasted for two years. At that time she was living with her father and stepmother. As regards problems, we are told that on occasion she was given to noisy overactivity which led to 'intervention by those around her'. Reference is also made to her clinging to her sixth-grade teacher and dominating him by 'her boisterous and turbulent behaviour'.

During therapy Esther described some of her fantasy life. Before going to sleep, she said, she was able to 'will' a special dream. This had gradually become embellished and currently took the following form. 'She rose from her bed, floated above the house and ascended to a cloudy area where her mother was. Her mother appeared in a long shimmering robe bedecked with beautiful jewels, and was surrounded by a special glowing aura. In the background was her mother's house on which was a sign "Here lives Miriam S".'

Esther also developed a game in which she pictured herself as president of a large bank or corporation. She was much sought after, indeed indispensable, and always busy, and she amassed huge profits. Whilst playing at it during her sessions she would on occasion turn to an imagined crowd around her, bow deeply to her 'fans', clasp her hands high over her head and murmur 'I'm great.'

As with Ruth, however, such sentiments were only skin deep. As therapy progressed Esther began to talk about feeling overlooked and forgotten. In the past this had led to her engaging in noisy overactivity; now she would often curl up on the couch and suck her thumb. She also found courage to describe how she had felt after her mother's death. 'After all the relatives had left and the funeral was over she had become very

---

[4] In the original this child is given the pseudonym Ruth which has been changed here to avoid confusion with the previous case. Virtually no information is given about the family relationships, the circumstances of mother's suicide or the reasons for Esther receiving treatment.

375

frightened. Everything in the house had begun to look like shadows. Nothing around her seemed real.' She also remembered how, after coming home from school one day, she had stood alone in the house calling out 'Mummy, Mummy, Mummy', and how no one had answered. Her voice had seemed nothing but an echo. It was the most scary thing she could remember. Whilst recounting it to a comforting adult during therapy she sobbed intensely.

Throughout Esther's treatment, it appears, issues regarding her relationship to her mother proved central. Amongst much else Esther described how after the suicide she had felt that her mother had abandoned her. She also felt torn between her loyalty to her mother and her tie to her stepmother.

Comment

In the original case report too little information is given about Esther and her parents to make much comment possible. Her mother, we can hardly doubt, had major emotional problems of her own and these had presumably had an adverse effect on the relationship between mother and daughter. A parent's death by suicide moreover, also poses special problems, of which leaving the survivors feeling abandoned is but one. In the next chapter these problems are discussed further.

Identificatory symptoms: accidents

In Chapter 9 it was noted that among adults whose mourning takes a pathological course there is a minority who develop a sense of the dead person being in some way within themselves. Particularly striking are those cases in which the bereaved develops symptoms that are replicas of those from which the dead person had suffered. A number of examples of such symptoms occurring also in children are reported in the literature. Two have already been mentioned.

In the account in Chapter 19 of Henry, whose mother died when he was eight and a half, a description is given of how during a therapeutic session he suddenly held his hand to his chest and claimed he had a terrible pain and was having a heart attack. The pain he linked immediately to the operation his mother had had for breast cancer. This led on to his reminding himself of his mother's insistence that he do his homework instead of coming to the clinic. It is probably relevant also that this episode occurred at a time when his stepmother was having a heart attack.

In the case of Addie, whose mother had died when Addie was four (this chapter), the stiff neck from which she suffered seemed clearly related to her mother's death, though what relationship it may have borne to any of mother's symptoms remains uncertain. Since mother had died of leukaemia and had also suffered injuries from father's assaults, a stiff neck could well have been one of her symptoms.

Two other examples of young children developing symptoms that replicate those suffered by a dying parent, or grandparent, may be given.

Krupp (1965) reports on a boy, Paul,[5] whose father had died suddenly of a cerebral haemorrhage when Paul was six. Shortly before his death father had complained of a splitting headache. Soon afterwards Paul, who had witnessed his father's death, began also to complain of headaches, and for the next three years, during periods of stress, he would claim to be having a 'splitting headache', always using the same words. Subsequently, Paul developed many other problems, among them anti-social behaviour, a strong sense of guilt and a constant fear of retribution. No clues are given as to why he might have developed in this way.

A further example is drawn from an account given by Erikson (1950, pp. 21–7) of a small boy, Sam, whose paternal grandmother died when he was three. Grandmother, who was on an extended visit to the family, was not in good health and Sam had been warned to be gentle with her. One day Sam was left with his grandmother whilst mother went out. On her return mother found Sam with his grandmother on the floor having a heart attack. She lived only a few months longer, and died in the house. Despite that, Sam's mother tried her hardest to keep the facts from him. In order to explain grandmother's sudden absence she had told him grandmother had gone to a distant town; and an attempt had been made to explain away the coffin by a story about its containing grandmother's books. Sam, it was evident, had not been deceived.

Five days after grandmother died Sam developed an attack of breathlessness during the night that was said to have resembled epilepsy. It was noted that before going to bed that night he had piled up his pillows in the way his grandmother had been used to doing to avoid congestion; and he had slept like her, sitting upright.

Accidents

Many clinicians believe that unhappy children, including those

[5] A pseudonym has been given this boy for ease of reference.

who have been bereaved, are more prone to accidents than other children. Much circumstantial evidence favours this view, though I know of no epidemiological evidence that bears on it.

Of the bereaved children already described in this and preceding chapters, two sustained accidents during the course of therapy. Soon after witnessing the funeral of President Kennedy and making her first references to her mother's funeral Geraldine fell in the gym and broke her leg (Chapter 19). Shortly before he was due to cease seeing his therapist Seth fell from a windowsill on to which he had climbed and broke his elbow. This six-year-old boy, it will be remembered, had been present when, two years earlier, his mother had fallen out of bed and been unable to get up.

Another child who sustained a fracture, in this case on a significant anniversary, is reported by Bonnard (1961). (In the original record this boy is referred to as John. Changing the name to Jack is to avoid duplication with the one-year-old referred to in Chapter 24.)

For some months Jack, now aged nearly thirteen, had not been attending school and for this reason was referred to a clinic. On investigation it turned out that he had also been pilfering housekeeping money from home for at least a year, though this was not known to the school. Until these difficulties began he had had the reputation of always being a well-behaved and reasonable boy.

Ten months before being seen at the clinic and when Jack was aged twelve his mother had died of carcinoma of the breast. She had had a mastectomy five years earlier; and during the ten months prior to her death she had been in hospital after a fall in which she had broken her thigh due to the presence of secondaries. Father had not been told of the fatal nature of the illness until the final five weeks. Jack had been kept in the dark until he had heard by chance shortly before she died.

Jack was one of three living children in a close-knit family. There was a brother four years older than him and a sister nine years younger who had been born a year after mother's mastectomy. In addition, a baby had been born a year before mother's operation but had not lived.

During interviews with father and with Jack it became clear that each was bitterly critical of the other. Father was in a state of fury and despair over his son's behaviour and had visions of him growing up to be a criminal. Conversely, Jack complained that his father had let his wife do everything in the home and for the children and had then grumbled at her. Now, he went on, father was simply spoiling the little girl who, amongst other things, shared his bed. For some months Jack had been doing much of the family cooking.

378

Ever since his mother died Jack had been bitter about having been kept in the dark about her illness and he was still much preoccupied about who or what might have been responsible for it. One idea was that after the baby had died his mother's milk had been left unused and had gone bad. Another, probably derived from his having overheard relatives talking, was that father was at fault for having made mother pregnant again so soon after her operation. As regards the fracture, he first blamed the dog because it had led her to lose her balance, and he next blamed the rest of the family, which of course included himself, for having lain abed and allowed mother to bring them their early morning tea even when she was unwell. It then transpired that on the first anniversary of mother's fall Jack had himself fractured his elbow.

Comment

Two features that stand out in this case are, first, the silence about mother's true condition with its attendant uncertainties about causation and, secondly, the strong tendency for each member of the family to direct blame either at other members or towards the self. The fact that Jack's accident had taken place on the anniversary of what, for him, was probably a crucial event in his mother's fatal illness, and about which all surviving members of the family had evidently felt much guilt, could hardly have been a coincidence.

From the relatively few cases on record it is not easy to identify what the precise conditions may be which result in certain children and not others either developing the same symptoms as a dead parent or sustaining an accident in circumstances that have a close connection with the parent's illness or death. The most that can be said is that in all the cases referred to here mourning was following a pathological course. In most of them the child had been present when the parent who subsequently died had suffered a severe attack of pain or an accident; and in most, too, there had been a great deal of attempted secrecy. Issues of blame were prominent also; and it may be that in all of them the child was in some degree blaming himself for the catastrophe. Nevertheless, frequent though all these conditions seem to be, each of them can occur also in cases in which the children do not develop in these particular ways so that none can be regarded as pathognomonic of the disorders in question.

Where a child or adult develops symptoms that are replicas of those suffered by a person who has died it is obviously convenient to refer to them as identificatory. As an explanation of why they should have occurred in certain individuals and not in others, however, this designation does not take us very far. Nor does it indicate in any clear way what the psychological processes at work may be. Fortunately for purposes of treatment our lack of understanding is no great handicap, since once the disorder is recognized as stemming from failed mourning the therapeutic task is clear.

The same is true in cases of accident. In some of them, and perhaps all, a major motive at work is a desire for reunion with the dead parent, associated more or less consciously with ideas of committing suicide. As we saw in Chapter 17 and also earlier in this chapter, these ideas are certainly prevalent in individuals, whether child, adolescent or adult, who have lost a parent during childhood.

Conclusion

In this long chapter an attempt is made to illustrate how a large variety of psychiatric disorders can be understood as being the responses of children to the death of a parent when the death is preceded by, or is followed by, certain specifiable conditions. For some disorders the causal connections are plain to see; for others they are more obscure even though discernible in outline. In regard to all of them more research is needed.

In the past far too little systematic attention has been given to the power of these environmental variables to influence the course of mourning. This has left the field clear for such traditional hypotheses as phase of development or autonomous phantasy. What we now know is that the more clearly the relevant conditions are specified and the more careful the investigation the more regularly are they found. With our present knowledge, therefore, I believe the only safe assumption for a clinician to make is that in every case, behind the smoke of a child's anxiety, self-blame or other symptom or problem, there burns a fire lit by some frightening or guilt-inducing experience of real life. In no situations are these sequences shown more clearly than after a parent has committed suicide.

CHAPTER 22

Effects of
A Parent's Suicide

Proportion of parents' deaths due to suicide

In earlier chapters attention is drawn to the fact that, although the death-rates for men and women of an age likely to have children are relatively low, the proportion of deaths due to suicide is high when compared to that for men and women in other age groups. This means that relative to deaths due to other causes the death of a child's parent by suicide is not altogether uncommon. Indeed, British figures suggest that for children born to parents in their twenties it may be as high as one father in fifteen and one mother in seventeen who die.[1]

Considering the traumatic circumstances surrounding a death due to suicide and the strong tendency to conceal the facts from children it would be no surprise were the loss of a parent by suicide to lead to an incidence of, and perhaps a degree of, psychopathology appreciably higher than for deaths due to other causes. Adequate data are lacking but such as are available point to both those propositions being likely.

Evidence stems both from survey data and from therapeutic studies.

[1] Figures for England and Wales for 1973, derived from the Registrar-General's Statistical Review (H.M.S.O. 1975), show the following percentages of deaths due to suicide in three age groups.

Age group	Men	Women
	%	%
15–24 years	6·2	7·1
25–44	7·0	5·8
45–64	1·1	1·5

These figures suggest that the estimate of 2·5 per cent made by Shepherd and Barraclough (1976) as the proportion of parent deaths due to suicide is too low. Their estimate is based on the number of child survivors left by 100 individuals who committed suicide; but many of these individuals were past the age when they would have been expected to have a child under 17.

Findings from surveys

There are three surveys, two of which are described in Chapter 18, that present findings suggesting that the incidence of psychiatric disturbance following a parent's suicide is unusually high.

In their study of a contrast group of people who had lost a parent during childhood and were now living an ordinary life in an area of California, Hilgard *et al.* (1960) note that for none of them had the parent's death been due to suicide. This compared with an incidence of 6·3 per cent among the comparable group who were psychiatric patients. In the second study, that of 83 Michigan children and adolescents who had lost a parent by death and had been referred because of psychiatric problems, Arthur and Kemme (1964) note that in ten (12 per cent) the parent's death had been due to suicide. Without relevant statistics of suicide rates for California and Michigan it is hardly possible to comment. None the less for the Michigan group the incidence seems high.

The third survey that reports relevant findings is the follow-up of the spouses of forty-four suicides in a county in southern England undertaken by Shepherd and Barraclough and described in part in Chapter 10. Amongst the forty-four survivors were thirteen mothers who between them had 28 children aged between two years and seventeen when their fathers committed suicide, and five fathers with a total of eight children in the same age-range when their mothers committed suicide. Information on the children was obtained from the surviving parent during two interviews, the first within a few weeks of the suicide and the second five to seven years later. Data on the 36 children (14 boys and 22 girls) are reported in Shepherd and Barraclough (1976).

When an overall assessment of these children was attempted on the basis of follow-up information and using criteria of health, school or work performance, relationship with the surviving parent and membership of a stable family unit, only fifteen were thought to be functioning adequately. Sixteen were assessed as functioning inadequately; and for the remaining five information was lacking. Amongst those functioning inadequately were five who had had treatment for psychological disorders since the parent's suicide; and the mother of a sixth said her son had been referred to a psychiatrist before the suicide and she was planning re-referral. This gives an incidence of declared psychiatric disorder of about 15 per cent of the group.

This incidence was significantly raised above that of a comparison group of children living in the same community. Whether it would also have been higher than that of a group of children one of whose parents had died from causes other than suicide is not clear, since the comparison was not made; but in view of the high incidence (15 per cent) among the children of suicides this seems not unlikely.

Disturbance in the children took the form principally of anxiety or misbehaviour. Fifteen had become more anxious after the suicide and, although in nine this was no longer evident five years later, in six it had persisted. It showed itself in constant enquiries about the health of the surviving parent and fear that he or she might leave home or die. The parents of fourteen complained of their children's behaviour; and four of these children were known to the police. Some of the children blamed themselves for the parent's suicide; others blamed the surviving parent. No child had attempted suicide but one had made threats.

The parents of half, eighteen, of the children, mainly the younger ones, had attempted to keep the suicide a secret. Nevertheless, four had discovered about it soon afterwards—from a newspaper, a relative or overhearing conversation—and a further two did so later; the parents of the other twelve believed the children still did not know. The parents of the remaining eighteen children had made an effort to inform them, though they had not always done so in a way a child could be expected to understand.

A comparison was made between the children who were doing reasonably well at follow-up with those who were not. In regard to age, sex, social class, family size and sex of parent lost, no differences were found. Differences were most marked in regard to conditions before the suicide had occurred. Children progressing less well were more likely to have had parents who had separated, at least temporarily, or who had exhibited an abnormal personality.

Findings from therapeutic studies

From the Shepherd and Barraclough study it might be concluded that, though the incidence of psychiatric disturbance after a parent's suicide is relatively high, nothing in the psychopathology is unusual.

Yet it must be remembered their data were all obtained second hand from the surviving parent. Had the children themselves been seen and the family interaction examined in greater depth the picture revealed might have been different.

It is therefore useful to turn to a study by Cain and Fast (1972) at the University of Michigan of a series of 45 children, aged between four and fourteen, all of whom had lost a parent by suicide and all of whom had become psychiatrically disturbed. Data are available from out-patient evaluations in all cases; from therapeutic interviews also in many; and from extended in-patient treatment as well in nine. The interval between the parent's suicide and the examination varied from a few days to over ten years.

About 60 per cent of the children fell into one of two main groups: (a) children who were sad, guilt-laden, withdrawn, fearful and inhibited; (b) children who were angry, truculent and defiant, and given to ill-organized and aggressive behaviour. The severity of psychopathology seen varied widely from relatively mild neurotic disorders to severe psychoses. The incidence of psychosis, eleven out of 45 children, was exceptionally high when compared to children from other backgrounds. Rightly or wrongly, the authors attribute this high incidence to a combination of the impact of the suicide with its chain of consequences and the pre-suicide family background which, as in the cases reported by Shepherd and Barraclough, had frequently been very disturbed.

In addition to finding a high incidence of severe psychopathology in this series of cases, Cain and Fast were struck by the very large roles played in the symptomatology of the children by their having been exposed to two special types of pathogenic situation. These are situations in which intense guilt is likely to be engendered and situations in which communications are gravely distorted. Let us consider the effects of each.

In cases in which the parent had been severely disturbed, and especially those in which threats of suicide or an attempt had been made, the child had often been warned or scolded by his other parent, or by the family physician, that he was 'upsetting Mom', that he was 'driving her crazy', that he must be very quiet and very good, that he must not argue or upset her. Within this guilt-inducing milieu it was almost inevitable that, should the suicide have followed some episode of friction, however trivial, between child and parent, the child should be convinced that it was that episode that had caused the suicide. This was especially likely should the parent have responded to the episode as though it had been a last straw.

In other cases a child had come to feel before the suicide that everything that was going wrong between his two parents was his fault. In some, moreover, he had come to feel that it was his responsibility to make sure that the threatening parent did not carry out his threats, with a consequent heavy sense of responsibility should the suicide eventually have occurred whilst he was out playing, or for some other reason was away from home. There were also cases in which a parent's repeated threats and gestures had driven an increasingly frightened and exasperated child to wish, consciously and angrily, that the parent would 'go ahead and do it'. Many of these children during therapy would not only describe how totally responsible they believed themselves to be but would continue to insist that that was so whatever the therapist might say. The case of Dan and his family described by Arthur (1972) provides a detailed and revealing account of a sequence of this kind.[2]

Dan was the eldest of six children of a hardworking father and disturbed and unstable mother. Both the parents had had difficult childhoods. Father had lost his own father when he was very young and, although his mother had worked hard to hold the home together, she had not been easy to live with.

Dan's mother had been brought up by an aunt and uncle where her life had been extremely unhappy; and she seems to have grown up 'with a deep sense of worthlessness, a hunger for love, and a determination to find a happier life'. She and Dan's father had got married on impulse, each hoping to find with the other the security neither had ever had. Quarrels began early. Mother felt progressively more tied down by her increasing family whilst father worked ever harder and was away from home longer. As time went on mother came to feel more and more lonely and unloved. 'Caught in her dilemma of being unable to accept love when it was offered and still needing excessive proof that she was loved, she became increasingly often depressed, more demanding of her husband and children and less involved in her home.' At length she began actively

---

[2] Dan's age is not given. From the fact that he was the eldest of six and from other information it appears that he was between about ten and fourteen at the time of his mother's suicide. Since Dan was first seen professionally only a few weeks afterwards it was possible to obtain a great deal of background information, both about the sequence of events and about mother's emotional problems, from Dan's father and other relatives as well as from Dan himself.

to seek love elsewhere. Although father became suspicious he said nothing.

The quarrels nevertheless became worse, with shouting and threats of separation and divorce, and they began throwing things at each other. On these occasions each parent sought the support of the children, and demanded they choose with whom they would stay if their parents separated. On occasion mother had threatened suicide.

One evening when father was away on a business trip, mother sought to kill herself and the six children by exposing them all to the car exhaust. All but the eldest child, Dan, died. The reason he did not was that he was roused by hearing the telephone ring which proved to be his father phoning his mother. In going to answer it Dan had stumbled over one of his dead siblings and had said something about it to his father, who, evidently suspecting the worst, then told the boy to look in the garage. Later, hearing what the boy had found, father told him to call the neighbours and the police.

The evening that mother had chosen for her action was the anniversary of their wedding. She had hoped for a celebration but instead her husband was away.

When found by the police Dan felt sick and dizzy and had a severe headache. He was taken to hospital and stayed there twenty-four hours. He then went to friends for a week, and thereafter to an uncle and aunt where he stayed, together with his father. Only gradually did he come to realize what had happened.

Fairly soon Dan began to complain again of feeling sick and dizzy and of having headaches; and, when no organic basis for them was found, he was referred for psychiatric help.

During the early talks Dan disputed that his mother and siblings were dead; they were just staying somewhere on a visit, he claimed. When he was reminded that they had been buried, he decided they should be exhumed so as to see whether they really were in the coffins. Later, as he began to accept the truth, he alternated between holding himself totally responsible and putting the blame on others. At one moment he thought the gas man was at fault; at another his father; but most often he blamed himself.

Not long before his mother's suicide, he explained, when his parents were quarrelling and the other children were opting to stay with mother, he said he would stay with father. This had caused her so much unhappiness, he believed, that she had done away with herself. Since his brothers and sisters had chosen to stay with mother, they were now with her and he had been left behind. He too had really wanted to stay with her but had chosen father in the hope that that would influence her to remain at home; but instead she had merely cried. Now he wished to be with her, like the other children. In addition he deserved to be punished, and so was best dead.

As Dan spoke about his mother it became evident that relations between them had never been easy and that his feelings towards her were intensely ambivalent. At her best she had been a loving mother and had given him and his siblings a lot of fun. Yet she had often neglected them so that they had had to fend for themselves, with the brunt falling on Dan because he was the eldest. On occasion, he admitted, she had made him very angry, and at least once he had told her he wished her dead. But again and again he came back to his own feeling of guilt. If only on the crucial occasion he had not chosen to stay with father his mother and siblings would still be alive.

Father came to the clinic only to provide background since he had no desire to participate in treatment. It was evident, however, that he had many problems. 'He alternated between praising his wife and criticizing her. He also alternated between saying that he had tried very hard to please her and intimating that she could not or would not be pleased. He . . . admitted that he had sometimes treated her in a very callous way by disregarding her needs for attention, by hitting her, and by deliberately refusing to give in to her. He, too, felt responsible for her death. He had made her stay married . . . and he had been cruel forcing the children to choose between them. This had hurt her deeply, he was certain.' He was worried also about his having been away so much and in particular about having been away on the night of their wedding anniversary.

Treatment in this case did not go well. Father began to threaten that he, too, would commit suicide. He also exhibited a violent temper both towards Dan and towards the uncle and aunt with whom the pair were staying. In addition Dan got into fights with other children. Then one day and without warning father left the city taking Dan with him.

Comment

Given the family problems it is no surprise that Dan should have been bewildered and disturbed by his mother's death. The extent to which he continued to direct blame towards himself, however, and his dwelling in particular on the occasion when he had chosen to stay with father instead of mother, calls for comment.

From the evidence presented it is plain that of the three of them —Dan, his mother and his father—Dan himself was the least to blame. Why then, we may ask, did he insist that he was? The most likely explanation, I believe, is that he harboured deep feelings of anger towards each of his parents, both of whom he blamed; but, for different reasons, he could not feel angry with either of them and, instead, directed anger towards himself. Towards his mother he had often had to be protective, consoling her especially when his father was away and she was depressed and lonely. Of his father he was clearly afraid, both when father lost his temper and also when he threatened suicide. If this assessment is correct, Dan's response to his mother's death was one of chronic mourning; and the prognosis for his future must be considered ominous.

The second type of pathogenic situation that Cain and Fast found to be prevalent in their series of families involved extremely distorted communication. In almost every one of them the surviving parent had not only avoided talking with the children about what had happened but had actively banned the subject from discussion. Some had prayed that the children would never ask. Some became furious with the clinicians for delving. Some, when their children did ask questions, refused to listen. Most of these children, however, had soon realized that it was a forbidden topic, so that the parent could later report, honestly but with relief, that 'they never asked'.

In about one-quarter of this series of cases the child had personally witnessed some aspect of the parent's death only to have the surviving parent insist that it had not been due to suicide but to some illness or accident. 'A boy who watched his father kill himself with a shotgun . . . was told later that night by his mother that his father had died of a heart attack; a girl who discovered her father's body hanging in a closet was told he had died in a car accident; and two brothers who had found their mother with her wrists slit were told she had drowned while swimming' (Cain and Fast 1972, p. 102). When a child described what he had seen, the surviving parent had sought to discredit it either by ridicule or by insisting that he was confused by what he had seen on TV or by some bad dream he had had. Such confusion was sometimes compounded, moreover, by the child hearing several different stories about the death from different people or even from his surviving parent him- or herself.

Many of the children's psychological problems seemed directly traceable to their having been exposed to situations of these kinds. Their problems included chronic distrust of other people, inhibition of their curiosity, distrust of their own senses and a tendency to find everything unreal. During therapy it was found that some of them were possessed of two or more distinct and incompatible systems of ideas, beliefs and plans, each with its corresponding feeling. The following is an account of an eleven-year-old boy, Bob, whose father had committed suicide two years earlier, and who, it was found, was possessed of three separate sets of belief system (Cain and Fast 1972, p. 104).

The first was that his father had died of a heart attack, which is what he had been told. To this system belonged some hypochondriacal pre-occupations and transient symptoms and also the belief that his own noisy behaviour might have caused the heart attack, leading to efforts on his part to stay quiet and subdued, and to a strong desire to become a doctor able to perform emergency operations.

The second belief system was that his father had died in a car accident. To this seemed to belong recurrent nightmares and a tendency to engage in dangerous activities and to sustain small injuries.

The third belief system was that his father had killed himself. To this belonged his belief that he had been responsible for his father's suicide, a loathing for himself and also for his father, and a distrust of all male authority.

In their valuable article Cain and Fast refer also to the strong urge to commit suicide that some of these children later develop themselves. The notion, advanced in the past, that a suicidal pro-pensity can somehow be transmitted through the genes is called sharply in question by the circumstances of the children's action which sometimes is linked in an almost uncanny way to the circum-stances of the parent's suicide. From many examples described by Cain and Fast, we can select two: one an eighteen-year-old girl who drowned herself alone at night in much the same fashion and at the same beach as had her mother many years earlier; the other a thirty-two-year-old man who drove his car over the same cliff that his father had driven over twenty-one years earlier. Some of these individuals, it seems, have lived for many years with a deep belief, amounting to a conviction, that they will one day die by suicide. Some quietly resign themselves to their fate. Others seek help.

Inevitably the concept of identification is invoked in the effort to understand these strange cases. An alternative approach, and one still to be explored, is that the urge to copy the parent experienced by these people springs from an urge literally to follow where the dead parent had led and then eventually to find him (or her). The suggestion is given credence by the way that one man spoke: before he was thirty, he said, he would be following his 'Pied Piper' father into the water. In due course he killed himself, leaving behind a simple, unrevealing suicide note.

CHAPTER 23

Responses to Loss
During the Third and Fourth Years

> I wept, and nothing happened, and you did not come.
> SARAH FERGUSON, *A Guard Within*

Questions remaining

In preceding chapters evidence is presented that shows that the ways in which children and adolescents respond to the loss of a parent differ little from the ways in which adults mourn a parent or a spouse. In so far as there are differences they turn mainly on the finding that children and adolescents are even more sensitive to the conditions that precede, surround and follow a loss than are adults.

The questions still at issue concern how children even younger than four years respond to loss. Do they, given favourable conditions, respond in ways similar to those of older children and adolescents? If they do, at what age do they begin to do so? If they do not, how do we understand the differences? And is the influence on their responses of unfavourable conditions similar or different to their influence on the responses of older children? These, of course, are the very questions with which this volume opened; but now we can examine them in a much broader perspective.

In this chapter we consider children in their third and fourth years of life, by which age they are likely to have a good understanding and command of language, leaving to the next the much more difficult problem of children in their first and second years.

Responses when conditions are favourable

In Chapter 16 we saw that, given favourable conditions, children as young as four years are as capable as are adults of retaining memories and images of the dead person and of sustaining repeated recurrences of yearning and sadness. By using their ability to keep their memories of the lost relationship and the intense feelings linked to it distinct from the present, they are, like adults in similar circumstances, enabled to make the best of whatever new relationship may be offered them. Although records of how children younger than that respond to the death of a parent are extremely scarce, there is reason to believe that, provided their questions and recollections are not discouraged, the responses of children as young even as two and a half differ little from those of their elders. We are indebted to Marion J. Barnes (1964) for the following detailed account of how one little girl responded to the death of her mother.

Winnie Mourns her Mother

In Chapter 16 an account is given of how Winnie's elder sister, the four-year-old Wendy, responded to their mother's sudden death, which followed a flare-up of the multiple sclerosis she had contracted but which had remained dormant during the previous seven years. Not only was much known about the family prior to this unforeseen tragedy but it was possible to keep in close touch with both children, Wendy aged four and Winnie aged two and a half, and with the bereaved father and maternal grandmother, during the twelve months after it. For details of the family and of the children's living conditions after mother died the reader is referred to the account given of Wendy.

Throughout her first two and a half years of life Winnie's development had been uneventful, and she had grown into 'a happy outgoing little girl well ahead of her age on all levels'. She was a great talker, never stopping from the time she rose till the time she went to bed.

At the time of their mother's death father decided to tell the children what had happened, that mother would be buried in the ground and that this was the end. We know that at one level Winnie registered this information correctly since, when three weeks later Wendy was chanting, 'My mommy is coming back, I know she's coming back', Winnie retorted, 'Mommy's dead and she's not coming back. She's in the ground by the "tower water".' On other occasions, too, Winnie came out with similar matter-of-fact statements: 'My mommy is dead. She's never coming back.'

Yet it is also clear that at another level Winnie was far from being convinced that her mother would never return. For some weeks she remained her usual cheerful self. She made no spontaneous references to her mother and she seemed actively to avoid the subject of her mother's absence. For example, although previously she had been very precise about who owned which car, now she referred to her mother's car as 'my daddy's car'. Nevertheless, there was clear evidence that mother was never far from Winnie's thoughts. For example, one evening when grandmother was wearing mother's apron, Winnie upbraided her: 'Take off that apron,' she ordered. On another occasion, six weeks after mother's death when the children were making valentines, Winnie asserted, 'I'm making mine for Mommy.' Wendy corrected her, 'You can't do that. She's dead.' To this Winnie replied, 'Tsh, don't say that.' On another occasion, when she had wet her bed one night she called for her mother.

Although during this period Winnie expressed no sadness and never referred to her mother's absence from home, she showed obvious signs of missing her. For example, she sought comfort in her blanket more frequently than before and also began pulling at her right ear so that it became red and swollen. Her appetite was poor and she lost a little weight. Instead of being an assertive little madam when asked to do something she disliked, she now became subdued and compliant; and she was unduly content to play quietly by herself.

During this time father and grandmother were having regular talks about the children's progress with the therapist. Concerned about Winnie's condition, the therapist recommended that grandmother and the maid give her a great deal of physical mothering: 'I advised them to hold Winnie and to talk to her as her mother had done, and to follow the mother's routines as much as possible. I also suggested that at these times they made appropriate references to the mother. For example, "You and Mommy used to go to the store. Now she is gone and I will take you." "Mommy read you a story every afternoon. Now I will do it." I suggested that the father talk to Winnie about how some little girls think their mothers get sick or even die if the children are naughty, but that this is not really so. With these few changes in handling, Winnie became her usual self again and the symptoms disappeared. She still made no spontaneous mention of her mother. The main characteristic of her behaviour was that she sought out mother-substitutes—her grandmother, the maid, the father, and sometimes her sister Wendy. She seemed happy and contented and showed no signs of disturbance as long as she was taken care of and loved, which she was.'

Seven months after mother's death when Winnie was three years and one month old, she suddenly began talking about her absent mother. Addressing her father one day she exclaimed, 'Daddy, I'm so sad. I miss my mommy very much.' During the days and weeks that followed she talked voluminously about her mother, asked questions about death, and wondered about her own health and that of members of her family. This was such a striking change that the question arises why it whould have occurred when it did.

The explanation given by the therapist, Marion J. Barnes, is that Winnie was able to express grief over losing her mother only after the grandmother had been able to express grief over losing her daughter.

This the grandmother had not found possible earlier owing, she herself thought, to her having to give so much attention to the children's welfare. The combination of a religious festival and of Winnie starting at nursery school she thought had acted as a trigger.

There were several occasions at nursery school when Winnie remarked that she had no mother. This she did especially when comparing herself with other children. Sometimes the emphasis was on the fact that her mother was dead. For example, when another child said to Winnie, 'When your mother comes for you', Winnie corrected her: 'My mother's dead, she's not coming.' On other occasions there was yearning for her mother's return. When another little girl referred to her mother coming to pick her up, Winnie replied, 'Me, too—but not really, because my mother's dead'; and once when the teacher was helping another child to write a greeting to her parents, Winnie remarked with feeling, 'I wish my mother would come back.' On another occasion when Wendy and Winnie had been referring to their mother being dead, Winnie withdrew to a corner and sat on the rocking-chair; for just a second or so she wept and then returned to play.

Throughout her first six months at nursery school Winnie was markedly sensitive to separations. From the first she looked to Wendy for security and when Wendy was unwell she was unduly quiet and did not eat her lunch. On another occasion when her nursery teacher was absent Winnie stayed close to Wendy all day and remained sad and subdued.

Winnie was also apprehensive lest she lose her other caregivers. One morning father and the maid exchanged sharp words over some triviality. When Winnie arrived at school with her grandmother she refused to be left, and so was taken home. Asked what was wrong, she explained that she was afraid lest when she returned home the maid would have gone. Winnie was upset, too, when grandmother was away on vacation; she resorted to nose-picking and produced a sore. Any reference to someone dying also caused her anxiety.

Although at the end of twelve months Winnie seemed to be developing reasonably well, Barnes expresses concern about her capacity to respond to stressful situations, especially long separations, and notes her ready resort to somatic symptoms.

Comment

This record shows that when conditions are favourable a child as young as two and a half when her mother dies is capable of going through a process of grieving that seems to show all the features typical of the healthy mourning of older children and adults. There was, it is true, a delay of six months between Winnie's verbal acceptance that her mother was dead and her overt expression of yearning. Barnes's explanation of the delay as being a reflection of the delayed mourning of grandmother is not unlikely; although without many more cases it is not possible to be confident.

Similarly, it is not easy to be sure which element of the advice given to father, grandmother and the maid effected the subsequent improvement in Winnie's condition. It seems very probable, however, that the most valuable change was the active physical mothering that she then was given.

Winnie's refusal to stay at school after hearing the sharp words exchanged between father and the maid, and her fear that she might return home to find the maid gone, can be seen as an example of school refusal (school 'phobia') occurring in a three-year-old child within the context of one of the patterns of family interaction postulated (in Chapter 18 of Volume II) as being characteristic of the condition.

Without many more such descriptive records of children bereaved during their third year of life and cared for with understanding it is not possible to know how common the responses shown by Winnie may be. There is, however, some evidence available of how children of this age respond to being separated from their mother-figure for periods of a few days or weeks which suggests that Winnie's responses may be fairly typical. Two examples follow.

Thomas, two years and four months old, and Kate, almost two and a half, were the elder pair of the four children whom James and Joyce Robertson fostered whilst the children's mothers were having a new baby (Robertson and Robertson 1971).[1] Thomas was away for only ten days, but Kate stayed twenty-seven. In the very favourable conditions of fostering provided both children retained a lively understanding of what was happening to them and both yearned explicitly for their absent mother. Yet there were also significant differences. These the Robertsons attribute, I believe correctly, to the very different ways in which the two children had been treated by their parents at home as regards both the behaviour expected of them and the methods of discipline employed.

Thomas's father was warm and outgoing and his mother gentle and affectionate. Both were understanding of their son and proud of his

[1] This project is described in the first chapter of Volume II where rather fuller accounts of the four children are given. Extracts are repeated here because of the relevance of the evidence to the present discussion.

achievements. Thomas himself was an active, secure and friendly child who talked well.

Having visited the foster home several times before going into care, Thomas soon settled happily. For most of the time he was good humoured, friendly, and able to enjoy the play and other activities offered. After two days, however, he began to express both sadness at his parents' absence and also anger about it. He talked much of his mother and sometimes cuddled her photograph. There were also times when he would spend long periods musing about his home, his toys and his parents. In a tearful mood one day he said, 'I'm thinking of my rocking-horse at home. My mummy says, "It's a nice day, Thomas." I like my mummy best.' On occasion he rejected his foster-mother's attentions and indicated that it was his mother's role to look after him: 'Don't cuddle me, my mummy cuddles me.' This very clear distinction between his relationship with his mother and that with his foster-mother was retained, as we might expect, after his return home. When a little later his foster-mother visited him there, although he was friendly to her he was also cautious and throughout kept close to his mother.

In their comments the Robertsons note that throughout his stay away Thomas was able to express his feelings freely: 'By the third day he was expressing his sadness and anxiety with almost adult understanding of the situation.'

The upbringing of the second of these children, Kate, aged two and a half, contrasted in certain ways with that of Thomas, though like him she came from a stable and affectionate home.

Kate's upbringing had been, in the Robertsons' words, 'on the rigid side. Her father employed smacks, but relied as much on prohibitions couched in quiet but threatening tones. Although the mother was softer . . . [her] demands were high.' In keeping with this treatment, Kate herself was more self-controlled than is usual in a child of her age.

During the twenty-seven days in foster-care Kate, like Thomas, was for the most part cheerful, active and co-operative. Yet, like him, she also expressed yearning for her absent parents and occasionally was angry with them for not taking her home.

During the first few days Kate made a special effort to be co-operative and cheerful and was heard repeating to herself her parents' instructions and prohibitions: 'Eat up your potatoes' or 'Be a good girl, don't cry.' So successful was she in this that it was not until the sixth day that she cried, on an occasion when, with her foster-mother, she was in a strange place with strange people. Soon afterwards, during the second week, she was expressing fear of getting lost and was more clinging than usual. She also cried more easily, and at times seemed preoccupied and dreamy. On one such occasion she murmured, 'What is Kate looking for?'—a remark that seems to indicate that she was temporarily losing track of the identity of the person for whom she was yearning and searching.

During the third and fourth weeks of her month's stay away, although Kate's relationship to her foster-mother deepened, her yearning for her own mother continued and was increasingly mingled with anger. First she would say sadly, 'I want my mummy and daddy'; then a little later her mood changed and she announced: 'I don't like my mummy. Mummy is naughty.' She also became apprehensive that her parents did not love her and might not want her back, fears that her foster-mother did her best to allay.

Eventually, when the day arrived for her to go home, Kate became tense and overactive. All the way across London by car she denied she was going home and sang gay nonsense songs. Only when she recognized her street did she drop the pretence, as she exclaimed, 'That's my mummy's house.' On entering she at once greeted her mother and for the next hour was busy rebuilding the relationship. By contrast, she completely ignored her foster-mother who had looked after her continuously for four weeks and who was sitting quietly by.

Throughout her stay away Kate was much more inhibited than Thomas in expressing her feelings; even during the journey home she still avoided admitting hope. This, I suspect, was because in Kate hope was mingled with fear, fear that she might get lost and, in particular, fear that her parents might not want her back. This, I believe, can be understood as stemming from the way they treated her. Not only did they insist she be a good girl and not cry but I infer also that in their efforts to discipline her they had often used the threat not to love her. An example of this might be: 'We don't want/love little girls when they're naughty!' which, were it to be expressed in the 'quiet but threatening tones' noted by the Robertsons and taken literally, would be extremely frightening for a small child of two and a half.

From the Robertsons' accounts of these two children it is plain that, apart from Kate's temporary lapse (to which reference is made later in the chapter), both these children retained a clear picture of the absent mother during separation from her and that, with the foster-mother's encouragement, neither had difficulty in distinguishing mother from foster-mother. Admittedly the periods during which they did so were relatively short (10 and 27 days respectively) and assurances that mother would return could repeatedly be given. Yet both children's responses were sufficiently similar to those of Winnie to suggest that the latter's were in no way atypical.

These findings lead to certain tentative conclusions. One is that children even as young as two and a half can, in favourable conditions, mourn a lost parent in ways that resemble very closely those of older children and adults; the second that, also like older children and adults, the pattern of response shown is much influenced by the experiences they have had with their parents before the loss takes place.

We turn now to consider how children in this age group respond when conditions are unfavourable, as all too often they are.

Responses when conditions are unfavourable

It is the fate of many young children away from their families to have no substitute mother to care lovingly for them. Moreover, even when a child has such care, his foster-mother may not realize that he regards her as no more than second best or that he continues to yearn for his absent mother; and, even should she recognize that, she may well neither sympathize with his feelings nor encourage their expression, especially when that would entail prolonged crying, periods of irritable dissatisfaction or outbursts of anger. Looking after a grieving child is exacting and unrewarding work; and it is small wonder if caregivers become impatient and irritable. After a small child has lost a parent, therefore, it is by no means unusual for him to be subjected to strong pressure to 'forget' his grief and, instead, to become interested in whatever his current caregiver thinks may distract him.

Not infrequently conditions of care differ according to whether a child's mother has died or is absent for some other reason. It is therefore unfortunate that no first-hand and detailed reports seem to be available of how children in their third and fourth years respond when conditions are unfavourable after mother has died. For that reason in what follows I have drawn solely on reports of how young children of this age respond when they are placed in a residential nursery or a hospital. These are situations in which conditions of care are often especially unfavourable, for as a rule not only is a child without any one nurse to care for him but he may also be competing for care with many other children of the same age.

Although in those respects the conditions for children whose mother has died are often no different to what they may be for children whose mother is expected to resume care, there are certain special circumstances that are more likely to apply to children who are only temporarily separated from mother than to children who have lost her permanently. For example, a child in hospital is likely to be confined in a cot and to be subjected to a variety of medical procedures that are always strange, perhaps painful, and certainly frightening. Again, before a mother leaves her child temporarily, whether in hospital or nursery, she may exert pressures on him of a kind that a dying mother probably would not. An example of that, which is of especial interest, is the mother who repeatedly admonishes her child not to cry whilst she is away and who instructs him to be a good boy, which means that he accept his lot without complaint. Furthermore, a bereaved child might perhaps elicit more sympathy from adults than a child pining for a mother who will soon return.

In reading what follows, therefore, it is necessary to bear in mind that certain of the adverse conditions described are likely to affect a smaller proportion of children who have lost a parent by death than of children who are undergoing no more than a temporary separation.

We start with the account of a boy of just over two who did not see his mother for eleven weeks whilst he was in a residential nursery.[2] It illustrates how, despite many adverse factors, a child of that age continues to hope for his mother's return. It illustrates much else besides; for example, how difficult it is for a child in these circumstances to maintain a trusting or even friendly relationship with his father at the times of visits, and the enormous emotional strain that is put on all parties at the time of reunion.

Owen Continues to Yearn for Mother

Owen was aged 2 years 2 months when he was placed in a residential nursery because his mother was to be in hospital for an operation on account of an old injury to her back. Although she herself was able to leave hospital after five weeks, Owen did not return home until after another six weeks, making eleven weeks and four days in all, far longer than had been foreseen. During that time he was visited regularly by his

---

[2] This boy was one of the ten young children whose responses during and after their stay in a residential nursery were observed systematically by my colleagues, Christoph Heinicke and Ilse Westheimer. The highly condensed account given here is derived from the unusually detailed one they give on pp. 112–58 of *Brief Separations* (1966).

father but saw nothing of his mother. Messages from her to him were delivered on the nine occasions when the research social worker who visited mother saw Owen in the nursery; but mother sent him no toys or other tangible reminders of herself.

Family. Owen was the second child in a stable, middle-class family with a sister, Sheila, six years older. His mother cared for the home and family full-time; father was employed as a civil servant.

Mother had had a rather unhappy childhood and had grown up to feel inadequate and uncertain of herself. This she covered by adopting an agreeable social manner, which made her popular with acquaintances. Within the home, however, she was excessively controlling. Unable to compromise, she felt she had to win every one of the ensuing battles. The result was a tendency to dominate and nag both her husband and the children.

Father, who had also had a difficult childhood, seemed always calm and conscientious, and towards mother and the children he showed remarkable patience and forbearance. Whether other feelings lay behind his placid demeanour was not discovered.

From what mother said about Owen's history during a number of long interviews the following picture emerged. He had been cared for always by her but, although relations between them were close, they had never run smoothly. She described him when a baby as having always been discontented and as having cried incessantly. During his second year, too, although much more cheerful by day, he had cried a great deal after being put to bed at night. Now, still only just over two, she described him critically as 'a little menace' with a will of his own. Battles between them were fairly frequent. On a recent occasion, when she had clearly been rather arbitrary with him, his temper tantrum had lasted more than two hours. Determined to win, she had put him in his room and told him to stay there until he was quiet. Later, subdued, he had come down seeking reassurances she still loved him.

Stay in nursery. On being left in the nursery by his father Owen cried bitterly and clung desperately. The rest of the afternoon he continued his bitter cries and refused to eat. During the night he woke and called 'Mummy, Daddy'. Next morning he had stopped crying and seemed to be trying his utmost to control himself; he looked bewildered and rubbed his eyes. When anything was expected of him he dissolved into tears and usually refused angrily.

Throughout the first week he fretted openly. After his father's visit on the third day he cried intensely and tried to follow him out. He made few approaches to the nurses, none of whose efforts to comfort him succeeded.

During the second week he cried much less and seemed often to be emotionally detached. For example, when his father visited he spoke not one word; and after his father's departure he sobbed quietly for a few moments only and then sat staring.

During later weeks behaviour of this kind became even more marked. Sometimes he greeted his father with a superficial smile, at others he seemed not to recognize him. All he wanted were the sweets he brought. Similarly, when father was ready to leave, Owen withdrew and refused to look at him despite father's repeated efforts to bid him a warm goodbye. After one of these visits Owen seemed twice to be on the verge of tears but each time he controlled himself.

Throughout the second and third months at times when his father visited Owen continued to treat him in the same distant way. Towards one of the nurses, however, he became more affectionate, and he seemed to desire a good deal of comfort when cuddling up to her. He was extremely possessive of toys and other items, and was quick to anger when anything was withheld.

Throughout these months, despite his not having seen his mother, it was clear he had not forgotten her. Every now and then he was heard to utter 'Mummy' in a quiet voice. On one occasion, six weeks after entering the nursery, he heard a voice down the corridor. Turning to the nearest adult he exclaimed, 'Mummy'; he was evidently thinking that his mother had come at last.

Reunion. On the morning that Owen was to go home he at first sobbed bitterly and then became docile, submissive and sad. When told his father had come to take him home he showed no response; nor did he respond when father greeted him. His only action was to cling tightly to all his possessions. During the first half of a ninety-minute drive home, Owen sat quietly on his father's knee; and it was only towards the end of the journey that he became more lively and began to comment on what he saw out of the car window. Yet when father announced, 'we are going home to mummy now' he seemed not to hear. When they arrived at the house, moreover, he looked bewildered and did not want to leave the car. He was willing, however, to be carried in by his father.

When his mother greeted him with 'Hello, Owen' he again appeared not to hear; instead, he remained silent and expressionless on his father's knee. When his mother handed him a new toy car he took it listlessly and then ignored it; a biscuit she offered he accepted and nibbled, but without interest. His only concern was to stay close to father. Even when twenty minutes later his elder sister came bursting in to greet him, all he did was to turn away from her. Like mother, Sheila was deeply troubled by his expression, 'It's not Owen's face,' she repeated, 'it's a different face.'

It was fifty minutes before Owen showed the first flicker of animation. This occurred after his mother had produced a favourite book which he looked at with her with signs of recognition and interest. Soon he was gathering to himself all his toys and possessions; and he also asked for orange juice. Subsequently he allowed his mother to put on his outdoor clothes and was willing to accompany his father to the shops. That evening father had to sit with him for twenty minutes before he went to sleep.

During his first days home Owen turned always to his father for comfort and ignored his mother's offers. By the second day, however, he was making small approaches to her, and by the fourth he was willing to let her comfort him. As the week went by he turned increasingly to her; but it was not until the eleventh day home that the full strength of his feeling for her found expression. At times he could then be heard murmuring to himself, 'my mummy, my mummy, my mummy'; and he began gradually to point things out to her with a 'Look, Mummy!', and also to turn to her for comfort.

During his second month home he was becoming more spontaneous with her: he wanted her to kiss his arm better when he hurt it, went to kiss her before going out with his father, would return to her briefly before resuming his play. But he could also be extremely obstinate (like his mother) and the conflicts between them recurred. He also cried a great deal before going to sleep unless someone would stay with him. Relations with his father were close; father took him for walks and put him to bed at night, and each seemed to enjoy the other's company.

By the third month relations between Owen and his mother seemed to have been restored. Even so he had not forgotten his experience, as was shown by an incident which occurred sixteen weeks after he had returned home. One of the research workers whom he had seen regularly during his stay in the nursery visited the home and, as it happened, left the house just as Owen was also leaving, to go out with his father. Owen screamed loudly; and only after he had been assured he would not be taken back to the nursery did he calm down.

Comment

When Owen's responses are compared with those of Winnie, Thomas and Kate, two features stand out. The first is the intensity of his distressed fretting during the first few days of his stay away, and the second the extent to which he became emotionally detached from his parents. Both types of response, and in the same sequence, occur regularly in children of this age group who are placed, as Owen was, in a strange place with strange people with no single person to act as substitute mother.

The phenomenon of emotional detachment is of special interest. Within about ten days of his entering the nursery all the responses he had habitually shown to his father are missing and he appears totally withdrawn and uninterested in him. The same is true when he first meets his mother. Yet there are also signs that his attachment to them remained. For example, on a few occasions after his father left at the end of a visit Owen was observed to be briefly on the verge of tears; and after returning home he kept close to his father and went to him for comfort. There is evidence, moreover, that during the whole of his time in the nursery he was still recalling his mother and had not entirely despaired of her return, as is witnessed by his repeated quiet references to her and by the hope he expressed when he heard a voice down the corridor. Moreover, although his relationship with his mother was much slower to regenerate than was that with his father, it was coming to life again after about ten days and thereafter took a form recognizably similar to what it had been before the separation.

In many of these respects Owen's condition resembles one of prolonged absence of grieving and can be understood in similar terms. Using the conceptual framework advocated, Owen's strange behaviour can be regarded as being the result of the systems governing his attachment behaviour, towards both his mother and his father, having been deactivated by means of the defensive exclusion of most, though not quite all, of the sensory inflow that would have activated it. Similarly, his recovery can be regarded as due to an increasing acceptance of such sensory inflow.

Although the study by Heinicke and Westheimer (1966), and earlier studies by Robertson, show that Owen's responses are fairly typical for children of his age placed as he was, it is not unlikely that the frequent conflicts he had had with his mother before the separation contributed to the intensity of his reactions. Bearing in mind his mother's modes of dealing with him, it is at least possible that his being placed in the nursery was construed by him as a punishment inflicted by her. In assessing the likelihood of his thinking in this way, a remark made by his mother to the research social worker is of great significance. Mother was complaining bitterly about Owen's continuing tantrums; she then went on to describe how she was by now feeling so fed up that she had threatened her husband she would 'pack up' and send the children to an institution.

Whereas in Owen's case the evidence that he was being deeply influenced by his previous exchanges with his mother may be thought inadequate, in accounts of other children evidence for it is unmistakable. For example, in Chapter 1 brief accounts are given of two young children, Patrick just over three and Laura aged two years and five months, whose responses during temporary separation from mother and home show plainly some of the effects of such exchanges. Both children had been enjoined by mother not to cry and both made strong efforts to conform but, because neither was wholly successful, telling fragments of the behaviour and feeling they were trying to suppress broke through. In each record (one by Anna Freud and Dorothy Burlingham, the other by James Robertson) sufficient detail is given for it to be possible to see both components of the conflict in which the child is caught, on the one hand his intense yearning for his absent mother and his strong urge to cry for her or to beg others to find her and, on the other, his strenuous efforts not to express any such feeling or behaviour and, instead, to accept the situation without demur.

Patrick Strives to Stifle his Yearning

One of these children, Patrick, a boy of three years and two months, had been admonished by his mother before she left him in a residential nursery to be a good boy and not to cry. She had added the threat, moreover, that, if he were not to conform, she would not visit him. From his subsequent behaviour it is evident that he had not only taken this threat extremely seriously but had probably interpreted it to mean that if he were not good she would leave him there for ever. For several days his main preoccupations were to avoid crying and to assure himself and anyone willing to listen that his mother *would* come for him and that she *would* take him home, assertions he made the more emphatic by an affirmative nod of his head. As the days went by these attempts to assure himself that his mother really would come became 'more compulsive and automatic' and were elaborated by reference to all the different items of clothing that he pictured her putting on him before taking him home with her.

The next step was that further pressure was brought on him, this time by one of the staff telling him to desist from monotonously repeating his assurances that his mother would be coming. Once again Patrick attempted to conform, and he no longer repeated the formula aloud. Yet, as his behaviour showed, he remained entirely preoccupied trying to assure himself that his mother would return; but, instead of words, he substituted gestures revealing how his mother would come, how she would dress him in his coat and pixie hat and take him home with her. A few days later the gestures were themselves reduced 'to a mere abortive flicker of his fingers'.

I believe the changes observed in Patrick's behaviour are a reliable guide to the kinds of psychological process going on within him. Yearning for his absent mother remains active throughout; but step by step its expression is stifled until signs have almost vanished.

From the first, crying for his mother is prohibited under threat of what he believes to be abandonment. Nevertheless, he is still able to find some comfort not only by assuring himself that his mother will be coming for him but also by inviting those caring for him to share his hopes and to confirm them. Later, however, even that measure of comfort is denied him. No longer is he allowed to communicate his sorrows or his hopes. As a result he retreats into himself standing alone in a corner, still attempting to reassure himself by the flickering movements of his hands and lips but wearing 'an absolutely tragic expression on his face'.

No more vivid account can be imagined, I believe, of how a state of natural sorrow can be transformed into one of pathological mourning. Not only do Patrick's hopes fade but, and even more important, he is prohibited, first by his mother and then by the nurse from taking any action known to him that might help him recover his missing mother. No protest is permissible since he must be 'good'. Crying also is forbidden and so, later, is enlisting the help of his caregivers. As a result he is rendered impotent; and thus he becomes ever more helpless and hopeless. His final state, were it seen in a grown-up, would quickly be diagnosed as one of depressive disorder.

The account of Patrick casts light not only on how yearning becomes inhibited and a sense of helplessness generated but also on the origin and function of identification with the lost person. It was clearly of the greatest importance to Patrick to be able to communicate, both to himself and to the nurses, what his hopes and expectations were. It was also vital for him to have those hopes confirmed, as is shown by his bursting into violent sobs whenever anyone contradicted him. Initially, he expressed himself directly and in speech. Later, however, speech was forbidden; and it was then that he resorted to gestures, using for the purpose just those actions of his mother's that he pictured her performing when at last she came for him.

In this case, therefore, it seems safe to say that behaviour that is quite correctly termed identificatory served as a means of communication: it was resorted to in place of speech when that was forbidden because it was the only means remaining to him for expressing, either to himself or to those around him, the hopes and expectations to which he clung. As such it is clearly part of a pathological condition.

Whether identificatory behaviour following loss is often serving as a deviant means of communication we cannot say; but it would be useful were examples to be examined in the light of this possibility.

Laura's Yearning becomes Disguised

The second child referred to in Chapter 1 in whom a conflict can be seen between distressed yearning and trying to be a 'good' child by not crying is Laura, the little girl of two years and five months who was observed and filmed by James Robertson during her eight-day stay in hospital (Robertson 1952). Here again injunctions by mother that the child not cry and efforts by nurses to divert her attention away from her missing mother both played major parts in engendering the conflict and in suppressing the child's yearning and its expression.[3]

Laura was two years and five months old and was due to go into hospital for eight days to have an umbilical hernia repaired.[4] Previously she had never been out of her mother's care. Although she was an only child, her mother was already five months' pregnant with her second baby. The marriage appeared stable and family relationships happy. Mother gave much time to Laura's care and expected much from her. In particular she insisted that Laura not cry. No doubt due to the combination of mother's loving care and her insistence on control, Laura cried rarely and in general showed control over the expression of feeling unusual for her age. The impression she gave was of an intelligent and relatively mature little girl.

Although Laura's parents had tried to prepare her for going into hospital it seems unlikely that she had understood that she would be there alone. At first she was friendly to the nurse, then cautious, and only when undressed did she start screaming for her mummy and attempting to

[3] The following account is taken from the guide to the film by James Robertson (1953) and a discussion of the psychological significance of Laura's behaviour by Bowlby, Robertson and Rosenbluth (1952). In addition to filming this child, with her parents and the hospital nurses when they were present, observers recorded Laura's behaviour throughout the waking hours of her stay. Details of how the film came to be made, how Laura came to be selected, and the schedule and method of filming are given in the guide.

[4] This is a painless condition which, it is now known, usually rights itself. In 1951 it was operated upon more commonly than nowadays. The operation itself is a minor procedure, often done in an out-patient department.

escape. Within ten minutes, however, her feelings were under control and she appeared calm. Thenceforward she oscillated between quiet resignation and overt yearning for her mother, expressed more or less strongly depending on the circumstances.

Much of the time Laura was alone in her cot. Often she was to be seen looking strained and sad, clutching in one arm her teddy bear and in the other the blanket she called her baby, both of which she had been allowed to bring from home. Since she did not cry or demand attention, it would have been easy for the uninformed to have regarded her as 'settled'. Yet, whenever a nurse appeared to take part in a brief play episode (specially arranged for the purposes of the study) Laura's feelings found expression. Her face crumpling into tears she repeated with greater or less emphasis, 'I want my mummy, I want my mummy now.' Never did she howl or scream as many children do; always there was some measure of restraint though the intensity of her feeling was never in doubt. When the nurse left, Laura resumed the sad control she had exercised before; but the constant picking of her face and nose, which had begun within two hours of her admission to hospital, told of the tension she was under.

Although she herself cried little, Laura was often much concerned when other children cried. On one such occasion a little boy was screaming piteously. Laura at once became solicitous and demanded that the boy's mother be brought. A little self-righteously Laura exclaimed, 'I not crying, see!' and then emphatically, 'Fetch that boy's Mummy!' A couple of days later Laura's yearning for her mother was disguised as she insisted to a nurse, 'My mummy's crying for me—go fetch her!' A day or two later when a newly admitted child was crying strongly Laura, very controlled herself, watched him with a tense expression and then attempted to reassure him: 'You're crying because you want your mummy, don't cry. She'll come tomorrow.'

Laura's mother was able to visit roughly every other day. Though Laura recognized her mother instantly, there was on each occasion a time-lag before she greeted her. At the first two visits Laura burst into tears when she saw her mother and, on the first of them, also turned away. There then followed an interval of some minutes (about two at the first visit and ten at the second) before she could begin to express any pleasure. Thereafter she quickly became the happy child playing intimately with her mother that she had been at home. When mother said she must go Laura became anxious; and as mother left she turned her head away. Though she did not cry, her expression changed and she became restless. Although still mid-afternoon, she asked to be tucked down with her various possessions and forbade the nurse to remove the chair on which her mother had been sitting.

On the third and fourth visits Laura did not cry but looked blank and made no attempt to get into contact with her mother. After a time she warmed up. At the fourth visit, when father arrived ten minutes after mother, he received a warmer welcome; and when he left Laura murmured quietly, 'I go with you.' But she did not insist and, when her parents left, she seemed to ignore their leaving her behind.

On the final morning Laura was sobbing: during the previous evening mother had told her she would be going home the next day. Laura had kept the news to herself; but her control had temporarily given way. Yet when her mother came to collect her Laura remained cautious in expressing any hope and not until mother produced her outdoor shoes did she permit herself to jump for joy. Then she gathered up all her precious possessions and marched away with her mother. On the way out she dropped a book and a nurse picked it up for her. Evidently supposing the nurse would keep it, Laura screamed in temper and snatched the book away—by far the fiercest feeling she had shown throughout the eight days.

Interim Comment

The observations of Laura leave no doubt that throughout her stay away she was constantly thinking about her mother and yearning for her. Nevertheless, but for a sensitive observer this evidence could easily have been missed and its significance ignored. Often Laura's potentially intense desire for her mother was disguised; for example, on the occasion she claimed that it was her mother who was crying for her, not the other way about. On other occasions she was heard to interpolate without emotion and as if irrelevantly the words, 'I want my mummy, where has my mummy gone?' into remarks about something quite different. On one such, as already reported in Chapter 1, she expressed her urgent wish to see the steam-roller that she had been watching from the hospital window and which had just gone out of sight. In the midst of her monologue, 'I want to see the steam-roller, I want to see the steam-roller,' there was interspersed occasionally, like a voice off-stage, 'I want to see my mummy!'

Laura's mother, it will be remembered, had high expectations of her and was especially insistent she not cry. The nurses, too, must have made their preferences clear. None of the adults wanted to see an unhappy little girl, crying piteously for her mother and deeply resenting the way she was being treated. Laura, no doubt aware of that, did her best to conform and to keep her desires and feelings to herself. Even when the moment came for her to return home Laura, like Kate, avoided hoping too much lest she be disappointed again. Her pleas having repeatedly been in vain, she was learning that effort to effect change is unavailing and so to resign herself to despair. Thus, like Patrick, Laura was growing daily to feel more helpless and more hopeless.

Another feature that is evident in the account of Laura is her strong disposition to care for others. Although she herself cried little, she was constantly concerned when other children cried and then did all she could to comfort them. This tendency for young children who are out of mother's care to mother each other was noted by Dorothy Burlingham and Anna Freud during the war years (Burlingham and Freud 1944, pp. 32–3). Although it is apparent that in comforting others a young child may find a measure of comfort for herself, opinions differ about how healthy it is for future development; this issue is referred to again at the end of the chapter.

Let us consider now how Laura behaved after her return home.

During her first days home Laura was unsettled and irritable and distressed whenever mother was even momentarily out of sight. After that, however, she seemed to have become her usual self and it might have been supposed that the eight days in hospital, however distressing they had been at the time, were now over and forgotten. Two episodes occurred, however, which made it plain that was not so.

The first occurred through a mischance. One evening six months after Laura's return home the film was being shown to her parents. Unknown to anyone Laura crept into the room and happened to see the final sequences of herself on the screen. When the lights were raised, agitated and flushed she exclaimed angrily: 'Where *was* you all the time, Mummy? Where *was* you?' Then she burst into loud crying, turned away from her mother and went to her father for comfort. Not unnaturally her parents were astonished by the strength of the feelings she revealed and were disturbed also that she should have turned angrily away from her mother.

The second episode occurred three months later, soon after Laura's third birthday. Taken by her parents to an exhibition Laura seemed happy to stay in the playroom provided for children despite the white-coated attendants who might have reminded her of the hospital nurses. When a photographer appeared, however, she became hysterical and it was an hour before her parents could console her. Apparently the camera had suddenly reminded her of her previous experience.

Further Comment

These two episodes strongly suggest that, despite Laura's apparent recovery from her distressing experience, she remained liable to respond to reminders of it with both anger and anxiety.

There was yet another episode in Laura's life to which her

responses may well have been influenced by her eight days in hospital. This was a period of four weeks during which she was cared for by her maternal grandmother whilst her mother was having the new baby. Laura's responses were not observed and information about them was received from her parents and grandmother. The interest lies in the way she treated her two parents at the time of her return.

Four months after the film was taken, when Laura was two years and nine months old, mother went to hospital to have the new baby. She was away for four weeks, during the whole of which Laura saw neither mother nor father. According to grandmother, whose account must be treated with caution, Laura had fretted at first but subsequently had been 'very happy'.

Laura's reunion with her mother began when mother, now at home, spoke to her by telephone. Laura was excited to hear her mother's voice and keen to return. Half an hour later she arrived and mother could hear her banging on the front door and calling 'Mummy, Mummy'. But when mother opened it, Laura looked at her blankly and said, 'But I want my *mummy*.' For the next two days Laura seemed not to recognize her mother and, although not unfriendly, was completely detached. This was naturally very upsetting for mother.

Laura's treatment of her father was quite different. When he returned home an hour or two after Laura's return, Laura was for a few moments mute; but she recovered quickly and was soon friendly. He had arranged to begin a holiday that day and during subsequent days he and Laura got on well. Puzzled by her attitude towards her mother, her parents thought she might have lost her memory. They therefore tried her out to see whether she recognized her favourite dolls and various household articles, which of course she did.

Two days after returning home Laura's relationship with her mother seemed to have recovered, though at times she addressed her as 'Nana', which mother found irritating. During these days Laura had shown no other signs of upset, no temper tantrums, no sleeping disturbances and no eating disturbances.

Distortions in Personality Development

The accounts of how Laura and Patrick responded during their days in a strange place, with no one to mother them or to sympathize with them in their plight, brings home both how intensely and continuously a young child in that situation pines for his absent mother and also how eager he is to obey any instructions she gives that he not protest, even if that means his exerting unrelenting effort to inhibit his every natural response—loud and angry protest against what is being done and strong demand for his mother's return. In complying with mother's wishes, it is clear, each child was striving to avoid the sanction he believed to lie behind her words, for Patrick the threat of her abandoning him, for Laura the threat of her disapproving and withholding her love.

For each child there is reason to infer that such awareness as he had of the pining and anger being engendered within him by his situation was becoming disconnected from his awareness of what that situation was—in traditional terms that certain processes of repression were operating. Laura's desires come to be focused on the steam-roller. Patrick, reproached for his constant repetitions, ceases to talk about his absent mother and, instead, becomes preoccupied with a set of movements that are rapidly losing their meaning. This leads me to suspect that each child was in danger of losing track of who it was he was wanting, in the same way that Kate appears to have done, if only momentarily, when she voiced her question, 'What is Kate looking for?'

The distortions in personality development that were occurring in these two children were taking rather different forms. With no one to sanction his yearning or to help him retain his awareness of who or what he was wanting, Patrick's grasp of what was making him unhappy was probably becoming steadily weaker. If this assessment is correct, Patrick's condition was becoming one of chronic mourning. Laura's condition, by contrast, tended towards excessive self-reliance and excessive caregiving. Admittedly she seemed much happier when she was comforting the other children than when she was grieving for her own mother. Yet I believe it would be dangerous to assume that her ability to find solace in comforting others represents a favourable step in the development of her personality. For it is not difficult to see how in a situation of prolonged lack of care Laura's concern for the miseries of others, combined with a strong tendency to inhibit expression of her own desire for care, could have become established as a firm pattern of compulsive caregiving.

In thus evaluating Laura's caregiving behaviour as potentially pathological my position is different to that of many others. For example, in a recent paper by McDevitt (1975), a member of Margaret Mahler's group, a traditional and contrasting view is expressed. First, McDevitt notes how, from the age of about sixteen months, a child whose mother is away 'may mother her doll in symbolic play, using this play to comfort herself . . .' and he then comments: 'This transfer of the mother–child relation to the inner world permits a continuing relationship with the love object during the latter's absence.' In saying this he implies that this 'transfer' is a step in healthy development. As already indicated, I do not share this optimism. In terms of the theory advanced here the behaviour in question is to be regarded as an *alternative* to seeking care. Because, moreover, it is a form of behaviour that is incompatible with seeking care and also because of the very fact that it does bring some measure of comfort, and is often highly approved by grown-ups, there is always risk that caregiving of others will be resorted to routinely whenever seeking care for the self would be the appropriate response.

CHAPTER 24

Responses to Loss
During the Second Year

A Transitional Period

The younger an infant the more difficult it is to know how his responses to loss of mother should best be conceptualized. Review of the evidence suggests the following. Before six months the responses are so different to what they are later that the concept of mourning seems certainly inappropriate. Between seven months and about seventeen months responses take forms that have sufficient resemblance to the responses of older children for their relation to mourning to call for careful discussion. From about seventeen months onwards the responses conform ever more closely to those described in the previous chapters so that the tentative conclusions reached in them begin to apply.

In order to limit discussion to manageable proportions, I have decided, reluctantly, to deal only very cursorily with responses to be observed in children younger than about sixteen months. This enables us to focus attention mainly on the responses to be seen during the last eight months of the second year. Not only is this a transitional period of great interest about which there is no lack of controversy, but the period is also one in regard to which there is a reasonable amount of evidence. This evidence, moreover, has been recorded by researchers working in two distinct traditions, clinicians studying problems of attachment, separation and loss, and psychologists concerned with cognitive development. Since I believe evidence from the two sources to be mutually compatible and since the theory developed by the cognitive psychologists is both closer to the data and better articulated than that developed by clinicians, I draw heavily on cognitive theory as well as attachment theory when interpreting the findings. Before dealing with theoretical issues, however, it is necessary to consider the evidence.

Responses when conditions are favourable

We start with the account of a little girl of seventeen months who was in foster-care with the Robertsons for ten days.

Jane, aged seventeen months when she came into care, was the youngest of the four children James and Joyce Robertson fostered whilst their mothers were having a new baby (Robertson and Robertson 1971). She was a lively, attractive child who had been cared for by her young mother with devotion and imagination. Both parents expected high standards of obedience and Jane already understood many of their prohibitions.

Familiarizing Jane with the foster-family was extended over several weeks and proved more difficult than it was with the two older children in the study, Thomas and Kate (see Chapter 23). By the time Jane came into care, however, she was fairly well at ease in her new surroundings, and, when the moment came, was willing to accept full mothering from the substitute at hand.

For the first three days Jane was gay and lively. Both the gaiety and the intense smiling she directed at her foster-parents seemed, however, rather artificial and intended to elicit answering smiles; and when she stopped smiling her face became tense and blank.

The impression gained by the Robertsons that these smiles were artificial and intended to placate was amply confirmed later by Jane's mother. After seeing the film record of these early days she commented, 'Jane smiles a lot like that after I've been angry with her and she's trying to placate me.'

By the fourth day Jane's mood had changed. No longer gay, she was often restless and cross, and was prone to cry irritably. She tended also to suck her thumb and wanted to be nursed. The impression she gave the foster-parents was of a child 'under stress and . . . at times bewildered'.

It happened that the foster-parents lived in the same block as Jane's parents so that when Jane was playing in the communal garden, which the families shared (with others), she was no distance from the gate to her parents' garden. For the first four days she seemed not to notice the gate. On the fifth, however, she went to it, tried to open it and failed. Looking over the wall into the empty garden, she shook her head, ran back to the communal garden and then seemed uncertain which way to go. The following day she tried the gate again and this time it opened. Running down the path she tried next to open the door to her parent's apartment. Unsuccessful, she returned, shut the garden gate carefully and then spent some minutes peering at the empty house. On returning to her foster-mother's home that day she resisted entering and for the first time since leaving her mother uttered the word 'Mama'.

On each of the ten days Jane was away her father visited for an hour. At first she played happily with him and cried when he left. Towards the end of her stay, however, she seemed pointedly to ignore him whilst he was there, but as soon as he made to leave she clung to him and cried.

When mother arrived to take her home Jane recognized her immediately. At first a little uncertain and shy, she was soon smiling in a sweet, perhaps placatory, way. The game of putting pennies into a purse that she had been playing with her foster-mother she switched quietly to her mother, who was thereafter expected by Jane to take over all her care.

For a time after Jane returned home relations between her and her parents were strained. Sometimes she conformed to their wishes, at others she did the opposite. Their attempts to correct her by smacks led to outbursts of crying of a strength not seen before.

By the end of her ten days in care Jane had seemed to be firmly attached to her foster-mother and reluctant to give her up. For that reason the foster-mother visited the home several times during the early weeks. At first she was warmly welcomed by Jane, but as Jane's renewed relationship to her mother became more secure the visits created conflict and Jane seemed hardly to know towards which of them to go.

Comment

Despite the very favourable conditions of care and her apparent gaiety during the early days, Jane's behaviour was, from the first, that of an insecure and perhaps bewildered child. Although no older than seventeen months and with only rudimentary beginnings of language, she was none the less able to distinguish clearly between her mother and her foster-mother. First, she recognizes her own house and garden; later she recalls her 'Mama'; and throughout she makes it abundantly clear where her preference lies. When her mother arrives to take her home, moreover, she switches at once from foster-mother to mother. These observations show that throughout her ten days away Jane was able to retain the memory of her absent mother in readily accessible form and so to respond with well-planned actions not only when she first sees her mother again but also as soon as she identifies the garden gate. Furthermore, her subsequent reference to 'Mama' is evidence that, given this reminder, she was capable of recalling the image of her absent mother.

In most respects the behaviour of Lucy, aged one year and nine months and the fourth of the Robertsons' foster-children, resembled Jane's. Although four months older than Jane, Lucy had no words. Nevertheless, there was evidence that she, too, was able to retain the memory of her absent mother in readily accessible form and to respond quickly both to a reminder of her mother during the period of separation[1] and to mother herself at the time of reunion.

[1] An account of Lucy is given in Chapter 1 of Volume II. The reminder of her mother was being taken to a park where she had often been before with her mother.

A question raised by the Robertsons is whether, in the absence of any tangible reminders of mother, either Jane or Lucy had the cognitive capacity to recall an image[2] of mother, without which, we may suppose, no child could either experience or express a yearning to be reunited with her. Whereas it was plain that the two older children, Thomas and Kate, had the capacity well developed (see Chapter 23), the ability of the two younger ones was certainly in doubt. Yet the observations made on the two children, taken alone, provide insufficient grounds for concluding, as the Robertsons are inclined to do, that children in the middle of their second year have no capacity for recall. Some children of this age unquestionably do have it, as certain of Piaget's observations make plain (see the next chapter). Nevertheless, many related questions remain to be answered. For how long, for example, can a child during his second year retain in recoverable form a model of his absent mother, either for recognition or recall? For how long does he continue to yearn for her? What happens to the model when it ceases to be recoverable? Firm answers are elusive.

What is certain is that great changes are occurring in a child's cognitive capacities during this second year so that operations that may be far beyond him during the early months are well within his compass at the end of it. In illustration of this is a rather brief account, by Furman (1974, p. 55) of a small boy, Clive, who had just reached his second birthday when his father died. It shows unmistakably that by that age a child has no difficulty over a period of at least several weeks in recalling an absent parent and mourning his absence.

Clive's mother helped him, it was thought successfully, to understand that his father would not return. Thereafter for several weeks Clive spent much time repeating the daily play activities which he had enjoyed with his father; and 'he also insisted, over and over, on taking the walks he had taken with his father, stopping at the stores where his father had stopped and recalling specific items'. Clive's mother, Furman notes, found these overt signs of Clive's sadness and longing difficult to tolerate.

We have noted repeatedly in earlier chapters that it is not easy for adults to bear the prolonged yearning of a bereaved child, especially when they have been bereaved themselves; and also that the

[2] Used in this context, the term 'image' has the same reference as the term 'representational model' used in this work.

difficulties of the adults increase the child's own difficulties. Despite his mother's attitude, however, Clive persisted in retaining his links with his dead father in a way that seems closely to resemble that of an older person engaged in healthy mourning.

Responses when conditions are unfavourable

We turn now to observations made of children of about the same age as Jane and Lucy but who, being in a residential nursery like the rather older Owen described in the previous chapter, had no continuous care from any one person. We draw on the accounts of two children, each reported at length by observers of much experience in the field and regarded by them as reasonably representative. One account, that of John aged seventeen months, is reported by James and Joyce Robertson (1971). The other, that of Dawn aged sixteen months, is reported by Christoph Heinicke and Ilse Westheimer (1966). The responses of the two children show many striking similarities. To simplify exposition, however, the description of John's responses and the comparison of them with those of Jane and also of Laura (Chapter 23) are given first and the description of Dawn deferred until later.

John despairs of being cared for

John was aged one year and five months when he spent nine days in a residential nursery because his mother was having a new baby; father was at a critical stage of his professional career and no relatives were available. The nursery was well recognized and approved for the training of nursery nurses; but at that time nurses were assigned to duties and not to children. As a result no one nurse had responsibility for John's care. Furthermore, John found himself one among many children most of whom, having been in the nursery from birth, were 'noisy, aggressive, self-assertive and demanding'.

Stay in Nursery. Mother's labour began during the night and John was left by her at the nursery on her way to hospital. When next morning he was greeted by Mary, a smiling young nurse, he responded in a friendly way and interacted with her as she dressed him. He was also friendly to the other young nurses as they came and went; but he received no extended care from any one of them. At nightfall Mary put him to bed, but she did not stay with him. Disappointed, John shouted in protest.

The second day also began fairly well. Much of the time John played quietly in a corner away from the other children, and occasionally he sought out a nurse who might mother him; but his tentative approaches were easily overlooked and he was likely to be pushed aside by other children. Most of the day he remained quiet and uncomplaining; but that changed when his father visited. As father left to go home, John cried and struggled to go with him. Nurse Mary was able to comfort him but when she, too, had to leave he became tearful once more.

From the third day onwards John became increasingly distressed, sometimes standing forlornly at one end of the room, at others engaged in a long spell of sad crying. Although he still attempted to get close to one or other of the nurses, more usually he played quietly in a corner or else crawled under a table to cry alone. By the fifth day his approaches to the nurses had grown fewer and even when one tried to comfort him he was likely to be unresponsive. Thereafter he turned instead to a giant teddy bear which he hugged. But he also cried a great deal 'in quiet despair, sometimes rolling about and wringing his hands. Occasionally he shouted angrily at no one in particular, and in a brief contact smacked nurse Mary's face.'

When on the sixth day father visited again, after missing two days, John pinched and smacked. Then his face brightened, he fetched his outdoor shoes and went hopefully to the door; but disappointment ensued when his father departed without him. Going over to nurse Mary he looked back at his father with an anguished expression. Then he turned away from Mary also and sat apart clutching his blanket.

During the following two days John was a picture of despair. 'He did not play, did not eat, did not make demands, did not respond for more than a few seconds to the fleeting attempts of the young nurses to cheer him.' When another child sought to oust him from a nurse's knee there was an angry note in his voice. But for long periods 'he lay in apathetic silence on the floor, his head on the large teddy bear. . .'.

When on the eighth day father came at teatime John cried convulsively and could neither eat nor drink. At the end of the visit he was abandoned to despair; and no one could comfort him. Squirming down from nurse Mary's knee, he crawled into a corner and lay crying beside the big teddy bear, unresponsive to the efforts of the troubled young nurse.

Return Home. On the morning of the ninth and last day John's condition was unchanged; and when his mother arrived to take him home he was slumped motionless on the lap of one of the nurses. At the sight of his mother he began throwing himself about and crying loudly. Several times he stole a glance at her, but each time he turned away 'with loud cries and a distraught expression'. After some minutes she took him on her knee, but he struggled and screamed, arched his back and ran, crying, away from his mother and towards Joyce Robertson (who was observing). The latter calmed him down and in due course passed him back to his mother. There he lay quietly on her knee but never once did he look at her.

When father arrived shortly afterwards John again struggled away from his mother. Then, lying in his father's arms, he stopped crying and for the first time looked directly at his mother. 'It was a long hard look,' mother commented, 'he has never looked at me like that before.'

At home during the first week John cried a great deal: he was impatient of the least delay and had many tantrums. 'He rejected his parents at all levels—would not accept affection or comforting, would not play with them, and removed himself physically by shutting himself up in his room.' During the second week he was quieter; but during the third he seemed more distressed than ever. The tantrums returned; he refused food, lost weight and slept badly; but he now began to cling. His parents, shocked by his condition, gave him maximum attention and did all they could to restore his confidence. Their efforts met with some success, and his relationship with his mother grew much better.

This improvement was precarious, however, as was shown when on two occasions Joyce Robertson who had observed him in the nursery visited. After her first visit, four weeks after John's return home, he reverted for some days to not eating and to refusing his parents' attentions. The same happened after her second visit, three weeks later: for five days John was extremely disturbed and for the first time was overtly hostile to his mother.

Follow-up. When visited three years later, when John was four and a half, he was a handsome lively boy who gave his parents much pleasure. Yet their reports indicated that he was still unduly afraid of losing his mother and always got upset when she was not where he had expected. There were also days when, apparently out of the blue, he became hostile and provocative towards her.

Comment

In considering John's responses to being out of his parents' care it is necessary to make two comparisons. In the first, age is held constant and the influence of varying the conditions examined; in the second, conditions are held constant and the influence of varying age examined.

For the first comparison John's responses can be compared to those of Jane, described in the previous section. John and Jane were the same age, seventeen months, and were away for the same length of time, nine and ten days respectively. Whereas, however, Jane was cared for by skilled foster-parents John had no one nurse to care for him.

Both John and Jane sought the company of such substitute figures as seemed available and both responded gladly to whatever attentions they received. In Jane's case the relationship was permitted to develop so that her behaviour came quickly to show some of the features characteristic of a stable attachment. In John's case, despite his every effort, this proved impossible. Again and again he approached a nurse, expecting and hoping for a motherly response, and again and again he was disappointed.

Thus each child sought to recreate with a substitute mother, or potential substitute mother, a version of the relationship each had had with his (her) own mother. At the same time, however, both children distinguished the substitute from the original with the utmost clarity, and by each child recognition of mother was immediate. Jane, whenever offered the choice, made her preference for her mother clear, whilst remaining appreciative of her foster-mother. John's reactions to his mother were far more complex, but there was never doubt that it was she who aroused in him his most intense emotions.

This brings us to the differences between John's and Jane's responses. Jane, with a substitute figure to whom she could become attached, was comparatively content during her stay away and responded pleasurably to her mother immediately they met. John, with no substitute figure able to give him time and attention, came to despair of being cared for by anyone. Gradually he gave up directing attachment behaviour towards the nurses and turned instead to the inanimate teddy. He played little and cried much. After a week of these experiences, moreover, he found no solace even when his father or a nurse sought to comfort him. The same was true when at last his mother reappeared. Instead of greeting her and welcoming her offer of loving care, he struggled away from her and glowered. His deep resentment at the way she had treated him and his persisting anxiety lest it be repeated were plain to see.

Thus, it is clear, both of these children retained in memory a readily available model of the absent mother and retained, too, the potential for responding to her with intense feeling as soon as they met her again. The question whether during his stay away John was able to recall his mother and to yearn actively for her must be left open.

For the second comparison John's responses can be compared to those of one of the older children, Laura. John and Laura were away for the same length of time (nine and eight days respectively) and neither had care from any one nurse. Whereas, however, John was only seventeen months old and had virtually no language, Laura was aged two years and four months and had a use of language good for her age.

In their responses the two children showed many similarities. Both were unhappy whilst away, both cried a lot and both turned for comfort to a teddy bear. Both played only desultorily. Both distinguished sharply between the nurses in the institution and their own parents. When mother reappeared both responded with strong feeling. Both showed deep resentment towards her for what had happened, John immediately and to the exclusion of almost all else, Laura belatedly and only after she had been reminded of the episode by seeing the film of herself leaving hospital with her mother. Before that the depth of Laura's resentment had been completely hidden.

The contrast between John who expressed his resentment openly and Laura who hid hers is part of a more general difference between the two children. Laura, clearly influenced by her parent's pressure to be a good girl and not to cry, strives throughout her stay away to restrain her tears and all other active expression of yearning for her mother and of anger at being deserted; and much of the time her control is effective. John, by contrast, shows little or no sign of attempting to control his expression of feeling. The difference reflects a difference in mental organization characteristic of the age-levels concerned. Laura, four months beyond her second birthday, is relatively well equipped to restrain, when necessary, forms of behaviour that are strongly aroused within her; whereas John, still only seventeen months, has yet to develop such mental equipment. In giving evidence that a capacity for control is present in children after passing their second birthday Laura is not alone: each of the other five children described in Chapter 23, including the youngest of them, Owen, also gave such evidence.

In addition to this major difference in the degree to which Laura and John controlled the expression of feeling, and the behaviour that goes with it, the two children differed markedly in the extent to which each gave evidence whilst away of being preoccupied with the missing mother. John gave no clear evidence that he was (though that does not preclude his having been so). Laura, by contrast, gave ample evidence that she was constantly thinking about her mother and also yearning for her. Nevertheless, it should be noted that had it not been for an informed and sensitive observer even this evidence might have been overlooked or its significance discounted.

In comparing John's responses with those, first, of Jane and, secondly, of Laura, the underlying assumption is that John's responses are fairly typical of a child in his age group cared for in the conditions described. Confidence in that assumption is strengthened by comparing John's responses with those of Dawn.[3]

Dawn Becomes Sad and Depressed

Dawn was sixteen months old when she spent fifteen days in a residential nursery. She came from a working-class family in which there was an elder boy of six. Father discriminated strongly in favour of Dawn and against the boy who was not his own. Mother, a rough-and-ready character, kept a spotless home and devoted herself to the children. She resented father's attitude to her son, which led to quarrels between them.

Stay in Nursery. During the first day Dawn was active and fairly cheerful, apparently unaware of the situation. Next morning, however, she cried desperately for 'Mummy, Daddy'. For long periods she stood by the door through which her father had disappeared. Attempts by staff to comfort her were to no avail. During the next three days she continued to fret inconsolably and was to be seen much of the time standing near the door.

On the fifth day, and for the only time, father visited. Dawn immediately recognized him and, when picked up, clung to him strongly, whining. Later she was willing to be put down for a time but as soon as he left she threw herself on the floor and screamed for him.

Bedtime was always difficult for the nurses until they discovered that Dawn was willing to be left if she was given a bottle with milk. At other times she sucked her comforter, interrupting only briefly to cry for her father. She also was often to be seen hugging her teddy bear.

At certain times Dawn could be extremely active and enjoyed pushing prams about. At others she appeared as though wandering and gave the impression she was looking for something.

During the last five days of her stay Dawn was often quiet and inclined to stare into space. At these times she seemed sad and forlorn and both observers used the word depressed to describe her. These depressed periods, however, were occasionally interrupted by sudden outbursts of laughter.

On several occasions there was clear evidence that Dawn was preoccupied with her absent parents. On the eleventh day she announced to one of the observers, 'Daddy come today.' Although at the time she did not seem upset when told he would not, when later another little girl's mother arrived she burst into uncontrollable sobs. On the thirteenth day, as soon as she spotted the observer, a woman, she ceased playing and started crying for her mother.

[3] This account is a much abbreviated version of the one given by Heinicke and Westheimer (1966, pp. 84–112).

During these final days, although Dawn seemed occasionally to be cheerful, she continued to cry a great deal and to wear a sad expression. At times she found comfort in the nurses, but she never sought it; nor did she seem to care which nurse attended her.

Return Home. When, ten days after his only visit, father came for her, Dawn cried loudly and put her arms out to be picked up. Quietening while in his arms, she again cried intensely when for a moment he put her down. Subsequently she clung tightly to him.

Unfortunately there was no opportunity to observe how Dawn would have greeted her mother, because as soon as mother sighted Dawn she rushed to take her from father and hugged her to herself in a tearful embrace. During the car journey home Dawn sat quietly on mother's lap. Arrived back in the flat Dawn was soon exploring the familiar environment and began playing intently with her favourite toys. The apathy and sadness seen in the nursery were gone and replaced by animated busy activity.

During the first days home Dawn seemed a little distant from her mother. For example, it was not until the sixth day that she uttered the word 'Mummy' and then only with prompting. As the days passed, however, she became more affectionate and began to climb on to her mother's lap; but she was anxious too to stay close to her mother and apt to fly into tantrums when thwarted. In these and other respects, Dawn's behaviour was much like that of other young children who have spent time in a strange place with strange people.

Comment

Since the similarities between Dawn's responses and those of John are so evident there is little call for comment. Both show a great deal of distress, both are eager to return home when father visits, neither finds much comfort in the nurse's attentions, both spend time hugging a teddy. At the end of the separation, however, Dawn's relationships with her parents are much less impaired than are John's with his; the reason for this is not clear.

Whereas during his stay away John gave no indication that he was thinking about his absent parents, Dawn did so. First, she announces that her father is going to visit, and later the same day she sobs uncontrollably when another child receives a visit. Two days later she begins crying for her mother as soon as she spots the woman observer. This observation suggests that Dawn may momentarily have supposed that the observer was her mother, much as Owen had mistaken the voice down the corridor.

There are observations of other children of the same age and even younger who have given evidence of their preoccupation with their absent parents. One, reported by Anna Freud and Dorothy Burlingham (1974, p. 39), concerns a little girl of seventeen months who said nothing but 'Mum, Mum, Mum' for three days and who, whilst liking to sit on nurse's knee and to have the nurse put her arm round her, insisted throughout on keeping her back to the nurse so as not to see her. Another, reported by James Robertson is already referred to in Chapter 1. Aged thirteen months and so too young to use words, Philip was seen, when fretting in the residential nursery in which he had been left, to make the motions associated with the rhyme 'round and round the garden' with which his mother used to humour him at home when he was upset.

In view of these observations I believe it safe to say that there are many children of sixteen months and over who have the capacity to retain in memory their model of a missing parent in accessible form and who recall that model at intervals during a stay with strange people; and, furthermore, that they can do so not only when they are presented with clear reminders but at other times as well. In view of Piaget's findings (referred to in the next chapter) there is no reason to be surprised by this. Nevertheless, we must bear in mind that there may be other children in whom the capacity is not present during the first half of the second year and in whom it develops only later.

In this chapter the unfavourable conditions to which attention is drawn are confined to the absence of a stable substitute mother. What part, it may be asked, do the many other unfavourable conditions discussed in previous chapters play during a child's second year. In particular, do things that are said to a child—injunctions not to cry, threats to reject or abandon him, attributions of blame—have an effect on children in their second year as they clearly do for those in their third year and beyond? One answer might be that they could not do so because children under two, being deficient in language, would not be able to grasp the meaning of what was being said. Others, however, might disagree, pointing to the fact that through a child's understanding of gesture his grasp of the gist of what is said to him is always far in advance of his capacity to express himself. A similar problem arises with children who have lost a parent by death. Can information that the parent will never return be understood in any way whatsoever by so young a child?

In my view we are in no position to answer these questions with confidence. Clearly a very young child's understanding is limited but it may not be zero. Furthermore, children differ greatly in their speed of development, and parents differ greatly in their willingness to communicate and in their skill in doing so. Until much more evidence is available we shall be wise to keep an open mind.

This brings us once more to the controversies about whether young children mourn with which we began. Since a large part of the disagreement turns on how different schools of thought conceive of the form and pace of early cognitive development, we consider in our final chapter what is now known about that and also what its implications for our problem seem to be.

CHAPTER 25

Young Children's Responses
in the Light of Early Cognitive Development

Developing the concept of person permanence

During the early decades of psychoanalysis very little was known about the development either of a child's cognitive abilities or of his relations with his parents during his first two or three years of life. As a result a variety of rather arbitrary guesses were made, many of them much influenced by the assumption that a child's interest in persons is necessarily secondary to, and derived from, his desire for food. Thus at one extreme it was confidently believed that a child as old as two years is still so dominated by his physiological needs that he switches his affections promptly to whoever at the moment is meeting them. At an opposite extreme complex cognitive abilities, and relationships with the breast as a part-object, were attributed to infants no more than a few months old. On the basis of these ideas two or more quite different theories of social development were elaborated by psychoanalysts, leading inevitably to widely divergent theories of mourning.

Today, thanks to the systematic studies of a steadily increasing band of developmental psychologists, it is no longer necessary to rely on guesses. Whilst a great deal still needs to be learned, a reliable outline of cognitive and socio-emotional development during the earliest years is becoming available. In this chapter I indicate briefly how children's responses to separation and loss can be considered in the light of these findings.

In giving attention to cognitive development I am drawing first and foremost on the work of Piaget (see especially *The Construction of Reality in the Child*, 1937 and *Play, Dreams and Imitation in Childhood*, 1951) and also on the work of Bower (1974), whose imaginative experiments have led him not only strongly to support Piaget's concepts but also to elaborate and clarify them. Bower's work suggests that during the first year of life an infant is appreciably more advanced in his cognitive development than Piaget initially supposed and much other work points also in that direction (see the critical review by Gratch, 1977). By cognitive development is meant the steps through which an infant progresses which result in his behaviour no longer being dependent exclusively on immediate stimulus input but becoming, instead, guided by rules that enable him to combine perceptual information with information from memory. By means of these rules he becomes able to predict more or less accurately what is likely to happen in his world and to plan and respond accordingly.

Piaget was the first to point out that it is not until half way through the first year of life that an infant makes any attempt to search for some interesting object he has seen disappear. Before that age not only does he make no attempt to search for it but when, later, the same object reappears he treats it as though it were a different one (as judged by latency of response and allied measures). Out of sight seems, therefore, to be truly out of mind. The reason for this, Bower suggests, is that prior to five months an infant seems able to identify an object by means of only two of its many possible identifying characteristics, namely either that it remains in the same place or else that it follows a consistent trajectory. Such obvious features as the object's size, shape and colour on which adults usually rely to identify particular objects are not used during these early months.

From about five months onwards, however, a marked change occurs. Henceforward size, shape and colour come to have significance. One result of this is that an object that reappears after an interval is recognized and treated as being the same object. Another is that it is credited with having a continuing existence even when out of sight, as is shown by its being searched for. Admittedly, for many months an infant's searching is sadly ill-guided and he makes many strange mistakes. For example, at first, even after being allowed to watch where an object is being hidden, perhaps under a cloth, he will none the less search for it not where he saw it put, but either in the place where he had last seen it or else in a place where he had found it previously. Later, having come to realize that missing objects can be hidden in any of a great variety of places, he still has difficulty in realizing that hidden objects may be moved from one place to another inside a container. For example, if a coin is hidden under one of two similar cups and the cups are then transposed in his presence he will nevertheless look for the coin under the wrong cup, namely the one which is now in the place where he had last seen the coin. Only after he has reached fifteen months or more is it likely that he will be able to solve this problem.

Thus, even after an infant has begun searching for an object he has seen disappear, it is only step by step that his knowledge of where to look for it improves and results finally in an efficient performance. From these observations Piaget and other students of cognitive development infer that, during the later months of the first year and the early months of the second, infants are becoming increasingly able to conceive of an object as an entity that exists independently of themselves. During these stages of development an infant is said to be achieving the concept of object permanence.

Piaget's own experiments were done mainly with small objects like keys and matchboxes, and the question arises whether his conclusions regarding the development of the concept of an object apply equally to the development of the concept of a person. Evidence at present available suggests that in principle they do though there are certain differences; for example, an infant's knowledge of persons develops rather earlier than his knowledge of things, as Piaget himself confidently predicted. What is especially interesting, however, is that, also as Piaget predicted, his skill in searching for and finding persons in successively more difficult situations seems to progress step by step through all the same stages as does his skill in searching for things (Décarie 1965; Bell 1970; Brossard in Décarie 1974).

An infant's attachment to a discriminated mother-figure is developing fast between the fourth and seventh month. Perceptual recognition comes early; but because before five months his concept of object is still primitive, some strange behaviour is observed. For example, as we have seen, evidence suggests that an infant of about twelve weeks thinks that an object is defined either by the place it occupies or else by the trajectory it follows, not both. As yet, therefore, he seems not to realize that one object may be first in one place and then move to another; nor that it cannot be in two places simultaneously. Evidence in keeping with these ideas is that when an infant of less than five months is shown multiple images of his mother (presented by means of some optical device) he is not disturbed but interacts happily with each of the 'mothers' in turn. Should, however, one or two of the mother-images be replaced by those of strangers, he knows well whom he prefers. Once past the age of five months, by contrast, his grasp of the properties of objects is such that the sight of multiple images of his mother becomes highly disturbing: by now he knows he has but one mother and that she cannot be visually present in two, or three, places at once (although as we see later he is not always certain about this).

From these and other observations it can be inferred that during these middle months of the first year an infant is developing some elemental representation of his mother-figure. Yet for him to be able to recognize her when present is not the same as his being able to recall her when absent; and there is reason to think that the latter capacity is not developing until the final months of the first year. An illustration of this developmental step is a finding, reported by Schaffer (1971) and already described in Chapter 3 of Volume II. When an infant of six months is placed with his mother sitting out of sight behind him and is then confronted with a strange object he behaves as though his mother were not there. When, by contrast, an infant of twelve months is placed in the same situation he habitually turns round to refer to her before deciding how to respond. Thus, within these admittedly narrow limits of space and time, one-year-olds brought up at home have no difficulty in knowing where their visually absent mother is or in utilizing that knowledge.

In keeping with this, by the last quarter of the first year a secure infant whose mother is responsive to his signals, is happy to play on his own for a time evidently aware that his mother, though visually absent, is available nearby should he want her (Stayton and Ainsworth 1973).

Not unexpectedly infants differ greatly in the age at which they develop all these cognitive abilities, whether applied to inanimate objects or to so important a person as mother. As regards the latter, some infants are already showing a limited degree of skill in finding her by seven months and can solve all or most of the problems by nine. Others are slower by several months (Bell 1970; Brossard in Décarie 1974). Also not unexpectedly, the age at which an infant develops these abilities is much influenced by his experiences. An infant whose mother is responsive to his signals and engages in plenty of social interaction with him is likely to be more advanced than is one whose mother is less attentive. Because infants differ so much in the age during which they are achieving the concept of person permanence or, more precisely, mother permanence, any statements linking stages of cognitive or emotional development to chronological age have to be treated with caution.

As a child develops his concept of person permanence he becomes increasingly capable of representing to himself the whereabouts and doings of absent persons. Thus, during the early months of the second year, a healthily developing child is becoming able to draw on his general knowledge in order to deduce where a vanished person may have got to and how he got there. In illustration of this achievement Piaget cites an incident in which one of his children, Laurent, a few days short of eighteen months, was asked, successively, where absent members of the family were. In reply he pointed each time to where he supposed them to be, evidently influenced in his opinion either by where they had been an hour previously or else by knowledge of their habitual occupations.

From observations such as these cognitive psychologists conclude that most children aged eighteen months and older, who have been reared in attentive homes, are able not only to represent the external world symbolically but also to manipulate their representations. By so doing a child can recapitulate actions of the past and anticipate actions of the future, including reaching a solution to a problem by purely cognitive means and without resort to action. These cognitive achievements, Piaget believes, and with him many linguists, provide a child with a necessary (though perhaps not a sufficient) basis to start comprehending and producing language (Cromer 1974).[1]

Although the work of Piaget, and of others working in the same tradition, suggests that a child is not capable of recalling and using his representational model of the world in all these more complex ways before the middle of the second year, it also shows that he is capable none the less of various embryonic degrees of representation throughout the preceding twelve months. Thus, it is extremely misleading to speak as though a child's representational model of his attachment figure is absent before a certain age or stage of development and present thereafter. Instead, the model is to be thought of as developing during the middle months of the first year from which time it is available for recognition and elementary search and, as the months pass, is becoming increasingly available also for recall and for cognitive operations. This way of conceptualizing early development I believe to have much more

[1] Because a child's use of language lags far behind his use of non-verbal modes of representation there is a persistent tendency for adults to underestimate a young child's cognitive capacities.

explanatory potential than those traditionally advanced by psycho-analysts. The serious shortcomings of the much invoked concept of 'libidinal object constancy' are discussed shortly.

Fields about which we still know too little are the length of an infant's or young child's memory span and the conditions that enable him to recognize or recall significant people and places after varying lapses of time. What is known, however, suggests that during the early months an infant has a memory span for visual information a good deal longer than is sometimes supposed (see reviews by Cohen and Gelber 1975, and Olson 1976[2]). For example, Fagan (1973) presents evidence that an infant of five months shown the photograph of a face for only two minutes can still recognize it when presented to him two weeks later. In the light of that it is hardly surprising that Bower (1974) should have observed that infants aged five and six months brought into the laboratory for a second visit often reveal that they remember what happened during their visit of a day or so earlier and begin rehearsing their responses before testing begins; nor that Ainsworth and her colleagues (Ainsworth *et al.* 1978) should have observed that infants aged twelve months put through the strange situation sequence for a second time two weeks after the first clearly foresaw what was going to happen and responded accordingly. As regards the development of spontaneous recall our information is still negligible and it would therefore be unwise to draw conclusions. In particular, until far more knowledge is available it is rash to conclude, as some clinicians do, that a child younger than eighteen months is wholly unable without reminders from adults to recall persons and places after an interval longer than a day or two.

In conclusion, it should be noted that experimental studies of young children's skill in recognizing items after a lapse of time would lead us confidently to expect that a child's capacity to recognize and recall his mother would be developing weeks and probably months in advance of his capacity to recognize and recall anything or anyone else. The reasons for this lie partly in the fact that she has far greater emotional salience for him than does anything else and partly in the fact that he has far greater and far more varied experi-

[2] After reviewing the evidence Olson concludes that 'the simplest generalization is that infants in the range of 3 to 6 months do not forget visual stimuli very rapidly if they have had sufficiently long initial exposure and if there is relatively little specific interference'.

ence of interacting with her—through sight, sound, smell and touch —than he has with anything or anyone else.

Libidinal Object Constancy: An Unsatisfactory Concept

In discussing problems of childhood mourning many psycho-analysts invoke the concept of 'object constancy', sometimes expanded to 'libidinal object constancy'. Since I believe this to be a most unsatisfactory concept, I do not use it. As Fraiberg (1969) points out, the term has come to be employed in a number of quite different ways, the variations reflecting in part the mixed parentage of the concept and in part a shift in the meaning given to the word 'constancy'.

The concept was introduced by Hartmann (1952) in connection with the contrast between what was, and by some psychoanalysts still is, believed to be a phase of development when an infant has no interest in any 'object' (person) except at the moments when it (she) is satisfying his physiological needs, and a much later phase when he is thought to become emotionally attached to a discrimi-nated person: in Hartmann's words, 'there is a long way from the object that exists only as long as it is need-satisfying to that form of satisfactory object relations that includes object constancy . . .'. The following year Hartmann (1953) linked his new concept to Piaget's already established concept of object permanence. Partly as a result of this linkage and partly for other reasons psychoanalysts have come to use the term object constancy in no less than three distinct ways.

(a) One usage is simply to equate object constancy with Piaget's object permanence. This is how Spitz (1957) used it and also how it is used by Furman (1974).

(b) A second usage rejects any linkage to cognitive psychology and reserves the term to denote 'the child's capacity to keep up object cathexis irrespective of frustration or satisfaction', a phase postu-lated to be contrasted sharply with a previous phase during which a child is held to consider the object as 'non-existent, unnecessary' whenever 'no need or libidinal wish is present . . .' (A. Freud 1968). This usage is in keeping with Hartmann's original proposal and is adopted by Anna Freud and those influenced by her.

(c) A third usage, which grows out of the second but is not the same, applies object constancy to the stage of development when a child can 'remain away from the mother for some length of time and still function with emotional poise, provided he is in a fairly familiar environment' (Mahler 1966). In Mahler's scheme of development this capacity is regarded as developing during the fourth sub-phase of separation–individuation, which extends from about 25 to 36 months. In addition to Mahler herself, this usage is adopted by her associates Pine (1974) and McDevitt (1975).

As a result of these different usages the age at which a child is held to attain libidinal object constancy varies from six months to late in his third year.

Let us consider these three usages in the light of the scheme of development proposed in this work.

Since the first usage is synonymous with the terms 'object permanence' and 'person permanence' already established in the field of cognitive psychology, the new term is redundant. Furthermore, use of object constancy in this sense risks confusion with the term 'perceptual constancy' which refers to the ability to perceive an object as staying the same size, shape and colour despite changes in its orientation and lighting that alter how it appears to the eye. (According to Bower (1974) this ability is already in evidence by 22 weeks.)

The second usage assumes two distinct phases of development, an early phase lasting well into the second year during which the 'object' is believed to exist for a child only so long as it is need-satisfying and a later phase, that of object constancy, when that is no longer so. Since, however, the assumption that there are two such phases is out of keeping with the evidence, there is no need to introduce a special term.

The concept to which the third usage applies looks at first sight to be an equivalent of the concept of secure attachment as it is manifested in the behaviour of children towards the end of their third year and which I have discussed in earlier volumes, notably in Chapter 21 of Volume II. It is, however, a little different.

In Mahler's thinking, the assumption tends to be made that it is only when a child is becoming able to sustain short separations with equanimity, e.g. a morning in a playgroup, that we can properly credit him with having developed the capacity to evoke mental representations of his missing mother (e.g. Mahler 1966). This seems to imply that as soon as he is able to evoke a mental representation of her he will be able to sustain brief separations with equanimity. I see no evidence that these two developmental steps occur simultaneously. On the contrary, the evidence shows that the capacity to evoke a representational model develops independently of the ability to sustain separations of the kind proposed and that it usually precedes the latter by a year or two; indeed in the case of pathological development it may do so by an indefinitely long period. This means that, although the capacity to evoke a representational model is necessary if a child who is approaching his third birthday is to sustain such separations with equanimity, it is far from being a sufficient condition (a point also made by McDevitt 1975). For conditions to be sufficient not only has the current external situation to be a familiar one and the child himself healthy and unfatigued but the model of the missing mother that he evokes must represent her as being reliably accessible and also well disposed towards him. This is a development that evidence shows is dependent not only on the maturation of certain cognitive skills but also on the form the child's model of his mother takes, which is in turn dependent in high degree on how she treats him. Thus the development of secure attachment is conceived not simply as a maturational stage but as a step along certain only of the array of developmental pathways that are initially available to a child.[3]

Although for purposes of theory building the differences between these formulations are of considerable consequence, for purposes of treating patients they are not necessarily so. It is of interest, for example, that the therapeutic principles advocated by Fleming (1975) and which she derives from Mahler's developmental scheme are extremely close to those I have myself derived from attachment theory (Bowlby 1977).

The role of person permanence in determining responses to separation and loss

When data on how infants and very young children respond to the

[3] A child developing compulsive self-reliance may also show a capacity to sustain brief separations with what appears to be equanimity; but the representational model of his mother that he is presumed to have developed is of course a very different one.

temporary absence of mother-figure are examined in the light of the findings described earlier no incompatibilities are apparent. Indeed, each set of data illumines the other.

At about six months of age an infant, if mobile, will attempt to follow his mother out of the room and will greet her on her return. Yet at that age there is no reason to suppose that during her absence he has access to whatever germinal representation he may be developing of her. As an illustration of this (though no proof) we note that in the experiment by Schaffer (1971) referred to earlier, infants of six months behaved quite differently to those of twelve months. When confronted by a strange object not one of these younger infants turned round to refer to his mother standing immediately behind him. Instead, each seemed totally absorbed by the object before him and totally oblivious of his mother's proximity.

As another illustration we note that when infants of twenty-six weeks and less are placed in a strange place without mother they appear to accept strangers as mother-substitutes without noticeable change in level of responsiveness and show little or none of the protest and fretting typical of the slightly older child. From the age of seven months onwards however a child in this situation not only notices the change but, by protest and crying and also by persistent fretting and rejection of the strange nurses, indicates his intense dislike of it. Furthermore, on returning home after periods in hospital lasting as long as three weeks about half those aged 7 to 9 months and almost all those over ten months become extremely clinging and cry excessively whenever mother is absent.[4] These observations are clearly consistent with the hypothesis that during the third quarter of the first year an infant's representational model of his mother is becoming readily accessible to him for purposes of comparison during her absence and for recognition after her return. They are consistent also with the view that during these months an infant is developing a capacity to conceive of his mother as a person existing independently of himself.

Before he can talk the only evidence we have that a child is thinking about his absent parent derives from observations of his behaviour. Since, however, only very few observers have been alert to

[4] These observations, which are reported by H. R. Schaffer (Schaffer 1958; Schaffer and Callender 1959), are consistent with those reported by Spitz (1946a) in his pioneer work. See also Yarrow (1963) on the responses of infants after transfer to adopting parents.

the relevance of such observations our knowledge remains scanty. The few records available are therefore of much interest. One, observed during a longitudinal study undertaken by Margaret Mahler, is reported by McDevitt (1975). It records the fairly typical behaviour of an infant who had achieved some degree of person permanence and who was left by her mother in what (for the infant) was a fairly strange place.

One morning, when Donna was nine months and two weeks old, her expression suddenly became very solemn as she watched her mother leave the room. When the door closed, she started fussing; immediately she sat herself down and mouthed a toy. During the half hour her mother was gone, Donna was constantly on the verge of tears, could not be distracted easily, and looked at the door over and over again, often with a worried expression.[5]

During the second year of life there is no lack of records of children left in hospital or nursery watching the door through which a parent has departed, and doing so persistently for several days in the evident hope of seeing him or her return through it. An example is the sixteen-month-old Dawn who, left in a residential nursery, stood for days near the door fretting inconsolably (Chapter 24). Similarly, the hopes raised both in the seventeen-month-old Jane when on her fifth day away she noticed the gate of her parents' garden and in the sixteen-month-old Dawn when on her thirteenth day in the nursery she apparently mistook the female observer for her mother (described in the previous chapter) are wholly in keeping with what present knowledge of early cognitive development might lead us to expect.

Persons and Places: Consequences of the Close Mental Link

Earlier in the chapter it was noted that observation shows that when searching for a missing object an infant under twelve months is extremely likely to search for it wherever he last saw it or else where he last found it, and that he behaves similarly with his missing mother. Although this tendency to locate persons in special places, and to find it difficult to think of them as being anywhere else, diminishes during development, it seems not to disappear altogether. Indeed common experience suggests that it stays with many

[5] Although McDevitt notes that Donna was more sensitive than other children to her mother's comings and goings, he regards the form of her response as typical of the phase of development in which she was.

people throughout life.[6] To its persistence, I suggest, can be traced certain common features of mourning.

One is the strong tendency for a mourner, of any age, to have the vivid experience of seeing or hearing a dead relative in a place he used often to be in. Another is the possibly universal tendency for a mourner to think of the departed as being located somewhere definite—perhaps in the grave, or in heaven, or in one of his favourite haunts, or, as in Japan, in a special shrine—and why being able to do so commonly brings a sense of stability and comfort. Yet a further feature may be the perplexing tendency of a mourner sometimes to think of the person lost as being in both of two places simultaneously. An example is a bereaved child who both knows that his parent has gone for ever and also expects him or her to return shortly.

In his discussion of the development of person permanence Piaget (1937) has reported observations that seem to throw much light on how such incompatible belief systems may develop. The observations that follow[7] concern his younger daughter, Lucienne.

At 15 months Lucienne is in the garden with her mother. Her father arrives. She sees him come, recognizes him and smiles. Her mother then asks her: 'Where is Papa?' Curiously enough, instead of pointing straight to him Lucienne turns towards the window of his office where she is accustomed to seeing him and points there. A moment later the experiment is repeated. Though she has just seen her father no more than a yard or so away yet, when her mother says 'Papa', Lucienne at once turns again towards his office.

Three months later, when aged 18 months, Lucienne behaves in a similar way, this time in reference to her elder sister. For a week Jacqueline had been unwell and confined to bed, and Lucienne had visited her there. This day Jacqueline was able to get up and so Lucienne has been playing with her downstairs. Despite this, however, Lucienne later climbs the stairs, clearly expecting to find Jacqueline still in her bedroom.

Similar episodes occur when Lucienne is $2\frac{1}{2}$ years old and again at $3\frac{1}{2}$.

[6] Experiments by von Wright *et al.* (1975) suggest that it may be a basic characteristic of human information processing that the location of an item is coded and stored in memory, routinely and automatically, with other information about the item. The experiments, using pictures, were done with children and young adults at several age-levels from 5 years to 18–23 years, with similar results at all age-levels. It is possible therefore that a strong association of person with place is a special example of a general tendency.

[7] The accounts given are abstracts of material presented in Observation 51 on pp. 58–9 of the English translation of 1955.

On the latter occasion, after seeing her godfather depart at the end of a visit, Lucienne returns to the house and goes straight to the room in which he had slept. 'I want to see if godfather has left,' she announces. Then, entering the room alone, she assures herself, 'Yes, he has gone.'

Not only do these observations demonstrate how closely tied to a particular location a person is in the world of a young child but they show also how easily this leads to a person being conceived as being in two places virtually at once. Furthermore, they call sharply in question the notions that such 'splits in the ego' are necessarily as pathological as it is customary for clinical theorists to suppose and that their origins must go back to the earliest months of life. On the contrary, Piaget's observations and conclusions strongly support the view, expressed in earlier chapters, that incompatible beliefs of this sort are of normal occurrence at all ages and that whether they lead to pathology turns on how much opportunity a bereaved child or older person has of discussing his uncertainties with an understanding and trusted companion.

Relevance to a Theory of Mourning

In the light of these ideas and of the observations reported earlier, there seem good grounds for attributing a germinal capacity for mourning to young children at least from sixteen months onwards. This implies that, as in the case of Jane, they have the ability to construct and to retain an image of their absent mother, to distinguish mother from foster-mother and to know well whom they prefer. It implies too that they relinquish the missing figure only reluctantly and that, when given the opportunity, become attached to the new figure only gradually.

At first it seems likely that the length of time during which the distinction between old and new and preference for the old can be maintained is a matter of weeks rather than months; and until about the second birthday doing so may require the active co-operation of the foster-mother. The reason for conceptualizing the responses of children of this age in the same terms as those of older children and adults is that the ontogenetic continuity of the responses is thereby emphasized so that differences of response at different ages can then be studied as variations on a common theme.

How best to characterize the responses of children aged between about six months and sixteen months, however, remains a puzzle. If the cognitive psychologists are right in believing that a child of less than about seventeen months has only the most limited capacity for symbolic functioning the term mourning may be inappropriate. Yet throughout this age-range a child shows manifest distress when his familiar attachment figure is missing and as the months pass searches for her with an increasing degree of competence. Even when he is receiving skilled foster-care, distress at separation and elements of search are present; and after reunion he shows a degree of recovery, the speed and extent of which turns both on the length of the separation and the conditions of care during it. Because the distress is so clearly a response to the absence of a highly discriminated individual there is, at the least, good reason to continue the practice of referring to it as grieving, as has for long been customary (see Chapter 1).

In considering these matters I am of course aware that much of the debate about whether very young children mourn arose as a result of the opinions I expressed in papers published during the late nineteen-fifties and early sixties. In those papers my aim was to emphasize that a child's attachment to a mother-figure develops during the first year of life, to a large extent independently of whoever feeds him, that after six months he is overtly distressed when he loses his mother and that, whatever the differences may be when the responses of the earliest years are compared to those of later ones, the similarities are both evident and important. Nothing in the subsequent debate—neither empirical observation nor theoretical argument—leads me to change that opinion.

Where my position has changed is that I now give much more weight than formerly to the influence on a child's responses of the conditions in which he is cared for whilst he is away from his mother, whether the separation be temporary or permanent. With regard to this the work of the Robertsons with children in their second and third years has been especially valuable by calling attention to the mitigating effects of good foster-care. Yet here again I am struck as much by the similarities in the ways that very young children, older children and adults respond as by any differences. For it is by no means only the responses to loss of very young children that are influenced by the family conditions that obtain after the loss. The same is true, as we saw in Chapters 15, 19 and 21, in regard to older children and adolescents; and the same again, as we saw in Chapter 10, in regard to adults. Indeed, in preparing this volume nothing has impressed me more deeply than the evidence showing the pervasive influence at all ages of the pattern of a human being's family life on the way he responds to loss.

Epilogue

This brings an already overlong work to an end. Most of the problems with which I set out have been explored and to aid their solution a new conceptual framework has been proposed.

Throughout the work I have concentrated on problems of aetiology and psychopathology, believing that it will only be when we have a good grasp of what the causes are of psychiatric disorder and how they operate that we shall be in a position to develop effective measures either for their treatment or for their prevention. My strategy has been to select one set of putative causal factors—the disruption or threatened disruption of an affectional bond—and to trace the consequences; and in doing so to identify so far as possible those other conditions that, occurring before, during or after the disruption, influence the consequences for better or worse. From an examination of the evidence, drawn from many disciplines and many lands, it has been possible to indicate how certain combinations of circumstance lead to certain forms of personality disturbance and how these affect not only the individual but almost invariably members of his family as well. Among such disturbances are to be counted many common clinical disorders, including states of anxiety and phobia, of depression and suicide, and also disturbances of parenting and marriage. Together, these are the kinds of disorder from which suffer a majority of all those who claim the attention of clinical workers in the Western world today.

Nevertheless, although disruptions of bonds, and experiences related to or consequent upon disruption, undoubtedly play a causal role in these and other conditions, we remain ignorant of how large a causal role they play and in precisely what circumstances they play it. In order to find out, continuing research, using a broad range of methods, will be necessary. Only when that is done, and the conceptual framework itself refined, elaborated and tested, shall we know how productive the enquiry described will turn out to be.

Meanwhile, there are conclusions on which I believe we can rely.

441

Intimate attachments to other human beings are the hub around which a person's life revolves, not only when he is an infant or a toddler or a schoolchild but throughout his adolescence and his years of maturity as well, and on into old age. From these intimate attachments a person draws his strength and enjoyment of life and, through what he contributes, he gives strength and enjoyment to others. These are matters about which current science and traditional wisdom are at one.

We may therefore hope that, despite all its deficiencies, our present knowledge may be sound enough to guide us in our efforts to help those already beset by difficulty and above all to prevent others becoming so.

Bibliography

Ablon, J. (1971). 'Bereavement in a Samoan Community.' *Brit. J. med. Psychol.* 44: 329–37.

Abraham, K. (1911). 'Notes on the Psycho-analytical Investigation and Treatment of Manic Depressive Insanity and Allied Conditions.' In Abraham, *Selected Papers on Psycho-analysis.* London: Hogarth, 1927. New edition, London: Hogarth, 1949; New York: Basic Books, 1953.

Abraham, K. (1924a). 'A Short Study of the Development of the Libido.' In Abraham, *Selected Papers on Psycho-analysis.* London: Hogarth, 1927. New edition, London: Hogarth 1949; New York: Basic Books, 1953.

Abraham, K. (1924b). 'The Influence of Oral-erotism on Character Formation.' In Abraham, *Selected Papers on Psycho-analysis.* London: Hogarth, 1927. New edition, London: Hogarth, 1949; New York: Basic Books, 1953.

Abraham, K. (1925). 'Character-formation on the Genital Level of Libido-development.' In Abraham, *Selected Papers on Psycho-analysis.* London: Hogarth, 1927. New edition, London, Hogarth, 1949; New York: Basic Books, 1953.

Adam, K. S. (1973). 'Childhood Parental Loss, Suicidal Ideation and Suicidal Behaviour.' In E. J. Anthony & C. Koupernik (eds.), *The Child in his Family; The Impact of Disease and Death.* New York and London: John Wiley.

Ainsworth, M. D., & Boston, M. (1952). 'Psychodiagnostic Assessments of a Child after Prolonged Separation in Early Childhood.' *Brit. J. med. Psychol.* 25: 169–201.

Ainsworth, M. D., Blehar, M. C., Waters, E., & Wall, S. (1978). *Patterns of Attachment: Assessed in the Strange Situation and at Home.* Hillsdale, N.J.: Lawrence Erlbaum.

Albino, R. C., & Thompson, V. J. (1956). 'The Effects of Sudden Weaning on Zulu Children.' *Brit. J. med. Psychol.* 29: 177–210.

Anderson, C. (1949). 'Aspects of Pathological Grief and Mourning.' *Int. J. Psycho-Anal,* 30: 48–55.

Anthony, E. J. (1973). 'A Working Model for Family Studies.' In E. J. Anthony & C. Koupernik (eds.), *The Child in his Family: The Impact of Disease and Death.* New York & London: John Wiley.

Anthony, S. (1971). *The Discovery of Death in Childhood and After.* London: Allen Lane, The Penguin Press.

Arthur, B. (1972). Parent suicide: A Family Affair. In A. C. Cain (ed.), *Survivors of Suicide.* Springfield, Illinois: C. C. Thomas.

443

Arthur, B., & Kemme, M. L. (1964). 'Bereavement in Childhood.' *J. Child Psychol. Psychiat.* **5**: 37–49.

Averill, J. R. (1968). 'Grief: Its Nature and Significance.' *Psychol. Bull.* **70**: 721–48.

Balint, M. (1952). 'New Beginning and the Paranoid and the Depressive Syndromes.' In Balint (ed.), *Primary Love and Psycho-Analytic Technique*. London: Hogarth, 1953.

Balint, M. (1960). 'Primary Narcissism and Primary Love.' *Psychoanal. Quart.* **29**: 6–43.

Barnes, M. J. (1964). 'Reactions to the Death of a Mother.' *Psychoanal. Study Child.* **19**: 334–57.

Barry, H. Jnr, Barry, H. III, & Lindemann, E. (1965). 'Dependency in Adult Patients following Early Maternal Bereavement.' *J. Nerv. Ment. Dis.* **140**: 196–206.

Beck, A. T. (1967). *Depression: Clinical, Experimental and Theoretical Aspects.* London: Staples Press; New York: Harper & Row. Republished by University of Pennsylvania Press with changed sub-title *Depression: Causes and Treatment*, 1972.

Beck, A. T., & Rush, A. J. (1978). 'Cognitive Approaches to Depression and Suicide.' In G. Serban (ed.), *Cognitive Defects in the Development of Mental Illness*. New York: Brunner Mazel.

Becker, D., & Margolin, F. (1967). 'How Surviving Parents Handled their Young Children's Adaptation to the Crisis of Loss.' *Amer J. Orthopsychiat.* **37**: 753–57.

Becker, H. (1933). 'The Sorrow of Bereavement.' *J. Amer. Soc. Psychol.* **27**: 391–410.

Bedell, J. (1973). 'The Maternal Orphan: Paternal Perceptions of Mother Loss.' Presented at symposium on bereavement, New York, Nov. 1973. Foundation of Thanatology.

Bell, S. M. (1970). 'The Development of the Concept of Object as related to Infant–Mother Attachment.' *Child Dev.* **41**: 291–311.

Bemporad, J. (1971). 'New Views on the Psycho-dynamics of the Depressive Character.' In S. Arieti (ed.), *World Biennial of Psychiatry and Psychotherapy*, Vol. 1. New York: Basic Books.

Bendiksen, R., & Fulton, R. (1975). 'Death and the Child: An Anterospective Test of the Childhood Bereavement and Later Behaviour Disorder Hypothesis.' *Omega* **6**: 45–59.

Berg, I. (1976). 'School Phobia in the Children of Agoraphobic Women.' *Brit. J. Psychiat.* **128**: 86–9.

Berg, I., Butler, A., & Hall, G. (1976). 'The Outcome of Adolescent School Phobia.' *Brit. J. Psychiat.* **128**: 80–5.

Bernfeld, S. (1925, Eng. trans. 1929). *The Psychology of the Infant.* London: Kegan Paul.

Bibring, E. (1953). 'The Mechanisms of Depression.' In P. Greenacre (ed.), *Affective Disorders*. New York: International Universities Press.

Binger, C. M., Ablin, A. R., Fuerstein, R. C., Kushner, J. H., Zoger, S., & Mikkelsen, C. (1969). 'Childhood Leukemia: Emotional Impact on Patient and Family.' *New England J. Med.* **280**: 414–18.

Binion, R. (1973). 'Hitler's Concept of Lebensraum: The Psychological Basis.' *History of Childhood Quarterly* **1**: 187–215.

Birtchnell, J. (1971). 'Early Death in relation to Sibship Size and Composition in Psychiatric Patients and General Population Controls.' *Acta Psychiatrica Scandinavica* **47**: 250–70.

Birtchnell, J. (1972). 'Early Parent Death and Psychiatric Diagnosis.' *Social Psychiat.* **7**: 202–10.

Birtchnell, J. (1975a). 'The Personality Characteristics of Early-bereaved Psychiatric Patients.' *Social Psychiat.* **10**: 97–103.

Birtchnell, J. (1975b). 'Psychiatric Breakdown following Recent Parent Death.' *Brit. J. med. Psychol.* **48**: 379–90.

Bond, D. D. (1953). 'The Common Psychological Defense to Stressful Situations and the Patterns of Breakdown when they Fail.' In *Symposium on Stress*, sponsored jointly by the Division of Medical Sciences National Research Council and the Army Medical Service Graduate School, Walter Reed Army Medical Center, Washington D.C., March 1953.

Bonnard, A. (1961). 'Truancy and Pilfering associated with Bereavement.' In S. Lorand & H. Schneer (eds.), *Adolescents*. New York: Hoeber.

Bornstein, P. E., Clayton, P. J., Halikas, J. A., Maurice, W. L., & Robins, E. (1973). 'The Depression of Widowhood after Thirteen Months.' *Brit. J. Psychiat.* **122**: 561–6.

Bower, T. G. R. (1974). *Development in Infancy*. San Francisco: W. H. Freeman.

Bowlby, J. (1944). 'Forty-four Juvenile Thieves: Their Characters and Home Life'. *Int. J. Psycho-Anal.* **25**, 19–52 and 107–27.

Bowlby, J. (1951). *Maternal Care and Mental Health*. Geneva: WHO; London: HMSO; New York: Columbia University Press. Abridged version, *Child Care and the Growth of Love*. Harmondsworth, Middx: Penguin Books, second edition, 1965.

Bowlby, J. (1953). 'Some Pathological Processes Set in Train by Early Mother–Child Separation.' *J. ment. Sci.* **99**: 265–72.

Bowlby, J. (1954). 'Psychopathological Processes Set in Train by Early Mother–Child Separation.' In *Proceedings of Seventh Conference on Infancy and Childhood* (March 1953). New York: Jos. Macy Jnr Foundation.

Bowlby, J. (1957). 'An Ethological Approach to Research in Child Development.' *Brit. J. med. Psychol.* **30**: 230–40. Reprinted in Bowlby 1979.

Bowlby, J. (1958). 'The Nature of the Child's Tie to his Mother.' *Int. J. Psycho-Anal.* **39**: 350–73.

Bowlby, J. (1960a). 'Separation Anxiety.' *Int. J. Psycho-Anal.* **41**, 89–113.

Bowlby, J. (1960b). 'Grief and Mourning in Infancy and Early Child-hood.' *Psychoanal. Study Child* 15: 9–52.

Bowlby, J. (1960c). 'Ethology and the Development of Object Relations.' *Int. J. Psycho-Anal.* 41: 313–17.

Bowlby, J. (1961a). 'Separation Anxiety: A Critical Review of the Literature.' *J. Child Psychol. and Psychiat.* 1: 251–69.

Bowlby, J. (1961b). 'Processes of Mourning.' *Int. J. Psycho-Anal.* 42: 317–40.

Bowlby, J. (1961c). 'Childhood Mourning and its Implications for Psychiatry.' *Amer. J. Psychiat.* 118: 481–98. Reprinted in Bowlby 1979.

Bowlby, J. (1963). 'Pathological Mourning and Childhood Mourning.' *J. Am. psychoanal. Ass.* 11: 500–41.

Bowlby, J. (1977). 'The Making and Breaking of Affectional Bonds.' *Brit. J. Psychiat.* 130: 201–10 and 421–31. Reprinted in Bowlby 1979.

Bowlby, J. (1979). *The Making and Breaking of Affectional Bonds.* London: Tavistock Publications.

Bowlby, J., Robertson, J., & Rosenbluth, D. (1952). 'A Two-year-old Goes to Hospital.' *Psychoanal. Study Child* 7:82–94.

Bozeman, M. F., Orbach, C. E., & Sutherland, A. M. (1955). 'Psychological Impact of Cancer and its treatment.' III The Adaptation of Mothers to the Threatened Loss of their Children through Leukemia: Part I. *Cancer* 8: 1–19.

Brown, F. (1961). 'Depression and Childhood Bereavement.' *J. ment. Sci.* 107: 754–77.

Brown, G. W., & Harris, T. (1978a). *The Social Origins of Depression: A Study of Psychiatric Disorder in Women.* London: Tavistock Publications.

Brown, G. W., & Harris, T. (1978b). 'Social Origins of Depression: A Reply.' *Psychol. Med.* 8: 577–88.

Brown, G. W., Harris, T., & Copeland, J. R. (1977). 'Depression and Loss.' *Brit. J. Psychiat.* 130: 1–18.

Bunch, J. (1972). 'Recent Bereavement in Relation to Suicide.' *J. Psychosomat. Res.* 16: 361–6.

Bunney, W. E. and others (1972). 'The "Switch Process" in Manic-depressive Illness.' Parts I, II and III. *Arch. Gen. Psychiat.* 27: 295–319.

Burlingham, D., & Freud, A. (1942). *Young Children in War-time.* London: Allen & Unwin.

Burlingham, D., & Freud, A. (1944). *Infants Without Families.* London: Allen and Unwin.

Cain, A. C. (ed.) (1972). *Survivors of Suicide.* Springfield, Illinois: C. C. Thomas.

Cain, A. C., & Cain, B. S. (1964). 'On Replacing a Child.' *J. Amer. Acad. Child Psychiat.* 3: 443–56.

Cain, A. C., & Fast, I. (1972). 'Children's Disturbed Reactions to Parent

Suicide. In Cain (ed.), *Survivors of Suicide*. Springfield, Illinois: C. C. Thomas.

Caplan, G. (1964). *Principles of Preventive Psychiatry*. New York: Basic Books.

Casey, K. L. (1973). 'Pain: A Current View of Neural Mechanisms.' *Amer. Scientist* **61**: 194–200.

Cecil, D. (1969). *Visionary and Dreamer*. London: Constable.

Chodoff, P., Friedman, S. B., & Hamburg, D. A. (1964). 'Stress, Defenses and Coping Behaviour: Observations on Parents of Children with Malignant Disease.' *Amer. J. Psychiat.* **120**: 743–9.

Clayton, P. J. (1975). 'The Effect of Living Alone on Bereavement Symptoms.' *Amer. J. Psychiat.* **132**: 133–7.

Clayton, P. J., Desmarais, L., & Winokur, G. (1968). 'A Study of Normal Bereavement.' *Amer. J. Psychiat.* **125**: 168–78.

Clayton, P. J., Halikas, J. A., & Maurice, W. L. (1972). 'The Depression of Widowhood.' *Brit. J. Psychiat.* **120**: 71–8.

Clayton, P. J., Halikas, J. A., Maurice, W. L., & Robins, E. (1973). 'Anticipatory Grief and Widowhood.' *Brit. J. Psychiat.* **122**: 47–51.

Clayton, P. J., Herjanic, M., Murphy, G. E., & Woodruff, R. Jnr (1974). 'Mourning and Dreams: Their Similarities and Differences.' *Can. Psychiat. Ass. Journal* **19**: 309–12.

Cohen, M. B., Baker, G., Cohen, R. A., Fromm-Reichmann, F., & Weigert, E. (1954). 'An Intensive Study of Twelve Cases of Manic-depressive Psychosis.' *Psychiatry* **17**: 103–37.

Cohen, L. B., & Gelber, E. R. (1975). 'Infant Visual Memory.' In L. B. Cohen & P. Salapatek (eds.), *Infant Perception: From Sensation to Cognition, Vol. I: Basic Visual Processes*. New York: Academic Press.

Corney, R. T., & Horton, F. J. (1974). 'Pathological Grief following Spontaneous Abortion.' *Amer. J. Psychiat.* **131**: 825–7.

Cromer, R. F. (1974). 'The Development of Language and Cognition: The Cognition Hypothesis.' In B. Foss (ed.), *New Perspectives in Child Development*. Harmondsworth, Middx: Penguin Books.

Darwin, C. (1872). *The Expression of the Emotions in Man and Animals*. London: Murray.

Décarie, T. Gouin (1965). *Intelligence and Affectivity in Early Childhood*. New York: International Universities Press.

Décarie, T. Gouin (1974). *The Infant's Reaction to Strangers*. New York: International Universities Press.

Deutsch, H. (1937). 'Absence of Grief.' *Psychoanal. Quart.* **6**: 12–22.

Dixon, N. F. (1971). *Subliminal Perception: The Nature of a Controversy*. London: McGraw-Hill.

Dunbar, J. (1970). *J. M. Barrie: The Man Behind the Image*. London: Collins.

Durkheim, E. (1915). *The Elementary Forms of the Religious Life*. London: Allen & Unwin.

447

Eliot, T. D. (1930). 'The Bereaved Family.' *Ann. Amer. Political and Social Sciences* 160: 184–90.

Eliot, T. D. (1955). 'Bereavement: Inevitable but not Insurmountable.' In H. Becker & R. Hill (eds.), *Family, Marriage and Parenthood*. Boston: Heath.

Engel, G. (1961). 'Is Grief a Disease?' *Psychosomat. med.* 23: 18–22.

Engel, G., & Reichsman, F. (1956). 'Spontaneous and Experimentally Induced Depressions in an Infant with a Gastric Fistula.' *J. Amer. Psychoanal. Ass.* 4: 428–52.

Erdelyi, M. H. (1974). 'A New Look at the New Look: Perceptual Defense and Vigilance.' *Psychol. Rev.* 81: 1–25.

Erikson, E. H. (1950). *Childhood and Society*. New York: W. W. Norton. Revised edition, Harmondsworth, Middx: Penguin Books, 1965.

Fagan, J. F. (1973). 'Infants' Delayed Recognition Memory and Forgetting.' *J. Experimental Child Psychol.* 16: 424–50.

Fast, I., & Chethik, M. (1976). 'Aspects of Depersonalization–derealization in the Experience of Children.' *Int. Rev. Psycho-Anal.* 3: 483–90.

Fairbairn, W. R. D. (1941). 'A Revised Psychopathology of the Psychoses and Psychoneuroses.' *Int. J. Psycho-Anal.* 22. Reprinted in *Psychoanalytic Studies of the Personality*. London: Tavistock Publications, 1952. Also in *Object-Relations Theory of the Personality*. New York: Basic Books, 1954.

Fairbairn, W. R. D. (1952). *Psychoanalytic Studies of the Personality*. London: Tavistock Publications. Published under the title of *Object-Relations Theory of the Personality*. New York: Basic Books, 1954.

Fenichel, O. (1945). *The Psychoanalytic Theory of Neurosis*. New York: Norton.

Ferguson, S. (1973). *A Guard Within*. London: Chatto & Windus.

Firth, R. (1961). *Elements of Social Organization*, 3rd edition. London: Tavistock Publications.

Flavell, J. H. (1974). 'The Development of Inferences about Others.' In T. Mischel (ed.), *On Understanding Other Persons*. Oxford: Blackwell.

Fleming, J. (1975). 'Some Observations on Object Constancy in the Psychoanalysis of Adults.' *J. Amer. Psychoanal. Ass.* 23: 742–59.

Fleming, J., & Altschul, S. (1963). 'Activation of Mourning and Growth by Psycho-analysis,' *Int. J. Psycho-Anal.* 44: 419–31.

Fraiberg, S. (1969). 'Libidinal Object Constancy and Mental Representation.' *Psychoanal. Study Child* 24: 9–47.

Frazer, J. G. (1933–4). *The Fear of the Dead in Primitive Religion*, 2 vols. London: Macmillan.

Freud, A. (1949). 'Certain Types and Stages of Social Maladjustment.' In K. R. Eissler (ed.), *Searchlights on Delinquency*. London: Imago.

Freud, A. (1960). 'A Discussion of Dr. John Bowlby's Paper "Grief and Mourning in Infancy and Early Childhood".' *Psychoanal. Study Child* 15: 53–62.

Freud, A. (1968). Contribution to Panel Discussion, 25th I.P.A. Conference, Amsterdam, 1967. *Int. J. Psycho-Anal.* **49**: 506–12.

Freud, A., & Burlingham, D. (1943). *War and Children.* New York: International Universities Press.

Freud, A., & Burlingham, D. (1974). *Infants Without Families and Reports on the Hampstead Nurseries 1939–1945.* London: Hogarth.

Freud, A., & Dann, S. (1951). 'An Experiment in Group Upbringing.' *Psychoanal. Study Child* **6**: 127–68.

Freud, E. L. (ed.) (1961). *Letters of Sigmund Freud.* London: Hogarth; New York: Basic Books.

Freud, S. (1912). 'The Dynamics of the Transference.' *SE* **12**: 97–108.[1]

Freud, S. (1912–13). *Totem and Taboo. SE* **13**: 1–162.

Freud, S. (1917). 'Mourning and Melancholia.' *SE* **14**: 243–58.

Freud. S. (1920). 'A Case of Homosexuality in a Woman.' *SE* **18**: 147–72.

Freud, S. (1921). *Group Psychology and the Analysis of the Ego. SE* **18**: 67–143.

Freud, S. (1923). *The Ego and the Id. SE* **19**: 12–66.

Freud, S. (1926). *Inhibitions, Symptoms and Anxiety. SE* **20**: 87–172.

Freud, S. (1927). 'Fetishism.' *SE* **21**: 149–57.

Freud, S. (1933). *New Introductory Lectures on Psycho-Analysis. SE* **22**: 7–182.

Freud, S. (1938). 'Splitting of the Ego in the Defensive Process.' *SE* **23**: 271–8.

Freud, S. (1954). *The Origins of Psychoanalysis: Letters to Wilhelm Fliess 1887–1902.* London: Imago.

Friedman, R. J., & Katz, M. M. (eds.) (1974). *The Psychology of Depression.* New York and London: John Wiley.

Friedman, S. B., Mason, J. W., & Hamburg, D. A. (1963). 'Urinary 17-hydroxycorticosteroid Levels in Parents of Children with Neoplastic Disease.' *Psychosom. Med.* **25**: 364–76.

Friedman, S. B., Chodoff, P., Mason, J. W., & Hamburg, D. A. (1963). 'Behavioral Observations on Parents Anticipating the Death of a Child.' *Pediatrics* **32**: 610–25.

Furman, E. (1974), *A Child's Parent Dies: Studies in Childhood Bereavement.* New Haven & London: Yale University Press.

Furman, R. A. (1964a). 'Death and the Young Child: Some Preliminary Considerations.' *Psychoanal. Study Child* **19**: 321–33.

Furman, R. A. (1964b). 'Death of a Six-year-old's Mother during his Analysis.' *Psychoanal. Study Child* **19**: 377–97.

Furman, R. A. (1968). 'Additional Remarks on Mourning and the Young Child.' *Bull. Philadelphia Ass. of Psychoanalysis* **18**: 51–64.

[1] The abbreviation *SE* denotes the Standard Edition of *The Complete Psychological Works of Sigmund Freud*, published in 24 volumes by the Hogarth Press Ltd, London and distributed in America by W. W. Norton, New York.

Furman, R. A. (1969). 'Sally'. In R. A. Furman & A. Katan (eds.), *The Therapeutic Nursery School*. New York: International Universities Press.

Furman, R. A. (1973). 'A Child's Capacity for Mourning.' In E. J. Anthony & C. Koupernik (eds.), *The Child in his Family: The Impact of Disease and Death*. New York: John Wiley.

Gardner, A., & Pritchard, M. (1977). 'Mourning, Mummification and Living with the Dead.' *Brit. J. Psychiat.* **130**: 23–8.

Garnett, D. (ed.) (1970). *Carrington: Letters and Abstracts from her Diaries*. London: Jonathan Cape.

Gartley, W., & Bernasconi, M. (1967). 'The Concept of Death in Children.' *J. Genet. Psychol.* **110**: 71–85.

Gero, G. (1936). 'The Construction of Depression.' *Int. J. Psycho-Anal.* **17**: 423–61.

Glick, I. O., Weiss, R. S., & Parkes, C. M. (1974). *The First Year of Bereavement*. New York: John Wiley, Interscience.

Glover, E. (1932). 'A Psycho-analytic Approach to the Classification of Mental Disorders.' *J. ment. Sci.* **78**, reprinted in *On the Early Development of Mind* by E. Glover. London: Imago (later by Allen & Unwin).

Gorer, G. (1965). *Death, Grief and Mourning in Contemporary Britain*. London: Tavistock Publications.

Gorer, G. (1973). 'Death, Grief and Mourning in Britain.' In E. J. Anthony & C. Koupernik (eds.), *The Child in his Family: The Impact of Disease and Death*. New York: John Wiley.

Granville-Grossman, K. L. (1968). 'The Early Environment of Affective Disorders.' In A. Coppen & A. Walk (eds.), *Recent Developments of Affective Disorders*. London: Headley Bros.

Gratch, G. (1977). 'Review of Piagetian Infancy Research; Object Concept Development.' In W. F. Overton & J. H. Gallagher (eds.), *Knowledge and Development*, Vol. 1. New York and London: Plenum Press.

Great Britain (1975). Office of Population Censuses and Surveys. *The Registrar-General's Statistical Review of England and Wales for the Year 1973*, Part I (A), tables, medical. London: HMSO.

Great Britain (1976). Office of Population Censuses and Surveys. *The Registrar-General's Statistical Review of England and Wales for the Year 1973*, Part I (B), tables, medical. London: HMSO.

Greer, S., Gunn, J. C., & Koller, K. M. (1966). 'Aetiological Factors in Attempted Suicides.' *Brit. Med. J.* **2**: 1352–5.

Halton, W. (1973). 'A Latency Boy's Reaction to his Father's Death.' *J. Child Psychotherapy* **3**: No. 3, 27–34.

Halpern, W. I. (1972). 'Some Psychiatric Sequelae to Crib Death.' *Amer. J. Psychiat.* **129**: 398–402.

Hamburg, D. A., Hamburg, B. A., & Barchas, J. D. (1975). 'Anger and Depression in Perspective of Behavioral Biology.' In L. Levi (ed.), *Parameters of Emotion*. New York: Raven Press.

Hansburg, H. G. (1972). *Adolescent Separation Anxiety: A Method for the Study of Adolescent Separation Problems.* Springfield, Illinois: C. C. Thomas.

Harris, M. (1973). 'The Complexity of Mental Pain Seen in a Six-year-old Child following Sudden Bereavement.' *J. Child Psychotherapy*, 3, No. 3, 35-45.

Harrison, S. I., Davenport, C. W., & McDermott, J. F. Jnr (1967). 'Children's Reactions to Bereavement: Adult Confusions and Misperceptions.' *Arch. Gen. Psychiat.* **17**: 593-7.

Hartmann, H. (1952). 'The Mutual Influences in the Development of Ego and Id.' *Psychoanal. Study Child* 7: 9-30, reprinted in *Essays on Ego Psychology* by H. Hartmann. New York: International Universities Press, 1964.

Hartmann, H. (1953). 'Contribution to the Metapsychology of Schizophrenia.' *Psychoanal. Study Child* 8: 177-98, reprinted in *Essays on Ego Psychology* by H. Hartmann. New York: International Universities Press, 1964.

Heinicke, C. M. (1956). 'Some Effects of Separating Two-year-old Children from their Parents: A Comparative study.' *Hum. Rel.* **9**: 105-76.

Heinicke, C. M., & Westheimer, I. (1966). *Brief Separations.* New York: International Universities Press; London: Longmans.

Hilgard, E. R. (1964). 'The Motivational Relevance of Hypnosis.' In D. Levine (ed.), *Nebraska Symposium on Motivation*, Vol. 12. Lincoln, Neb.: University of Nebraska Press.

Hilgard, E. R. (1973). 'A Neodissociation Interpretation of Pain Reduction in Hypnosis.' *Psychol. Rev.* **80**: 396-411.

Hilgard, E. R. (1974). 'Toward a Neo-dissociation Theory: Multiple Cognitive Controls in Human Functioning.' *Perspectives in Biology and Med.* **17**: 301-16.

Hilgard, J. R., & Newman, M. F. (1959). 'Anniversaries in Mental Illness.' *Psychiatry* **22**: 113-21.

Hilgard, J. R., Newman, M. F., & Fisk, F. (1960). 'Strength of Adult Ego following Childhood Bereavement. *Amer. J. Orthopsychiat.* **30**: 788-98.

Hobson, C. J. (1964). 'Widows of Blackton.' *New Society* 24 Sept. 1964.

Hofer, M. A., Wolff, C. T., Friedman, S. B., & Mason, J. W. (1972). 'A Psychoendocrine Study of Bereavement.' *Psychosomat. Med.* **34**: 481-504.

Horn, G. (1965). 'Physiological and Psychological Aspects of Selective Perception.' In D. Lehrman, R. A. Hinde, & E. Shaw (eds.), *Advances in the Study of Animal Behaviour*, Vol. 1. New York: Academic Press.

Horn, G. (1976). 'Physiological Studies of Attention and Arousal.' In T. Desiraju (ed.), *Mechanisms in Transmission of Signals for Conscious Behaviour.* Amsterdam: Elsevier.

Jacobson, E. (1943). 'Depression: The Oedipus Conflict in the Development of Depressive Mechanisms.' *Psychoanal. Quart.* **12**: 541-60.

Jacobson, E. (1946). 'The Effect of Disappointment on Ego and Super-ego Formation in Normal and Depressive Development.' *Psychoanal. Rev.* 33: 129–47.

Jacobson, E. (1957). 'Denial and Repression.' *J. Amer. Psychoanal. Assoc.* 5: 61–92.

Jacobson, E. (1965). 'The Return of the Lost Parent'. In M. Schur (ed.), *Drives, Affects, Behaviour*. New York: International Universities Press.

Jeffcoate, W. J. and others (1978). 'β-endorphin in Human Cerebrospinal Fluid.' *Lancet* 2: 119–21.

Jones, E. (1953). *Sigmund Freud: Life and Work*, Vol. 1. London: Hogarth; New York: Basic Books.

Kaplan, D. M., & Mason, E. A. (1960). 'Maternal Reactions to Premature Birth Viewed as an Acute Emotional Disorder.' *Amer. J. Orthopsychiat.* 30: 539–47.

Kaplan, D. M., Smith, A., Grobstein, R., & Fischman, S. E. (1973). 'Family Mediation of Stress.' *Social Work* 18: 60–9.

Kay, D. W., Roth, M., & Hopkins, B. (1955). 'Aetiological Factors in the Causation of Affective Disorders in Old Age.' *J. ment. Sci.* 101: 302–16.

Keddie, K. M. G. (1977). 'Pathological Mourning after the Death of a Domestic Pet.' *Brit. J. Psychiat.* 131: 21–5.

Kennard, E. A. (1937). 'Hopi Reactions to Death.' *Amer. Anthropologist* 29: 491–4.

Klagsbrun, M., & Bowlby, J. (1976). 'Responses to Separation from Parents: A Clinical Test for Young Children.' *Brit. J. Projective Psychology and Personality Study* 21: No. 2, 7–27.

Klaus, M. H., & Kennell, J. H. (1976). *Maternal-infant Bonding*. St Louis, Mo.: C. V. Mosby.

Klein, M. (1926). 'The Psychological Principles of Infant Analysis.' In *Love, Guilt and Reparation and Other Papers, 1921–1946*. London: Hogarth, 1947. Boston: Seymour Lawrence/Delacorte.

Klein, M. (1932). *The Psycho-analysis of Children*. New edition, London: Hogarth; Boston: Seymour Lawrence/Delacorte.

Klein, M. (1935). 'A Contribution to the Psychogenesis of Manic-Depressive States.' In *Love, Guilt and Reparation and Other Papers, 1921–1946*. London: Hogarth, 1947; Boston: Seymour Lawrence/Delacorte.

Klein, M. (1936). 'Weaning.' In J. Rickman (ed.), *On the Bringing Up of Children*. London: Kegan Paul. Reprinted in *Love, Guilt and Reparation and Other Papers, 1921–1946*.

Klein, M. (1940). 'Mourning and its Relation to Manic-depressive States.' In *Love, Guilt and Reparation and Other Papers, 1921–1946*.

Klein, M. (1945). 'The Oedipus Complex in the Light of Early Anxieties.' In *Love, Guilt and Reparation and Other Papers, 1921–1946*.

Klein, M. (1948). *Contributions to Psycho-Analysis 1921–1945*. London:

Hogarth. Reprinted, with additional papers, in *Love, Guilt and Reparation and Other Papers, 1921–1946.*

Klein, M., Heimann, P., Isaacs, S., & Riviere, J. (1952). *Developments in Psycho-analysis.* London: Hogarth.

Kliman, G. (1965). *Psychological Emergencies of Childhood.* New York: Grune & Stratton.

Kliman, G., Feinberg, D., Buchsbaum, B., Kliman, A., Lubin, H., Ronald, D., & Stein, M. (1973). 'Facilitation of Mourning During Childhood.' Presented at symposium on bereavement at New York Foundation of Thanatology.

Kluckhohn, C. (1947). 'Some Aspects of Navaho Infancy and Early Childhood.' In *Psychoanalysis and the Social Sciences,* Vol. 1. New York: International Universities Press.

Knox, V. J., Morgan, A. H., & Hilgard, E. R. (1974). 'Pain and Suffering in Ischemia: The Paradox of Hypnotically Suggested Anesthesia as Contradicted by Reports from "The Hidden Observer".' *Arch. Gen. Psychiat.* 30: 840–7.

Koller, K. M., & Castanos, J. N. (1968). 'The Influence of Parental Deprivation in Attempted Suicide.' *Med. J. Australia* 1: 396–9.

Kovacs, M., & Beck, A. T. (1977). 'An Empirical-clinical Approach toward a Definition of Childhood Depression.' In J. G. Schulterbrandt & A. Raskin (eds.), *Depression in Childhood: Diagnosis, Treatment and Conceptual Models.* New York: Raven Press.

Kris, E. (1956). 'The Recovery of Childhood Memories in Psychoanalysis.' *Psychoanal. Study Child* 11: 54–88.

Krupp, G. (1965). 'Identification as a Defense against Anxiety in Coping with Loss.' *Int. J. Psycho-Anal.* 46: 303–14.

Krupp, G. R., & Kligfeld, B. (1962). 'The Bereavement Reaction: A Cross-cultural Evaluation.' *J. of Religion and Health* 1: 222–46.

Leff, M. J., Roatch, J. F., & Bunney, W. E. (1970). 'Environmental Factors Preceding the Onset of Severe Depressions.' *Psychiatry* 33: 293–311.

Lehrman, S. R. (1956). 'Reactions to Untimely Death.' *Psychiat. Quart.* 30: 564–8.

Levinson, P. (1972). 'On Sudden Death.' *Psychiatry* 35: 160–73.

Lewis, C. S. (1955). *Surprised by Joy: the Shape of my Early Life.* London: G. Bles (reprinted Fontana 1959).

Lewis, C. S. (1961). *A Grief Observed.* London: Faber.

Lewis, E. (1976). 'The Management of Stillbirth: Coping with an Unreality.' *Lancet* 2: 619–20.

Lewis, E., & Page, A. (1978). 'Failure to Mourn a Stillbirth: An Overlooked Catastrophe.' *Brit. J. med. Psychol.* 51: 237–41.

Lewis, W. H. (ed.) (1966). *Letters of C. S. Lewis: with a Memoir by W. H. Lewis.* London: G. Bles.

Lieberman, S. (1978). 'Nineteen Cases of Morbid Grief.' *Brit. J. Psychiat.* 132: 159–63.

Lind, E. (1973). 'From False-self to True-self Functioning: A Case in Brief Psychotherapy.' *Brit. J. med. Psychol.* 46: 381–9.

Lindemann, E. (1944). 'Symptomatology and Management of Acute Grief.' *Amer. J. Psychiat.* 101: 141–9.

Lindemann, E. (1960). 'Psycho-social Factors as Stressor Agents.' In J. M. Tanner (ed.), *Stress and Psychiatric Disorder*. Oxford: Blackwell.

Lipson, C. T. (1963). 'Denial and Mourning.' *Int. J. Psycho-Anal.* 44: 104–7.

Longford, E. (1964). *Victoria R.I.* London: Wiedenfeld & Nicolson.

Lord, R., Ritvo, S., & Solnit, A. J. (1978). 'Patients' Reactions to the Death of the Psychoanalyst.' *Int. J. Psycho-Anal.* 59: 189–97.

MacCurdy, J. T. (1925). *The Psychology of Emotion*. London: Kegan Paul.

McDevitt, J. B. (1975). 'Separation-individuation and Object Constancy.' *J. Amer. Psychoanal. Ass.* 23: 713–42.

McDonald, M. (1964). 'A Study of the Reaction of Nursery School Children to the Death of a Child's Mother.' *Psychoanal. Study Child* 19: 358–76.

MacKay, D. M. (1972). 'Formal Analysis of Communicative Processes.' In R. A. Hinde (ed.), *Non-verbal Communication*. Cambridge: Cambridge University Press.

Mackay, D. G. (1973). 'Aspects of the Theory of Comprehension, Memory and Attention.' *Q. J. Exp. Psychol.* 25: 22–40.

McKinney, W. T. Jnr (1977). 'Animal Behavioral/biological Models relevant to Depressive and Affective Disorders in humans.' In J. G. Shulterbrandt & A. Raskin (eds.), *Depression in Childhood: Diagnosis, Treatment and Conceptual Models*. New York: Raven Press.

Maddison, D. (1968). 'The Relevance of Conjugal Bereavement to Preventive Psychiatry.' *Brit. J. med. Psychol.* 41: 223–33.

Maddison, D., & Viola, A. (1968). 'The Health of Widows in the Year following Bereavement.' *J. Psychosomat. Res.* 12: 297–306.

Maddison, D., Viola, A., & Walker, W. L. (1969). 'Further Studies in Bereavement.' *Aust. & N.Z. J. Psychiat.* 3: 63–6.

Maddison, D., & Walker, W. L. (1967). 'Factors Affecting the Outcome of Conjugal Bereavement.' *Brit. J. Psychiat.* 113: 1057–67.

Magee, B. (1977). *Facing Death*. London: Kimber.

Mahler, M. S. (1961). 'On Sadness and Grief in Infancy and Childhood.' *Psychoanal. Study Child* 16: 332–51.

Mahler, M. (1966). 'Notes on the Development of Basic Moods: The Depressive Affect.' In R. M. Loewenstein, L. M. Newman, M. Schur & A. J. Solnit (eds.), *Psychoanalysis: A General Psychology. Essays in Honor of Heinz Hartmann*. New York: International Universities Press.

Main, M. B. (1977). 'Analysis of a Peculiar Form of Reunion Behavior in Some Day-care Children: Its History and Sequelae in Children who are Home-reared.' In R. Webb (ed.), *Social Development in Child-*

hood: Day-care Programs and Research. Baltimore: Johns Hopkins University Press.

Malinowski, B. (1925). 'Magic, Science and Religion.' In J. Needham (ed.), *Science, Religion and Reality.* London: The Sheldon Press, reprinted in: *Magic, Science and Religion and Other Essays* by B. Malinowski. Boston, Mass: Beacon Press, 1948.

Mandelbaum, D. (1959), 'Social Use of Funeral Rites.' In H. Feifel (ed.), *The Meaning of Death.* New York: McGraw Hill.

Mandler, G. (1975). *Mind and Emotion.* New York: John Wiley.

Marris, P. (1958). *Widows and their Families.* London: Routledge & Kegan Paul.

Marris, P. (1974). *Loss and Change.* London: Routledge & Kegan Paul.

Marsden, D. (1969). *Mothers Alone.* London: Allen Lane, the Penguin Press.

Mattinson, J., & Sinclair, I. A. C. (1979). *Mate and Stalemate: Working with Marital Problems in a Social Services Department.* Oxford: Blackwell.

Mendelson, M. (1974). *Psychoanalytic Concepts of Depression,* 2nd edition. New York: Halsted Press (John Wiley).

Miller, J. B. M. (1971). 'Children's Reactions to the Death of a Parent: A Review of the Psychoanalytic Literature.' *J. Amer. Psychoanal. Ass.* 19: 697–719.

Miller, S. I., & Schoenfeld, L. (1973). 'Grief in the Navajo: Psycho-dynamics and Culture.' *Int. J. Soc. Psychiat.* 19: 187–91.

Mintz, T. (1976). 'Contribution to Panel Report on Effects on Adults of Object Loss in the First Five Years,' reported by M. Wolfenstein. *J. Amer. Psychoanal. Ass.* 24: 662–5.

Mitchell, M. E. (1966). *The Child's Attitude Toward Death.* London: Barry & Rockliff; New York: Schocken Books.

Moss, C. S. (1960) 'Brief Successful Psychotherapy of a Chronic Phobic Reaction.' *J. Abnorm. and Soc. Psychol.* 60: 266–70.

Murray, H. A. (1937). 'Visceral Manifestations of Personality. *J. Abnorm. and Soc. Psychol.* 32: 161–84.

Nagera, H. (1970). 'Children's Reactions to the Death of Important Objects: A Developmental Approach.' *Psychoanal. Study Child* 25: 360–400.

Nagy, M. (1948). 'The Child's Theories Concerning Death. *J. Genet. Psychol.* 73: 3–27.

Neisser, U. (1967). *Cognitive Psychology.* New York: Appleton-Century-Crofts.

Norman, D. A. (1976). *Memory and Attention: Introduction to Human Information Processing,* 2nd edition. New York: John Wiley.

Olson, G. M. (1976). 'An Information Processing Analysis of Visual Memory and Habituation in Infants.' In T. J. Tighe & R. N. Leaton (eds.), *Habituation: Perspectives from Child Development, Animal Behavior and Neurophysiology.* Hillsdale, N.J.: Lawrence Erlbaum.

O'Neill, E. (1956). *Long Day's Journey into Night*. London: Jonathan Cape.

Orbach, C. E., Sutherland, A. M., & Bozeman, M. F. (1955). 'Psychological Impact of Cancer and its Treatment.' III The Adaptation of Mothers to the Threatened Loss of their Children through Leukemia. *Cancer* 8: 20–33.

Palgi, P. (1973). 'The Socio-cultural Expressions and Implications of Death, Mourning and Bereavement arising out of the War Situation in Israel.' *Israel Ann. Psychiatry* 11: 301–29.

Pantin, C. F. A. (1968). *The Relation between the Sciences*. London: Cambridge University Press.

Parker, G. (1979). 'Parental Characteristics in Relation to Depressive Disorders.' *Brit. J. Psychiat.* 134: 138–47.

Parkes, C. M. (1964a). 'Recent Bereavement as a Cause of Mental Illness.' *Brit. J. Psychiat.* 110: 198–204.

Parkes, C. M. (1964b). 'The Effects of Bereavement on Physical and Mental Health: A Study of the Case-Records of Widows'. *Brit. Med. J.* 2: 274–9.

Parkes, C. M. (1965). 'Bereavement and Mental Illness.' *Brit. J. med. Psychol.* 38: 1–26.

Parkes, C. M. (1969). 'Separation Anxiety: An Aspect of the Search for a Lost Object.' In M. H. Lader (ed.), *Studies of Anxiety*. British Journal of Psychiatry Special Publication No. 3. Published by authority of the World Psychiatric Association and the Royal Medico-Psychological Association.

Parkes, C. M. (1970a). 'The First Year of Bereavement.' *Psychiatry* 33: 444–67.

Parkes, C. M. (1970b). ' "Seeking" and "Finding" a Lost Object: Evidence from Recent Studies of the Reaction to Bereavement.' *Soc. Sci. & Med.* 4: 187–201.

Parkes, C. M. (1970c). 'The Psychosomatic Effects of Bereavement.' In O. W. Hill (ed.), *Modern Trends in Psychosomatic Medicine*. London: Butterworth.

Parkes, C. M. (1971). 'Psycho-social Transitions: A Field of Study.' *Soc. Sci. & Med.* 5: 101–15.

Parkes, C. M. (1972), *Bereavement: Studies of Grief in Adult Life*, London: Tavistock Publications; New York: International Universities Press.

Parkes, C. M. (1975a). 'Unexpected and Untimely Bereavement: A Statistical Study of Young Boston Widows.' In B. Schoenberg *et al.* (eds.), *Bereavement: Its Psychosocial Aspects*. New York: Columbia University Press.

Parkes, C. M. (1975b). 'Determinants of Outcome following Bereavement.' *Omega* 6: 303–23.

Parkes, C. M. (1975c). 'What Becomes of Redundant World Models? A Contribution to the Study of Adaptation to Change.' *Brit. J. med. Psychol.* 48: 131–7.

Parkes, C. M. (in preparation). *Stress of Illness.*

Parkes, C. M., Benjamin, B., & Fitzgerald, R. G. (1969). 'Broken Heart: A Statistical Study of Increased Mortality among Widowers.' *Brit. Med. J.* 1: 740–3.

Parkes, C. M., & Brown, R. (1972). 'Health after Bereavement: A Controlled Study of Young Boston Widows and Widowers.' *Psychosomat. Med.* 34: 449–61.

Paul, N. L. (1966). 'Effects of Playback on Family Members of their own Previously Recorded Conjoint Therapy Material.' *Psychiat. Res. Reports* 20: 175–87.

Paul, N. L., & Grosser, G. (1965). 'Operational Mourning and its Role in Conjoint Family Therapy.' *Community Mental Health J.* 1: 339–45.

Paykel, E. (1974). 'Recent Life Events and Clinical Depression.' In E. K. E. Gunderson & R. D. Rahe (eds.), *Life Stress and Illness.* Springfield, Illinois: C. C. Thomas.

Paykel, E. S., Prusoff, A. B., & Klerman, G. L. (1971). 'The Endogenous-neurotic Continuum in Depression: Rater Independence and Factor Distributions. *J. Psychiat. Res.* 8: 73–90.

Peterfreund, E. (1971). '*Information, Systems, and Psychoanalysis.*' Psychological Issues, Vol. VII, Monogr. 25/26. New York: International Universities Press.

Peterfreund, E. (in press). 'On Information and Systems Models for Psychoanalysis.' *Int. Rev. Psycho-Anal.*

Piaget, J. (1937, Eng. trans. 1954). *The Construction of Reality in the Child.* New York: Basic Books. Also published under the title *The Child's Construction of Reality.* London: Routledge & Kegan Paul, 1955.

Piaget, J. (1951). *Play, Dreams and Imitation in Childhood.* London: Routledge & Kegan Paul; New York: Norton.

Pine, F. (1974). 'Libidinal Object Constancy: A Theoretical Note.' In L. Goldberger & V. H. Rosen (eds.), *Psychoanalysis and Contemporary Science*, Vol. 3. New York: International Universities Press.

Pollock, G. H. (1961). 'Mourning and Adaptation.' *Int. J. Psycho-Anal.* 42: 341–61.

Pollock, G. (1972). 'On Mourning and Anniversaries: The Relationship of Culturally Constituted Defence Systems to Intra-psychic Adaptive Processes.' *Israel Ann. Psychiat.* 10: 9–40.

Prugh, D. G., & Harlow, R. G. (1962). ' "Masked Deprivation" in Infants and Young Children.' In *Deprivation of Maternal Care: a Reassessment of its Effects*, WHO Public Health Papers, 14. Geneva: WHO.

Purisman, R., & Maoz, B. (1977). 'Adjustment and War Bereavement—Some Considerations.' *Brit. J. med. Psychol.* 50: 1–9.

Rado, S. (1928a). 'An Anxious Mother.' *Int. J. Psycho-Anal.* 9: 219–26.

Rado, S. (1928b). 'The Problem of Melancholia.' *Inst. J. Psycho-Anal.* 9: 420–8.

Raphael, B. (1973). 'Care-eliciting Behaviour of Bereaved Children and their Families.' Paper presented at section on Child Psychiatry, Australian and New Zealand College of Psychiatrists.

Raphael, B. (1975). 'The Management of Pathological Grief.' *Aust. and N.Z. J. Psychiat.* 9: 173–80.

Raphael, B. (1976). 'Preventive Intervention with the Crisis of Conjugal Bereavement.' Thesis submitted for degree of M.D., University of Sydney.

Raphael, B. (1977). 'Preventive Intervention with the Recently Bereaved.' *Arch. Gen. Psychiat.* 34: 1450–4.

Raphael, B., Field, J., & Kvelde, H. (1978). 'Childhood Bereavement: A Prospective Study.' Paper presented at 9th International Congress of Child Psychiatry and Allied Professions, Melbourne, 1978.

Raphael, B., & Maddison, D. C. (1976). 'The Care of Bereaved Adults.' In O. W. Hill (ed.), *Modern Trends in Psychosomatic Medicine.* London: Butterworth.

Rees, W. D. (1971). 'The Hallucinations of Widowhood.' *Brit. Med. J.* 4: 37–41.

Rees, W. D., & Lutkins, S. G. (1967). 'Mortality of Bereavement.' *Brit. Med. J.* 1: 13–16.

Rickarby, G. A. (1977). 'Four Cases of Mania associated with Bereavement.' *J. Nerv. and Ment. Dis.* 165: 255–62.

Rickman, J. (1951). 'Methodology and Research in Psychopathology.' *Brit. J. med. Psychol.* 24: 1–25.

Robertson, J. (1952). Film: *A Two-year-old Goes to Hospital.* (16 mm, 45 mins; guidebook supplied; also abridged version, 30 mins), London: Tavistock Child Development Research Unit; New York: New York University Film Library.

Robertson, J. (1953). *A Guide to the Film 'A Two-year-old Goes to Hospital'.* London: Tavistock Child Development Research Unit, 3rd edition, 1965.

Robertson, J., & Robertson, J. (1971). 'Young Children in Brief Separation: A Fresh Look.' *Psychoanal. Study Child* 26: 264–315.

Rochlin, G. (1953). 'Loss and Restitution.' *Psychoanal. Study Child* 8: 288–309.

Rochlin, G. (1967). 'How Younger Children View Death and Themselves.' In E. A. Grollman (ed.), *Explaining Death to Children.* Boston: Beacon.

Root, N. (1957). 'A Neurosis in Adolescence.' *Psychoanal. Study Child* 12: 320–34.

Rosenblatt, A. D., & Thickstun, J. T. (1977). '*Modern Psychoanalytic Concepts in a General Psychology*', Parts 1 and 2. Psychological Issues Monogr. 42/43. New York: International Universities Press.

Rosenblatt, P. C. (1975). 'Uses of Ethnography in Understanding Grief and Mourning.' In B. Schoenberg *et al.* (eds.), *Bereavement: Its Psychosocial Aspects.* New York: Columbia University Press.

Roth, M. (1959). 'The Phobic Anxiety-depersonalisation Syndrome.' *Proc. Royal Soc. Med.* 52: 587–95.

Rutter, M. (1966). *Children of Sick Parents*. London: Oxford University Press.

Rutter, M. (1972). *Maternal Deprivation Reassessed*. Harmondsworth, Middx: Penguin Books.

Rutter, M. (1976). 'Separation, Loss and Family Relationships.' In M. Rutter & L. Hersov (eds.), *Child Psychiatry*, Ch. 3. Oxford: Blackwell.

Rynearson, E. K. (1978). 'Humans and Pets and Attachment.' *Brit. J. Psychiat.* 133: 550–5.

Sachar, E. J., Mackenzie, J. M., Binstock, W. A., & Mack, J. E. (1967). 'Corticosteroid Responses to the Psychotherapy of Reactive Depressions. I. Elevations during Confrontation of Loss.' *Arch. Gen. Psychiat.* 16: 461–70.

Sachar, E. J., Mackenzie, J. M., Binstock, W. A., & Mack, J. E. (1968). 'Corticosteroid Responses to the Psychotherapy of Reactive Depressions. II. Further Clinical and Physiological Implications.' *Psychosomat. Med.* 30: 23–44.

Schaffer, H. R. (1958). 'Objective Observations on Personality Development in Early Infancy.' *Brit. J. med. Psych.* 31: 174–83.

Schaffer, H. R. (1971). *The Growth of Sociability*. Harmondsworth, Middx: Penguin Books.

Schaffer, H. R., & Callender, W. M. (1959). 'Psychological Effects of Hospitalization in Infancy.' *Pediatrics* 24: 528–39.

Searles, H. E. (1958). 'Positive Feelings between a Schizophrenic and his Mother.' *Int. J. Psycho. Anal.* 39: 569–86.

Seligman, M. E. P. (1975). *Helplessness: On Depression, Development and Death*. San Francisco: W. H. Freeman.

Shallice, T. (1972). 'Dual Functions of Consciousness.' *Psychol. Rev.* 79: 383–93.

Shambaugh, B. (1961). 'A Study of Loss Reactions in a Seven-year-old.' *Psychoanal. Study Child* 16: 510–22.

Shand, A. F. (1920). *The Foundations of Character*, 2nd edition. London: Macmillan.

Shepherd, D., & Barraclough, B. M. (1974). 'The Aftermath of Suicide.' *Brit. Med. J.* 1: 600–3.

Shepherd, D. M., & Barraclough, B. M. (1976). 'The Aftermath of Parental Suicide for Children.' *Brit. J. Psychiat.* 129: 267–76.

Siggins, L. D. (1966). 'Mourning: A Critical Survey of the Literature.' *Int. J. Psycho-Anal.* 47: 14–25.

Smith, J. H. (1971). 'Identificatory Styles in Depression and Grief.' *Int. J. Psycho-Anal.* 52: 259–66.

Sperling, S. J. (1958). 'On Denial and the Essential Nature of Defence.' *Int. J. Psycho-Anal* 39: 25–38.

Spitz, R. A. (1946a). 'Anaclitic Depression.' *Psychoanal. Study Child* 2: 313–42.

Spitz, R. A. (1946b). Film: *Grief, a Peril in Infancy*. New York: New York University Film Library.

Spitz, R. A. (1953). 'Aggression: Its Role in the Establishment of Object Relations.' In R. M. Loewenstein (ed.), *Drives, Affects and Behaviour*. New York: International Universities Press.

Spitz, R. A. (1957). *No and Yes*. New York: International Universities Press.

Stayton, D. J., & Ainsworth, M. D. S. (1973). 'Individual Differences in Infant Responses to Brief Everyday Separations as related to Other Infant and Maternal Behaviors.' *Developmental Psychol.* 9: 226–35.

Stengel, E. (1939). 'Studies on the Psychopathology of Compulsive Wandering.' *Brit. J. med. Psychol.* 18: 250–4.

Stengel, E. (1941). 'On the Aetiology of the Fugue States.' *J. Ment. Sci.* 87: 572–99.

Stengel, E. (1943). 'Further Studies on Pathological Wandering.' *J. Ment. Sci.* 89: 224–41.

Strachey, J. (1957). Editor's Note to the Standard Edition of Freud's 'Mourning and Melancholia'. *SE* 14: 239–42.

Sullivan, H. S. (1953). *Conceptions of Modern Psychiatry*, 2nd edition. New York: Norton.

Tanner, J. M. (ed.) (1960). *Stress and Psychiatric Disorder*. Oxford: Blackwell.

Tennant, C., & Bebbington, P. (1978). 'The Social Causation of Depression: A Critique of the Work of Brown and his Colleagues.' *Psychological Medicine* 8: 565–75.

Tessman, L. H. (1978). *Children of Parting Parents*. New York: Jason Aronson.

Tooley, K. (1975). 'The Choice of Surviving Sibling as "Scapegoat" in Some Cases of Maternal Bereavement: A Case Report.' *J. Child Psychol. and Psychiat.* 16: 331–41.

Trivers, R. L. (1971). 'The Evolution of Reciprocal Altruism.' *Quart. Rev. Biol.* 46: 35–57.

Tulving, E. (1972). 'Episodic and Semantic Memory.' In E. Tulving & W. Donaldson (eds.), *Organization of Memory*. New York: Academic Press.

Tuters, E. (1974). 'Short-term Contracts: Visha.' *Social Work To-day* 5: 226–31. Reprinted in J. Hutten (ed.), *Short-term Contracts in Social Work*. London: Routledge & Kegan Paul, 1977.

Volkan, V. (1970). 'Typical Findings in Pathological Grief.' *Psychiat. Quart.* 44: 231–50.

Volkan, V. (1972). 'The Linking Objects of Pathological Mourners.' *Arch. Gen. Psychiat.* 27: 215–21.

Volkan, V. (1975). ' "Re-grief" Therapy.' In B. Schoenberg *et al.* (eds.), *Bereavement: Its Psychosocial Aspects*. New York: Columbia University Press.

Waller, W. W. (1951). *The Family: A Dynamic Interpretation.* New York: Dryden.

Ward, A. W. M. (1976). 'Mortality of Bereavement.' *Brit. Med. J.* 1: 700–2.

Wear, L. E. (1963). 'Disorders of Communion: Some Observations on Interpersonal Tensions in General Practice.' *Lancet,* Jan. 1963, 103–4.

Weiss, R. S. (ed.) (1974). *Loneliness.* Camb., Mass.: MIT Press.

Weiss, R. S. (1975a). 'The Provisions of Social Relationships.' In Z. Rubin (ed.), *Doing Unto Others.* New York: Prentice Hall.

Weiss, R. S. (1975b). *Marital Separation.* New York: Basic Books.

Wing, J. K., Cooper, J. E., & Sartorius, N. (1974). *The Measurement and Classification of Psychiatric Symptoms: An Instruction Manual for the Present State Examination and CATEGO Programme.* London: Cambridge University Press.

Winnicott, D. W. (1945). 'Primitive Emotional Development'. *Int. J. Psycho-Anal.* 26: 137–43. Reprinted in *Through Paediatrics to Psycho-Analysis* by D. W. Winnicott. London: Hogarth, 1957; New York: Basic Books.

Winnicott, D. W. (1953a). 'Psychoses and Child Care'. *Brit. J. med. Psychol.* 26: 68–74. Reprinted in *Through Paediatrics to Psycho-Analysis.*

Winnicott, D. W. (1953b). 'Transitional Objects and Transitional Phenomena.' *Int. J. Psycho-Anal.* 34: 89–97. Reprinted in *Through Paediatrics to Psycho-Analysis.*

Winnicott, D. W. (1954). 'Mind and its Relation to Psyche-soma.' *Brit. J. med. Psychol.* 27: 201–9. Reprinted in *Through Paediatrics to Psycho-Analysis.*

Winnicott, D. W. (1960). 'Ego Distortion in Terms of True and False Self.' Reprinted in *The Maturational Processes and the Facilitating Environment* by D. W. Winnicott. London: Hogarth, 1965. New York: International Universities Press.

Winnicott, D. W. (1965). 'A Child Psychiatry Case Illustrating Delayed Reaction to Loss.' In M. Schur (ed.), *Drives, Affects, Behavior,* Vol. 2. New York: International Universities Press.

Wolfenstein, M. (1966). 'How Is Mourning Possible?' *Psychoanal. Study Child* 21: 93–123.

Wolfenstein, M. (1969). 'Loss, Rage and Repetition.' *Psychoanal. Study Child* 24: 432–60.

Wolff, C. T., Friedman, S. B., Hofer, M. A., & Mason, J. W. (1964a). 'Relationship between Psychological Defenses and Mean Urinary-17-Hydroxy-corticosteroid Excretion Rates. I A Predictive Study of Parents of Fatally Ill Children.' *Psychosomatic Med.* 26: 576–91.

Wolff, C. T., Hofer, M. A., & Mason, J. W. (1964b). 'Relationship between Psychological Defenses and Mean Urinary 17-Hydroxy-corticosteroid Excretion Rates. II. Methodologic and Theoretical Considerations. *Psychomatic Med.* 26: 592–609.

Wolff, J. R., Nielson, P. E., & Schiller, P. (1970). 'The Emotional Reaction to a Stillbirth.' *Am. J. Obstet. and Gynaecol.* 108: 73–6.

Wretmark, G. (1950). 'A Study in Grief Reaction.' *Act. Psychiat. et Neurol. Scand. Suppl.* 136.

von Wright, J. M., Gebhard, P., & Karttunen, M. (1975). 'A Developmental Study of the Recall of Spatial Location.' *J. Exp. Child Psychol.* 20: 181–90.

Yamomoto, J., Okonogi, K., Iwasaki, T., & Yoshimura, S. (1969). 'Mourning in Japan.' *Am. J. Psychiat.* 125: 1660–5.

Yarrow, L. J., (1963). 'Research in Dimensions of Early Maternal Care.' *Merill-Palmer Quart.* 9: 101–11.

Author Index

Subject Index

accidents, 292, 376–80
adaptive behaviour, 72–4
affectional bonds, 1, 39, 42, 124–5, 202, 212–13, 216, 224–5, 231, 247
  see also independence of affectional bonds; compulsive self-reliance
age
  at time of bereavement, 84, 95, 107, 172, 178–9, 300
  at which children can be said to mourn, 9–19, 265, 276–90, 317, 390–4, 397, 412, 424, 437–9
aggression, 36, 235–6, 316, 361–5
  see also anger; hostility
agoraphobia, 138, 223–4
alcoholism, 105, 153, 179, 186, 225, 300
ambivalent behaviour, 28–9, 202–6, 218, 222
ancestors, worship of, 134
anger, 13–14, 28–30, 68, 87, 90–3, 104, 116–18, 128–30, 134, 136, 141, 148, 161, 188, 238, 271, 288, 293, 346, 362–3, 387, 408
anniversaries, 148, 158–60, 256, 287, 313, 324, 338, 346, 348, 378–9
anthropology, 126–34, 190–1
anxiety, 23, 26–7, 36–7, 138, 180, 286, 351–4
anxious attachment, see under attachment
attachment
  anxious attachment, 14, 202–6, 218–22, 301, 304–6
  behaviour, 2, 38–43, 55, 66, 69–70, 73, 102, 171, 217, 224–5, 228, 345, 348
  theory of, 38–43, 441–2
automated systems, 54–6

beliefs, 190–1, 270–1, 354–8
  see also mourning customs
bereavement, see loss
blame, 128–9, 136, 146, 183–4, 238, 288–9, 358–61, 363, 379, 383, 387–8
Buddhist mourning customs, 134–136

caregiving, see compulsive caregiving
cases
  Addie, 359–60
  Arnold, 361–2
  Bob, 389
  Clive, 415
  Dan, 385–7
  Dawn, 421–2
  Donna, 435
  Esther, 375–6
  Geraldine, 338–43
  Henry, 327–30
  Howard, 362–3
  Jack, 378–9
  James, 356–8
  Jane, 413–14
  Jenny, 352
  John, 416–18
  Julia, 157, 219–20
  Kate, 395–6
  Kathy, 282–5
  Laura, 11, 405–7, 408, 409
  Lucienne, 436–7
  Lucy, 414
  Mary, 318n
  Norma, 352–3
  Owen, 21, 398–401
  Patricia, 366–7
  Patrick, 12, 13, 403
  Paul, 377
  Peggy, 33
  Peter, 321–4, 325–6
  Philip, 11, 423

467